The First Socialist Society

Geoffrey Hosking

The First Socialist Society

A History of the Soviet Union from Within

ENLARGED EDITION

Harvard University Press
Cambridge, Massachusetts

This book is printed on acid-free paper,
and its binding materials have been
chosen for strength and durability.

Library of Congress Cataloging-in-Publication Data

Hosking, Geoffrey A.
    The first socialist society.

    Includes bibliographical references (p.   ) and index.
    1. Soviet Union—History—1917–   . I. Title.
DK266.H58   1990   947.084   90–4554
ISBN 0–674–30442–X

Contents

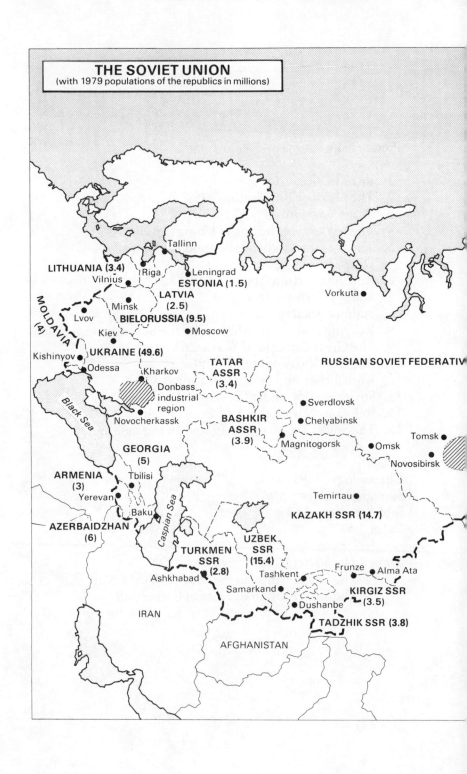

THE SOVIET UNION
(with 1979 populations of the republics in millions)

Tallinn

LITHUANIA (3.4)

Riga • Leningrad

Vilnius •

ESTONIA (1.5)

Vorkuta •

LATVIA
(2.5)

Minsk •

Lvov •

BIELORUSSIA (9.5)

Kiev •

• Moscow

RUSSIAN SOVIET FEDERATIV

Kishinyov •

UKRAINE (49.6)

Odessa •

Kharkov •

TATAR
ASSR
(3.4)

Donbass
industrial
region

• Sverdlovsk

Novocherkassk •

BASHKIR
ASSR
(3.9)

• Chelyabinsk

Tomsk •

Black Sea

GEORGIA
(5)

Magnitogorsk •

• Omsk

Novosibirsk

ARMENIA
(3)

Tbilisi •

Temirtau •

Yerevan •

Caspian Sea

Baku •

KAZAKH SSR (14.7)

AZERBAIDZHAN
(6)

UZBEK
SSR
(15.4)

Frunze •

• Alma Ata

TURKMEN
SSR
(2.8)

Tashkent •

KIRGIZ SSR
(3.5)

Ashkhabad •

Samarkand •

IRAN

Dushanbe •

TADZHIK SSR (3.8)

AFGHANISTAN

MOLDAVIA
(4)

Kolyma Labour
camp complex

Magadan

SOCIALIST REPUBLIC

(Jewish
autonomous
oblast)
Birobidzhan

Kuzbass
industrial
region

Irkutsk

Vladivostok

MONGOLIA

KOREA

CHINA

THE SOVIET UNION IN THE SECOND WORLD WAR

Front line December 1941
Front line October 1942
Front line July 1943
Front line June 1944

0   200
Miles

Leningrad
ESTONIA
Pskov
Riga
LATVIA
LITHUANIA
Smolensk
EAST PRUSSIA
Moscow
U   S   S   R
Kursk
Voronezh
Brest-Litovsk
POLAND
Kiev
Kharkov
Stalingrad
HUNGARY
Kishinyov
Odessa
Rostov-on-Don
ROMANIA
BULGARIA
TURKEY

THE SOVIET UNION IN EASTERN EUROPE

Adapted from Martin Gilbert, *Russian History Atlas* (1972)

Preface to the Enlarged Edition

By a strange coincidence, the first edition of this book was published on the very day that Gorbachev became General Secretary of the Soviet Communist Party. That made for good publicity, but it meant that the text rapidly became overtaken by the remarkable events which began to take place under the new leadership. It is true that in the last pages of the old edition I remarked that change, when it came, would be rapid and far-reaching, and that the Soviet public would prove to be more ready for it than we were then accustomed to think. As a pointer to the future, that now seems to have been reasonably apt, but all the same, a mere four years into the new era, a generous extension of the last chapter seemed essential to give some idea of the momentous changes which have been occurring and to relate them to earlier Soviet history. I have taken this opportunity to correct a few errors earlier in the text, and thank those reviewers and readers who have pointed them out to me.

School of Slavonic & East European Studies,
University of London,
July 1989

Preface

Viewed from the West, the peoples of the Soviet Union tend to seem grey, anonymous and rather supine. When we see them on our television screens, marching in serried ranks past the mausoleum on Red Square, it is difficult to imagine them as more than appendages – or potential cannon fodder – for the stolid leaders whom they salute on the reviewing stand. This is, of course, partly the image the Soviet propaganda machine wishes to project. But is it not also partly the result of our way of studying the country? So many general works on the Soviet Union concentrate either on its leaders, or on its role in international affairs, as seen from the West.

There is plenty on the Soviet leaders in this book, too. No one could ignore them in so centralized and politicized a society. But I have also tried to penetrate a little more into their interaction with the various social strata, the religious and national groups, over which they rule. Fortunately, in the last ten to fifteen years, quite a large number of good monographs have been published in the West and (to a lesser extent, because of censorship) in the Soviet Union itself, which enable us to say more about the way of life of the working class, the peasantry, the professional strata, and even the ruling elite itself. In addition, many recent émigrés have, since leaving, given us candid accounts of their lives in their homeland, and these have afforded us a much more vivid insight into the way ordinary people think, act and react.

In order to focus on this material and give, as far as possible in brief compass, a rounded picture of Soviet society, I have deliberately said little or nothing about foreign policy or international affairs. There are already many excellent studies from which the reader can learn about the Soviet Union's role in world affairs: to add to them is not the purpose of this book. I have, however, given some consideration to the Soviet Union's relationship with the other socialist countries lying within its sphere of influence. As I argue in Chapter 11, developments in those countries have a claim to be considered almost as Soviet internal affairs; besides, East European efforts to discover their own distinctive 'roads to socialism' have brought out elements in the socialist tradition which have been obscured or overlaid in the Soviet Union itself. These elements may yet be of great importance, and therefore it is essential to give them due weight.

I have, moreover, again in the interests of concentration, consciously laid the strongest emphasis on the years of Stalin's personal rule – roughly from the start of the first Five Year Plan in 1928 until his death in 1953 – because this seems to me the most crucial period for understanding the Soviet Union today. It is also the one on which recently published works throw the greatest light.

In order to avoid cluttering the narrative and to allow a smoother flow of argument, I have dealt with some individual topics – such as literature, religion, education and law – not within each chapter, but in large sections confined to a few chapters. Thus, for example, the reader interested in the Russian Orthodox Church will find most of the material on it concentrated in Chapters 9 and 14. The index indicates these principal sections in italics.

This history is the product of some fifteen years' teaching on the Russian Studies programme at the University of Essex, and it reflects the often stated needs of my students on the post-1917 history course. I owe a considerable debt to them, especially to the inquisitive ones, who tried to encourage me to depart from vague generalization and tell them what life has really been like in a distant and important country they had never seen. I have also learnt a great deal over the years from my colleagues in the History Department and in the

Russian and Soviet Studies Centre at Essex University. The marvellous Russian collection in the Essex University Library has provided me with most of the materials I needed, and I am particularly thankful to the collection's custodian, Stuart Rees, for his unfailing attention to my wants.

I am most grateful to my colleagues who have read all or part of an earlier draft: the late Professor Leonard Schapiro, Peter Frank, Steve Smith, Bob Service and, the most tireless of my students, Philip Hills. At crucial stages of the writing, I have benefited from conversations with Mike Bowker, William Rosenberg and George Kolankiewicz. Where I have ignored their advice and gone my own way, I acknowledge full responsibility.

I am much beholden to the support and encouragement of my wife Anne, and my daughters Katherine and Janet. Without their endless patience and indulgence, this book would have been abandoned long ago, and then they might have seen more of me.

School of Slavonic Studies,
University of London.
July 1984

Administrative Divisions

Often in the text I refer to one or other of the main administrative divisions of the Soviet Union. These may be schematically laid out as follows:

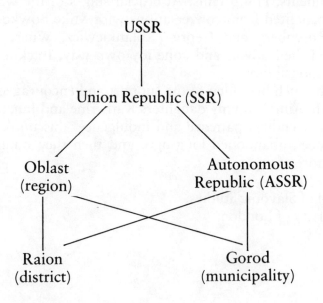

1

Introduction

'The philosophers have only explained the world; the point is to change it.' This famous dictum of Marx invites us to judge his doctrine by its practical consequences, in other words by examining the kind of society which has resulted from its application. Yet, paradoxically, many Marxists themselves will deny the validity of such a judgement. They will dismiss the example of Soviet society as an unfortunate aberration, the outcome of a historical accident, by which the first socialist revolution took place in a country unsuited to socialism, in backward, autocratic Russia.

It is important, therefore, to begin by asking ourselves just why this happened. Was it indeed a historical accident? Or were there elements in Russia's pre-revolutionary traditions which predisposed the country to accept the kind of rule which the followers of Marx were to impose?

It is true that Russia was, in some ways, backward and it was certainly autocratic. Economically speaking – in agriculture, commerce and industry – Russia had lagged behind Western Europe from the late Middle Ages onward, largely as a result of two centuries of relative isolation under Tatar rule. There is, however, no single track along which history advances, and this backwardness had positive as well as negative features. It made the mass of the people more adaptable, better able to survive in harsh circumstances. It may also have helped to preserve a more intimate sense of local community, in the peasants' commune (*mir*) and the workmen's cooperative (*artel*).

Politically, on the other hand, nineteenth-century Russia might be thought of as rather 'advanced', if by that we mean resembling twentieth-century Western European political systems. It was an increasingly centralized, bureaucratized and in many ways secular state; its hierarchy had strong meritocratic features; it devoted a considerable share of its resources to defence, and operated a system of universal male conscription; and it accepted an ever more interventionist role in the economy. Furthermore, the state's opponents, the radicals and revolutionaries, pursued secular utopias with the same mixture of altruism, heroism and intense self-absorption which characterized, for example, the West German and Italian terrorists of the 1960s and 1970s. What Russia did *not* have, of course, was parliamentary democracy, though even that was developing, in embryonic form, from 1906.

As for autocracy, there were very good reasons why it should have proved the dominant political form in Russia, and why it should have been acceptable to most of the people. It is unnecessary to postulate an inborn 'slave mentality', as many Westerners are prone to do. First, there are Russia's flat, open frontiers, which have been both her strength and her weakness. Her strength, because they gave Russia's people the chance to spread eastwards, colonizing the whole of northern Asia and occupying in the end one-sixth of the earth's surface. Her weakness, because they have rendered Russia ever vulnerable to attack, from the east, the south and, especially in recent centuries, from the west. For that reason all Russian governments have made the securing of their territory their chief priority, and have received the whole-hearted support of the population in so doing. National security has been, in fact, more than a priority – an obsession to which, when necessary, everything else has been sacrificed with the enthusiastic approval of the people. Any other people in such circumstances would react the same way. That is not to say that Russian governments have not abused the trust their subjects have placed in them: on the contrary they have found it possible to do so again and again. But the geographical and historical motives for accepting strong authority have nearly always prevailed.

Another reason for the popular identification with the

autocrat is that, historically speaking, Russia's formation as a self-conscious nation began unusually early. The Tatar occupation of the thirteenth century generated, by reaction, intense Russian national feeling, which centred on the Orthodox Church, as the one national institution which had survived the disaster. And because the church conducted its liturgy not in Latin but in a Slavonic tongue close to the vernacular, this national feeling had deep roots among the ordinary people. All this imparted to Russian national consciousness from early times a demotic quality, a defensiveness, and an earth-boundness which still have strong echoes today. Its religious basis was celebrated as soon as Russia was able, thanks to strong Muscovite rulers, to throw off the Tatar yoke. Moscow Grand Dukes proclaimed themselves Tsars (Caesars), claiming the heritage of Byzantium, which had fallen to the infidels in 1453: 'Two Romes have fallen, the third Rome stands, and there shall be no fourth.' Russia became Holy Russia, the one true Christian empire on earth.

In order to ensure that armies could be raised and the country defended, the tsars imposed a tight hierarchy of service on the whole population. Nobles were awarded land in the form of *pomestya,* or service estates, on condition that they performed civilian or military service, usually the latter. They also had to raise a unit of fighting men from among the peasants committed to their charge. In this way the old independent aristocrats, the boyars, were gradually displaced, while the peasants became enserfed, fixed to the land, bound to serve their lord, to pay taxes, and to provide recruits for the army. For nobles and peasants alike, their function and status in society was defined by state service. Society became almost an appendage to the state.

In the end, even the church was taken into service. The process began in the seventeenth century, when its head, Patriarch Nikon, tried to provide for the church's imperial role by correcting liturgical mistakes which had crept into the prayer books over the centuries, and which he felt would shame the Russian Orthodox Church in its relations with other churches. He was also ambitious for the church to play a stronger role in the state. Although Tsar Alexei dismissed him as a dangerous rival, the reforms he had sponsored were ratified by a Church Council. These reforms aroused vehement opposition among both priests and laity, who felt that the integrity of the Russian faith was being violated by foreign importations. All the strength, exclusiveness and defensiveness of Russian national feeling was exhibited by the Old Believers, those who clung to the old liturgical practices, and were prepared to be imprisoned or exiled, or even commit mass suicide, rather than submit to the new and alien practices. The Old Belief survived right up to the revolution of 1917, and beyond, depriving the official church of many of its natural, indeed most fervent, supporters.

Perhaps the most significant aspect of this schism, whose importance for Russian history can scarcely be exaggerated, was that the church became dependent on the full coercive support of the state in implementing its reforms. The way was thus prepared for Peter I, in the early eighteenth century, to abolish the Patriarchate, symbol of the independent standing of the church, and replace it with a so-called Holy Synod, essentially a department of state, headed moreover by a layman. Peter did this with the same aims as Henry VIII in England: to bring the church under firm state control, to discipline it and make it fitter to fulfil the tasks the state had in mind for it, such as education, social welfare and the pastoral care and supervision of the common people. His principal ecclesiastical theorist, Feofan Prokopovich, insisted that the state should have undivided and indisputable sovereignty on earth, including the right to interpret God's law. Any less clear arrangement he deemed dangerous, since it might mislead ordinary, gullible people to entertain the 'hope of obtaining help for their rebellions from the clergy'. This secular approach to church–state relations, and the obsession with civil disorder, was close to the thinking of many European Protestant thinkers at the time, notably

Thomas Hobbes. Shades of the Leviathan hung over Russian society from then on.

Peter I also impugned Russian traditions in numerous other ways. He moved the capital from Moscow to a swampy outpost on the Baltic coast, simply because that sea gave direct access to the ports of Europe, in whose more 'progressive' ways Peter hoped for salvation. In the new city of St Petersburg, he required his nobility to adopt European fashions in everything from education to clothing. When some of his courtiers refused to shave their beards – honoured as a sign of manhood in Muscovite custom – Peter took the shears and did the job personally. Both the changes he promoted, and his uncouth manner of imposing them, aroused considerable opposition. Old Believers, indeed, regarded him as the Antichrist.

Catherine II completed the subordination of church to state by expropriating the church's huge landholdings, which left the priesthood poor and dependent on their parishioners for subsistence. The clergy became in effect a subordinate estate, having neither the education nor the financial independence to cultivate a distinctive stand, even in spiritual matters. They were also a more or less closed order, since clergy sons usually had little choice but to take their education in a church seminary, and then to follow in father's footsteps. The high culture and politics of the period were essentially secular: priests were regarded by most intellectuals as beings of inferior education and status, peddling superstition to pacify the plebs. It would be difficult to overstate the importance of this subordination of the church. It meant that Holy Russia, still haunted by visions of unique religious rectitude, was governed in a radically secular manner, outdoing most Protestant states, and was acquiring an almost aggressively secular culture.

Russian government in the nineteenth century is often described as 'reactionary', but this view is based on superficial comparisons with West European political systems. In fact, from the time of Peter I, Russian governments were radical and modernizing to an almost dangerous degree. They were so because they felt they faced a potential military threat from European nations which on the whole were technically better equipped. It was to face this challenge that Peter sacrificed so much to the creation of a strong army and navy, with a modern armaments industry to back them up, and overhauled the administration of the country, the tax system, education and even social mores. He regarded all the country's resources – material, cultural and spiritual – as being at the service of the state for the good of society as a whole. His successors continued his work, but they faced both the advantages and disadvantages of weak social institutions. Advantages, in that no fractious nobility or urban patriciate possessed the independence to impede the monarch's commands. Disadvantages, in that the existing aristocratic and urban institutions (the elites of town and country) were often not even strong enough to act as transmission belts for orders from above, as they did in other European countries; in their absence the government's intentions often petered out ineffectually in the vast expanses of the landscape.

For that reason some Russian monarchs, notably Catherine II in the late eighteenth century, and Alexander II in the 1860s, actually tried to create or strengthen what Montesquieu would have called 'intermediary bodies', that is, self-governing associations of nobility and of townsmen, with a direct responsibility for local government. Others – Paul I, for example, and Nicholas I – regarded such associations as self-seeking and divisive, tried to curb them and to rule through monarchical agents, controlled from the centre. Much of the history of Imperial Russia's government between Peter I and the revolution of 1917 is to be found in this swing to and fro between local autonomy and strict centralization, between support of local elites and distrust of them.

The radical intelligentsia of the nineteenth century were in some ways the unnatural offspring of this frustrating relationship. Most of the radicals came from the social strata from which the tsarist government recruited its central and local officials – the minor nobility, the clergy, army officers and professional men – and they typically went through the same education system as the country's civil servants. They espoused many of the ideals of the modernizing wing of the bureaucracy: progress, equality, material welfare for all, the curbing of privilege. Frustrated, however, by the hierarchy and authoritarianism of the state service, and by the gross discrepancy between ideal and reality, they underwent a conversion, usually as early as their student days, and harnessed their vision to a revolutionary ideology.

In the absence of a genuinely conservative political theory, and lacking the support of an independent church, the Russian imperial state often found itself extraordinarily vulnerable when faced with the activists of the revolutionary movement. In effect the state's own ideals had been hijacked by its opponents, and as a result the government found itself being deserted by those who should have been its natural supporters. Even Dostoevsky, a writer of conservative views, once said that, if he knew that revolutionaries were going to blow up the Winter Palace, he would not report the plot to the police, for fear of 'being thought an informer': 'The liberals would never let me hear the end of it.' Without necessarily approving of terrorism, in fact, members of the nobility and liberal professions sometimes felt a kind of sympathy for the terrorists' world outlook. The impeccably liberal Kadet Party in 1906, for example, refused publicly to condemn terrorism for fear of discrediting itself in the eyes of public opinion. In this way the revolutionaries came to constitute a kind of 'alternative establishment'.

This did not make the practical dilemmas of the radicals any easier. It was not at all clear how they were to achieve their aims. Alexander Herzen, perhaps the first thoroughgoing Russian socialist, thought the peasant commune should function as the nucleus of the new society, but he was ambivalent about how and even whether a revolution should take place to bring that about. Mikhail Bakunin urged that the only essential thing was to spark off a massive popular uprising by the *narod* (the common people), and this would of itself purge and destroy the evils of existing society, leaving men free to improvise. Petr Lavrov, on the contrary, hoped that revolution would not be necessary at all: he felt that the educated strata had a debt to the narod, their education having been made possible by the latter's toil. They should pay this debt off by 'going to the people' and passing on the fruits of their education to them, teaching them how they might create a truly humane society on the basis of their own institutions, the mir and the artel. In the 1870s several hundred students tried to fulfil Lavrov's vision, learning handcrafts and dressing in smocks and felt boots in order to live in the village, practise a trade and pass on the good word. Most, though not all, of the peasants met them with incomprehension and some suspicion: for the time being at least their faith in the 'little father' tsar was still unshaken. Many of the student idealists who 'went to the people' finished up in prison.

Their failure lent strength to those who argued that a revolutionary movement must *lead* and it must use violence, disorganizing the government apparatus by terror, and if possible seizing power by a coup d'état. An organization called the People's Will (*Narodnaya volya*) was set up to achieve this, and in 1881 it actually succeeded in assassinating the Emperor Alexander II. But setting up a different regime, or even putting effective pressure on Alexander's successor – that proved beyond their capacities. Their victory was a pyrrhic one: all it produced was more determined repression.

By the 1880s, in fact, the Russian revolutionary movement seemed to be in a blind alley, unable to achieve its aims either by peaceful propaganda or by terrorism. It was in this situation that Marxism presented itself as a panacea in troubled times. Its first Russian exponent, Georgy Plekhanov, was the leader of those who had refused to accept the methods of the People's Will. He welcomed Marxism because it suggested he had been right all along in rejecting the idea of a coup d'état: no revolution could yet come about in Russia, by *any* means, simply because objective social and economic circumstances were not yet ripe. Plekhanov's interpretation thus emphasized Marxism's *determinist* features: he argued that capitalism had not yet even begun in Russia, so that naturally the socialist revolution, which could only take place as a result of the contradictions of capitalist society, had no chance of success yet. In his view, Russia must first accept the coming of capitalism, with the concomitant breakdown of the peasant commune and the creation of large-scale industry, because these processes would generate a genuinely revolutionary class, the factory proletariat, which would not let down the hopes of the radical intelligentsia, as the peasantry had done. Plekhanov took up Marxism with such enthusiasm because he discerned in it a *scientific* explanation of history, and hence the certainty that the revolutionaries, if they followed it, would no longer sacrifice their hopes, and indeed their lives, in vain. Previous revolutionaries he dismissed contemptuously as 'Populists'.

Historians of Russia often approach Marxism as though it came to the country as a completely formed and internally consistent doctrine. In fact this was far from being the case. Marxism was itself the product of European experiences not unlike those which had troubled the Russian revolutionaries of the 1860s and 1870s, especially the disappointments of the French revolution, and of the European risings of 1848–9. Each time, the shortfall between revolutionary expectation and subsequent reality had been immense. Marx claimed that this was because the revolutionaries had not heeded objective socioeconomic conditions: they were in fact mere 'utopian socialists'. His kind of socialism, on the contrary, he described as 'scientific'. He argued that the proletariat, growing now uncontrollably with the expansion of capitalist industry, would overcome the gap between ideal and reality. The factory worker was in a uniquely favourable position to achieve this, since he was both the 'subject' and the 'object' of history: the object in that he was the victim of its economic laws, the subject in that he was conscious of the fact that he had nothing to lose and he was impelled by the vision of the more just and prosperous society that would come out of his revolt. As the unavoidable contradictions of capitalism bore ever more heavily on the workers, so they would inevitably rise and overthrow their oppressors, creating of their shared destitution a more just and humane society.

In this way Marx overcame, to his own satisfaction and that of most of his followers, the troubling gap between ideal and fulfilment. The trouble is, there was and is no necessary connection between Marx's vision of intensifying socioeconomic crisis, with everyone moved by their own material interests, and the world of harmony and brotherhood which was supposed to succeed the revolution. Indeed, logically speaking, if the workers were impelled by their own economic interests in making revolution, then the more likely sequel of such a revolution would be further economic struggle, but with a different set of masters. Nevertheless, the idea that the workers' revolution would somehow magically cancel out all the conflicts of society had enormous attraction. It seemed to be both realistic and optimistic at the same time. It had the simultaneous attractions of a science and a religion. That is what made it so appealing, and nowhere more so than in Russia, where the intelligentsia already had its own troubles with a secular state claiming religious prerogatives.

Certainly the young Vladimir Ulyanov – or Lenin, as he became known – was attracted by precisely this dual nature of Marxism. He had been deeply affected by the execution in 1887 of his elder brother Alexander for membership of a conspiracy to murder the emperor. Lenin was attracted by his brother's idealism and self-sacrifice, but at the same time he was determined not to give up his own life in vain. He wanted to pursue Alexander's aim of revolutionary social transformation with *certainty*. Hence the scientific claims of Marxism were very important to him. Reading Marx's *Capital* was, as he later said, a revelation to him, because it seemed to demonstrate that revolution was embedded in the objective evolution of society, if one only had the patience and consistency to await its unfolding. In his own early writings, Lenin made a similar analysis of Russia's own socioeconomic structure, aiming to show that capitalism was already destroying the economy of the peasant commune, and that capitalism – and therefore ultimately revolution – was inevitable in Russia. Admittedly Lenin felt that Russia had further to go than most of Europe, and, following Plekhanov, he envisaged a revolution in two stages: (i) the 'bourgeois democratic' one, when the feudal system, still not entirely destroyed in Russia, would be finally overthrown by an alliance of the 'bourgeois liberals' with the as yet small workers' party; (ii) the later socialist stage, which would come in the fullness of time, when capitalism was fully developed and the working class had reached maturity.

All this had the merit of apparent certainty. But it was predicated on a formidably extensive time scale, and would require daunting patience and self-restraint to realize in full. In fact Lenin did not for long adhere to the full schema, but began to cast around for ways of telescoping the two stages. Furthermore, in his own way, he was aware of the gap between science and prophecy in Marx. He did not share the master's confidence that the workers would automatically grasp the full significance of their destitution in existing society and how it might be ended. On the contrary, in his pamphlet *What is to be Done?* (1902) he expressed his fear that, left to themselves, workers would not attempt a revolution but would fight for more limited goals, such as higher wages, better working conditions and more humane treatment from their employers. His own experience of propaganda work in the St Petersburg factories of the 1890s led him to the conclusion that 'The workers did not have, nor was it possible for them to have, an awareness of the irreconcilable contradiction of their interests with the whole modern political and social system.' This did not apply just to Russian workers: 'The history of all countries shows that by itself the working class can only develop a trade union consciousness, that is to say a conviction of the necessity to form trade unions, struggle with the employers, obtain from the government this or that law.' Only the 'educated representatives of the propertied classes – the intelligentsia' could fully understand the real, as distinct from the superficial, needs of the workers. To bring about a revolution, a genuinely revolutionary party was needed, that is, one 'embracing primarily and chiefly people whose profession consists of revolutionary activity'. That seemed, on the face of it, to exclude any workers, since their profession, perforce, was factory labour.

This was a most important clarification of a weak point in Marxist theory. In actual practice, Lenin never tried to run his party in this way. But he always stuck theoretically to his definition of the revolutionary party, and indeed made it his touchstone of the true revolutionary spirit. For the sake of it he was prepared to break with other Marxists who took a different view. At what was, in effect, the founding congress of the Russian Social Democratic Party, in Brussels and London in 1903, Lenin insisted that 'personal participation in one of the party's organizations' was to be the key qualification for membership. His principal opponent, Yuly Martov, wanted a more relaxed formulation: 'regular personal support under the guidance of one of the party's organizations'. This would make it easier for workers to become full party members, even in conditions of illegality. Lenin lost that particular vote, but nevertheless emerged from the congress with a majority, and henceforth called his faction the 'Bolsheviks' or 'men of the majority', while Martov's had to content themselves with the sobriquet 'Mensheviks' or 'men of the minority'.

The issue which provoked the great split in the Russian Social Democratic Party sounds like a minor organizational quibble. In fact, however, this quibble turned out to symbolize more profound disagreements, which drove the Bolsheviks and Mensheviks ever further apart. With time it became clear that they were envisaging two different kinds of revolution. The Mensheviks laid great store by the coming of a parliamentary 'bourgeois' republic, in which a mass working-class party would act as a legal opposition until they were numerous enough to take power on their own account. Lenin, however, became increasingly impatient with the protracted timetable entailed by this vision. He hankered after telescoping the whole process, running the two revolutions together by enlisting the peasants (carrying out a 'bourgeois-democratic' revolution against the landlords) as auxiliaries of the workers (carrying out their 'socialist' revolution against the capitalists). However, he did not fully clarify his ideas on this issue until his final return to Russia from exile in 1917.

In effect, Lenin reintegrated into Russian Marxism certain elements of the Populist tradition: the leadership of a small group of intelligentsia revolutionaries, the readiness to regard the peasants as a revolutionary class, and the telescoping of the 'bourgeois' phase of the revolution.

The Populists had, however, their own views. They recovered from their prostration of the 1880s, and by 1901 managed to form a new political party, with its centre in emigration, the Socialist Revolutionary Party. Their theoreticians no longer disputed the proposition that industrial capitalism had come to Russia, but they maintained that it had taken a very different form from the one Marx envisaged. First, it was heavily dominated by the state. Secondly, most of the workers had not really broken away from the countryside: they were 'peasant-workers', not proletarians in the Marxist sense. The Socialist Revolutionaries refused, in fact, to recognize any fundamental distinction between workers and peasants: they organized themselves, and with some success, to work among both. They also set up a 'fighting detachment' to continue the work of the People's Will by terrorism directed against officials: they succeeded between 1901 and 1908 in murdering a Grand Duke, several ministers and over a hundred other senior officials.

In 1905, risings broke out in both town and countryside. These outbursts owed little to the organizational efforts of the Social Democrats and the Socialist Revolutionaries, but rather more to their long-term inspiration. The most powerful ingredient of all, however, was the enduring discontent felt by the peasants and workers who made up the great majority of Russia's population.

The Emancipation Act promulgated by Alexander II in 1861 had released the peasants from personal bondage, but it had not relieved any of their other hardships, and indeed had burdened them with an additional grievance. This was the obligation to *pay* for land which they already regarded as their own – and indeed, in the Lockean sense that they 'mixed their labour with it', so it was. The peasants' collective legal sense had never accepted the legitimacy of the awards of land made by the tsars to the nobles.

In order to ensure that the peasants would pay for the land 'newly allotted' to them, and would discharge their other taxes, the government bound them to a 'village society', which was often, though not always, equivalent to the old 'commune', or mir. This institution has been the subject of more myth-making and less solid empirical research than perhaps any other in Russian history, partly because its members left little or no written testimony, and partly because ideologists of left and right hoped and feared great things from it. The government saw it as a guarantor of law and order, as well as of primitive social security, while the revolutionaries, at least the Populists, regarded its practices as a kind of rudimentary socialism, which might enable Russian society to proceed straight to real socialism without the unpleasant intermediate stage of capitalism. In Great Russia the mir assembly, consisting of heads of household, periodically redistributed land, adding to the allotments of families grown larger (along with the obligation to pay higher taxes) and subtracting from the allotments of those which had lost members. In the Ukraine and Bielorussia, on the other hand, rather different customs prevailed: land was usually passed down the family hereditarily, and was not subject to periodic redistribution. In both types of commune, timber, meadows, pastures and water-courses were held in common.

The communal land tenure system, though it provided a safety net in time of difficulty, had real economic dis-advantages. All the villagers were compelled to adopt a safe but primitive and underproductive form of agriculture: the open three-field system with strip farming. At a time when the peasant population was growing very fast – from around 55 million in 1863 to 82 million in 1897 – the mir in effect impeded the introduction of improved seeds, fertilizers or machines; and it offered a disincentive to land improvement, since the cultivator never knew when his plot might be taken away from him and awarded to someone else.

The low level of agricultural productivity was only partly a result of communal tenure. Partly, too, it was a function of low urbanization. Where, as in most of western Europe, there was a dense network of towns and good communications between them, then a receptive market existed for a wide variety of agricultural produce. In Russia this was the case only around St Petersburg and Moscow. Over the remaining expanses of Russia's main agricultural regions, peasants scratched the soil with wooden ploughs, grew rye and oats, lived on a diet of 'cabbage soup and gruel' (as a popular saying had it) and sold very little to the outside world, except when economic need made it unavoidable.

As a result, though the picture varied from area to area, it seems clear enough that most peasants were poor, threatened by hunger in bad years, and that the problem was getting worse. In 1890 more than 60 per cent of peasants called up for the army were declared unfit on health grounds: and that was *before* the famine of 1891.

The peasants themselves felt that the explanation for all this was obvious: they needed more land, and they had a right to it. In the neighbouring nobles' fields they saw their own potential salvation. This was an illusion: the total area of peasant landholdings exceeded that of the landowners by nearly three to one, so that simple expropriation of the latter would not solve the problem. But in 1905 the peasants were convinced that it would, and that their grievance was justified. Acting in common, by decision of their mir assemblies, they began to take the law into their own hands, seizing estates and driving the landowners out. It took a long time for the government to restore order.

In fact, there was no simple solution to Russia's agrarian problem, as the later experience of developing countries confirms. Only a patient combination of improvements in land tenure and in agricultural methods with the gradual development of the commercial and industrial life of the country could in the end have brought greater prosperity to the village. But the myth that there *was* a simple solution, and that the peasants had a natural right to all the land, was the single most explosive factor in Russian politics in the last years of the tsarist regime.

Peter Stolypin, prime minister from 1906 to 1911, tried to make a start to the process of patient improvement by giving peasant households the right to withdraw from the village commune, set up on their own and enclose their holdings. After a promising start, however, this programme was abruptly curtailed by war and revolution.

Workers, the other great factor in the revolutionary upheaval of 1905, were also restless to an unusual degree in Russia compared with their West European counterparts. This may have been because they had unusually close ties with the land. Under the Emancipation legislation of 1861, a peasant who went into the town to work permanently was still registered with his 'village society' and remained legally a peasant. His family still paid taxes there, and he probably sent back money regularly to help them out; perhaps he would return at Christmas or Easter for family celebrations, or in the late summer to help with the harvest. Some workers, especially those in construction and transport, organized themselves in an artisan cooperative, or artel, which had its origins in village life, and was sometimes found even in heavy industry. Individual factories often perpetuated the rural link by recruiting most of their workforce from a particular province; and workers themselves would often form a *zemlyachestvo*, or regional association, to keep in touch with each other and with their home villages.

Compared with the workers who had lived in the towns for a generation or more, these 'peasant-workers' seem to have been unusually prone to unrest at times of crisis. This may have been partly because their right to allotment land in the village gave them something to fall back on, and hence an extra sense of security. Or it may have been because, in the absence of legalized trade unions in the towns, the tradition of collective action was far stronger in the countryside. In their case, too, the newly discovered urban discontents, over housing, pay, working conditions or overbearing foremen, were superimposed on the grievances which they had brought with them from the village. As R. E. Johnson, the most recent student of this subject, has suggested, 'the fusion of rural and urban discontents and propensities produced an especially explosive mix'.

At any rate, the experience of 1905 suggested that Russian workers, in times of crisis, were unusually good at improvising their own institutions. The body which sparked off the unrest of that year was, ironically, organized by Father Gapon, a priest who wished to *save* the monarchy. On Sunday 9 January 1905 he led a huge demonstration in the capital, St Petersburg, bearing ikons and portraits of the tsar: they were to march to the Winter Palace with a petition appealing for a living wage and for civil rights. The troops stationed in the streets panicked in the face of the crowd and opened fire: nearly two hundred people were killed and many more wounded.

This incident, which has passed into history as Bloody Sunday, had a dramatic effect: more than any other, it undermined the popular image of the tsar as the benevolent 'little father'. It helped to release the restraint which the peasants had previously felt about taking the law into their own hands. And it certainly contributed to the wave of strikes, demonstrations and sometimes violence which swept Russia's industrial cities. In the course of this, workers set up trade unions for the first time, rather begrudgingly legalized by the government. They also improvised councils (or *soviets*) of workers' deputies. Beginning as strike committees elected at the workplace, these bodies often found themselves temporarily exercising local government functions as well, in cities whose normal administration was paralysed by strikes. They also negotiated with the employers and the government. In short, they gained a brief but intense experience of self-government, unforgettable to workers who had never before been allowed to organize in their own interests.

The mass popular unrest gave the professional strata and the intelligentsia the chance to press their demands for an elected parliament, or even a constituent assembly, to decide on Russia's future form of government. Political parties were formed, of which the most prominent were the Constitutional Democrats (or Kadets for short), under their leader, the Moscow University history professor, P. N. Milyukov. Their ideal was a constitutional monarchy on the British model, or even a parliamentary republic, as in France.

In the end, faced with a general strike, Tsar Nicholas II reluctantly conceded much of what the Kadets were demanding. In the October Manifesto of 1905 he promised that henceforth the civil rights of all citizens would be observed, and he granted a parliament, the *Duma*, to be elected on an indirect but fairly broad franchise. Written into its statute was the provision that 'without [its] consent no law can take effect'. This concession relieved him of the outright opposition of the liberals, and Nicholas was then able to instruct the police and army – which remained almost completely loyal – to crush the workers' and peasants' movement.

During the few years of its existence, the Duma was sometimes harassed, sometimes ignored by the government, and indeed twice summarily dissolved. Nevertheless, its mere presence made a great difference to political life. Its electoral assemblies remained as a minimal focus for working-class and peasant political education and activity, even at a time when the government was trying to withdraw some of its concessions of 1905. And the existence of a relatively free press alongside it meant that the reading public (now growing very fast) were incomparably better informed about political issues than they ever had been before. Combined with the rapid growth in literacy, with the bitter political conflicts resulting from 1905, and with ever-accelerating social and economic change, all this was potentially very explosive.

The tsarist monarchy was finally overthrown in the midst of the First World War. Major wars, of course, raise all the stakes in domestic politics, since survival itself is at issue. Furthermore, the government fought this one before a Duma which proved watchful and at times bitterly critical, while the press, though under wartime censorship, remained freer than at any time before 1905. Whether the constitutional monarchy founded by the October Manifesto could have survived if there had been no war is an open question. What is certain is that the war caught it at a very vulnerable moment, when it had not yet fully established itself in the eyes of the public, yet was already suffering from the exposure to fierce criticism which civil liberties made possible. Bloody Sunday had weakened the reputation of the tsar. His standing was now further undermined by rumours – bandied around in the press though never substantiated – that the royal family was being compromised by a 'holy man' of dubious credentials, Rasputin, and that the court even had treacherous connections with the enemy, Germany. As the normally restrained Milyukov put it in a famous Duma speech of November 1916, 'Is this stupidity or is it treason?'

Against the background of such public accusations, the more or less normal difficulties of war, military defeat, shortages of guns and food, became magnified into matters involving the very survival of the monarchy.

The end came relatively suddenly, and to at least the revolutionary parties, unexpectedly, in February 1917, when food queues in Petrograd suddenly turned into political demonstrations, demanding an end to what many still called the 'autocracy'. When even the Cossacks, long the faithful upholders of order, refused to disperse the crowds, Nicholas II suddenly found that he had no supporters. Liberals and socialists were in agreement, for the first time since 1905, and what they agreed was that the monarchy must go. Fearing for national unity, not even the army generals attempted to resist the demand. Two Duma deputies were sent to see the tsar, who tendered his abdication in a railway carriage outside Pskov, on 2 March 1917.

As we now know, the collapse of the monarchy opened the way to eventual rule by Marxist revolutionaries. Russia became the first country to fall under Marxist socialist domination. In the light of Russia's previous history it is perhaps possible to see why this should have been so. The country's life had long been arranged on highly authoritarian lines (at least until 1905), dominated by an ideology which was ostensibly religious but was imposed by secular means and thus forfeited most of its spiritual authority. In this sense Russia was ripe for takeover by a self-avowedly secular ideology bearing unacknowledged religious overtones — which is what Marxism was, especially in its Bolshevik form.

In a very real sense, in fact, the Russian autocracy, especially since Peter I, provided a pattern for socialist rule: the notion of the ideological state to which all ranks of the population owed service absolutely and in equal measure. Much, however, was yet to happen before *this* variant of Marxist socialism gained the upper hand.

2

The October Revolution

It was a mark of the abruptness of political change in Russia that when the monarchy fell, what replaced it was not one regime, but two. On the one hand, the politicians surviving from the Duma established a Provisional Government, in which the principal parties were at first the Kadets, later the Mensheviks and Socialist Revolutionaries. It was called 'provisional' because it was to exercise power only until a Constituent Assembly could be convened, elected by all the people. On the other hand, the workers of Petrograd (as St Petersburg was now called) hastened to revive their memories of the days of freedom in 1905 by re-establishing the Petrograd Soviet. They were joined by the soldiers of the capital city's garrison, active participants in the revolution for the first time, and their joint tribune was known as the Soviet of Workers' and Soldiers' Deputies.

But government and soviet refrained from trying to oust each other – for good reason. The Provisional Government, which began by abolishing the tsarist police and security services, had no effective power of coercion, and therefore had to tolerate the soviets as expressions of the popular will, at least in the big cities. As the minister of war, Guchkov, said, 'The Provisional Government does not possess any real power; and its directives are carried out only to the extent that it is permitted by the Soviet of Workers' and Soldiers' Deputies, which enjoys all the essential elements of real power, since the troops, the railroads, the post and telegraph are all in its hands.' The leaders of the soviets, for their part, recognized that the Provisional Government contained experienced politicians, that it could command the loyalty of the army officers, reduce the chances of counterrevolution, and gain international recognition. The theoretically inclined among them regarded the Provisional Government as a 'bourgeois' institution, which the soviets would 'supervise', on the workers' behalf, until such time as the socialist revolution became possible.

The Provisional Government was from the start in a very difficult, arguably an untenable position. It had not been brought to power by election, but nor could it claim direct descent from the old imperial government or the Duma. Prince Lvov, its first prime minister, proclaimed that it had been created by the 'unanimous revolutionary enthusiasm of the people'. That was to prove a shaky basis, especially since the new government found itself in a situation where it was unable to carry out the reforms that the 'people' were expecting. The fundamental difficulty was the war. The peasants might be crying out for a redistribution of the land in their favour, but could such a complex operation be carried out equitably without first a thorough land survey, and while millions of peasant-soldiers, with an impeccable claim to their own shares, were far away from the village at the front, and unable to take part in the share-out? The workers began to organize themselves to exercise a greater share in the running of factories and enterprises, but was it responsible to attempt such intricate reorganization in the middle of keeping up industrial output for the war effort? Could the supplies problems, which had brought the tsarist government down, be solved while the war was on? Most important of all, was the soldiers' demand to elect their own committees and to take part in the running of their units compatible with the discipline needed at the front line?

While the war continued, none of these questions could be solved without serious and damaging political conflict. And yet, to stop the war proved almost impossible (I say 'almost', since the Bolsheviks did eventually achieve it, but at a price which nearly split the party in two). The leaders of the Petrograd Soviet tried to organize a conference of socialists from all the combatant states, to put pressure on their governments to negotiate a peace 'without annexations or indemnities'. The British and French governments, however, put paid to this plan by refusing to allow representatives from their parliaments to attend. The alternative would have been to sign a separate peace with Germany and Austria-Hungary, but this would have amounted to a capitulation, and not until the Provisional Government was in its final days did any of its members recommend such a desperate step. So the war went on. Its problems continued to undermine the Provisional Government's efforts to establish a new political system, until the popular expectations aroused by the February revolution finally brought the Bolsheviks to power.

The new-found freedoms of February caused a tremendous upsurge in the ordinary people's capacity to organize themselves. It is often supposed that the Russians are a passive people, accustomed to doing what their rulers tell them. Actually, this is far from being the case. Partly because of the huge distances, many Russian communities remained, at least up to the early twentieth century, relatively unaffected by central government, and had to improvise their own arrangements. But even where government has been near and ever-pressing, Russians have always been highly inventive in devising social forms such that they appear to be obeying their rulers, whilst in fact running matters as far as possible to their own advantage. This was the centuries-old basis of the peasant commune, which the government had always intended as an agency for taxation and military recruitment. Now, in 1917, with government repression suddenly removed, there was a veritable explosion of 'self-help' organizations among Russian workers, peasants and soldiers, each with their own, often exaggerated demands.

The peasants saw in the February revolution an opportunity to rectify what they considered a very long-standing injustice, that much of the land they worked did not belong to them. As a resolution from Samara province put it, 'The land must belong to those who work it with their hands, to those whose sweat flows.' Peasants were prepared to support the Provisional Government as long as it appeared to be actively promoting a wholesale transfer of land to them. As the months passed, and the Provisional Government did nothing, they lost interest in it and turned instead to direct action. Ironically, the government helped them to create the institutions which made this possible: the local land committees, which it set up to carry out a land survey and prepare for the ultimate land reform, actually became dominated at the lowest level by the peasants themselves, and increasingly proceeded to direct land seizures. This was especially the case after the army began to break up. A typical scenario was for a deserter to return to the village from the front, bringing news of land seizures elsewhere. The peasants would gather in their traditional mir assembly, or use the facade of the local land committees; they would discuss the situation and decide to take the local landowner's estate for themselves. They would then all march together up to the steward's office, demand the keys, proclaim the land, tools and livestock sequestered and give the owners forty-eight hours to leave. Then they would divide up the land among themselves, using the time-honoured criteria employed in the mir, the 'labour norm' or the 'consumption norm' (i.e. the number of working hands available, or the number of mouths to feed), whichever prevailed in local custom. They used violence where they thought it necessary, or where things got out of hand.

Inevitably, then, a gulf of mistrust opened between the peasants and the Provisional Government. It was widened by the government's supplies policy. Because of the problem of supplying the towns with bread, the tsarist government in its last months had instituted a grain monopoly at fixed prices. The Provisional Government felt it had no alternative but to continue this, though the belatedly adjusted prices in a period of high inflation inevitably caused resentment among the peasants. Ultimately, indeed, it led to the peasants' refusing to part with their produce in the quantities needed. This is where the backward nature of the rural economy became a positive strength to the peasants. It was, of course, more convenient for them to buy matches, paraffin, salt, ironmongery and vodka from the urban market, but, if the terms of trade turned badly against them, then peasants could always turn their backs on the market and make do with the primitive products they could manufacture for themselves. During the summer and autumn of 1917 this is what many of them began to do, resuming a natural economy which their fathers and grandfathers had gradually been leaving behind, shutting themselves off from the market and refusing to provide food for anyone outside their own village. All Russian governments had to face this potential isolationism of the peasant communities until Stalin broke open the village economy by brute force in 1929–30.

Nowhere was the exuberant improvisation of the revolutionary period so evident as in the multiplicity of organizations created by the workers of Russia's cities. Pride of place, of course, belonged to the soviets, to which the workers of Petrograd streamed back as soon as they had a chance in February 1917. It cannot be said, however, that the Petrograd Soviet, or any other large city soviet, lived up to its original ideals. Perhaps that was impossible. The Petrograd Soviet's plenary assembly consisted of three thousand members, and even its executive committee soon grew to an unmanageable size, so that many of its functions had to be delegated to a bureau of twenty-four members, on which each of the main socialist parties had a prearranged quota of representatives. Naturally enough, these representatives tended to be established politicians and professional men rather than workers or soldiers. In fact, the attempt to introduce direct democracy led to an engaging but unproductive chaos, so that the real business had to be transferred upstairs to a small number of elected officials. This engendered a feeling among the rank and file that their voices no longer counted for anything. As we shall see, this discontent played an important part in the events of 1917, and helped to provide the Bolsheviks with the impetus that carried them to power.

In reaction, workers tended to devote more of their energies to lower level organizations which expressed their aspirations more directly. In some cases this meant the trade unions. These, however, were not well suited to a fast-changing revolutionary situation. They were bodies with some local roots but also strong national organizations: a few of them had managed to survive in shadowy form since 1905, in spite of persecution. They were organized on the 'production' principle, that is to say by branch of industry, whatever the precise skill, qualification or rank of their members. This tended to produce hierarchical splits *within* unions, which weakened their influence. They were also, of course, designed to function within a relatively stable economic and political environment, promoting their members' interests within that setting. They were not well adapted to fast-changing circumstances or to attempts to assume real power. It is not surprising that the Mensheviks and Socialist Revolutionaries retained a grip on many unions up to and beyond October.

In this respect, the factory or shop committees (*fabzavkomy*) were more suited to the circumstances of 1917. Often their origins were similar to those of the soviets of 1905: they began as informal strike committees during the February-March days, but this time at the level of the individual factory or even shop. The question of how they should develop caused controversy. Many Socialist Revolutionaries and most Mensheviks wanted them to run cultural and welfare facilities for the workers and to represent their interests in negotiations with the employers. That, however, would have reduced them virtually to the status of local trade union branches. The Anarchists, on the other hand, and in the short run the Bolsheviks, wanted fabzavkomy actually to *run* the factories, or at the very least to supervise the management's discharge of that duty. The Anarchists intended that in that way they should become units in a self-governing society, while the Bolsheviks planned to subordinate them to the state economic administration of an embryonic socialist society. For both of them, however, the immediate watchword was 'workers' control', and they persuaded a Petrograd congress of fabzavkomy to adopt it at the end of May – the first institution to pass a Bolshevik resolution.

The factory committees were thus in the vanguard of all the workers' struggles between February and October – for the eight-hour day, for higher pay and better conditions, and then increasingly for 'control' itself. At first the pressure was directed particularly against harsh foremen or staff: workers sometimes dealt with unpopular figures by bundling them into a wheelbarrow and carting them out of the factory gates, to the accompaniment of jeers and catcalls, for a ducking in the nearest river. Increasingly, however, the struggles concerned the very survival of enterprises. Faced with newly militant workers, as well as the more familiar problems of shortages of raw materials, fuel and spare parts, employers sometimes decided that the game was not worth the candle, and that their capital would be better invested in something safer. There was a wave of factory closures. The workers regarded these as lockouts, and often reacted by occupying the factory, and trying to keep production going under their own management.

Right from the beginning, some soviets and factory committees had armed contingents at their disposal. These bodies, often formed during the heady days of February, gradually assumed the name of 'Red Guards'. They were able to provide themselves with weapons and ammunition by courtesy of garrison soldiers, or by pilfering from armaments works. They patrolled factory premises and maintained order in industrial areas (where the writ of the Provisional Government's militia never really ran). Not until the Kornilov affair at the end of August did they assume real political importance. At that stage, however, the Bolsheviks, now in control of the Petrograd and many other urban soviets, mobilized them as paramilitary units under the soviets' Military Revolutionary Committees, originally set up to forestall a military coup (see below, page 48). In that form they made a major contribution to the October seizure of power.

The real troubleshooters of 1917, however, were the soldiers, both at the front and in the rear. Their charter was the famous Order No. 1, passed in full session by a seething and chaotic Petrograd Soviet, before any Provisional Government had even been established. It was intended originally for the Petrograd garrison alone, but it soon spread far more widely, probably because it met soldiers' wishes, and was swiftly taken up in most units. It called on servicemen to elect committees to run all units down to company level, and to send their delegates to the new soviets of workers' and soldiers' deputies. Soldiers were to recognize the soviets (rather than the Duma) as their political authority. In combat situations, officers were to be obeyed as before, but the committees would control the issue of weapons, and off-duty officers were no longer to be recognized as superiors. In practice, in some units the committees actually arrogated to themselves the authority, not mentioned in Order No. 1, of electing and dismissing officers.

The position of officers during 1917 was not enviable. Because of the high casualty rate at the front during two and a half years of war, most of the junior officers were quite recent appointees, from the same social class as their men, often raw and unsure of their new-found superiority. Though some reacted flexibly to the new situation and found a common language with their men, others retreated into an exaggeratedly rigid defence of their recently acquired authority. Among the senior officers were rather more survivors from pre-1914, but they were mostly men who had been taught to regard politics as subversive, an affair of which they were properly ignorant. It is not surprising, therefore, that at all levels of the officer corps there was support for a return to the unquestioning discipline of pre-February.

Evidence suggests that the soldiers, especially at the front line, remained patriotic in outlook even after February, and determined at least to prevent the Germans advancing any further into Russia. The revolution did, however, induce in the men a feeling that they no longer had to obey *all* orders unquestioningly. The soviets' peace programme circulated among them, and led to a widespread conviction that only a *defensive* war was still justified: the formula 'without annexations or indemnities' was very popular. The peace offensive also aroused expectations that the war would be over soon and that they could return home. These expectations were further sharpened by intensive propaganda from the Bolsheviks, who sent agitators, newspapers and broadsheets to popularize the idea of a *separate* peace to be concluded without reference to the Allies.

These expectations were rudely jolted by Minister of Defence Kerensky, who in June ordered an offensive on the south-western front. This was timed partly in order to aid the Allies (the mutinies in the French army looked at that stage more serious than the Russian ones), but partly because the officers hoped it would restore a sense of purpose and discipline among their men. The opposite turned out to be the case. Soldiers' committees discussed the order to advance at great length: some refused, some went ahead initially and then pulled back when they saw the casualty rate. At any rate, the offensive soon turned into a rout in which the Russian army *lost* territory. Far more serious than that was the effect on morale. Whole units abandoned their positions, and some of them murdered officers who tried to restore order. Then the mutinous soldiers seized freight wagons, or even whole trains, and held them at gunpoint until they were transported deep into the rear. From there they could return home, rifles at the ready, to take a decisive part, as we have seen, in the share-out of land.

The mood of the garrison troops was, if anything, even more radical than that of those at the front. Many of them were recently mobilized peasants or workers, undergoing their training, and still identifying strongly with the class from which they came. The Provisional Government's initial agreement with the Petrograd Soviet stipulated that these troops would not be sent to the front, but would stay in the capital to 'defend the revolution'. And in fact the refusal of a machine-gun regiment to be sent to the front sparked off the July Days in Petrograd, when an undisciplined armed mob caused havoc on the streets.

Even at this stage, however, the army did not disintegrate altogether. Some units remained loyal, particularly Cossack ones, with their special traditions, or specialist units, like those from the artillery, cavalry or engineers. Nowhere was the collapse so complete that the Germans felt they could advance without risk. Indeed, the German High Command deliberately held back, fearing that a major advance might be the one factor which could yet restore morale in the Russian army.

At the time of the February revolution the Bolsheviks numbered, at the highest estimate, no more than 20,000, and their leaders were scattered in exile, at home and abroad. For that reason they had even more difficulty than the other parties in adjusting to the sudden changes. They were seriously divided about what to do, but the dominant figures inside Russia, notably Kamenev and Stalin, inclined towards cooperation with the other socialist parties in the soviets in exercising 'vigilant supervision' over the Provisional Government. Some even talked of a rapprochement with the Mensheviks.

Lenin had quite different ideas. He was still in Switzerland in February. He returned to Russia with the help of the German High Command, taking a specially provided 'sealed train' through Germany to Sweden. The Germans were anxious to facilitate his return, so that he could begin fomenting unrest inside Russia and spread his idea of a separate peace. They also provided the Bolsheviks with considerable funds thereafter, which helped to pay for the newspapers and political agitators who proved so effective among the soldiers and workers.

As soon as he arrived back in Petrograd, Lenin poured scorn on the notion of 'revolutionary defencism', conditional support for the Provisional Government, or cooperation with the other socialist parties. The 'bourgeois' stage of the revolution, he maintained, was already over, and it was time for the workers to take power, which they could do through the soviets. Russia should unilaterally pull out of the war, calling on the workers of all the combatant nations to convert it into an international civil war by rising against their rulers. Landed estates should be expropriated forthwith, and all other land nationalized and put at the disposal of 'Soviets of Agricultural Labourers and Peasant Deputies'.

Lenin's new programme should not have been a complete surprise to those who had read his writings since 1905, but all the same it did represent something of a shift in his thinking. His study of imperialism had led him to the view that the socialist revolution would take place on an international scale, with the colonized nations of the world rising against their exploiters. In this perspective, Russia, as the weakest of the imperialist powers, but also the strongest of the colonies (in the sense that it was exploited by French, German and other capital), was the natural setting for the initial spark of the revolution – though it would need swift support from within economically stronger nations if it was not to die away. Lenin, in fact, had moved close to the position of Trotsky, who since 1905 had been preaching 'permanent revolution' on an international scale. Trotsky acknowledged this rapprochement by joining the Bolsheviks in the course of the summer.

Another new facet of Lenin's thinking was his view that imperialism created the *economic* prerequisites of socialism – trusts and syndicates, large banks, railways, telegraph and postal services – and that when the imperialist *state* was smashed, these structures would survive and be taken over by the new proletarian government. Since they were sophisticated and self-regulating, all that would be needed was to ensure that they were used in the interests of the people as a whole, not of a small class of exploiters, and this would be essentially a matter of 'book-keeping and monitoring' (*uchet i kontrol*). 'Capitalism', he asserted, 'has simplified the work of book-keeping and monitoring, has reduced it to a comparatively simple system of accounting, which any literate person can do.'

This vision was the real source of Lenin's confidence in 1917. He seems to have really believed that, through the soviets, ordinary working people could take power into their own hands, and administer complex economic systems. He called his vision the 'commune state', taking as his model the Paris Commune of 1871. This introduced a certain contradiction into his ideas, since of course the Paris Commune had originated in precisely the kind of 'revolutionary defencism' which Lenin rejected. But the image was to prove useful to him and to confuse some of his opponents. At any rate there proved to be a good deal of support among Bolsheviks for Lenin's heightened radicalism, and by May most of his programme had been accepted as party policy.

Initially, the Bolsheviks' position in the new popular institutions was very weak. With the disappointments of the summer and autumn, however, some existing delegates swung over towards the Bolsheviks, while new ones were elected on a Bolshevik mandate. The appeal of the Bolsheviks lay in their programme of 'peace, land and bread'. Facing a Provisional Government which could not end the war, and which was therefore incapable of carrying out land reform or ensuring food supplies either, the Bolsheviks were able to offer something which nearly all workers, peasants and soldiers wanted. Bearing these promises in their hands, Bolshevik speakers were often able to win over audiences and gradually the new grass-roots popular insitutions as well. This was the case first of all in the factory committees, then in the soviets of workers' deputies, then in the soldiers' committees and in some of the trade unions. The failure of the July uprising and the public revelations about German backing for Lenin reduced this support for a time, but it revived and redoubled with the Kornilov affair at the end of August.

This affair has been the subject of much historical controversy, and it cannot be said that it is clear even now exactly what happened. In the last week of August General Kornilov, commander-in-chief of the Russian army, sent troops from the front to Petrograd, evidently with the intention of dispersing the soviets and arresting all the leading Bolsheviks, probably in order to set up a military government. He was thwarted by the action of Kerensky (now prime minister) in declaring him under arrest, by the railwaymen, who blocked the passage of his troops, and by the soldiers of the garrisons south and west of Petrograd, who fraternized with Kornilov's troops and persuaded them they were fighting on the wrong side. General Krymov, their commander, committed suicide at this disgrace.

The mysterious aspect of the affair is that Kornilov had been appointed by Kerensky only shortly before, with an apparent mandate to tighten the discipline in the army. Indeed, the early stages of the coup itself were coordinated with Kerensky, who then abruptly changed his mind. The whole business seems, in fact, to have been dogged by the insoluble ambiguities of the Provisional Government's position. Kerensky wanted to restore military discipline in order to be able to go on fighting the war, especially after the débâcle of the June offensive, but at the same time he knew that the measures Kornilov proposed – abolishing soldiers' committees at the front, restoring the full power of officers, imposition of full military discipline among rear garrisons, in armament factories and on the railways – would alienate his allies in the soviets, and probably provoke a popular rising with Bolshevik backing. In the end Kerensky could not have it both ways, and he came down on the side of the soviets, in a manner that exposed Kornilov to maximum humiliation.

What is quite certain is that this fiasco dramatically revived the fortunes of the Bolsheviks. It left the High Command confused, demoralized and resentful of the Provisional Government. Alexeyev, Kornilov's immediate successor, resigned in disgust in the middle of September, saying, 'We have no army', and describing his fellow officers as 'martyrs' in the face of the general indiscipline. By contrast, the workers' militias, especially in Petrograd itself, gained enormously in status and self-esteem: under their new name of 'Red Guards' they gained many new recruits during September and October. The Bolsheviks' view of events generally seemed to have been vindicated, and nearly all popular institutions, especially the soviets, swung sharply in their direction. From the beginning of September the Bolsheviks had a majority in the crucial Petrograd Soviet, and Trotsky became its chairman. Moscow soon followed suit, and it became clear that the elections to the second All-Russian Congress of Soviets would result in the Bolsheviks becoming the largest single party.

To forestall any possible repeat of the Kornilov affair, the Petrograd Soviet established on 9 October a Military Revolutionary Committee (MRC), to organize the 'revolutionary defence' of the capital against either a military putsch or Kerensky's reported intention of evacuating the city and letting the Germans (already in Riga, only 300 miles away) occupy it and crush the soviet. The motion to establish MRC was supported by left-wing Mensheviks and Socialist Revolutionaries; its first chairman was a Socialist Revolutionary. All the same, the majority of its members were Bolsheviks. The new body immediately set about coordinating the Red Guards and, helped by the impassioned oratory of Trotsky, persuading the garrison troops to recognize *it* rather than the Provisional Government as their ultimate source of authority.

Throughout September, Lenin, at first from the safety of Finland (a warrant had been out for his arrest since the July Days), then from hiding in Petrograd, bombarded the party Central Committee with letters urging that the moment for the insurrection had come. He cited as evidence the Bolshevik majorities in the soviets, the rising wave of peasant unrest, the intended surrender of Petrograd (which would produce the 'Paris Commune' situation), and in the international dimension the recent mutiny in the German Baltic Fleet. Once MRC was in existence, that seemed to him the appropriate instrument for the seizure of power. And indeed, it was on the day after its establishment, 10 October, that he at last persuaded his colleagues on the Central Committee that a rising was 'on the agenda'.

Even at this stage, however, there were sceptics among Lenin's closest colleagues, notably Zinoviev and Kamenev, two of the longest standing members of the Bolshevik Party. Their arguments are worth dwelling on, as they represent an important strand in Bolshevik thinking at the time. They maintained that the Bolsheviks had more to gain by working with the other socialist parties in a coalition government based on the soviets, than by going it alone and risking a violent seizure of power. Bolshevik support was rising among peasants, workers and soldiers: they would soon dominate the soviets, and would gain a substantial share of the seats in the Constituent Assembly, whose elections were approaching. Why jeopardize all this by a violent coup, which would alienate everyone? And even if it succeeded, then the Bolsheviks would be left bearing the responsibility *alone* for the huge tasks of improving the food supply, restoring the industrial economy, and, most difficult of all, either securing peace with Germany or else leading a 'revolutionary war' against her. For such tasks a coalition was needed, and, moreover, the Bolsheviks were already in a position to lead it.

Of course, it can be argued that Zinoviev and Kamenev were pleading merely for different *tactics*, for what became known after the Second World War as the 'popular front' policy. Yet major differences of conception underlay their argument. Lenin's attitude was utopian, even apocalyptic: for him, the Bolsheviks embodied, in some mystical sense, the people, and once they seized power that power would *ipso facto* be in the hands of the people. Zinoviev and Kamenev, by contrast, were practical politicians, worried about how power could actually be exercised. Probably their views were closer to those of the majority of Bolsheviks in the soviets.

One significant observation they made: 'Insofar as the choice depends on us, we can and must confine ourselves now to a *defensive position*.' That was precisely what, in the event, MRC did, and this fact may have been crucial to the success of the insurrection. For what finally provoked the seizure of power was Kerensky's action, on the night of 23–24 October, in trying to close down two Bolshevik newspapers and to arrest some Bolsheviks on charges of anti-government agitation. On the initiative of Trotsky, MRC responded by reopening the newspaper offices, and then, to ensure the safety of the second All-Russian Congress of Soviets, due to open the next day in Petrograd, its troops began to occupy bridges, road junctions and railway stations, moving on to take over telegraph offices and government ministries during the following night. Lenin came out of hiding and went to the Smolny Institute, now the headquarters of MRC, to persuade them not to confine themselves to a defensive operation, but to carry on and arrest the Provisional Government. This is certainly what happened, whether because of Lenin's influence or from the natural dynamic of events. MRC called in Baltic sailors from Kronstadt and Helsingfors, while Kerensky's attempts to raise units from the front line were almost wholly unavailing, so low was the stock of the Provisional Government among army officers. In the end Kerensky slipped out of the city in a car to continue his efforts in person. The rest of the Provisional Government was duly arrested in the Winter Palace late on the night of the 25th–26th.

Already on the 25th Lenin felt able to issue a proclamation announcing that power had passed into the hands of the soviets. He did not, however, significantly, identify the Congress of Soviets or even the Petrograd Soviet as the new source of authority, but rather MRC, 'which has placed itself at the head of the proletariat and the garrison of Petrograd'. He thus specifically located power in the institution where the Bolsheviks had perhaps the greatest weight. When the Congress of Soviets met that evening, a large and influential group of Mensheviks and Socialist Revolutionaries, including most of the members of the executive committee of the First All-Russian Congress of Soviets (back in June), condemned this step as a usurpation and walked out of the assembly, to form a Committee of Public Safety and to try to organize resistance to unilateral Bolshevik rule. A few Mensheviks remained behind, while the much larger number of Socialist Revolutionaries who did so reconstituted themselves as the Left Socialist Revolutionary party, finalizing a break which had existed for some months in all but name.

Now that power was in the hands of the soviets, one might have expected that it would be exercised by the All-Russian Executive Committee (VTsIK), which was elected by the congress to conduct its business between sessions and to hold authority in the soviet movement. This, of course, contained representatives of several socialist parties. Lenin, however, announced that the supreme body in the new 'Workers' and Peasants' Government' would be the so-called Council of People's Commissars (*Sovnarkom*), a kind of 'council of ministers', whose members would all be Bolshevik. The Left Socialist Revolutionaries were invited to participate, but were unwilling to do so without other socialist parties also being represented.

As a result of the way Lenin and the Central Committee interacted, then, the Bolsheviks had seized power under the guise of defending the soviets against a Provisional Government bent on undermining them. That was the basis on which most of the participants in the seizure of power had acted, and most of them expected a coalition socialist government to follow, resting on the authority of the soviets.

There was indeed an attempt to form just such a government, sponsored by the railwaymen's union, Vikzhel, which welcomed the departure of the Provisional Government, but condemned the Bolsheviks' unilateral seizure of power, and invited representatives of the major parties and political institutions to try to reach agreement on the formation of a socialist coalition. Vikzhel backed their invitation with the threat of a railway strike. Against Lenin's opposition, several leading Bolsheviks did take part in these negotiations, and indeed discussed political options which would have entailed removing Lenin and Trotsky from the government. They were worried by the intolerant and arbitrary measures their government was taking, such as the suspension of non-socialist newspapers. On 4 November five of them – Zinoviev, Kamenev, Rykov, Nogin and Milyutin – resigned from the party's Central Committee, declaring that 'we cannot take responsibility for the Central Committee's disastrous policy, which is being pursued against the will of the vast majority of workers and soldiers.' Other Bolsheviks resigned from Sovnarkom, warning that 'there is only one way to keep a purely Bolshevik government in power – by political terror.'

This Fronde in the upper levels of the party soon dissipated, however. The Vikzhel negotiations got nowhere, partly because of Lenin's obstruction of them, partly because the Socialist Revolutionaries and Mensheviks were unwilling to go on parleying with a party which was suppressing the freedom of the press. The five dissident members of the Central Committee suddenly found themselves isolated, and begged their way back by renouncing their personal opinion. Zinoviev commented, 'We would prefer to make mistakes together with millions of workers and soldiers, and die together with them, rather than withdraw from events at this decisive historical moment.' This was to be only the first of many occasions on which doubting Bolsheviks suppressed their personal scruples in the face of the simple fact that their party held power, and of their judgement that this was all that really mattered. As Leonard Schapiro has commented, 'The greatest weakness of the opposition was that, having supported thus far a policy of insurrection without foreseeing its full implications, they felt it was too late for them to withdraw.' This is not wholly fair to Zinoviev and Kamenev, who had publicly expressed their doubts before the insurrection, but it well captures the essential dilemma of all Bolsheviks who disagreed with Lenin.

In the event, Vikzhel proved unable to mobilize the railway workers to carry out their threat of a strike. For his part, Lenin decided to broaden somewhat the basis of his regime by admitting seven Left Socialist Revolutionaries to Sovnarkom. They stayed for only three months, before resigning over the Brest-Litovsk Treaty (see below, pages 61–2).

In the provinces, as in Petrograd, power also passed to the Bolsheviks in the form of a soviet takeover of some variety. Their opponents were either the scanty and poorly armed forces of the old tsarist local government bodies, the *zemstvos* and municipalities, or else Committees of Public Safety on the Petrograd model. Where the Bolsheviks had a majority in the local soviet, they assumed power smoothly, and used their domination of the local *revkom* (equivalent of MRC) to suppress their opponents. Where they did not have such a majority, they formed a soviet consisting simply of workers, or called directly on Red Guards or sympathetic garrison units to form a revkom and take power. Some of the bitterest fighting was in Moscow, where the soviet did not set up a revkom till the Petrograd seizure was already accomplished and the soviet troops needed a further week, with artillery barrages, to overcome the Committee of Public Safety.

The only places where the Bolsheviks' methods were used successfully *against* them were, significantly, the national areas, where local support could be secured for a policy directed against the 'Russians' or the 'Muscovites'. A notable example of this was Kiev, where the Ukrainian nationalists managed to swamp the local congress of soviets.

The one body that might successfully have resisted the Bolshevik coup was the officer corps. They, however, after the experience of the Kornilov affair, were less than lukewarm in their support for the Provisional Government. General Cheremisov, commander of the northern front, refused to divert any troops from his sector to defend Kerensky. The latter's desperate personal mission to the front only succeeded in raising some seven hundred Cossacks comman-

ded by General Krasnov: these advanced as far as the
Pulkovo Heights, outside Petrograd, but were resisted and
eventually thrown back by a large force of Red Guards and of
sailors from the Baltic Fleet. A rising of officer cadets within
the city was not coordinated with this expedition and was
crushed separately by Red Guards.

In this way, during November and December, the
Bolsheviks succeeded in extending their control to most of
the country which had been ruled by the Provisional Government. There remained, however, a final potential limit to
their authority. This was the Constituent Assembly, whose
nationwide elections were imminent even as the seizure of
power took place. This body had been the aspiration of
Russian democrats and socialists since before the 1905 revolution. The Bolsheviks themselves had criticized the Provisional Government for not hastening its convocation, and
even after taking power they called their new 'Workers' and
Peasants' Government' 'provisional' in deference to the
claims of the assembly.

Privately Lenin had strong forebodings that the Constituent Assembly would not support the Bolsheviks, but he
decided that his new government could not allow itself the
outrageous inconsistency of forbidding its convocation. His
fears were confirmed by the results of the elections, held in
November. The Socialist Revolutionaries polled 15.8 million
votes and emerged as the largest single party, with 380 seats,
while the Bolsheviks, with 9.8 million votes and 168 seats,
were a respectable but clear second. Once that was evident,
Lenin began to speak of the Assembly as if it were on a level
with the Provisional Government, an institution of
'bourgeois democratic type' whose only function must be to
yield to a 'democratic institution of a higher order', namely
the soviets.

Even though they had lost the election, the Bolsheviks did
permit the assembly to meet. They did everything possible,
however, to instil in its members the impression that they
were on sufferance, even under direct threat, from the new

government. Sovnarkom issued a decree outlawing the leading members of the Kadet Party (which had 17 seats in the assembly), as a party of 'enemies of the people' (the first use of a phrase which was to have terrifying implications under Stalin); their newspapers were closed down, and some Socialist Revolutionaries and Kadet delegates were in fact arrested. On the day the assembly opened, 5 January 1918, Red Guards were posted all over Petrograd, especially around the Tauride Palace, where the assembly was to meet. Even during the session itself, soldiers leered at the delegates from the balconies, and took symbolic aim at them with their rifles.

The Bolsheviks put before the assembly a resolution recognizing the authority of the new Soviet government. The assembly rejected it, and went on to pass the first ten articles of a new Basic Land Law, intended to supplant the new Bolshevik legislation on the subject. The guards then requested the chairman to adjourn the session, and locked and sealed the building so that the delegates could not meet the next day. Rejection of the Bolshevik resolution had meant the forcible end of the Constituent Assembly.

Some Socialist Revolutionaries had recognized before the Assembly met that its fate would be decided by force. They had set up a Committee for the Defence of the Constituent Assembly, and, like MRC before them, had appealed for the support of the garrison troops in the city. According to one of their members, Boris Sokolov, the Semenov and Preobrazhensky regiments were prepared to come to their support, but the Socialist Revolutionary Central Committee decided against using arms in defence of the assembly. They anticipated that the government would win any armed confrontation in the capital, and decided therefore to rely on the moral appeal of the Constituent Assembly and the broad support which the Socialist Revolutionaries enjoyed in the country at large. When a workers' demonstration took place in support of the assembly, then, it was unarmed and was forcibly dispersed by the Red Guards, with the loss of some lives.

The dissolution of the Constituent Assembly was confirmed the next day by the Third All-Russian Congress of Soviets, and the Soviet government finally removed the word 'provisional' from its title.

Looking at the resistance offered by the moderate socialists, one cannot but conclude that they misjudged both the historical situation and the nature of the Bolshevik Party. They all considered the October seizure of power to be an adventurist putsch, morally reprehensible and objectively unjustified by Russia's social and economic development. They tended to regard the Bolsheviks as misguided comrades who would be taught a lesson both by history and by the Russian people. None of them thought the Bolsheviks could last long in power. For that reason the reaction of most Socialist Revolutionaries and Mensheviks was to keep their moral record clean for the battles of the future by walking out of the soviets and assemblies where the Bolsheviks had just taken control. In that way they more or less capitulated without putting up a fight (though one should note the places, notably Moscow, which were exceptional in this respect). Only belatedly and reluctantly did many of them come to realize that if the Bolsheviks were to be effectively resisted, then it must be by force.

In the long run, some army officers, the liberal parties and many of the Socialist Revolutionaries did come round to the view that it was necessary to fight the Bolsheviks. By that time, however, this meant a civil war in which the Bolsheviks already held many of the advantages.

3

War Communism

Even after the dissolution of the Constituent Assembly, it was not clear what form of government the Bolsheviks would be able to install, what its relations would be with local soviets as local centres of power, nor what kind of support it would receive from the various sectors of the population. The Bolsheviks had called for 'All Power to the Soviets', but Lenin clearly had reservations about that slogan, and the manner in which he had established Sovnarkom did not augur well for the future of decentralized government. The Bolsheviks had also talked a great deal of the 'dictatorship of the proletariat' and had called their new government a 'Workers' and Peasants' Government'; but how was the proletariat to put their new-found authority into effect? What was to be the relation between the new centralized institutions of the Soviet government (admittedly as yet largely on paper) and bodies like trade unions and factory committees, which had their own narrower interests to defend?

The Bolsheviks had absolutely no clear answer to these questions. As we have seen, they were divided over how and even whether to seize power.

Even Lenin himself had no clear conception of how he was going to run the enormous, divided, war-torn country. He fully admitted this. Not long before the seizure of power, he said, 'We do not pretend that Marx or Marxists know the road to socialism in detail. That is nonsense. We know the direction of the road, we know what class forces lead along it, but concretely, practically, this will be shown by the *experience of millions* when they decide to act.' He did have a general vision, expounded in *State and Revolution*, of ordinary workers and peasants taking over the smoothly running mechanism of the imperialist economy. He evoked this vision frequently in the early days of the new regime, in language which mixed democratic voluntarism with ruthless authoritarianism. 'Comrade workers,' he exhorted them on 5 November 1917, 'remember that *you yourselves* are administering the state. Nobody is going to help you if you do not yourselves unite and take over *all* state affairs. Rally round your soviets: make them strong. Get to work right there, at the grass roots, without waiting for orders. Institute the strictest revolutionary order, suppress without mercy the anarchic excesses of drunken hooligans, counterrevolution- ary cadets [*yunkera*], Kornilovites, etc. Institute rigorous supervision over production and accounting over products. Arrest and deliver to the tribunal of the revolutionary people whoever dares to raise his hand against the people's cause.' This was the language of the utopian, confident that he is already on the threshold of the ideal society.

Some of the very early Bolshevik legislation did seem to be putting this vision into practice by creating or strengthening institutions through which workers, peasants and soldiers could gain greater control over their own fate and also over the running of the country.

1. The land decree of 26 October 1917 abolished all pri- vate landownership without compensation, and called on village and *volost* (rural district) land committees to re- distribute the land thus secured to the peasants on an egalitarian basis. The decree was couched in the words of a Peasant Congress of June 1917. It reflected the Socialist Revolutionary programme and gave the peasants what most of them wanted at the time, while making no mention of the ultimate Bolshevik aim of nationalization of the land.

2. The decree of 14 November 1917 on workers' control gave elected factory committees the power of supervision (*kontrol*) over industrial and commercial enterprises, for which purpose commercial secrecy was to be abolished.

3. Decrees of November and December 1917 abolished all ranks, insignia and hierarchical greetings in the army and subordinated all military formations to elected committees of soldiers, among whose duties would be the election of their officers.

4. Existing judicial institutions were replaced, in a decree of 22 November 1917, by 'people's courts', whose judges would be elected by the working population. Special revolutionary tribunals were to be elected forthwith by the soviets to deal with counterrevolutionary activity, profiteering, speculation and sabotage.

On the other hand, some of the Bolsheviks' very earliest measures pointed in the other direction, towards tighter central authority. On 2 December 1917 a Supreme Council of the National Economy was set up, almost universally known by its initials, VSNKh (or *Vesenkha*), to 'elaborate general norms and a plan for regulating the economic life of the country' as well as to 'reconcile and coordinate' the activities of other economic agencies, among them the trade unions and factory committees. In January 1918 the factory committees were converted into local branches of the trade unions, and the whole structure subordinated to Vesenkha. This was not necessarily done against the wishes of the workers themselves: indeed there is a good deal of evidence that, to keep production going at all in the desperately difficult economic circumstances, many factory committees were only too glad to seek support from some larger entity. Nevertheless, in practice it meant that the economy was becoming very centralized even before the civil war broke out.

The same was true of the decision to set up the *Cheka* – or, to give it its full name, the Extraordinary Commission for Struggle with Counterrevolution and Sabotage – instituted by Sovnarkom on 7 December 1917. Its immediate task was to combat looting, hooliganism and black market trading, which had increased alarmingly, and to keep watch on organizations known to be opposed to the Bolsheviks. In its early appeals it tried to mobilize the population in the same style as Lenin: 'The Commission appeals to all workers, soldiers and peasants to come to its aid in the struggle with enemies of the Revolution. Send all news and facts about organizations and individual persons whose activity is harmful to the Revolution and the people's power to the Commission . . .' In practice, the Cheka was never subordinated to any soviet institution, nor indeed to any party body, only to Sovnarkom, and was able to extend its powers unchecked.

Another source of uncertainty about the new Soviet regime was its relation to the outside world. Lenin had encouraged the seizure of power in the expectation that its example would provoke workers' revolutions in other countries of Europe, especially in Germany. As the months passed and this did not happen, it became clear that the Bolsheviks were going to have to honour their pledge to end the war, not through negotiations with a friendly, socialist Germany, but by reaching some kind of agreement with the old imperial Germany. Given the weakness of the Russian army, which the Bolsheviks themselves had fostered, this could only mean acceptance of whatever terms the German generals cared to dictate. Trotsky, as the newly appointed commissar for foreign affairs, tried to put the new-style 'public diplomacy' into effect by addressing the German people directly over the heads of their leaders, but his words produced no immediate effect.

The dilemma of how to deal with this situation very nearly tore the Bolshevik Party in two once again. The Germans were demanding the Baltic provinces and the whole of Bielorussia and the Ukraine, which meant losing a substantial proportion of Russia's industrial and agricultural wealth. The Left Communists, led by Bukharin, argued that to accept this meant capitulating to imperialism and losing a golden opportunity to continue the world revolution which October had started. Bukharin agreed with Lenin that the Russian army was no longer capable of holding back the Germans in regular warfare, but he rejected this concept of warfare:

Comrade Lenin has chosen to define revolutionary war exclusively as a war of large armies with defeats in accordance with all the rules of military science. We propose that war from our side – at least to start with – will inevitably be a partisan war of flying detachments. . . . In the very process of the struggle . . . more and more of the masses will gradually be drawn over to our side, while in the imperialist camp, on the contrary, there will be ever increasing elements of disintegration. The peasants will be drawn into the struggle when they hear, see and know that their land, boots and grain are being taken from them – this is the only real perspective.

Bukharin's views certainly had wide support in the party. They may appear quixotic, but his recipe for involving the masses, especially the peasants, in the revolution through partisan warfare against an occupying power does closely resemble the methods of later successful Communist leaders, such as Mao, Tito and Ho Chiminh. Lenin, however, took the line of strict Realpolitik. The most precious possession of the world revolution, he argued, was that a Soviet government existed in Russia. That, above all, must not be placed in jeopardy. It followed that the only possible policy was to gain a 'breathing space' by capitulating to the German demands and preserving what could be preserved while postponing international revolution to the distant future.

In this controversy we see Lenin on the opposite side from the one he took in October. Then he had been an internationalist in perspective, trusting to the revolutionary élan of the workers all over the world. Now he became distrustful of any working-class revolutionary spirit not guided by the Bolshevik Party (as in *What is to be Done?* so many years before) and retreated into the one 'socialist fortress'. The party eventually accepted his arguments, and Soviet Russia signed a treaty at Brest-Litovsk, acceding in full to the German demands. Much flowed from that decision, especially the creation of a relatively conventional army (see

below) and the abandonment of 'open diplomacy'. One
might even see here the first glimmerings of 'socialism in one
country', later to be developed by Stalin. However that may
be, Germany's subsequent defeat by the Western Allies rescued Lenin from the most damaging consequences of his
decision: the Germans withdrew from the occupied
territories after November 1918.

The Left Socialist Revolutionaries agreed with the Left
Communists on this issue and resigned from the government
in indignation, calling the Brest-Litovsk Treaty a 'betrayal'.
Thenceforth the Bolsheviks exercised literally 'one-party
rule'. As if to mark this break, they renamed themselves the
Communist Party (in memory of the Paris Commune).

The Bolsheviks' method of seizing and consolidating
power led naturally to civil war. This was something Lenin
had always accepted. He had repeatedly urged that the First
World War should be turned into a class struggle or 'international civil war'. The same logic underlay his determination in 1917 to shun all agreements with other
parties, even from the socialist camp, and to promote a
violent seizure of power single-handed.

It took some time, however, for the various anti-Bolshevik
forces to grasp the reality of the situation, and to retrieve
themselves from their initial reverses. Senior officers from the
Imperial Army made their way to the Don Cossack territory
in the south, where they tried to assemble an anti-Bolshevik
Volunteer Army. Because of the divisions among the
Cossacks, however, it took them a long time to secure a base
area. Long before they did so, an opportunity for
anti-Bolshevik activity was created in quite another part of
Russia, namely Siberia. Following the termination of
hostilities on the German front, the Czech Legion was being
evacuated on the Trans-Siberian Railway, when fighting
broke out between them and Red Guards at Chelyabinsk.
Using the telegraph system, the Czechs managed to gain
control over the entire length of the railway. Since this is the
one vital artery of Siberia, that meant the whole of that

enormous territory, together with the Urals and part of the Volga basin, became an area where anti-Bolshevik forces could gather.

The first to take advantage of the situation were the Socialist Revolutionaries. Since the October revolution they had been uncertain and divided about how to meet the Bolshevik threat. On walking out of the Second Congress of Soviets they had declared the seizure of power 'a crime against homeland and revolution, which means the beginning of civil war'. But they had been reluctant to back this declaration with actions. One inhibiting factor was the fear of finding themselves along with the 'Kornilovites' on the side of counterrevolution: they still felt the lingering ties of socialist brotherhood with the Bolsheviks. All the same some Socialist Revolutionaries, without the approval of their Central Committee, did organize the assassination of the German ambassador and attempted to seize power by a coup in the new capital, Moscow, in July 1918. This coup was supplemented by an armed rising in Yaroslavl and one or two other northern towns, timed to coincide with an Allied landing at Arkhangelsk. The landing, however, was postponed, and the risings put down.

Taking advantage of the Czech revolt, the Socialist Revolutionaries set up a government at Samara on the Volga, which they called the Committee of Members of the Constituent Assembly, or *Komuch*. As their title implied, they wanted to reconvene the Constituent Assembly on non-Bolshevik territory. They saw themselves as a 'third force', between the emerging 'Red' and 'White' orientations. Their programme declared, for example, that the land was 'irrevocably the property of the people', which was not to the taste of most of the generals. In Omsk a Provisional Government headed by the Kadet, P. Vologodsky, promised, on the contrary, that all nationalized property, including land, would be restored to its former owners. The two governments eventually reached a compromise and formed a joint Directory, but this in its turn was overthrown by officers and Cossacks, who objected to its (moderately) left-wing programme, and installed Admiral Kolchak as supreme ruler and 'commander-in-chief of all the land and naval forces of Russia'. In this way political uncertainty and disunity undermined the efforts of the Whites, while the attempts to found a 'third force' all failed, since such a force always needed support from army officers, which meant the Whites.

The emerging White armies did have some degree of foreign support, from Russia's former allies, especially Britain and France. The effectiveness of this support should not, however, be exaggerated. The truth was that Allied governments, though worried by the incipient power vacuum in Russia, and by the growth of communism there, were not sure what they wanted to achieve, nor of the best means for doing so. In the summer and autumn of 1918 the main aim was to get the Russians back into the war against Germany. When that objective lapsed in November 1918, some Western politicians still took the view that it was necessary to rid Russia of Bolshevism, which might otherwise sweep Europe like the plague (Trotsky's vision in reverse). The majority, on the other hand, felt that after a long war the first priority must be to bring the troops home at last, and that in any case anti-communism was a policy that would split public opinion at home. Some British soldiers, indeed, mutinied. For that reason, most Allied troops left Russia during 1919, though the Japanese stayed on longer in the Far East, where they had more durable geopolitical interests.

Perhaps the most important contribution the Allies made was to supply the Whites with arms, ammunition and equipment, without which they could scarely have mounted an effective military challenge to the Communists. On the other hand, they never committed enough men to make a decisive difference to the outcome of the war, and, by committing what they *did*, they opened the Whites to the charge of being unpatriotic, of encouraging foreigners to intervene in Russian affairs. They also gave the Communists impeccable grounds for believing, as Lenin had warned them, that the imperialists were out to crush the young Soviet state. The foundations of many a myth were laid by the Allied intervention.

The Whites were able, at any rate, to mount a very serious threat to the Soviet Republic. Two moments of crisis stand out in particular. The first was in August 1918, when the Czechs and other White forces captured Kazan, on the Volga. This was some four hundred miles from Moscow, but there was no significant force of the infant Red Army ready to interpose itself, so that the capital was very vulnerable. Trotsky, now commissar for war, rushed in what was to become his famous armoured train, to assemble a force to defend the town of Svyazhsk, on the road to Moscow. He succeeded in doing so, and in recapturing Kazan. This was when he issued his command, 'I give a warning: if a unit retreats, the commissar will be shot, then the commander.' This crisis gave the decisive impulse towards the creation of a full-scale Red Army, as well as to the declaration of the Red Terror (see below, page 70).

The second period when it seemed as if the Reds might be defeated was in the autumn of 1919. The Volunteer Army, having finally become a formidable force under General Denikin, took advantage of a Cossack rising against the Reds to conquer most of the south and the Ukraine, and by October had advanced as far as Chernigov and Orel, the latter less than two hundred miles from Moscow. At the same time, General Yudenich, using the Baltic region as a base, advanced on Petrograd, and penetrated as far as the suburbs of the city by October. In both cases the Red Army proved equal to the challenge, and was able to drive the attackers back.

The Whites were, then, ultimately unsuccessful. This was partly because of political disunity, as has been suggested: at the very least they failed to act as a focus for all the various anti-Bolshevik forces. They failed even to attract a mass following among the population, though both the workers and the peasants were becoming very disillusioned with Bolshevik rule as it had turned out in practice. The Whites' political programmes were vague and inadequate: they did nothing to reassure the peasants that the land they had won in 1917 would not be taken away from them again in the event of a White victory. They failed to offer the workers a secure status for the trade unions, factory committees and other new representative organizations of 1917. In fact their only consistent political message was 'Russia one and indivisible' – which of course alienated the non-Russian nationalities who might otherwise have been inclined to support the Whites as Bolshevik nationality policy began to reveal itself in practice.

All this might not have mattered so much if the Whites had demonstrated by their behaviour towards the population that they were fairer and more responsible rulers than the Bolsheviks. But this was not the case. Dependent for quartering and food supplies on the regions where they were fighting, they requisitioned and pillaged less systematically, but scarcely less ruthlessly, than the Bolsheviks. They never glorified in terror as a system of rule, but they often applied it nevertheless. Moreover, the White generals continually lost control of their subordinates, so that, even if Kolchak and Denikin were themselves morally blameless, they proved powerless to prevent their armies committing excesses. As Kolchak wrote to his wife: 'Many of the Whites are no better than the Bolsheviks. They have no conscience, no sense of honour or duty, only a cynical spirit of competition and money-grabbing.' That was no recipe for winning a civil war, especially against opponents who were such masters of political propaganda.

The creation of the Red Army was one of the clearest examples of the way in which the Communists reversed the slogans of the revolution. The Bolsheviks had come to power by undermining the old army. Insofar as they had thought about what might replace it, they had envisaged an armed people's militia, on the model of the Red Guards. This was what made the Left Communists' programme for a 'revolutionary war' against the Germans so logical and appealing. Even for some time after Lenin had secured the defeat of that idea at Brest-Litovsk, the regime left itself with only a small new army, the so-called Workers' and Peasants' Red Army, structured on the principles the Bolsheviks had proclaimed in 1917: there were no insignia or ranks, and each unit was run by an elected committee, one of whose jobs was to choose officers. Military discipline was recognized only in active combat, and even there unit commanders had to operate for the time being without the sanction of the death penalty.

This structure, however, did not last for long. During the confusion of the Brest-Litovsk negotiations, the Germans actually resumed their advance for a time. This was a cruel reminder of just how helpless and quixotic the new Russian army was. Trotsky decided to scrap it, and to rebuild on more traditional principles. He set up a Supreme Military Council, under the tsarist General Bonch-Bruevich, to organize the task of creating a new army. A network of military commissariats was distributed over Red-controlled territory to raise recruits, at first voluntarily, then, after the Czech revolt, by compulsory conscription. Most of the Red Guard and militia units were disbanded as unreliable, with a few party members drawn from each to constitute the nucleus of newly formed and conventionally constituted regiments. But who was to command the new units? The party did not possess anywhere near enough men with the necessary degree of military training and experience to lead troops in modern warfare. With Lenin's support, Trotsky turned to officers of the old Imperial Army, at least those who had not fled to serve with the Whites: their insignia and ranks were not restored, but otherwise they were given the disciplinary powers to which they had been accustomed, up to and including the death penalty. There was no longer any nonsense about 'soldiers' committees': they were simply abolished and replaced by 'political commissars'. These were party-approved appointees, placed at the side of the officers – some of whom, at least initially, were reluctant to serve the Reds –

to ensure their loyalty, pass on political instructions and raise
the level of political consciousness among the conscripts. The
commissar was explicitly not subordinated to the officer but
was his equal, with the right to execute him if he committed
treason towards the Red Army.

Trotsky's methods aroused much criticism, both in and
outside the party. In VTsIK the Menshevik, Dan, exclaimed,
'Thus the Napoleons make their appearance', while inside the
party a so-called Military Opposition called for a return to
the militia principle and the dismissal of old-regime officers.
However that might be, Trotsky did create an effective fighting organization under ultimate party control. Considering
how hastily it was put together, and the magnitude of the
tasks it faced, the Red Army fought remarkably well, and it
can probably be asserted that morale inside it was better than
in any other section of the Russian population. Its troops
were, of course, better fed than almost anyone else at the
time, and service in the Red Army was an excellent means of
advancing oneself in the new society. Hundreds of thousands
of workers and peasants in the Red Army joined the party,
and some of them later advanced through it to positions of
power and responsibility in the new society. Trotsky, in fact,
did his best to ensure that Red soldiers were given special
training and promoted to command positions as soon as
possible. By the end of the civil war, these new promotees
constituted two-thirds of the officer corps: among them were
some destined to become household names during the Second
World War. All this had a profound effect upon the social
structure of the party (see below, pages 86–7).

The revolutionary regime's other main instrument was the
Cheka. As we have seen, this was established in such a way
that it was not subject to the supervision either of the party or
of the soviets. It arose outside even the rough and ready legal
norms which the new regime set before itself. It might be said,
indeed, that the Cheka directly embodied Lenin's ambivalence about democracy and authoritarianism. 'The workers
and soldiers', he exhorted the presidium of the Petrograd

Soviet in January 1918, 'must realize that no one will help them except themselves. Malpractices are blatant, profiteering is monstrous, but what have the masses of soldiers and peasants done to combat this? Unless the masses are aroused to spontaneous action, we won't get anywhere. . . . Until we apply terror to speculators – shooting on the spot – we won't get anywhere.'

From the beginning it was the Cheka, as the 'avenging sword' of the proletariat, which in fact carried out these functions, though Lenin talked of 'spontaneous mass action'. With Lenin's at least implicit encouragement, it soon overstepped the restrictions that had initially been placed on it: it proceeded from mere investigation of counterrevolutionary crime to the arrest of suspects, and from there to staging trials, deciding sentences and even carrying them out. The first person shot by the Cheka was a certain exotically named Prince Eboli, an extortionist who particularly offended the Cheka head, Felix Dzerzhinsky because he claimed to be a member of his organization. 'Thus', said Dzerzhinsky, 'does the Cheka keep its name clean.' The Cheka also received the right to create its own armed formations to carry out its growing duties.

From January to July 1918 the Left Socialist Revolutionaries were represented on the ruling Collegium of the Cheka, and they resisted summary justice and the application of the death penalty (traditionally abhorred by Russian revolutionaries). Steinberg, the Left Socialist Revolutionary commissar for justice, sought to restrict the Cheka's judiciary functions in the name of the 'revolutionary tribunals', which, though not necessarily gentle with their accused, were at least elected by the soviets and to some extent under their control. They more nearly, in fact, embodied popular involvement in justice.

After the rising of July 1918, however, the Left Socialist Revolutionaries were expelled from the Cheka, and the republic entered a more dangerous period, when emergency justice became more acceptable. A start was made with the insurgents of Yaroslavl. The future prime minister, N. A. Bulganin, there headed a Cheka detachment which summarily shot 57 rebels, mostly officers, while a commission of investigation selected a further 350 captives for execution. This was still an isolated incident, but with the proclamation on 5 September of the Red Terror, such operations became routine. The decree stated that 'it is essential to protect the Soviet Republic against its class enemies by isolating these in concentration camps; all persons involved in White Guard organizations, plots and insurrections are to be shot.' It became unnecessary for an actual crime to be proven against any person of non-worker and non-peasant origin. His very existence could be held to imply that he was at war with the Soviet system, and therefore with the people as a whole. The sinister term 'enemy of the people' began to creep into official instructions and propaganda. Latsis, chairman of the eastern front Cheka, told his officers in November 1918:

> We are not waging war against individual persons. We are exterminating the bourgeoisie as a class. During the investigation, do not look for evidence that the accused acted in deed or word against soviet power. The first questions that you ought to put are: To what class does he belong? What is his origin? What is his education or profession? And it is these questions that ought to determine the fate of the accused. In this lies the significance and essence of the Red Terror.

The imagery of public hygiene became part of the standard language of Soviet propaganda. Already in December 1917 Lenin had called for 'a purge of the Russian land from all vermin', by which he meant the 'idle rich', 'priests', 'bureaucrats' and 'slovenly and hysterical intellectuals'. And on 31 August 1918 *Pravda* exhorted: 'The towns must be cleansed of this bourgeois putrefaction. . . . All who are dangerous to the cause of the revolution must be exterminated.'

Concentration camps served the same sanitary purposes, by isolating the class enemy from the ordinary people. Lenin first proposed their establishment in a letter to the Penza provincial soviet on 9 August 1918 (the town was in an exposed position on the vulnerable eastern front): 'It is essential to organize a reinforced guard of reliable persons to carry out mass terror against *kulaks* [rich peasants], priests and White Guardists; unreliable elements should be locked up in a concentration camp outside the town.' Such camps were mentioned again in the decree on Red Terror, and were evidently already in existence, although the enactment authorizing them was not passed by VTsIK till 11 April 1919. By 1922 it appears from official figures that there were some 190 camps containing 85,000 inmates. According to Solzhenitsyn and others, conditions in most of them (there were notorious exceptions) were still tolerable compared with later days: prisoners still worked an eight-hour day and received a small regular wage. Perhaps something of the genuine notion of 'corrective labour' still survived. On the other hand, the inmates were hostages, liable to be summarily shot or taken out in a barge and drowned in a river in retribution for some action of the Whites in the civil war.

It is impossible to know how many people died at the hands of the Cheka during this period. Latsis stated that 12,733 persons were shot by them up to December 1920. Chamberlin in his standard history of the revolution makes an estimate of more like 50,000, while more recently Robert Conquest has given a figure of 200,000 for the period 1917–23, reckoning that a further 300,000 died as a result of other repressive measures, such as the suppression of peasant risings, strikes and mutinies.

These figures yield something by comparison with Stalin's later efforts, and of course it must be remembered that they occurred in a period of genuine civil war, when the other side was also committing atrocities. One has the impression that White brutality was sporadic and sometimes committed without the knowledge of White leaders, while the Reds frankly and proudly acknowledged terror to be part of their system. Lenin's attitude we have seen above, and Trotsky (in *Terrorism and Communism*, 1920) called terror 'no more than a continuation . . . of armed insurrection'. Perhaps these distinctions are tenuous. What one can say with certainty is that Lenin introduced and made habitual the ruthless use of violence against all real and imagined 'enemies', while also creating, outside soviet or party control, the extra-legal institutions to enable this to be done.

Whatever may have been the Bolsheviks' intentions when they came to power, there can be no doubt that during the civil war they withdrew or nullified most of the benefits they had given to the people in October, while submitting the democratic institutions they had helped create to rigid and often brutal control from above. 'During the civil war' does not, however, necessarily mean 'because of the civil war': in fact, there is considerable controversy among historians on this point. Soviet historians, and some Western ones, would attribute the extreme authoritarianism of Bolshevik rule at this time to the emergencies which the regime faced. Many Western historians, on the other hand, have always insisted that such authoritarianism was to be found in Lenin's attitudes from the outset and in the way he organized his own faction and broke with all those who were unable to agree with him wholeheartedly.

There is in fact no need no posit any total incompatibility between these two views. By their very method of seizing power the Bolsheviks plunged Russia into a situation akin to civil war – which later developed into actual civil war. Futhermore, some of their most authoritarian measures were taken either before or after the most critical phases of the civil war. The war, in fact, merely offered the Bolsheviks the first *occasion* to grapple with reality, to move out of the realm of fantasy into that of practical politics. They were guided by the vague but powerful preconceptions they had brought to the situation. Wartime, moreover, in some ways provided them with the best opportunity to combine democracy (in the sense of contact with the masses) and authoritarianism in the manner of Lenin's exhortations of November and December 1917. In *State and Revolution* he had urged that 'to organize the *whole* national economy on the lines of the postal service . . . all under the control and leadership of the armed proletariat – this is our immediate aim.' If one substitutes for 'armed proletariat' 'the party and the Red Army' that is a pretty close approximation to what War Communism actually was. But of course that substitution is the whole point. Lenin easily made the transition from the concept of 'proletariat' to that of 'party', without seeing the enormity of the questions begged. He displayed the same ambivalence in his article 'The immediate tasks of Soviet power', of April 1918, in which he was able to assert at one and the same time that 'without full-scale state accounting and supervision of production and the distribution of products, the workers' rule cannot hold, and a return to the yoke of capitalism is inevitable', yet also that 'each factory, each village is a producers' and consumers' commune, with the right . . . of deciding in its own way the problem of acounting for production and distributing the products'. Perhaps such ambivalence was natural in what was still largely a utopian programme being tempered by reality.

At any rate, there can be no doubt that the actual measures adopted even before, but especially during and after the civil war increased the power of the state enormously, and withdrew or nullified the benefits the Bolsheviks had granted to the people in October. The essence of War Communism consisted in (i) the nationalization of virtually all industry, combined with central allocation of resources; (ii) a state trade monopoly (which, because it could not satisfy people's needs, was accompanied by a vigorous black market); (iii) runaway inflation, leading to a partial suspension of money transactions (welcomed by those Bolsheviks who considered that money had no place in socialist society) and the widespread resumption of barter and of wage payments in kind; (iv) requisitioning of peasant surplus (or even non-surplus) produce. Alec Nove has summed it up trenchantly: 'A siege economy with a communist ideology. A partly organized chaos. Sleepless, leather-jacketed commissars working round the clock in a vain effort to replace the free market.'

Already gravely overstrained by more than three years of a huge war, and then by the fears and conflicts of revolution, the economy finally collapsed. By 1921 heavy industrial production was at about a fifth of its 1913 level, and in some spheres had virtually ceased altogether. Food production declined somewhat less severely, as far as we can tell from the inevitably unreliable figures we have, but the trading and transport systems to bring it to the consumer had broken down. The situation of both cities and countryside was indescribable. Evgeny Zamyatin thus evoked Petrograd in the winters of War Communism: 'Glaciers, mammoths, wastes. Black nocturnal cliffs, somehow resembling houses; in the cliffs, caves. . . . Cave men, wrapped in hides, blankets, wraps, retreated from cave to cave.' And Pasternak, in *Doctor Zhivago*, depicted the devastation on the railways:

> Train after train, abandoned by the Whites, stood idle, stopped by the defeat of Kolchak, by running out of fuel and by snowdrifts. Immobilized for good and buried in the snow, they stretched almost uninterruptedly for miles on end. Some of them served as fortresses for armed bands of robbers or as hideouts for escaping criminals or political fugitives – the involuntary vagrants of those days – but most of them were communal mortuaries, mass graves of the victims of the cold and typhus raging all along the railway line and mowing down whole villages in its neighbourhood.

In the countryside the peasants had already set about the welcome task of expropriating private land and dividing it up among themselves. Under the terms of the Bolshevik Land Decree, this process was mainly managed by the old village communes, which of course tended to be dominated by the more established and wealthier (or less poor) village families. The redistribution engendered a lot of friction, was probably not strictly egalitarian in its results, and was in any case vitiated by the discovery that, even when all private, church and state land had been absorbed, each peasant household could only add, on average, half a *desyatina* (just over an acre) to their holding.

Before the process was complete, moreover, the peasants were being importuned by supply officials looking for produce and unable to offer much in the way of money or goods to pay for it. This problem, of course, was inherited from the Provisional Government, but with the increasing hunger of the towns in the winter of 1917–18 it now became much more severe, and clashes became more bitter. Given their political philosophy, the Bolsheviks were bound to regard this problem as one of class warfare, and therefore to react much more sharply than the Provisional Government. In January Lenin suggested that the Petrograd Soviet should send out armed detachments to find and confiscate grain, and that they should be empowered to shoot the recalcitrant. And in May VTsIK and Sovnarkom issued a joint decree dubbing those who were reluctant to deliver grain to the state as a 'peasant bourgeoisie' and 'village kulaks'. 'Only one way out remains: to answer the violence of the grain owners against the starving poor with violence against the grain hoarders.' To organize class war in the village, and to make the search for hidden stocks more effective, 'committees of poor peasants' (*kombedy*) were set up in every village and volost. Theoretically these were to consist of all peasants whose holdings did not exceed the local norms laid down at the land redistribution. But, in practice, whatever the village's internal disputes, peasants were more and more reacting with united resentment against outsiders. Few except down-and-outs were prepared to help the hated intruders, and the kombedy degenerated into bands of louts looting for their own benefit or getting senselessly drunk on home-brewed 'moonshine'. The Bolsheviks themselves quickly came to the conclusion that the kombedy were doing more harm than good, and abolished them in November 1918.

In fact, then, much of the provisioning of the towns was carried on outside the state supplies monopoly. Peasants trudged with their sacks of produce into the towns and there either sold it for high prices or – in view of the unreliability of money – bartered it for manufactured items tendered directly by artisans or workers. Intellectuals and non-manual workers bargained away furniture and family heirlooms in the desperate struggle to stay alive, sometimes themselves going out to the villages to do so: Zoshchenko's story in which a bewildered peasant accepts a grand piano in return for a sack of grain was only a slight exaggeration. Half of Russia was on the roads or railways, carrying or trundling objects with which to trade. These were the so-called *meshochniki*, or 'bagmen', who became part of the daily scene. Such urban markets as the famous (or notorious) Sukharevka in Moscow became arenas of permanent lively and desperate haggling, as people sought the means to survive. Of course the Communists deeply disapproved of this commerce: it offended their trade monopoly and their ideological instincts. At times they set up road blocks round cities to apprehend the 'bagmen'. But they never really tried to eradicate the illicit trade, since they knew that to do so would finally bring mass starvation.

These experiences, and the kombedy episode, naturally inflamed peasant feelings against the Communists. Further fuel was added to the flames by the closures of churches and the arrests of priests, as well as by compulsory conscription for the Red Army. Between the spring and autumn of 1918 rural violence against Communists and against supply officials increased markedly. It was still somewhat restrained, perhaps, by the fear that if the Communists were overthrown by the Whites, then the peasants would lose the land they had recently gained. But in the autumn of 1920 and spring of 1921, when the Whites no longer represented any danger, sporadic violence broke out into full-scale peasant insurrection.

According to the Dutch historian Jan Meijer, a typical peasant rising would begin with a meeting of the *skhod*, the traditional gathering of heads of households. There an act of condemnation would be formulated, and local Communists or members of kombedy taken prisoner or shot. Arms would be seized from the local military training unit (set up by the Red Army), and the requisition team driven off. The peasants would then endeavour to cut themselves completely off from the outside world and to defend this isolation by force.

These risings culminated in the huge insurrections of the black-earth provinces, the Volga basin, North Caucasus and Siberia (the major grain-producing areas) in 1920–1. The largest of them was probably that in western Siberia, where armed rebels may have numbered as many as 60,000: they occupied two large towns (Tobolsk and Petropavlovsk) and cut several stretches of the Trans-Siberian Railway for three weeks in February-March 1921. We know very little about this rising, however, whereas that in the black-earth province of Tambov left somewhat more in the way of written evidence, which has been exhaustively investigated by the American historian, Oliver Radkey. Much of what he discovered may well be true of other risings too.

The Tambov movement was a peasant rising in the classical sense, with no direct influence or support from any political party. The Socialist Revolutionary Party, who would have been their natural sponsors, were reticent in their support for the insurrection, perhaps because their civil war experience suggested to them that fighting meant subordination to generals, and they wanted no more of that. It is true that the leader of the rising, Antonov, had once been a Left Socialist Revolutionary, and that there were Socialist Revolutionary features in the programme issued by the Union of the Toiling Peasantry, which was the civilian branch of the movement: reconvening the Constituent Assembly, renewed guarantees of civil liberties, full socialization of the land, and restoration of the mixed economy. But the latter two were natural peasant demands anyway.

At first Antonov's men consisted of odd bands of deserters from the Red Army, dispossessed peasants and other people 'on the run' for a variety of reasons. It was not until the final defeat of Denikin that Antonov extended his forces any further. Then began a campaign of murdering Bolshevik and soviet officials, raiding village soviets and court rooms (burning documents, like the French peasants of 1789), railway stations, and grain collection points.

Full-scale insurrection came only in August-September 1920, with the appearance of the requisition teams to claim their share of the harvest, which that year was a poor one. Battles broke out between grain teams and villagers, to whose aid Antonov came. At first he was very successful: thousands of peasants flocked into the Green Army (as it became known), and, since Bolshevik morale and strength in Tambov was low, they were able to liberate whole rural districts and establish a civilian administration. The Green Army was in some ways remarkably like the Red Army in structure, complete with political commissars, though naturally with few trained officers: even the Reds' opponents found themselves imitating Red methods. At its height the Green Army numbered up to 20,000 men, with a good many more fighting as irregulars. It cut no fewer than three main railway lines on which the Bolshevik government depended for communications with the Volga and North Caucasus. By December 1920 Lenin was so alarmed by the situation that he created a Special Commission for Struggle with Banditry, initially under Dzerzhinsky. Surviving local Bolsheviks and Cheka officials were pulled out of Tambov province, and special troops sent in under the command of Antonov-Ovseyenko (formerly of the Petrograd MRC) and later Tukhachevsky (fresh from suppressing the Kronstadt rising – see below, pages 90–1). These troops took control of villages one by one, shooting whole batches of peasants suspected of having fought with Antonov's army. Some villages they actually burned down. At the same time they flushed the Green forces out of the relatively sparse woodland into the open fields, where armoured units with machine-guns could function more effectively against them.

Repression was, however, combined with concessions. Grain requisitioning was abolished in Tambov on Lenin's specific order, and scarce supplies were brought in from elsewhere. In effect, the New Economic Policy (see below, page 119) was given a preliminary trial in Tambov, and seemed to work well, when combined with ruthless repression, in reducing the peasant will to fight.

It remains to be explained, however, why this and other peasant risings failed. After all, their aims were shared by most peasant communities, especially in the grain-producing regions, and even in some measure by urban workers. Yet there was never any consistent link, either between individual peasant movements, or with the workers. The peasants remained too localized and rural in their consciousness. The Green Army did once mount an attack on the town of Tambov, but seems to have been repulsed relatively easily by Red Guards. Above all, there was a lack of political coordination, such as might have been supplied by the Social Revolutionaries, had they not been already organizationally weakened and reluctant to take up arms; and in any case the peasants were by now distrustful of all political parties and of all help from urban intellectuals.

In some ways, given the anti-rural prejudices of most Marxists, it was not surprising that relations between the Bolsheviks and the peasants should have deteriorated so sharply. Matters were not much better, however, among the workers, who should have been the new government's natural allies. We have already seen that by the summer of 1918 the Bolsheviks had nationalized most of industry and subordinated the factory committees to the trade unions, centralizing 'workers' control' to a point where it no longer came from the workers. This certainly contributed to the revolution's loss of its ideals, but nevertheless such centralization was often accepted by the workforce as an alternative to the even graver threat of hunger. The fact was that the peace policies of the Bolsheviks, popular though they undoubtedly were, created a great deal of unemployment. It has been estimated that as many as 70 per cent of Russia's factories were working in some way for the war effort – and these tended to be the larger enterprises, employing large numbers of workers. State defence contracts ended abruptly with the ceasefire of December 1917, and in Petrograd some 60 per cent of the workforce was laid off between January and April 1918. The factories which survived very often went over to one-man management, since Lenin was now very keen on clear lines of authority, and began to pay piecework wages. Since the managers who took over were sometimes the old capitalist ones, now working under state supervision, factory discipline became once again reminiscent of pre-revolutionary days.

At the same time, food prices rose: in Moscow the price of potatoes doubled between January and April 1918, while rye flour (the main ingredient of the staple Russian loaf) quadrupled. In Petrograd rations fell to 900 calories a day, as against 2300 considered necessary for *non*-manual labour. Productivity declined as workers became malnourished and exhausted. To supplement their rations, many pilfered, resorted to the black market, went out to the villages to barter, or even to resettle there permanently, if they still had relatives or communal rights. Many workers of course joined the Red Army. The great depopulation of the major cities began. Between mid-1917 and late 1920 the number of factory workers declined from around 3½ million to barely over a million. Those who stayed behind either sought a career in the new party and state institutions (which gave preference to entrants from the proletariat), or they remained cold, hungry, insecure and powerless.

The demonstrations over the Constituent Assembly offered the first opportunity for the workers to express their new discontents. The shooting of unarmed workers by the Red Guards was widely denounced, while workers in a number of factories condemned Sovnarkom, demanded the disarming of the Red Guards (in some resolutions compared to the tsarist gendarmerie) and called for new elections to the soviets. On 9 January (which happened to be the anniversary of Bloody Sunday in 1905) a huge procession accompanied the funeral of those killed.

The non-Bolshevik political parties were too restrained and disorganized to offer effective articulation to the movement. All the same, some dissident Mensheviks managed to organize in Petrograd a so-called Extraordinary Assembly of Delegates from Works and Factories, which met in March 1918. It is not clear how the assembly was elected, but it did contain a number of working-class activists of 1917, especially from among the Mensheviks and Socialist Revolutionaries. Their speeches gave abundant evidence of renewed discontent among the workers: at hunger, unemployment, the closure and evacuation of factories – the capital had just been moved to Moscow – at arbitrary arrests by the Cheka, and the muzzling of the soviets. Above all, the workers felt powerless: they no longer had any institutions speaking for them. The factory committees were turning into obedient organs of government, the trade unions were no longer in a position to protect their interests, the soviets would no longer permit them to recall delegates of whom they disapproved in order to choose new ones. 'Wherever you turn', complained one worker delegate, 'you come across armed people who look like bourgeois and treat the workers like dirt. Who they are we don't know.' In general, they felt that they had been promised bread and peace, but given food shortages and civil war; they had been promised freedom and given something nearer to slavery. The assembly called for the resignation of Sovnarkom, the repudiation of the Brest-Litovsk Treaty and the reconvocation of the Constituent Assembly.

The Assembly movement did spread to other parts of Russia, and organized a number of stoppages and protests directed against Communist policy. It looks as if the movement mainly attracted workers from sectors such as metalworking and armaments, which had suffered particularly severe dislocation at the end of the war. The assembly's debates reflect the alarm and disorientation of such workers. On the other hand, many workers continued to identify 'soviet power' with the Communists, seeing them as their best hope in a bewildering and dangerous world. In June 1918 the Communists received working-class support in the elections to the Petrograd Soviet, while the general strike called by the assembly on 2 July fizzled out. Its failure was partly due to increased governmental pressure. The whole Moscow bureau of the Extraordinary Assembly was arrested, and the Red Army cordoned off the entire Nevsky district of Petrograd (the southern industrial area where the assembly was especially strong) and declared martial law there.

By the summer of 1918, though many, perhaps most workers were profoundly disillusioned with Communist rule, they had no convincing alternative to which to look. This may account for the haphazard and inconclusive nature of their activity, compared with the previous year. Most, in any case, were more preoccupied with survival. In 1917 they had felt themselves to be on an upswing, creating the future through the new democratic institutions they had themselves brought into being. Now they had ostensibly achieved their aims, yet were faced by poverty, insecurity and oppression such as they had never known before. The institutions they had created were now being used against them. Of the two political parties who might have articulated and channelled their grievances, the Mensheviks had pledged themselves to strictly legal activities through the soviets, while the Socialist Revolutionaries were divided and ambivalent about whether to oppose the Bolsheviks outright. One Menshevik summed up the workers' political mood in June 1918 as follows: 'To hell with you all, Bolsheviks, Mensheviks, and the whole of your political claptrap.'

This disillusionment and uncertainty, combined with the increasing repression now being applied by the Communists, probably explain the failure of the Assembly movement. On 21 July, the Cheka finally arrested all 150 participants at a congress and took them to the Lubyanka, where they were accused of plotting against the Soviet government and threatened with the death penalty. In the event, however, they were all gradually released over the next few months. The age of rigged trials against supporters of the October revolution had not quite arrived.

The workers were not again able to mount such a widespread challenge to Communist rule, but their voting behaviour in the soviets during 1919–21 showed the extent to which they had become disillusioned. Some of their support went to the Mensheviks, who maintained a strong presence in the trade unions, especially among the printers. The Mensheviks also sent an increasing number of delegates to the soviets, even though they were banned from them for several months after June 1918. Even after they were readmitted they faced constant official harassment: the candidates would be detained shortly before an election, or Menshevik votes would be disqualified on technical grounds. Since soviet voting was by show of hands, moreover, it was easy for Menshevik voters to be victimized. In view of all this, it is a tribute to their tenacity that they still had any deputies at all in the soviets: one or two were elected as late as 1922, after which the party's Central Committee (or its surviving members in emigration) forbade further participation in soviet elections, as too dangerous for the voters. By that time, anyway, all the party's leaders still inside Russia had been arrested by the Cheka. The Mensheviks' main political activity thereafter was to publish an émigré journal, *Sotsialisticheskii vestnik* (The Socialist Herald), which evidently claimed an extensive network of correspondents inside the country: over the next decade it published abundant accounts of working-class life in the Soviet Union, which are invaluable to historians.

The working-class movement was also, of course, gravely weakened by hunger, poverty and the drain of so many town-dwellers. By 1921 the industrial working population was at about a third of its 1917 level, and was poorer in every respect. The Communists had their own ideas about how to restore this supposed social base of their rule. To absorb soldiers coming out of the Red Army at the end of the civil war, the Central Committee resolved early in 1920 to convert certain army units into 'labour armies' – thus the Third Army became the First Labour Army. The railways and certain key industrial enterprises were placed under military discipline, and political commissars from the Red Army were brought in to replace trade union officials. 'Labour soldiers' felled trees, cleared roads, rebuilt bridges and restored railway lines. All this was supposed to facilitate the transition to a peacetime planned economy, without the disruption which demobilization would have brought. Some Communists thought that in any case the 'labour army' was the appropriate industrial unit in a socialist society. 'In a proletarian state, militarization is the self-organization of the working class,' proclaimed Trotsky. And in an Order of the Day he exhorted them, 'Begin and complete your work . . . to the sound of socialist songs and anthems. Your work is not slave labour but high service to the socialist fatherland.'

Not everyone agreed. The Workers' Opposition (see below, pages 89–90) were strongly resistant to the idea, and in the great crisis of February-March 1921 (pages 90–2) Lenin came over to their way of thinking (on this issue alone). Apart from the enormous resentment the labour armies aroused among soldiers who wanted to get back home, their actual work achievements were unimpressive. In 1921 they were abolished.

By 1921, the Communists were the only significant political force in Soviet Russia. They were also an enormously important *social* force. Most of the other classes of Russian society had been destroyed or gravely weakened in the revolution and civil war – even the working class in whose name the Communists ruled. In the absence of any ruling class, the full-time officials of the Communist Party and the Soviet state came closest to fulfilling that function. Of course they could not yet be regarded as a social class in the full sense: their power and their institutions were as yet embryonic, likewise their customs and their culture, and they certainly had not devised a means of perpetuating their power and privilege. In many ways the history of Soviet Russia might be regarded as the history of their efforts to extend this embryonic power and privilege into a permanent, secure and accepted acquisition, such as any ruling class expects to have.

Anyone who had known the Bolsheviks in February, or even October, 1917, would have found them in many ways difficult to recognize in 1921. In February they had been a party of underground and exile, small, loosely organized (in spite of Lenin's principles), quarrelsome, but lively, spontaneous, and beginning to make real contact with the mass of the population, especially the workers and soldiers. In October the party still looked much the same, though by then it had perhaps ten times as many members, and close contact with the mass of workers and soldiers, to whose aspirations it was far more sensitive than any other party at the time. By 1921, it had changed in almost every respect. It now had a mass membership, including many who were in it for careerist reasons; it was tightly organized, rigid, intolerant of divergent views, and out of touch with the mass of the people, indeed regarded by most of them with resentment and fear. The Tenth Party Congress in March 1921 sanctified the final stages of this transformation.

What had made this difference? Basically it had been the experience of holding power and of conducting a civil war; and both those experiences had resulted directly from Lenin's decision to go it alone in seizing power in October.

The most obvious external change was the growth in membership. After their rapid rise in 1917, numbers grew a further three- to fourfold by March 1921, when officially membership stood at nearly three quarters of a million. The climb had been by no means smooth. There was, for example, a considerable influx immediately after October, but then a large-scale exodus, probably mainly of workers disillusioned with Bolshevik rule. Growth resumed during the civil war as Red Army soldiers joined, but there were also periodic 'purges' designed to weed out the half-hearted, the corrupt and the merely careerist.

These ups and downs reflected in part anxiety in the leadership about their rank and file. Membership policy was dictated by two considerations which were in tension with one another. The Communists were unequivocally the ruling party, but on the other hand they also called themselves a mass party. Now, ruling parties inevitably have many members who, whatever their social origin, become unmistakably middle-class in their lifestyle. With the working-class base fading away, and the peasants increasingly alienated by the party, it constantly faced the threat of becoming largely a party of officials. Between 1917 and 1921 working-class membership reportedly sank from 60 per cent to 40 per cent. In reality, it probably fell a good deal further than that, since many who declared themselves workers were actually by now administrators, commissars, Red Army commanders and the like. Indeed, party records show that in October 1919 only 11 per cent of members were actually working in factories, and even some of them were in administrative posts.

Another natural result of numerical growth was that the proportion of pre-October Bolsheviks declined. In the summer of 1919 it was discovered that only one fifth of the members had been in the party since before the revolution. This proportion must have declined further thereafter. The formative experience of most Communists was no longer the revolutionary struggle in the factories (still less the deprivations and theoretical wrangles of underground and exile), but rather the fighting of the civil war. The archetypal Communist was no longer a shabbily dressed intellectual, but rather a leather-jacketed commissar with a Mauser at his hip, and promotion in party ranks now tended to go to the poorly educated, theoretically unsophisticated, direct, resourceful, often brutal types who had risen to prominence in the Red Army. If they were of worker or peasant origin – and most were – they were only too glad to have risen beyond it. It would be too much to say that the party now became militarist in outlook, but it is true that most party officials were by now used to solving problems by willpower, effort and coercion. This wartime experience reinforced Lenin's dictum that politics was essentially about who defeats whom (*kto kogo*).

The civil war and the experience of power also profoundly affected the party's internal organization. If in 1917 it had been possible for Sverdlov and Stasova, in the Secretariat, to handle all the party leadership's correspondence and to keep the membership records more or less in their heads, that was clearly no longer satisfactory once the party had governmental responsibility. All the same, it took quite a long time before the party's structure assumed clearly defined forms, and for a year or more after October improvization was often the order of the day.

When it did come, the hardening of the party's institutional structure owed as much to pressure from below as from above, as emerges clearly from recent research by Robert Service. During the emergencies of the civil war, local party organizations often found themselves desperately short of capable organizers, since their best men had gone off to fight. They were only too glad to be sent emissaries or instructions from the Central Committee in Moscow. Local party secretaries, deprived of colleagues or assistants, would take important decisions themselves: party meetings would become perfunctory formalities, with resolutions passed 'at a cavalry gallop', as someone complained. The practice of electing party officials, and of seriously discussing alternative candidates and policies, withered away. It became the norm for officials and committees to be appointed from the next higher level, and for commissars from the centre to arrive in an emergency and take all the really important decisions.

Of course, all this suited Lenin's leadership style – and Trotsky's too, for that matter. Both men were used to dealing with local difficulties by firing off peremptory telegrams cutting through Gordian knots. What happened now was that their instinctive authoritarianism received institutional form.

This meant that, especially at the medium and upper levels

of the party, a stratum of full-time officials was emerging, whose main function, given the grip the party now had over the soviets and the Red Army, was simply the exercise of power. At the very top, 1919 also saw further hardening of the structures, owing both to the war and to Sverdlov's death in March. The Central Committee, currently a body of nineteen full members and eight candidates, was already too large for speedy decision-making, and the Eighth Party Congress (March 1919) set up a Political Bureau (or *Politburo*) of five to do this. Its initial five members were Lenin, Trotsky, Stalin, Kamenev and Krestinsky. Alongside it an *Orgburo* was installed to concentrate on the organizational and personnel work of the Central Committee, and this soon developed a formidable array of files and card indices on *cadres* (as the party's staff came to be called) all over the country. Originally there were only two joint members of the Politburo and Orgburo: Krestinsky and Stalin. The Secretariat was also now formalized to conduct the party's correspondence and deal with 'current questions of an organizational and executive character', the Orgburo being entrusted with 'the general direction of the organizational work'. In practice these two bodies had overlapping functions. Stalin did not move into the Secretariat until 1922, but when he did so, he not only took charge of it as General Secretary, but also became the only man to sit on all three of the party's directive committees.

From the outset, the new bodies, especially the Politburo, took over much of the *de facto* power of the Central Committee. In theory the latter was supposed to meet once a fortnight, but during the rest of 1919 it met less than half that often, while between April and November the Politburo held 29 separate meetings, and 19 joint ones with the Orgburo, while the latter met no less than 110 times on its own.

The party's relationship with the rest of society was also beginning to take shape. The party rules passed in December 1919 laid down that, where there were three or more party members in any organization whatever, they had the duty to form a party cell 'whose task it is to increase party influence in every direction, carry out party policies in non-party milieux, and effect party supervision over the work of all the organizations and institutions indicated'. To ensure that suitable people were selected for this authoritative role, the Ninth Party Congress recommended party committees at all levels to keep lists of employees suitable for particular kinds of work and for promotion within their field. Such lists, coordinated and extended by the Secretariat, became the nucleus of the *nomenklatura* system of appointments, not just in the party, but in all walks of life.

Not everyone in the party approved of these developments. Some prominent members, not in the top leadership, were disturbed by them, feeling that they ran counter to the ideals which had brought the party to power. Two groups in particular emerged during 1919–20. The Democratic Centralists called for restoration of the 'democratic' element in Lenin's theory of party organization: that is, the restoration of genuine elections and genuine debate over matters of principle. The Workers' Opposition were worried by what they saw as the 'growing chasm' between the workers and the party which claimed to act in their name. They spoke in the language Lenin had used in October 1917, calling for 'self-activity of the masses', and proposing specifically that industry should be run by the trade unions, rather than by the managers and specialists that the government had installed under Vesenkha. Alexandra Kollontai, the most flamboyant and imaginative member of this group, argued that what had taken the place of 'self-activity' was 'bureaucracy', buttressed by the system of appointments within the party, and she therefore also urged a return to genuine elections and spontaneous debate by the rank and file. Although fundamental research on this issue still needs to be done, it does seem that the Workers' Opposition had substantial support among the industrial workers.

Before binding discussion of these issues took place, however, the party was faced by a crisis even more threatening to its ideals than the civil war. Towards the end of February 1921, first of all in Moscow, then in Petrograd, strikes and demonstrations broke out among the industrial workers. Their immediate cause was a further cut in the bread ration, but the workers' demands rapidly took on a political colouring as well, and began to reflect the effects of more than three years of hunger and repression. The demands, in fact, were remarkably similar to those being made at the same time by the peasants of Tambov province (see above, page 77). The workers called for free trade, an end to grain requisitioning, and abolition of the privileges and extra rations enjoyed by specialists and by Bolshevik officials. Their political demands reflected the influence of both the Socialist Revolutionaries and the Mensheviks, who were regaining popularity, despite their semi-legal status: freedom of speech, press and assembly, the restoration of free elections to factory committees, trade unions and soviets, an amnesty for socialist political prisoners. There were some calls for the reconvening of the Constituent Assembly.

Zinoviev, the party leader in Petrograd, closed down some of the most affected factories (in effect instituting a 'lockout') and declared martial law in the city. Special troops and *kursanty* (Red Army officer cadets) were drafted in and posted to key positions. Selected workers and the most prominent Socialist Revolutionaries and Mensheviks were arrested. At the same time emergency supplies were rushed into the city, road blocks were dismantled, and Zinoviev let it be known that there were plans to abolish grain requisitioning.

These measures did eventually quieten the Petrograd disorders, but not before they had spread to the nearby naval base of Kronstadt, where the Baltic Fleet had its headquarters. The sailors of Kronstadt had a long revolutionary tradition, dating back to 1905, when a soviet had first been set up there. They had played a vital part in the October seizure of power. Central to the anarchism which had been the dominant mood in Kronstadt was the original conception of the soviet as a free and self-governing revolutionary community. This ideal of course had been unceremoniously pushed aside by the Bolsheviks, and now, more than a year after the virtual end of the civil war, there was still no sign of an improvement.

A delegation of sailors went to meet the Petrograd workers and reported back to a general meeting of the sailors on 1 March. In spite of the presence of Mikhail Kalinin (president of the Russian Soviet Republic), the meeting unanimously passed a resolution which repeated the demands of the Petrograd workers (though there was no mention of the Constituent Assembly). Pride of place was given to the following demand: 'In view of the fact that the present soviets do not express the will of the workers and peasants, immediately to hold new elections by secret ballot, the pre-election campaign to have full freedom of agitation among the workers and peasants.'

The Soviet government reacted forthwith by declaring the Kronstadt movement 'a counterrevolutionary conspiracy'. They claimed it was led by one General Kozlovsky – who was actually one of Trotsky's numerous appointees from the former Imperial Army, sent to take charge of the Kronstadt artillery. The Communists appointed their own army commander, Tukhachevsky, to head a special task force and storm the fortress across the ice before the March thaw. Once again, special duty troops and kursanty were used, in larger numbers. On 17 March they finally stormed Kronstadt, capturing it with huge losses on both sides. These were compounded on the rebel side by the subsequent repression, in which the Cheka shot hundreds of those involved.

Assembling under the direct shadow of these events, the Tenth Party Congress took some decisions which confirmed the rigid centralization the party had developed since 1917. Lenin admitted that the Kronstadt revolt had awakened echoes in many industrial towns, and warned that this 'petty bourgeois counterrevolution' was 'undoubtedly more dangerous than Denikin, Yudenich and Kolchak combined'. He admitted, too, that relations between the party and the

working class were poor: much more 'solidarity and concentration of forces' was required, he exhorted. He submitted
two resolutions, one explicitly condemning the Workers'
Opposition as a 'syndicalist and anarchist deviation', the other,
entitled 'On Party Unity', condemning the practice of forming
'factions' and ordering that all future proposals, criticisms and
analyses be submitted for discussion, not by closed groups, but
by the party as a whole. 'The Congress orders the immediate
dissolution, without exception, of all groups that have been
formed on the basis of some platform or other, and instructs all
organizations to be very strict in ensuring that no manifestations
of factionalism of any sort be tolerated. Failure to comply with
this resolution of the Congress is to entail unconditional and
immediate expulsion from the party.' Such was the besieged
mood at the Congress that these resolutions were passed by
overwhelming majorities, which even included members of the
Workers' Opposition. One of the delegates, Karl Radek, made a
portentous and perceptive comment: 'In voting for this resolution I feel that it can well be turned against us, and
nevertheless I support it ... Let the Central Committee in a
moment of danger take the severest measures against the best
party comrades if it finds this necessary ... That is less
dangerous than the wavering which is now observable.'

No less important was the justification which Lenin gave
for the suppression of all opposition parties, as was now
finally done. 'Marxism teaches us that only the political party
of the working class, i.e. the Communist Party, is capable of
uniting, educating and organizing such a vanguard of the
proletariat and of the working masses as is capable of resisting the inevitable petty bourgeois waverings of those
masses ... [and] their trade union prejudices.'

It is true that factions and programmes survived a few
years longer, in spite of these resolutions. Nevertheless, with
the Tenth Congress the party finally sanctified the substitution of itself for the working class, and gave into the
hands of its leaders the means for the suppression of all
serious criticism and discussion.

4

The Making of the Soviet Union

The country which the Bolsheviks took over in 1917 was the largest territorial state on earth. It was also a great multinational empire, containing a bewildering variety of peoples: their formation as nations and their absorption into Russia had been going on ever since the Middle Ages.

The Tatar invasion began the process. We saw in the first chapter that the rule of the eastern hordes did much to develop Russians' sense of their identity as a nation. But it also divided them. Those Russians in the north-west who remained outside the Tatar empire developed their language and culture (Bielorussian) separately: this later became the official language of a Lithuanian state, which in its turn amalgamated with Poland. Thereafter Bielorussian became largely a peasant language, which absorbed marked Polish elements, while agriculture and land tenure tended to follow Polish patterns. In the south and south-west another branch of the old Russian nation, the Ukrainians (which means 'border folk'), also evolved separately, first under Tatar, then Polish rule. Like the Bielorussians, some of them became Catholics, while even some of those who remained Orthodox in their liturgy recognized the Pope as head of their church (the so-called Uniate Church). They absorbed many Cossacks, or 'freemen', fleeing from taxation, military service and serfdom in Muscovy. These became fiercely independent local communities of fighting men, living in a kind of no man's land between Russia, Poland and Turkey. Their traditions were invoked when Ukrainian national feeling began to revive in the nineteenth century, even though by that time Cossack units had been reintegrated into the Russian army, and indeed were performing internal security duties for the tsar.

By the time the Bielorussians and most Ukrainians were reabsorbed into Russia during the partitions of Poland in the late eighteenth century, their languages and cultures were very distinct from that of Great or Muscovite Russia; but the nations themselves were largely peasant, while the urban and rural elites were composed of Russians, Poles or even Jews.

Over the centuries the course of Russian expansion brought under Russian rule many people who had no kinship with Russia at all. Already in the sixteenth century the Russians were beginning to reverse the Tatar invasion (though at a much slower pace), conquering territories in the Volga basin still inhabited by Tatars as well as by Bashkirs and other pagan or Islamic peoples. In the eighteenth century the Russians conquered the last independent Tatar Khanate, in the Crimea, and began the subjugation of the Islamic mountain peoples of the Caucasus – which, however, took them nearly a century. The Caucasians proved to be fierce fighters and under their leader, Shamil, waged a *jihad* or 'holy war' against the infidel invaders.

During the mid- and late nineteenth century Russian armies struck across the steppes and deserts of Central Asia, into the oasis regions beyond, in the foothills of the mountains, where a variety of Turkic peoples lived, again of Islamic faith. The aim of the advance was partly better to secure existing frontiers, partly to acquire Central Asian cotton, and partly the desire for sheer military glory. Once the armies had passed, the nomad Kazakh people of the steppes were gradually displaced from their best grazing land by Russian and Ukrainian peasant settlers, while in the oasis regions of Turkestan, colonies of Russian workers immigrated to the towns, including eventually large numbers of railwaymen, as the railway followed conquest and trade. The resentment aroused among the local population by this incursion culminated in a major anti-European rising in 1916: much blood was shed on both sides, and many Central Asian Muslims fled across the border into China.

Just beyond the Caucasus mountains, surrounded by Muslims on all sides (and with Turkey just across the border), were two of the oldest Christian peoples in the world, the Georgians and the Armenians. They both came under Russian rule in the early nineteenth century. Although they tended to regard the Russians as uncouth upstarts, both peoples acquiesced in Russian suzerainty, for it meant the protection of a strong Christian power against Islam. In other respects the Georgians and Armenians were very different from one another. The Georgians were a rural people, mostly nobles or peasants, though with a lively intelligentsia: they had a reputation for immense national pride, love of their homeland and lavish hospitality. The Armenians, on the other hand, were more urban and cosmopolitan, successful bankers and traders, often to be found outside their homeland, throughout the Caucasian region, and indeed the whole Middle East.

Along the coast of the Baltic Sea, Peter the Great in the early eighteenth century conquered regions which had been ruled since the Middle Ages by the Teutonic Knights and their German descendants. There German landowners and burghers of Lutheran faith ruled over a largely peasant population of Estonians, Latvians and Lithuanians. The Estonians spoke a language related to Finnish, but the other two nations were completely isolated in the European community of languages. During the nineteenth century they began to generate their own native intelligentsia, often centred on the church to begin with: by the early twentieth century, with the coming of industry to these relatively advanced regions, a native working class was beginning to develop. In fact the growing national consciousness led to especially violent clashes there in the 1905 revolution.

The annexations of Poland in the late eighteenth century

brought several million Jews into the Russian Empire. Speaking Yiddish and practising their own faith, they ruled themselves in self-governing communities (the *kahal*) under the general protection of the crown. Most of them· were traders, artisans, innkeepers and the like. They were usually prohibited from owning land, so that very few practised agriculture. The Imperial government decided to restrict them to the territories where they already lived, which became known as the Pale of Settlement. Only Jews with higher education or certain professional qualifications were permitted to live elsewhere. Official discrimination against them was aggravated by powerful popular prejudice, which sometimes flared up into violent pogroms, especially from the 1880s onwards. Jews began to seek a way out of their situation, some by setting up their own socialist party (the Bund), others by calling for the establishment of a Jewish national homeland in Palestine (the Zionists).

Altogether, the peoples of the Russian Empire were at very different stages of national integration by the early twentieth century: some were still primitive nomadic clans, while others had their own literate intelligentsia and working class. In all cases, however, the social changes of the time – urbanization, industrialization, the growth in commerce, the rise of primary education – tended to intensify and accentuate national feelings, both among Russians and non-Russians. More and more citizens of the empire were faced with the question: do I belong primarily to the Russian Empire or to my national homeland? On the answer depended language, culture, career, often religion.

The 1917 revolution posed the same question again, in even sharper form. Marxism had no ready formula for the national question. Marx himself had tended to underestimate the whole thing, assuming that the existing industrial nations of Europe had a natural right, at least for the time being, to speak for the proletariat everywhere, while ultimately national differences were less important than economic ones.

In the spectrum of European Marxism, Lenin occupied an

intermediate position on the national question. Unlike the Austrian Marxists, Otto Bauer and Karl Renner, he did not regard nations as permanent historical entities: he held that they were conditioned, like all other social formations, by economic forces. On the other hand, he did not believe, like Rosa Luxemburg, that as soon as the socialist revolution took place they could all be merged forthwith in an international community. Like most Marxists, Lenin was inclined to underestimate the strength of national consciousness as a social force, but he was very well aware that in the circumstances of 1917, the desire of the subject nations of the former Russian Empire to enjoy greater independence was a powerful potential ally. His observations of the Austro-Hungarian Empire had made him conscious of the power of national feelings during what he called the 'bourgeois' revolution.

Besides, during the First World War, Lenin became increasingly impressed by the revolutionary potential of the colonized nations of the world, especially those in Asia. In *Imperialism, the Highest Stage of Capitalism* (1916) he developed the view that the class struggle was now taking place on an international scale, and that the colonized nations *as a whole* were being exploited by the advanced industrial nations of Europe and North America. It followed that, at the present stage of history, the slogan of national self-determination was a revolutionary one, and in particular that the subject nationalities of Russia, led if necessary by their 'national bourgeoisie', should be encouraged to overthrow their oppressors and decide their own future.

Lenin, then, viewed national aspirations as real and powerful. Nevertheless, he did believe that in the long run they were secondary. And since Lenin always tended to hope that 'the long run' might be speeded up, the result was considerable ambivalence on the national question, an ambivalence reflected in his policy after October. His intention was that nations of the old Russian Empire should be allowed either to declare their complete independence from

Soviet Russia or to join the new state as a constituent part of it. He did not envisage any intermediary position. In fact, however, as it turned out, what most nations actually desired in 1917 was neither complete independence nor total assimilation, but some form of associate or autonomous status within a multinational federal state.

In this significant way, the Bolsheviks were out of tune with the aspirations of the nationalities. Furthermore, in the absence of world revolution, Lenin was in no position to offer them genuine internationalism: the most he could extend to them was membership in a multinational state dominated in numbers, language, culture and administrative power by Russians. Without the safeguards of a federal structure, this threatened to mean actual Russification, the very evil against which they had struggled, with Lenin's support, under the tsars. This danger was intensified by the Bolsheviks' explicit subordination, in theoretical terms, of national independence to 'proletarian internationalism': as Lenin frequently reiterated, the primary concern of the proletarian party was 'the self-determination, not of peoples, but of the proletariat within each nation'.

In order to meet these dilemmas, the Bolsheviks in government had from the beginning to compromise, and to accept in practice what they denied in theory, a federal structure. The Declaration of the Rights of the Toiling and Exploited People, of January 1918, explicitly called the new Soviet state 'a federation of Soviet national republics'. At that stage, of course, even this was a mere aspiration, since the Bolsheviks did not control most of the outlying regions of the empire in which the intended national republics were situated: federation was accepted temporarily as preferable to disintegration. Nevertheless, the use of the word had long-term implications. It harmonized with the Declaration of the Rights of the Peoples of Russia (2 November 1917), which recognized the equality and sovereignty of all peoples, abolished all national privileges and restrictions, and established the right to self-determination 'up to and including secession and the formation of an independent state'.

To deal with the manifold and delicate problems of relations with the nationalities, Lenin set up a People's Commissariat of Nationality Affairs (*Narkomnats* for short) under Stalin. It mediated in conflicts between national groups, and advised generally on the ways in which Bolshevik policies would affect the non-Russians. As more nationalities gradually passed under Soviet rule, Narkomnats also became a real instrument of political influence. At its head was a 'collegium', a kind of large committee on which elected representatives of the nationalities sat. Narkomnats thus collated and aggregated national opinion as well as providing a means by which orders could be passed down from above.

Whenever national self-determination clashed with 'proletarian internationalism', it was the latter which took precedence. This can be seen even in the case of Finland, which had been a Russian protectorate for only a century. It is true that when a non-socialist government led by Svinhufvud declared independence, the Soviet government in Petrograd recognized this. It also, however, simultaneously supported a Red rising inside Finland, designed to instal a pro-Soviet government in Helsinki. This rising was crushed after the Treaty of Brest-Litovsk, when the Germans intervened on the side of the Finnish Whites. Here for the first time a danger appeared which was to recur frequently: that of Red troops being regarded by the local population as Russifiers and being therefore resisted as foreign invaders.

The history of Estonia, Latvia and Lithuania was somewhat similar. In Estonia and Latvia a National Council took advantage of the Soviet Declaration of the Rights of the Peoples and announced their independence from Russia, only to be arrested by Red Guards who installed a Soviet regime. These in their turn were swept aside by the German occupation troops following the Treaty of Brest-Litovsk. Then, after November 1918, with the defeat of the Germans, all three national movements struggled to consolidate the existence of independent republics in a dual war against both the Red Army and local socialists (who were especially strong in Latvia). They succeeded in this, at least partly owing to armed support both from irregular German units and from the British navy, which was trying to clear the region of both Russian and German influence. In this way Estonia, Latvia and Lithuania became independent republics which lasted till 1940.

Poland's independence from Russia was already a *fait accompli* when the Bolsheviks came to power, since the whole of the Congress Kingdom (the Russian sector of Poland) had been occupied by the Germans in 1915. Recognition of this was a pure formality. What reopened the question was the decision of Pilsudski, the Polish leader, in 1920, to invade the Ukraine and attempt to reincorporate territory which had been ruled over by the Poles before the partitions of the late eighteenth century. The Poles did very well at first, and in fact captured Kiev, but the Red Army then regrouped itself from its victories over Denikin and managed to drive the Poles back out of the Ukraine. The question then arose: should the Red Army profit by its impetus, pursue the enemy into Poland itself, and try to set up a Soviet republic in Warsaw? On this the Soviet leaders were themselves divided, and their divisions were significant. Trotsky took the immaculately internationalist line that socialist revolution in Poland should proceed from the efforts of the Polish workers themselves: for the Red Army to invade would merely persuade them that the Russians had returned, albeit under a new banner, to occupy and rule over their country as before. Lenin, on the other hand, took the view that circumstances were once again favourable for world revolution: encouraged by the heroism of the Red Army against their own bourgeoisie and landowners, the Polish workers would rise against their native oppressors and overthrow their government. Beyond that, too, the revolution might spread to Germany and even the rest of Europe. For a brief intoxicating moment the dreams of October 1917 returned: a Polish

Provisional Revolutionary Committee, headed by the Social Democrat Marchlewski, waited in Moscow to take up the reins of power in Warsaw (a scene to become familiar in Europe in 1944–5), while Stalin began to elaborate plans for the creation of a super-confederation of Soviet republics, to include Poland, Hungary and Germany.

This Polish war brought the final stage in the reintegration of part of the old officer corps into the new Red Army. General Brusilov, perhaps the most distinguished of the former tsarist commanders, and a man who had hitherto held aloof from the Communists, published an appeal in *Pravda*: 'Forget the wrongs you have suffered. It is now your duty to defend our beloved Russia with all your strength, and to give your lives to save her from irretrievable subjugation.' Many fellow officers responded to his words. And in case anyone should worry about the revival of Russian nationalism in Communist guise, the internationalist Radek provided a ready justification: 'Since Russia is the only country where the working class has taken power, the workers of the whole world ought now to become Russian patriots. . . .' This was of course only an extension of the arguments Lenin had used to justify the Treaty of Brest-Litovsk: it marked a stage in the eventual emergence of the doctrine of 'socialism in one country'.

In the end, the Red Army failed to capture Warsaw for reasons which have been the subject of controversy ever since (Trotsky ascribed the failure to Stalin's military insubordination). Lenin, however, summed it up as follows: 'The Poles thought and acted, not in a social, revolutionary manner, but as nationalists, as imperialists. The revolution in Poland which we counted on did not take place. The workers and peasants, deceived by Pilsudski, . . . defended their class enemy and let our brave Red soldiers starve, ambushed them and beat them to death.'

The war of 1920 showed, in fact, that Soviet Russia was prepared to act as a new kind of great power with a traditional army, and that its actions would be so interpreted by its neighbours, even where the ostensible aim was the promotion of international proletarian brotherhood. The ambiguity of Soviet 'fraternal aid' has remained to the days of the 'Brezhnev doctrine'.

The immediate result was a frontier settlement relatively favourable to the Poles. By the Treaty of Riga, concluded in October 1920, Poland was awarded territories that included large numbers of Bielorussian and Ukrainian peasants, and until 1939 her eastern frontier ran only just west of the capital of the Soviet Bielorussian Republic, Minsk.

The Ukraine offers an example of a national movement which, though far from negligible in pre-revolutionary Russia, received considerable fresh impetus from the revolutions of 1917. Ukrainian nationalism had been slow to develop in nineteenth-century Russia, partly because of government repression (it was livelier across the border in Austria-Hungary, where the authorities were less opposed to it). Something of a flowering followed the revolution of 1905, with the easing of national restrictions, and a Ukrainian urban intelligentsia began to develop, particularly in Kiev and the western regions. It remained true, however, that the great majority of Ukrainian speakers were peasants, and that the towns were very strongly influenced by Russian, Jewish and Polish cultural life. Many of the industrial workers were Russian, especially in the modern industries of Kharkov (the largest city in the Ukraine), the Krivoi Rog region and the Donbass: generally the eastern Ukraine had a much higher proportion of Russians than the west.

After the February revolution, a Ukrainian central *Rada* (Ukrainian for soviet) convened in Kiev, elected rather haphazardly (though no more so than the Russian soviets of the time) by those inhabitants, particularly in the towns, who felt themselves to be Ukrainian. In June, after abortive negotiations with the Provisional Government, this rada issued a 'Universal' (or decree, in old Cossack usage) proclaiming an 'autonomous Ukrainian republic'. The rada was under pressure from a Ukrainian Military Congress, representing Ukrainian officers and soldiers from the Imperial Army: they had gathered in St Sophia's Square in Kiev and vowed not to disperse until such a proclamation appeared.

During the summer of 1917 a great variety of congresses met, representing Ukrainians from all walks of life: from peasant communes and agricultural cooperatives, from zemstvos and municipalities, from universities and schools, from hospitals and army units. All of them took a pride in using the Ukrainian language and in stressing those traditions which distinguished them from the Russians. What was taking place was the explosive creation of a Ukrainian nation, discovering and confirming its identity in this multiplicity of organizations and meetings, rather as the Russian working class was doing at the same time. For most urban Ukrainians at this moment, however, national, not social, consciousness was paramount. It is not clear that the same was true of the peasants, many of whom shared the grievances and aspirations of their Russian counterparts, and wanted above all more land.

After the October revolution in Petrograd, the rada (in its Third Universal, of 7 November 1917), supported again by the Ukrainian Military Congress, confirmed the existence of a Ukrainian People's Republic, and promised an early land reform and the convening of a Ukrainian Constituent Assembly. At this stage the rada did not insist on complete independence from Soviet Russia – Ukrainian intellectuals had always thought of themselves as part of Russia, but wanted to be a self-ruling part – yet, all the same, bitter disputes soon broke out between Kiev and Petrograd. With encouragement from the Bolsheviks in Petrograd, soviets of workers' and soldiers' deputies, separate from the rada, were established in Kiev and other Ukrainian towns: because of the national composition of the population, these were normally dominated by Russians. Troops loyal to the rada closed some of these soviets down, rather as the Bolsheviks themselves were doing to their opponents in other parts of Russia; but in fact Ukrainian national feeling was so strong, even in the soviets, that when an all-Ukrainian Congress of Soviets opened in Kiev in December , it turned out to have a non-Bolshevik majority anyway. The Bolsheviks, dismayed by this result, withdrew from it and called an alternative congress in Kharkov, where they could be surer of working-class Russian support. So in the Ukraine too the Bolsheviks found themselves acting as agents of Russification.

In this way the scene was set for civil war on Ukrainian territory, with Red troops and Ukrainian military formations facing one another. The Reds succeeded in capturing Kiev before the fighting was halted by the German occupation of the Ukraine in March 1918.

During the following two and a half years at least eight different kinds of regime ruled in the Ukraine, and not one of them was able to consolidate itself, or even to claim the adherence of a majority of the population. This was not only because of the multiplicity of forces interested in the region, but also because of the divisions of interest in the population itself. It is scarcely surprising that the Germans, the Poles and the Whites under Denikin (who would have crushed Ukrainian autonomy) were unable to command mass support. But it is perhaps more surprising that the rada, or the later Ukrainian nationalist government under Petlyura, were not able to attract a more stable following. This may have been because, as Vinnichenko, leader of the rada government, later confessed, the rada had not done enough to win over the peasants by carrying through a thorough land reform. After all, the great majority of Ukrainian speakers *were* peasants, for whom the agrarian issue was at least as important as the national one: to ignore their interests was to deprive oneself of a vital source of support. This impression is strengthened by the enthusiastic support given by many Ukrainian peasants to Makhno, the Anarchist leader, who seems to have filled a much-felt need, without being able to lay the foundations of stable and lasting government because he had so little support *outside* the peasantry.

Lacking a convinced peasant following, the Ukrainian nationalists could expect little enthusiasm from the Russians, who preferred rule from Moscow to that from Kiev, and still less from the Jews, whom Petlyura alienated by his encouragement of vicious pogroms against them. The Ukrainian national movement was thus defeated in its hour of apparent victory, and the Reds were eventually able to establish themselves permanently in Kiev.

The Ukraine's brief and turbulent independence did, however, leave a heritage. The victorious Ukrainian Bolsheviks were themselves affected by it. It is true that in October 1919 the Ukrainian Communist Party had its own Central Committee abolished and was directly subordinated to the Russian Communist Party in Moscow. But many Ukrainian Communists never really accepted this decision: indeed they protested to Moscow and succeeded in provoking from Lenin a ringing denunciation of Great (i.e. Muscovite) Russian chauvinism. He recommended that the Ukrainian Communist Party should rule in a coalition government with the Borotbisty (equivalents of the Left Socialist Revolutionaries), and that party members should 'act by all means available against any obstacles to the free development of the Ukrainian language and culture', for example by making it a condition that all administrative offices should have a kernel of Ukrainian speakers, and that no one should be officially employed who did not have some knowledge of Ukrainian.

Under a regime of this kind, the Ukraine did in fact in the 1920s experience an unprecedented flowering of its language, its culture and its education system. But it was to prove fragile, since all the elements of tight subordination to Moscow remained in place.

Rather similar developments took place in Bielorussia, where two imperfectly elected radas arose, one in Minsk and the other in Vilnius. They amalgamated for a time, and declared national independence under German protection (following the Treaty of Brest-Litovsk). When the Germans withdrew in November 1918, the Bielorussian state collapsed, and the territory it claimed was subsequently divided between Poland and Soviet Russia at the Treaty of Riga. All the same, its brief, precarious independence served as the basis for later nationalist myths.

The nations of the Transcaucasus broke away from Russia not so much from determination to do so, as because circumstances detached them from the empire. The three main nations of the region, the Georgians, Armenians and Azerbaidjanis, had little in common with one another. The Azerbaidjanis were Muslims, the other two Christians: but whereas the Georgians were a settled people of peasants and nobles (some 5 per cent of the population belonged to the nobility), among the Armenians was a fair number of active and thrusting merchants, many of whom lived outside their homeland, and were resented as successful foreign businessmen usually are. There were substantial Russian minorities, administrators, professional men and workers, in most of the main cities of the region.

All three local nations had territorial claims on each other, and the Armenians and Azerbaidjanis, in particular, had got into the habit of inflicting violence on one another. The numerous nationalist and socialist parties of the region wanted an easing of Russian dominance, but, with the exception of the Muslim movements, they did not seek secession from Russia: their fear and dislike of each other was too great for that, and the Armenians still welcomed Russian protection as an insurance against a repetition of the horrifying Turkish massacre among their countrymen in the 1890s and in 1915.

It is scarcely surprising, in view of all this, that an attempt at a Transcaucasian federation in 1917–18 swiftly broke down, and that each nation tried to go its own way, seeking armed support from abroad. The Georgians received it first from the Germans, then from the British; the Azerbaidjanis from their fellow Muslims, the Turks; and the Armenians from the Whites under Denikin, who, though insensitive to national aspirations, at least offered protection from the hated Turks.

The Germans, the Turks and Denikin were, however, all in turn defeated, while the British withdrew. This left the three republics open to Soviet Russia. During 1920 Armenia and Azerbaidjan, weakened by internal conflicts and border disputes, were reintegrated into Russia by the technique which the Bolsheviks had tried in Finland and the Baltic: military invasion coordinated with an internal coup by the local Reds. Azerbaidjan, with its large colony of Russian oil workers in Baku, was especially vulnerable to such means, while Armenia was weakened by a Turkish attack.

The Georgian Republic was a somewhat more formidable adversary. Alone of the three it had established a stable government, under the Menshevik, Noi Zhordania, and it was carrying out a land reform which brought it solid peasant support. Nevertheless, in February 1921 the Red Army invaded, and was able to conquer the country after a month or so of stubborn fighting. Lenin was doubtful about the timing of this invasion, and he insisted afterwards that a gentler occupation policy should be pursued than in Armenia and Azerbaidjan. He was on the eve of announcing the New Economic Policy in Russia proper, and he was aware of the resentment that brutal Communist policies had aroused elsewhere. 'It is imperative', he exhorted, 'to enforce a special policy of concessions towards Georgian intellectuals and small traders.' He even talked of a compromise with Zhordania and the Mensheviks. Nothing came of this, not entirely through Lenin's fault. Stalin was anxious to establish a tightly controlled regime in his own homeland, and, as we shall see, came into direct conflict with Lenin over this.

The relationship between Islam and Bolshevism was an ambivalent one. There was, of course, a basic incompatibility between the atheism of the Marxists and the staunch monotheism of Islam. All the same, many politically active Muslims had become socialists of one kind or another in the decade or so before the revolution. This was partly for instrumental reasons: they had seen socialism in 1905 as a form of politics able to organize an underground party, mobilize the masses and threaten an oppressive government. They saw in it too the means of attracting international support for their own movements. But the adoption of socialism by Muslim intellectuals sprang from reasons of substance too: as a doctrine, socialism offered them, in theory, the brotherhood and equality of all nations, and solidarity in the struggle against Western imperialism. As Hanafi Muzaffar, a Volga Tatar radical intellectual, predicted, 'Muslim people will unite themselves to communism: like communism, Islam rejects narrow nationalism.'

Significantly, however, he continued: 'Islam is international and recognizes only the brotherhood and the unity of all nations under the banner of Islam.' That sentence sums up both what was to attract Muslims to communism, and what was to alienate them from it. The ideal of the *Umma*, the worldwide Muslim community, was still very different from 'proletarian internationalism'. It was not a vision to which Lenin could accommodate himself save for passing expediency, especially when combined, as it often was, with the idea of a 'pan-Turkic' state – a federation joining all the peoples, both inside and outside Russia, of Turkic language and ethnic origin.

All the same, in the late months of 1917, there was much on which Muslims and Bolsheviks could agree. Muslims had been infuriated by the temporization of the Provisional Government, which had declined to concede the separate educational, religious and military institutions demanded by the All-Russian Muslim Congress in May 1917. As against this, the Bolsheviks opened their eastern policy with a declaration of 20 November 1917 'To all Toiling Muslims of Russia and the East', which expressed abhorrence of religious and national oppression under the tsars, and promised: 'Henceforth your beliefs and customs, your national and cultural institutions are declared to be free and inviolate. . . . Know that your rights, like the rights of all the peoples of Russia, are protected by the whole might of the revolution and its organs, the Soviets of Workers', Soldiers' and Peasants' Deputies.'

This promise was to be belied by events soon enough, but for the first two or three months the Bolsheviks were actually in no position to prevent the emergence of Islamic governing institutions, since this usually happened in areas where soviet power was insecure. As a result, soviets and Muslim committees often existed side by side. It soon became clear, however, that the divide between them was a national as well as a religious one. The soviets were usually entirely composed of Russians, and their attitude to the Muslim committees was often suspicious and hostile, especially in Central Asia, where the memory of the 1916 massacres was still vivid. There were also ideological reasons why no indigenous delegates were admitted to the soviets or to responsible party posts in Islamic regions. As Kolesov, chairman of the Tashkent Congress of Soviets, explained, 'It is impossible to admit Muslims to the supreme organs of the Communist Party, because they do not possess any proletarian organization.' And indeed, the working class of Tashkent (mostly either railway or textile workers) were largely Russian. The Tashkent Soviet, consequently, was 100 per cent Russian, and the local native population tended to regard it as the bearer of a relabelled but familiar Russian colonialist oppression. Soviet moves to expropriate *waqf* (religious endowment) lands, and to close mosques, Koranic schools and *sharia* (Islamic law) courts, vividly exemplified this oppression: indeed the tsarist regime had never attempted religious discrimination on this scale.

The tension between the two communities burst into the open in February 1918, when units of the Tashkent Soviet stormed and destroyed the city of Kokand, where a Muslim People's Council had proclaimed the autonomy of Turkestan. Similarly in Kazan, the capital of the Volga Tatars, the soviet decreed martial law, arrested the leaders of the Harbi Shuro, the Muslim military council, and stormed the suburb in which its surving members took refuge.

As a result of these ferocious attacks, some Muslims allied

themselves with the Whites. But they did not usually stay with them for long, for the Whites were no less ruthless with those who opposed them – they shot the prominent Tatar leader, Mulla-Nur Vakhitov, for example, in August 1919 – and they did not even have any theoretical commitment to national or religious freedom: on the contrary, they proclaimed their intention of restoring Russian supremacy over other nations within the empire. This may explain the fact that most Muslims continued to try to work with the Communists, despite the frequent brutality of their policy in the localities.

For their part, the Communist government in Moscow did come half way to meet them, at least as long as they needed their support in the civil war. As part of Narkomnats, Stalin set up a Central Muslim Commissariat, headed by Vakhitov (until his death), to coordinate Muslim affairs, and to articulate the views of the Muslim population. They were even allowed for a time to run a Muslim Military College, directed by the Tatar, Mir-Said Sultan Galiev: at one stage nearly half the Red troops on the eastern front facing Kolchak were Muslim, so that the Bolsheviks had an overwhelming interest in their morale and training, in spite of the obvious dangers, from their point of view, of authorizing separate Islamic fighting units.

Stalin even held out the hope that the Soviet government would create a large Tatar-Bashkir Republic, to act as an arena for the development of Islamic socialism: though less than a pan-Turkic republic, it could be seen as the first step towards such a state. The Russian Communist Party also recognized at this stage the existence of an independent Muslim Communist Party, not directly subordinated to Moscow.

At the height of their fortunes, in the summer of 1918, the Muslim socialists had succeeded in creating the embryos from which an Islamic socialist state could grow: a state apparatus, a party, an army. The potential ideology of such a state was adumbrated by Sultan Galiev in *Zhizn natsionalnostei* (The Life of the Nationalities), the organ of Narkomnats. He extended Lenin's view, expounded in *Imperialism, the Highest Stage of Capitalism*, that the class struggle was now taking place on an international scale: Sultan Galiev actually claimed that European nations *as a whole* objectively exploited the colonized nations *as a whole*.

All Muslim colonized peoples are proletarian peoples and as almost all classes in Muslim society have been oppressed by the colonialists, all classes have the right to be called 'proletarians'. . . . Therefore it is legitimate to say that the national liberation movement in Muslim countries has the character of a socialist revolution.

This was the first statement of a thesis which has become enormously influential in the twentieth century, as developed by Mao Tsetung, Ho Chiminh, and other Asian, African and Latin American Marxists. Like them, Sultan Galiev increasingly suspected that only the colonized peoples were really revolutionary in spirit. He feared that the Russian people, having achieved supremacy in a revived empire, albeit now socialist in name, would resume their oppression of other peoples. He could not give vent to such fears in *Zhizn natsionalnostei*, but he did express the conviction, unwelcome to most Bolsheviks at the time, that revolution was to be expected, not from Western Europe, where the workers were already, from an international viewpoint, 'bourgeois', but from the East, where colonized and oppressed peoples could be united by the joint Islamic and Communist battle cry of anti-imperialism. Like Mao, he saw the army – in his case the Muslim units of the Red Army – as a nucleus and training ground for a revolutionary movement, and ultimately for a legitimate and popular socialist government. In Tashkent a similar line was taken by the Kazakh Tarar Ryskulov, who hoped to establish an autonomous Turkic Republic and Turkic Communist Party.

As soon as the Bolsheviks had a little more confidence in

their military position, they moved to inhibit any developments which might impart substance to Sultan Galiev's vision. Already in November 1918 they merged the Muslim Communist Party with the Russian Communist Party, as a subordinate unit. The scheme for a Tatar-Bashkir Republic was dropped and instead two smaller republics, Tatarstan and Bashkiria, were set up within the Russian Republic: in this way hopes of a homeland for Islamic socialism were dashed.

Once the civil war was safely over, and Sultan Galiev's doubts became even more irksome to the Bolsheviks, in 1923 he was arrested on Stalin's orders, charged with collaborating with the Basmachi (see below), and expelled from the Communist Party. He was released for a time, but finally rearrested in 1928, and sent to the concentration camp of Solovki. Once the Bolsheviks were securely in power, they unambiguously disavowed the temporary alliance with Muslim 'national communism'.

This way having been closed, there remained to Muslims only meek submission or outright armed resistance. The latter began with the Soviets' overthrow of the Kokand government, whose chief of militia escaped and began to organize raids against Russian settlements and Red Army detachments. Gradually more and more partisan bands came into existence, contesting Soviet control over the whole of Turkestan, at a time when the region was cut off from European Russia by White armies.

To begin with, the partisans came from all social classes. The various bands were not always in agreement with one another: they fought under different leaders and for different aims. Some continued the anti-Russian tradition of 1916; some wanted to reverse the Bolsheviks' anti-Islamic legislation; yet others actually fought alongside Russian peasants in anti-Bolshevik movements. Nearly all of them, however, believed that they were fulfilling a religious duty in resisting Russian and infidel domination. In Fergana they called themselves an 'army of Islam', and proclaimed a jihad, or 'holy war . . . in the name of our founder and prophet, Muhammad'. Traditionalist and reformist Muslims were at one in their estimation that Bolshevik policy posed a grave threat to Islam. The term *basmachi* (brigands) was fastened on these various partisan groups by their opponents: they referred to themselves, however, as 'freemen'.

The fall of the Central Asian Khanates of Khiva and Bukhara during 1920 brought more recruits to these irregular armies, and a new element of political organization and coordination was injected the following year by the arrival of Enver Pasha, former leader of the Young Turk government in Istanbul. Ironically, he had come determined to convert the Muslims of Turkestan to the cause of communism: what he saw there changed his mind completely, and he began planning the overthrow of Bolshevism and the establishment of Turkestan as a base for an international pan-Turkic state. He made considerable progress towards the formation of a unified army with its own, partly Turkish, officer corps. He regularized communications with the Afghans who, long accustomed to anti-Russian resistance from tsarist days, were supplying the Basmachi with arms and affording them asylum.

By 1921 the Communist government had realized that the Basmachi posed a serious threat to their control of Central Asia. They began to send in European Red Army troops, with aerial support, and they devoted an all-out effort to the capture of Enver Pasha. In this they succeeded, capturing and killing him in August 1922.

As in their treatment of the Tambov peasant revolt, the Communists combined repression with a degree of appeasement. In May 1922 they restored waqf land to the mosques, reinstated the sharia courts and relegalized the Koranic schools. At least for a time they were prepared to compromise with Islam in its traditional forms (while turning against Islamic reformism and socialism).

This combination was quite successful. Popular support for the partisans dwindled sharply from 1922, and was largely confined to the mountainous regions thereafter, at least until it revived with compulsory collectivization of agriculture (see below), which once again entailed a direct assault on Islamic values and institutions.

By the beginning of 1921 the territorial and national composition of the new Soviet Russia was becoming clearer. Lenin had hoped, of course, for a worldwide union of Soviet republics, but with the collapse of the short-lived Bavarian and Hungarian Soviet regimes, and the defeat of the Red Army in Poland, this vision had receded.

The Communists found themselves the masters of ethnic Russia — now called the RSFSR (Russian Soviet Federative Socialist Republic) — surrounded by a network of theoretically independent Soviet republics, whose territory covered approximately the same area as the former tsarist empire, with the significant exceptions of Finland, Poland and the Baltic area.

The Soviet republics now within the Russian sphere of influence were of two types. There were those on the borders (later to be known as 'union republics'), which had known at least a period of genuine independence during the turmoil of 1917–21, and had established diplomatic relations with foreign powers: these were the republics already mentioned in this chapter. Then there were the republics surrounded by Russian territory, known as 'autonomous republics', the largest of which were Tatarstan and Bashkiria, which had never been in a position to exercise any real sovereignty. The situation of these 'autonomous republics' was fairly straightforward from Moscow's point of view: they were permitted their own governmental bodies (people's commissariats), but subordinate to those in Moscow, while their local Communist Party organizations were equivalent to those of the Russian provinces. The border republics, however, posed greater problems. They had been led to believe that they would be able to exercise genuine self-determination, and all of them had done so, at least briefly, during

1917–21, notably Georgia, whose new Communist rulers proved almost as anxious to assert the nation's self-government as their Menshevik predecessors.

With these republics – Ukraine, Bielorussia, Georgia, Armenia, Azerbaidjan, Bukhara, Khoresm (formerly Khiva) and the Far Eastern Republic – Soviet Russia concluded bilateral treaties which varied somewhat from one another, and were highly ambiguous in form. In some respects they were worded like treaties with separate sovereign states, yet in others they were more like articles of federation: they reflected, in fact, the ambiguities of 'proletarian internationalism'. They began as military treaties, offering guarantees in case of external attack; but the military clauses were supplemented by economic ones, which placed decisive authority in most economic matters in the hands of organizations in Moscow. Anomalously, some of the republics actually retained a separate diplomatic service, and foreign representation, for a year or two, but this was lost when the RSFSR claimed and secured the right, in 1922, to negotiate for all the republics at the European conference of Genoa.

These anomalies and ambiguities could not last for long. Already during the civil war, the population of the border republics had mostly become accustomed to accepting the authority of certain centralized institutions controlled from Moscow: Sovnarkom, the Red Army, the Council of Labour and Defence (which since November 1918 had coordinated the civilian war effort) and the Revolutionary Military Council of the Republic (the political branch of the army). Except in the special case of Georgia, it did not stretch custom and expectation too much to extend and formalize these arrangements and establish a unitary Soviet Russian Republic containing all these disparate political entities.

That was precisely what Stalin, as people's commissar for nationalities, had in mind. He wanted to see a political framework which would give expression to the dominance Russia had assumed in the world revolutionary movement. As one delegate at the Tenth Party Congress proudly declared: 'The fact that Russia had first entered on the road of revolution, that Russia had transformed itself from a colony – an actual colony of Western Europe – into the centre of the world revolutionary movement, this fact has filled with pride the hearts of those who have been connected with the Russian revolution, and has engendered a peculiar Red Russian patriotism.'

This process might have been accomplished unproblematically had it not been that Lenin himself became concerned by the Russian nationalist implications of Stalin's project, as exemplified in such speeches. His fears were deepened when Stalin and his local lieutenant, Sergei Ordjonikidze, came into conflict with the Georgian Bolshevik leaders, Budu Mdivani and Filip Makharadze, over the place of Georgia in the new state. Stalin wanted Georgia to enter the proposed new republic merely as part of a 'Transcaucasian federation, which would also include Armenia and Azerbaidjan. Mdivani and Makharadze objected vehemently to this downgrading of their homeland. Lenin eventually gave his blessing to Stalin's scheme, but during an argument on the subject, Ordjonikidze became very heated and actually struck one of Mdivani's followers. Lenin was incensed at this uncouth behaviour, which confirmed his worst fears about Stalin, and he ordered an investigation into the incident; but he suffered his third and most serious stroke before it could be completed, and was never able to intervene effectively and ensure that the lessons of the incident were absorbed.

He did, however, prepare a memorandum on the national question for the forthcoming Twelfth Party Congress: it was suppressed by Stalin (with the scarcely explicable connivance of Trotsky), and did not come to light until 1956. In it Lenin recognized that 'self-determination', embodied in the theoretical right to secede from the Soviet state, had been reduced in practice to 'a scrap of paper', and that as a result the minority nationalities were in danger of being delivered up to 'this 100 per cent Russian phenomenon, Great Russian chauvinism, which is characteristic of the Russian bureaucracy'. He demanded 'exemplary punishment' for Ordjonikidze, to demonstrate that this would not be tolerated, and recommended that the Soviet constitution should guarantee real governmental power to the minority nationalities, in the form of people's commissariats for all except diplomatic and military matters, as well as enshrining in an explicit code the right to use local language.

Although Lenin's memorandum was not publicly discussed, some of its spirit did find its way into the formal provisions of the Soviet constitution of 1923. For one thing the new state did not bear the appellation 'Russia': it was called the 'Union of Soviet Socialist Republics' (USSR), and was formally a federal union between its various constituent republics, in which none of them was supreme. Also Narkomnats as a forum for national opinion survived as a second chamber of the All-Union Executive Committee of the Soviets (VTsIK): called the Council of Nationalities, it gave equal representation to each union and autonomous republic, regardless of population. Significantly, though, Lenin did not recommend any change in the highly centralized functioning of the party: his conversion to the cause of the nationalities was never more than partial.

In most respects the new constitution embodied Stalin's conceptions rather than Lenin's. The distribution of governmental powers between the republics and the Union as a whole left the latter with all real authority not only in diplomatic and military matters, but also in the running of the economy, while the Union also secured the right to lay down general principles in the fields of justice, labour, education and public health. With the notable exception of culture and linguistic policy, this left most power in internal affairs, as well as external, in the hands of the Union.

Another strong centralizing factor, in practice, was the disparity between the Russian Republic and all the others. The RSFSR contained 90 per cent of the land-area and 72 per cent of the population of the Soviet Union, so that its constitutional status as just one republic among seven was a fiction. Add to this the fact that 72 per cent of members of the Communist Party were Russian, and it will be clear that only ironclad constitutional guarantees could have restrained Russia from dominating the Union. In the words of E. H. Carr, the Soviet Union was 'the RSFSR writ large'. Or, to put it another way, the Soviet constitution of 1923 was Leninist in form, but Stalinist in content.

All the same, just a few residuary ambiguities remained in practice. The revolution and civil war *had* given most of the nationalities of the former tsarist empire at least a brief experience of real independence, such as they had not known for centuries, or in some cases had never known. This gave a tremendous impetus to feelings of national identity, and, taken together with the policies of cultural and linguistic autonomy pursued for some years yet, rendered non-Russian national identity far stronger than it had ever been under the tsars. This fact built permanent tensions into the working of the Soviet system.

March 1917: the last traces of the tsarist regime, the imperial double eagle, being removed from public buildings and carted away (*Keystone*)

The motley origins of the Red Army are reflected in this picture of recruits drilling in 1920 (*BBC Hulton Picture Library*)

A Red Army court martial in Poland, 1920 (*BBC Hulton Picture Library*)

ГРАМОТНЫЙ НАРОД СЧАСТЛИВО ЖИВЕТ.

The reading room in the Samara Peasant House, mid-1920s. The self-conscious poses suggest that a *likbez* (liquidation of illiteracy) class is in progress. The inscription reads, 'A literate people lives happily' (*H. F. Toogood Archive, School of Slavonic Studies, University of London*)

5

The New Economic Policy and its Political Dilemmas

Even as the delegates to the Tenth Party Congress were voting for tight party discipline and the violent repression of the Kronstadt revolt, they also approved a radical change in economic policy, this time towards greater freedom. This was the abolition of grain requisitioning and its replacement by a tax in kind set at a much lower level than the compulsory deliveries. This measure was being tried out in Tambov and had been announced in Petrograd: it was conceived as a way of taking the sting out of popular discontent without making political concessions.

The abandonment of requisitioning had, however, profound economic consequences. Since the tax was both lower and more predictable than the requisitions had been, it gave the peasant an incentive once again to maximize the productivity of his plot of land, secure in the knowledge that whatever surplus he achieved could be sold for profit on the market. This meant, of course, that the government had to restore freedom of private trade. Since, moreover, peasants could not be expected to trade unless there was something to buy with the proceeds, it was obviously important to generate at least a reasonable supply of consumer goods. In practice, the easiest way to do this was to abolish the state monopoly of small- and medium-scale manufacture, retail trade and services.

This was in fact what the government did during 1921, while keeping heavy industry, banking and foreign trade in the hands of the state. Taken together, these measures became known as the New Economic Policy (NEP). In the urban markets the results were apparent immediately. When a hero of the novelist Andrei Platonov returned to his native town in 1921:

> At first he thought the Whites must be in town. At the station was a café where they were selling white rolls without ration cards or queuing. . . . In the shop he came across all the normal equipment of trade, once seen in his long forgotten youth: counters under glass, shelves along the walls, proper scales instead of steelyards, courteous assistants instead of supply officials, a lively crowd of purchasers, and stocks of food which breathed an air of well-being.

Although some private trade recovered remarkably quickly, in general the economy was still in deep crisis. Years of war, conscription and food requisitioning had devastated agriculture, particularly in the most fertile regions. On top of this, the Volga basin experienced drought in 1920 and 1921. Unprotected by any reserves, peasant households faced two very poor harvests in succession. The result was famine on a scale that the government simply could not meet. For the one and only time, it allowed direct foreign aid inside Soviet Russia. An international relief committee was formed, which included prominent Russian non-Communists (who were all arrested once the emergency was over). But in spite of its efforts, probably about 5 million people died.

Industry, too, was in a desperate state. In the major branches of manufacture, output in 1921 was a fifth or less of the 1913 level: in the case of iron and steel it was actually below 5 per cent. The number of workers employed to generate this output did not fall below 40 per cent of the 1913 level, and here lay one of the major problems of the new era. For these underemployed workers were soon joined by a flood of new job-seekers, heading in from the countryside as soon as there was any prospect of a job, and also by millions of former soldiers demobilized from the Red Army. They joined the labour market at the very time when industrial concerns were having to adjust to the new conditions. Whether they were nationalized or private firms made no difference: henceforth there were to be no direct state subsidies. That meant the expenditure for fuel, raw materials, wages and further investment had to be met out of sales revenue. Firms had to balance their books, or they could well go out of business. This was a reality which workers, party and trade unions had to recognize.

The industrial recovery thus started on a very shaky basis. Initially this led to an imbalance in the terms of trade with agriculture. In spite of the famine, the ploughing and sowing of underused fields proved to be a much faster process than the re-equipment of damaged and dilapidated factories. By the summer of 1923 the shortage of industrial products in relation to agricultural ones had reached such a pitch that the ratio of industrial to agricultural prices stood at more than three times its 1913 level. What this meant in practice was that peasants who sold their produce on the market were not thereby raising enough revenue to buy the industrial goods they wanted. The danger was that repeated experiences of this kind would induce them to cut back their sowings – as they had done during the civil war – and food shortages would resume. Industrial products would then remain unsold, to everyone's mutual disadvantage. Although the fact was not immediately recognized, this 'scissors crisis' (as it was called in reference to the divergent parabolas of industrial and agricultural prices) proved to pose a fundamental threat to NEP. The disputes generated by it formed the first stage in the long-term debate on the economic development strategy of the Soviet government (see below, pages 136–40).

Another result of the uncertain industrial recovery was that the workers, who were theoretically the inheritors of the new society, in practice found it very difficult to understand their place within it. The large reserve of unemployed ensured that their wages remained low: in 1925, Sokolnikov, people's commissar for finance, admitted that the pay of miners, metal workers and engine drivers was still lower than it had been before 1914. This in turn meant that workers' housing and nourishment was often inadequate. The factory committee of a cement works in Smolensk reported, for example, in 1929: 'Every day there are many complaints about apartments: many workers have families of six and seven people, and live in one room. . . . [We] have about 500 applications from workers who do not have apartments.' Food supplies, though far better than before 1922, fluctuated and so prices were unstable: again from Smolensk it was reported that wheat flour doubled in price and rye flour trebled between the end of 1926 and early 1929. 'Workers are being inadequately supplied by consumers' cooperatives [run by the soviets to cushion the workers from the worst effects of price fluctuation] . . . , and as a result, private traders virtually occupy a dominant position in the market.' It is understandable that workers consequently felt resentment about the peasants, who charged them such high prices, and about the specialists and officials, who were paid so much better. How was this possible in a society allegedly 'moving towards socialism' under the 'dictatorship of the proletariat'?

The structure of industrial enterprises was also a disappointment to workers who recalled the heady days of October. All remnants of 'workers' control' had now finally disappeared. Factory administration was once more hierarchical, with clearly identifiable individual managers in charge (sometimes drawn from pre-revolutionary managerial staff, for their expertise and experience), while technical specialists and foremen enjoyed unambiguous authority over the ordinary operatives. Since efficiency and productivity were paramount, some enterprises (though not enough for Lenin) were experimenting with 'Taylorite' schemes for time-and-motion rationalization and conveyor-belt mass production. Lenin had once regarded such schemes as the quintessence of capitalist exploitation, but now favoured them for the higher output they generated. As a further incentive, most workers were paid on a piece-rate system, which tied their income directly to productivity.

Before 1917 the workers would have expected the trade union or indeed the party to act on their behalf. But both these organizations were now explicitly part of the state economic mechanism, and hence tended only to support workers in conflict with private employers. In 1925 the trade union newspaper *Trud* (Labour) itself complained that unions seemed to be 'occupied in dismissing and fining workers, instead of defending their interests'. The mood on the shop floor seems to have been volatile (though research on worker attitudes in this period is still embryonic), and quite a lot of labour disputes and strikes did break out, typically over housing, supplies, late or inadequate pay, or conflicts with specific administrators. The unions hardly ever supported the workers in such disputes.

Although further research on this needs to be done, there appears to be no link between industrial protests and any of the opposition groups within the party. Most workers, in fact, seem to have regarded the party as 'them', a part of the structure of authority with which they had to deal. Political and production meetings were shunned as 'boring', unless they dealt with something of immediate interest to the workman, such as pay or housing. Some workers, of course, looked on the party as a way to get on in life, seeking training, promotion, and ultimately perhaps escape from the shop floor. Party workers, for their part, often complained that the workers were 'contaminated by bourgeois tendencies' and 'petty bourgeois individualism'.

Mutual relationships between the party and the class they claimed to represent were, in fact, by the late 1920s, rather cool. For a 'working-class' party about to embark on a major industrialization programme, that was a discouraging, not to say dangerous, situation.

Relations with the peasants were even worse. In the peasantry the Bolsheviks faced the only social class which had survived the revolution in substantially its previous form. Indeed revolution and civil war had actually strengthened the more traditional and underproductive aspects of Russian agriculture. The landowners, who had by and large used more modern equipment and methods and who had provided much of the pre-1914 grain surplus, had been expropriated, and their estates had mostly been divided up among the peasants. The 'Stolypin' peasants likewise had their enclosed plots of land taken away from them, and they were either expelled from the village or reabsorbed into the mir. Enclosed holdings were once again divided up into strips and often made subject to periodic redistribution; modern crop rotations were abandoned where they did not fit the communal pattern. The mir, in short, achieved a dominance in Russian rural life which it had never known before. This was a direct consequence of the Bolsheviks having adopted the Socialist Revolutionary programme in 1917, but that did not mean to say it was welcome to them now.

Landholdings, even among peasants themselves, had also tended to get smaller since 1917, in spite of the new awards of land. The problem was that millions of unemployed and hungry workers had streamed out of the towns, looking to resettle on the land, and many of them were awarded communal strips, where they still had claims. The revolution also seems to have intensified strains and disputes within peasant households, which provoked younger family members to break away and claim holdings of their own. As a result of all these new awards, the total number of family holdings rose from 17–18 million in 1917 to 23 million in 1924 and 25 million in 1927. The average size of each holding naturally fell also, in *spite* of the annexations from landowners, church and state in 1917, as did the proportion of the crop from each holding which was sold on the market rather than used for subsistence.

For the government the implications of this fragmentation of holdings, and of the reversion to primitive techniques were very alarming. As they began to conceive ambitious industrial projects, they needed more food to be both produced and sold. Yet their own policies aggravated the situation. The better-off and more productive peasants were usually taxed more heavily and felt themselves to be under stronger political pressure than their poorer colleagues. They always suspected, moreover, that the policies of 1918–21 might return.

These factors are reflected in the agricultural production figures, especially for grain, the most vital crop for the regime. It is true that output recovered rapidly from the catastrophic levels of 1920–1, but it never quite returned to pre-war levels. Compared with 81.6 million tonnes in 1913 (admittedly an unusually good year), grain output never exceeded 76.8 million tonnes in 1926, and fell off thereafter. Livestock production did reach pre-war levels in 1926, but declined subsequently. And there were some 14 million extra mouths to feed: in 1914, grain production had been 584 kg. per head of the population, in 1928–9 it was only 484 kg., while the government was planning for an enormous growth in the number of industrial workers, who would not produce food but would certainly need to consume it. Furthermore, of the amount produced, somewhat less was being marketed than in 1914 – though Stalin exaggerated this factor in order to produce the impression that grain was deliberately being hoarded on a large scale. In fact, since official grain prices remained low, many peasants preferred to turn their grain into *samogon* (unlicensed liquor), or even not to grow it at all.

Of course it had never been the Bolsheviks' intention to let Russian agriculture stagnate in small and primitively cultivated holdings. They had always envisaged large farms, collectively owned and mechanized. Their 1917 Land Decree had been a tactical diversion from this strategy, and they intended now to return to the main highway. In the last years of his life Lenin on the whole thought that this 'collectivization' of agriculture should take place gradually, with the party encouraging the creation of model collectives whose high productivity and prosperity would in time persuade the rest of the peasantry to join them.

A certain number of collective farms did already exist, some of which had started during the civil war, with party encouragement and help. Broadly speaking, these were of three types: (i) the *kommuna*, in which all property was held in common, sometimes with communal living quarters and childrearing; (ii) the artel in which each household owned its own dwelling and small plot of land, together with such tools as were needed to cultivate it, but all other land and resources were shared; (iii) the *TOZ*, or 'association for common cultivation', in which some or all of the fields were cultivated collectively. The last category might be barely distinguishable from the traditional village community, with its custom of *pomochi*, or mutual aid at busy times of year. It is no surprise, then, to find that the majority of collectives were of the TOZ variety, and there is evidence to show that some of them at least were ordinary village communes relabelled to draw the tax advantages of 'collective' status.

In addition, there were some state farms (*sovkhozy*), in which the labourers were paid a regular wage, like industrial workers. Even taken together, however, all state and collective farms accounted in 1927 for less than 2 per cent of cultivated land. It is significant, though, that their share of marketed produce was much higher: about 7.5 per cent in 1927. In view of this, one might have expected that the party would have begun a programme of 'collectivization' much earlier. In fact, however, the party was remarkably dilatory during most of the 1920s about pursuing its own official policy.

In part this was because of the weakness of the village soviets. In theory the soviets were supposed to take over local administration, leaving the peasant mir (renamed 'land society') to cope with questions of land tenure and cultivation. In practice, however, the mir continued to collect local taxes and to perform administrative functions, as before the revolution. A study published by *Izvestiya* in 1927 showed that the mir, not the soviet, was still the basic unit of local government in most villages, and that this was creating problems in the relations with the next tier above, the volost soviet.

Nor was the party any more successful than the soviets in rooting itself in the countryside. The Communists were townspeople by mentality and inclination, and most of them regarded village life with indifference or distaste. It is true that the revolution and civil war did bring an influx of rural members into the party, mostly Red Army soldiers. Yet these were often the first to be expelled in purges against the corrupt or insufficiently active, and in any case they constituted a negligible proportion of the rural population. The 1922 party census reported that party members formed a mere 0.13 per cent of the villages' inhabitants, and many of these were teachers, doctors, agronomists and officials of volost soviets. By 1928 this proportion had only doubled: out of an estimated rural population of 120 million, about 300,000 (0.25 per cent) were Communists, and of that number only some 170,000 were actual peasants.

By and large, the weakness of the party meant domination of the village by the traditional notables. While all adults, including women, enjoyed a vote for the soviet, the commune was, by custom, a gathering of the heads of household, almost invariably male. Younger men, women and the landless were usually excluded. This meant that, in spite of the equalizing tendencies of the revolution, a degree of stratification soon reappeared in the villages. Indeed, it had never entirely disappeared. Since the commune had usually controlled the process of redistribution in 1917–18, the village notables had typically tried to ensure that some elements of greater wealth – whether in the form of acreage, livestock, or tools – remained in their own hands, or with the families whom they trusted. The former landless were better off than before, but they never became the equals of their 'betters'.

This stratification is greatly emphasized in the Soviet

studies of the subject, both contemporary and subsequent. They divide peasants into so-called 'kulaks' ('fists' or moneylenders, by nineteenth-century usage, but a term now loosely applied to better-off peasants), middle peasants, poor peasants and landless labourers. The definitions of these terms fluctuated, and they were used by the party on the whole for political rather than scientific purposes. Their use was intended to suggest that class war was brewing in the countryside between the richer and poorer strata. However, Teodor Shanin's examination of the Soviet data tends to invalidate this hypothesis. He shows that the incomes of kulak households were only marginally higher than those of the 'middle peasants': they might own two horses, hire labour at busy times of year and have more produce left over for the market, but they were in no sense a separate, capitalist stratum. As for the 'poor peasants', while clearly a real category, their poverty was typically due to circumstances that were temporary – illness, natural disaster, military service of the breadwinner, shortage of working hands. 'The chance of a hard core of poor peasants showing lasting cohesion and ability for political action emerging was very limited, therefore.' Nevertheless, this was the layer which the party was to try once more to organize, from 1927, in the form of 'committees of poor peasants'.

Nor is there much evidence of systematic conflict *between* different classes of rural dwellers. What Soviet sources call 'kulak outrages' usually turn out, when one can look more closely at the sources, to have involved more than just the wealthier peasants, and often the whole village. It would be much closer to the truth, in fact, to say that the great dividing line was not that between classes of the peasantry, but that between peasants and the rest of society, in particular anything that smelt of the towns. Gorky, writing of his conversations with peasants in 1922, reports that they felt 'suspicious and distrustful . . . not of the clergy, not of authority, but simply of the town as a complex organization of cunning people who live on the labour and grain of the countryside and make many things useless to the peasant whom they strive in every way to deceive, and skilfully do so.' There was much in recent peasant experience to substantiate this view. Since 1914 the town had called up the peasant's sons to fight in a war for aims quite irrelevant to the village, it had requisitioned his horse for the cavalry, it had taxed him extra and offered him derisory sums for his grain; then, after a paltry land allotment in 1917, it had called up his sons yet again and also extorted his produce by force, paying him nothing for it. Quite often, furthermore, the town had closed down his church, sometimes destroying it in the process, and arrested his village priest.

The peasants' distrust, in fact, was wholly understandable, indeed rational. And although they found the products of the town useful, most peasants were still at a sufficiently primitive economic level to be able to fall back on their own resources if they had to. It was very convenient to buy candles, kerosene, matches, nails and vodka in the town, but if really up against it, a peasant could devise his own substitutes for most of these things, and cottage industry was still lively enough to satisfy many of the needs which in more 'advanced' societies are supplied from the town. If they found market conditions not to their liking, in other words, peasants could react, not by working harder and trying to make more money, but by withdrawing from the market altogether. That had been demonstrated in 1918–21, and the threat of a repeat performance always hung over Bolshevik calculations.

Altogether, then, NEP was the party's creation, but it also faced the party with unforeseen and bewildering dilemmas. During the last couple of years of his life, Lenin began to reflect on these. He suffered a stroke in May 1922, which left him partly paralysed, and another in March 1923, which deprived him of speech, but he did not die till January 1924. Between the first two strokes, at least, he remained politically partly active. For the first time since October 1917 he was able to stand back to some extent from the immediate pressures of decision-making and come to some conclusions about what he and his party had done. His reflections were ambivalent, and his writings of these months sometimes betray a note of uncertainty which had never been present earlier.

On the credit side was the fact that the Bolsheviks had seized power and held it, in spite of grave emergencies. In almost all respects, however, the premises on which Lenin had urged an uprising in October 1917 had proved false. No international revolution had taken place: on the contrary, the revolution had remained confined to Russia, which as a result was now surrounded by suspicious or hostile states and was rapidly resuming the outward forms of the old tsarist empire. The proletariat and poorer peasantry had not proved capable of exercising any kind of class dictatorship: the proletariat was dispersed and impoverished, and the poorer peasants, as a result of the Land Decree, had more or less merged with the rest of the peasantry. Ordinary working people had never had a chance to try their hand at administration: in their place, a growing host of appointed officials (some of them inherited from the old regime) was running the country, especially in the localities. The Bolsheviks had seized power with few definite ideas about how they would govern, and such ideas as they had possessed had been swept away by civil war, deindustrialization and famine. Lenin spent the rest of his life grappling with these unintended consequences of his own revolution, and after his death his successors quarrelled and then split over the heritage. Utopia had failed. The party now divided between those who wanted to restore utopia by coercion (the left), and those who were inclined tacitly to recognize its failure and try to come to terms with the new reality (the right).

For all that he might *talk* of the 'dictatorship of the proletariat', Lenin recognized the actual situation and was deeply worried by it. 'Those who get jobs in factories now', he commented at the Eleventh Party Congress in March 1922, 'are usually not real proletarians, but just people who happen to turn up [*vsyachesky sluchainy element*].' 'Marx', he added, 'was not writing about present-day Russia.' Alexander Shlyapnikov, a leader of the Workers' Opposition, taunted him from his seat: 'Permit me to congratulate you on being the vanguard of a non-existent class.' This put the matter in a nutshell. Lacking a secure social base, the party could not direct NEP as it wanted to. The economy was like a car not being driven by the man who thought he was at the steering wheel: 'Speculators, private capitalists, goodness knows who is actually driving the car . . . but it often goes not at all in the direction imagined by the person at the wheel.'

This feeling of being out of control was shared by many at the congress. Lenin attributed it partly to what he called cultural factors. Since the Communists would now have to play a more active role than they had envisaged in the construction of a new economy, it was vital that they should possess the basic skills to do this. In practice, he warned, that was not at all the case. Capitalists and private traders were usually more competent. Communist officials often lacked 'culture' – by which he meant education, tact, honesty, public spirit and efficiency – and so, *faute de mieux*, they were being swamped by the bad old ways of the pre-revolutionary regime. 'If we take Moscow – 4700 responsible Communists – and then take the whole contraption of bureaucracy there. Who is directing whom? I very much doubt whether one can say that the Communists are doing the directing. . . . The culture [of the bureaucrats] is wretched and contemptible, but still it is higher than ours.'

Although he could see some problems clearly enough, Lenin was unable to devise any solutions to them. In some ways, he thought the most important thing to do was to ensure that the best *individuals* were in charge – people of proven ability and probity. In his Testament he reflected on the characteristics of his possible successors from that point of view – and, significantly, he found them all wanting. He expressed particular misgivings about Stalin, on the grounds that he might not be able to use his 'unlimited authority' as party General Secretary 'with sufficient caution'. He later added in an appendix: 'Stalin is too rude, and this defect, though quite tolerable in our midst and in dealings among us Communists, becomes intolerable in a General Secretary. That is why I suggest that the comrades think about a way to remove Stalin from that post . . .' He also proposed administrative reorganizations: enlarging the Workers' and Peasants' Inspectorate (which had inherited the powers of the tsarist auditor-general) and merging it with the Party Control Commission (a kind of party inspectorate), so that the more capable and trustworthy people at the top could better monitor what was going on lower down. Actually that was a recipe for compounding the problems of overcentralized control, especially in view of the fact that the Workers' and Peasants' Inspectorate was headed by Stalin.

Lenin died before he was able to try to effect any of the changes he proposed, and the party leaders kept his unflattering personal comments secret from the rank and file. With Lenin's death, the nature of politics and public life changed quite considerably. Lenin had always been confident that he was right in his ideas, but he acted by persuasion: until 1921 he had never tried to silence debate within the party, and even thereafter he often tolerated it in practice. Certainly he had never demanded consecrated status for his own ideas. Now, however, a very real change began to take place. Perhaps it is significant that two members of the commission in charge of Lenin's funeral ceremony, Anatoly Lunacharsky and Leonid Krasin, were past adherents of 'God-building', the pre-revolutionary intellectual tendency which had claimed to be a 'socialist religion of humanity', indeed 'the most religious of all religions'. Its main tenet had been that the proletariat, in creating a new and more humane kind of society, were building a new man, who would cease to alienate himself in illusions about a transcendental God, but instead would fulfil a more genuine earthly religious mission. Lenin had been scathing in his denunciation of this tendency, but, as far as is known, Lunacharsky had never abjured it, while Krasin had been a sympathizer of Bogdanov, who as the philosopher of Proletkult (see below, page 180) tried to revive God-building in a new form after the revolution.

At any rate, the form of ceremony chosen for Lenin had strong traditional religious overtones, especially the decision to embalm his body and preserve it for public display in a mausoleum on Red Square, in the middle of Moscow. This was comparable with the Orthodox cult of 'relics' of saints. But it was also different: Orthodoxy had never preserved a whole body. This was, in fact, a religious gesture of a new kind. Stalin approved of the decision to embalm Lenin – indeed he may have initiated it – and although he was never a God-builder, he had a shrewd idea of the value of religious symbolism to the state, derived perhaps from his youthful study in the Tiflis seminary. In accord with the new spirit, at a session of the Congress of Soviets on the eve of the funeral, he carefully enumerated Lenin's 'commandments' and pledged himself to fulfil them, as if consciously assuming the mantle of disciple and heir.

During 1924–5 he continued this work by assembling a doctrine, drawn selectively from the dead man's writings, which he published as *The Foundations of Leninism*. Two special institutes were set up, the Marx-Engels Institute and the Lenin Institute, to gather and study the heritage of the founding fathers of the new ideology, and a journal, *Bolshevik*, was founded to publish the results. Claiming for himself the home ground of these ideological temples, Stalin could assail the ideas of opponents of the new orthodoxy, not just as misguided, but as somehow illegitimate. Traditional religions would have used the term 'heresy'; Stalin called them 'deviations'.

The first issue on which Stalin tried thus to isolate and discredit his opponents was the fundamental question of the nature of the revolutionary state and the nation it claimed to represent. NEP had initially been launched in the expectation that it constituted a 'retreat', a temporary concession to capitalism in order to restore the economy until such time as

socialist revolutions could break out elsewhere and backward, war-torn Soviet Russia receive fraternal help from
outside. By the autumn of 1923, however, with the failure of
yet another attempt at a Communist coup in Germany, it was
becoming clear that, for the foreseeable future, Russia was
going to be on its own. Did that mean that the Soviet state
should indefinitely prolong a 'provisional' economic system,
or did it mean that the Russians should abandon hope of
external help, and buckle down to build socialism on their
own?

Almost ever since the October revolution, some Bolsheviks
had tacitly accepted the proposition that, for the moment at
least, proletarian internationalism must mean Soviet (and
even Russian?) patriotism, since Russia was the only country
in which a 'proletarian' state had been established. We have
seen this at the time of the Brest-Litovsk Treaty and during
the Soviet-Polish war. At the same time many non-Bolsheviks
took a partly compatible view: that the Bolsheviks had
succeeded in holding on to power because, in circumstances
which threatened the disintegration of the Russian Empire,
they had proved themselves to be the party best able to hold
that empire together. This stream of thought crystallized in
1920 in the form of *smenovekhovstvo* (from the collection of
essays, *Change of Landmarks*, which appeared in that year).
Nikolai Ustryalov, its leading exponent, now in emigration in
Kharbin, argued that the defeat of the Whites had demonstrated that the Bolsheviks were now the only truly Russian
national force: they had succeeded in holding Russia together
against all the attempts of foreigners and non-Russian
nationalities to dismember her. His case was strengthened by
the reincorporation of the remaining non-Russian nations
into the new Soviet Union, and by the introduction of NEP,
which seemed to show that, in social and economic terms as
well, the new Russian state was becoming more like the old
one. In a famous image, Ustryalov likened Soviet Russia to a
radish – 'red outside and white inside'.

This point of view found some support among émigrés, but

even more perhaps inside Russia itself. It was close to the outlook of probably the majority of former Imperial Army officers who had joined the Red Army. Many of the 'bourgeois specialists' would also have sympathized with it: indeed, Jeremy Azrael, the historian of the managerial stratum in Soviet society, goes so far as to call smenovekhovstvo 'the ideology of the specialists'. Some writers (especially the 'fellow travellers') and clergy took a similar view. At a time when émigré books were still published inside Russia, and links between Soviet citizens and émigrés were strong, these ideas, while not universally accepted (especially in emigration) did play a part in reconciling the traditional professional classes to the new system.

Obviously the Soviet leadership could not simply take over smenovekhovstvo, since it was avowedly non-socialist and anti-internationalist. But there were good reasons why they should evolve their own version of Russian patriotism. First, because they needed to appeal to the specialists on whom they still depended so much: and it was cheaper and more effective to gain their willing compliance than to rely on compulsion alone. Secondly, even the party apparatus itself, now growing so fast under the guidance of Stalin's card-indexers, could not be expected indefinitely to work enthusiastically for a system that was only provisional. They too needed to feel that they were doing something constructive, 'building socialism', even if only in Russia, and not just marking time till the world revolution, now apparently receding, should at last break out.

It was with them above all in mind that Stalin began in 1924 to reconsider the party's theoretically absolute commitment to international revolution. In an article entitled 'October and Trotsky's theory of permanent revolution', published in the newspapers in December 1924, he first raised the possibility that socialism might be achieved in one country alone, even if that country were less developed economically than its neighbours which had remained capitalist. Such a victory he deemed 'perfectly possible and even probable'.

It is significant that this idea, backed with scanty but authentic quotations from Lenin, was directed against Trotsky. Stalin's article was in fact a salvo in the power struggle for Lenin's succession. The theoretical differences between Stalin and Trotsky were mainly ones of emphasis: even Stalin conceded that the 'final victory', as distinct from just the 'victory', of socialism required an international proletarian community. But Stalin depicted Trotsky as someone who lacked confidence in Soviet Russia, and in the 'alliance of the proletariat and the toiling peasantry', which had brought about the socialist revolution in Russia, and could, according to Stalin, now make possible the construction of a socialist society. This was a classic example of a weapon Stalin was to use increasingly: exaggerating and distorting the views of his opponents, and applying crude labels to them, as though from a position of unique and guaranteed rectitude. 'Trotskyism', 'the left deviation', 'the right deviation' – these gradually became equivalent in Stalin's rhetoric to 'non-Leninism', and hence to 'anti-Leninism', which 'objectively' meant supporting the imperialists. By stages, in fact, Stalin was able to insinuate that all his opponents were nothing less than enemies of the soviet system.

At any rate, as far as 'socialism in one country' was concerned, there was at least as much justification in Lenin's writings for Trotsky's assertions that primacy should be given to international revolution. But it was Stalin who managed to occupy the temple, to represent *his* interpretation as the only truly Leninist one, and to gain the institutional backing for it. The Fourteenth Party Conference, in April 1925, resolved that 'in general the victory of socialism (*not* in the sense of *final* victory) is unconditionally possible in one country'.

Thereby 'socialism in one country' became official party doctrine, and its implications had to be absorbed. The economic ones were the most pressing. It was generally assumed that 'building socialism' meant developing Russia's industry. Lenin had hoped to do this by attracting foreign concessions to the country, recognizing frankly that Russia needed help from abroad, even from capitalists. But, although a few significant deals were concluded, foreign concessions still accounted for only 0.6 per cent of industrial output in 1928. This was scarcely surprising, in view of the fact that the Bolsheviks had deliberately defaulted on all past Russian debts: it took them many years to regain a reputation for financial probity.

At any rate, it looked as if economic development would have to come out of Russia's own resources. The Opposition, which was beginning to crystallize around Trotsky, felt this could only be done through rigorous state planning and the diversion of resources from the private sector to feed heavy industry. The manufactured products thus created would feed into all sectors of the economy, including consumer industry and agriculture, and would ultimately make them all more productive. Admittedly, there would probably be some years of austerity, while consumption was cut in order to concentrate resources on industrial investment. The Opposition's main economic spokesman, Evgeny Preobrazhensky, even called this process 'primitive socialist accumulation', and likened it to the 'primitive capitalist accumulation', which Marx had described in *Capital*. He argued, however, that it would be far less objectionable than the capitalist variety, since (a) it would bear mostly on the 'bourgeois' sector of the economy, and (b) the surplus value generated would be used for the ultimate benefit of everyone, not just for the conspicuous consumption of the few.

The Oppositionists were moved by a dislike of NEP which was widely shared in the party. They were repelled by the raucous, untidy, money-grabbing peasant markets, by the debauchery of the nightclubs, by the furs and silk dresses at the theatre, all to be seen again just as if the revolution had never taken place. Even prostitutes had reappeared on the streets. Preobrazhensky warned, with Trotsky's support, that if the socialist sector of the economy were not given deliberate advantages, then the country was in danger of being dominated by kulaks and *nepmen* (as the traders, retailers and small manufacturers were contemptuously known). Fast industrialization, on the other hand, would enable agriculture to be mechanized, and this in turn would draw the peasants into collective farms, as Lenin had recommended. 'Only a powerful socialized industry can help the peasants transform agriculture along collectivist lines,' Trotsky argued in the Opposition's platform of September 1927.

Spokesmen for NEP were quick to point out the drawbacks in the Opposition programme. 'Squeezing the private economy' meant above all squeezing the peasantry: might the result not be the same as during the civil war — severe shortages and the revival of the black market? If Russia was now really on its own, could the nation afford a policy which would endanger the relatively smooth trading arrangements between town and country created by NEP? Or, to put it in Leninist terms, was it prudent to jeopardize the 'alliance between the proletariat and peasantry' which had made the October revolution possible? In his Testament Lenin had warned: 'Our party rests upon two classes, and for that reason its instability is possible, and if there cannot exist an agreement between those classes its fall is inevitable.'

It was precisely in order to preserve this alliance that Bukharin and the party's right wing, including initially Stalin, rejected the recipes of the Opposition. With experience of NEP, especially in its contrast to War Communism, Bukharin increasingly came to see the peasant economy as bearing the key to Russia's economic future. For that reason, during the 'scissors crisis' he recommended easing the terms of trade for the peasants by cutting industrial prices. For the same reason in 1924–5 he recommended easing restrictions on peasant hiring of labour and leasing of land. Both these proposals were put into effect, and helped to stimulate an upswing in agricultural production and marketing. If the peasant economy developed at its own pace, he argued, then the benefits would be felt in all sectors of the economy. The produce the peasants grew would feed the urban workers, their buying power would create a reliable market for industrial products, and their taxes and savings would fuel future industrial investment. The artificial forcing of industry, on the other hand, as Bukharin saw it, would create an unbalanced economy, in which workers in highly modern steel works would not have proper food, clothing or housing. This would be to the detriment of all sectors of the economy. At one stage, in 1925, Bukharin went so far as to call upon all strata of the peasantry: 'Enrich yourselves, accumulate, develop your economy!'

Bukharin never fully faced the political consequences of what he was saying, but his opponents did. As they saw it, giving primacy to a non-socialist sector of the economy would result in conceding to the 'petty bourgeoisie' a great deal of political influence. Bukharin partly accepted the logic of this. He did not favour the establishment of opposition political parties, but he did envisage a degree of pluralism. He thought it important to encourage the emergence of 'hundreds of thousands of small and large rapidly expanding voluntary societies, circles and associations' in the economic, cultural and social fields. These associations, from agricultural cooperatives to learned societies and chess clubs would express the interests of the different strata of the population and foster 'mass initiative at lower levels', opening channels through which the people could influence the government, learn about politics, and thus gradually 'grow into socialism'. The existence of such legally protected voluntary organizations he saw as a guarantee against the 'bureaucratization' of society, a danger which, like Trotsky, he increasingly discerned behind the growth of the party-state apparatus.

This vision, though Bukharin never really developed it fully himself, has remained, though in embryo only, an alternative view of socialist society, as a one-party system in which the rule of law would guarantee individuals and groups against the otherwise crushing power of the state. It has never been properly tried out – but more than a quarter of a century later Bukharin's views, unacknowledged, were to influence some of the post-Stalin attempts to find 'alternative roads to socialism', especially in Eastern Europe.

Since the economic component of Bukharin's theories in fact underlay party policy in 1921–7, it is important to inquire why the party never accepted the social and political corollaries.

Fundamentally the answer seems to lie in the nature of the emerging party apparatus and of its leadership. As we have seen, by 1922, when Stalin became general secretary, the system of appointing all party officials from the centre was already well established, and was being extended to the regular appointment of non-party posts in all social and public organizations. This system was not created by Stalin: it grew naturally out of Lenin's theories as well as the exigencies of the civil war. But it was Stalin who now perfected it and transformed it into a base for his own personal power. To his comrades in the party leadership he was known, rather condescendingly, as 'Comrade Card-Index' (*Tovarishch Kartotekov*): they were content to leave him to assemble and classify the personnel files, not yet realizing what power was accumulating therein. Most of them, being well read in the history of past revolutions, were obsessed by a very different danger: that of finding the revolution hijacked by a general, another Bonaparte. One can understand their fears. In 1917–21 power had certainly 'grown out of the barrel of a gun' (to use a later expression). If there was any authoritarian figure waiting to take over, then most would have guessed it to be not Stalin, but Trotsky, the man who had hired the old regime generals to win the civil war. It was in fear of him that Lenin's two closest old colleagues, Zinoviev and Kamenev, principal party secretaries in Petrograd and Moscow, initially allied themselves with Stalin, forming what was generally known as the 'triumvirate'.

Trotsky was no less authoritarian a figure than Stalin, but in rather a different way. In his pamphlet *Terrorism and*

Communism, and in his schemes of 'labour armies' he had
conceived some of the most extreme versions of the 'dictatorship of the proletariat'. But for him authoritarianism was
always indissolubly linked to the revolutionary spirit, to the
emotional impetus of defeating enemies and creating a new
world. Stalin, though no stranger to this type of authoritarianism, could accommodate himself to more peaceful and
settled conditions – indeed he needed them to consolidate
and perfect his kind of politics, which Trotsky contemptuously
and somewhat misleadingly stigmatized as 'bureaucratism'.
This basic incompatibility of temperament, as well as long-
standing personal differences, engendered the split between
them which came into the open after Lenin's death.

In this way Trotsky himself became from 1923 what earlier
observers would least have expected, a spokesman for all
those in the party who were worried about the increasing
rigidity and unresponsiveness of the apparatus. He had rejected earlier warnings, from Rosa Luxemburg, from the
Mensheviks, that suppression of free elections, freedom of
the press, of association etc., would be bound to cause the
atrophying of the body politic and the triumph of
'bureaucracy'. Yet now, though without making the causal
connection, this was precisely the sin he castigated.

The first immediate occasion was an outbreak of working-
class unrest in the summer and early autumn of 1923, in
which members of two underground groups in the party were
said to be involved ('underground' because of the resolutions
of the Tenth Party Congress). Their leaders were arrested. In
October, Dzerzhinsky requested that members of the party
should be placed under a formal obligation to report to the
GPU (as the Cheka was now known) on 'fractions' opposing
the official leadership. In a letter to the Central Committee,
Trotsky objected that the encouragement of 'spying and
denunciations' was symptomatic of the unhealthy atmosphere that had grown up inside the party. Participation of the
masses in the party had now become completely 'illusory', in
fact 'the present regime . . . is much further from any workers'

democracy than was the regime of the fiercest period of war communism.' The election of party officials had atrophied, and 'appointment of the secretaries of provincial committees is now the rule. That creates for the secretary a position essentially independent of the local organization.' As a result, 'secretarial psychology' had grown up, 'the principal trait of which is that the secretary is capable of deciding everything'.

The events of 1923 amply substantiated Trotsky's new-found perspicacity. Criticism of NEP, of concessions to the 'bourgeoisie', suppression of the workers, was by now very widespread in provincial party organizations, in the *Komsomol* (the party's youth organization) and in university and army party cells. It found expression in a 'platform of 46', circulated to members of the Central Committee only a week after Trotsky's letter. Although he himself did not sign this platform, many of those who did had been associated with him in the past, and its sentiments closely echoed his own. Starting from wide-ranging censure of the regime's economic policy, the signatories traced its shortcomings back to a 'one-sided recruitment policy', to a division which had opened up between 'a secretarial hierarchy and "the quiet folk" . . . who do not participate in the common life'. Serious discussion of issues had stopped, because 'members of the party who are privately dissatisfied with this or that decision of the central committee . . . , who privately note this or that error, irregularity or disorder, are afraid to speak about it at party meetings, or even in conversation, unless the partner in the conversation is thoroughly reliable from the point of view of "discretion".'

Like Trotsky, the 46 were not in favour of inner party democracy on principle: they too wanted to restore 'real unity in opinions and actions', but of a different kind from Stalin.

The triumvirate decided to respond by promising free discussion of serious issues within the party, and opening up the pages of *Pravda* for the expression of opinions. It soon turned out that Trotsky and the 46 did indeed have widespread support.

Meetings were held in party organizations: it transpired that the Opposition had a majority not only in many of the provinces, but even in the Moscow city party organization, and indeed in the enormous party cell of the Central Committee itself. Stalin got his personal assistants to collate the voting figures and keep records of them, and in the following months used them to start making changes in the personnel of party organizations: Antonov-Ovseenko, for example, was dismissed as head of the Political Department of the Red Army, and a selective purge of secretaries was carried out in the Komsomol, as well as in provincial organizations which had voted for the Opposition.

At the same time Stalin used a ploy suggested to him by Trotsky, and thus gave the appearance of making concessions to the Opposition. Trotsky had pointed out that workers formed only a small minority, approximately one-sixth, of the party's membership. The reason for this was that some workers had left since 1921 (when working-class membership of 40 per cent had been reported) in disillusionment, some had been promoted to official positions and ceased to be 'working-class', while yet others had been expelled for belonging to the Workers' Opposition or other 'underground' groups. For Trotsky this was ample evidence of the 'degeneration' and 'bureaucratization' he discerned. Stalin responded with two massive recruitments of workers in the year after Lenin's death. This 'Lenin Enrolment' brought in some 500,000 workers, doubling party membership and dramatically improving the proletarian share of it. The effects, however, were opposite to those Trotsky had intended. The entrants were admitted with the minimum of scrutiny and formality, in contravention, strictly speaking, of the party rules. They were of course beholden to the secretaries who recruited them, who in their turn were beholden to Stalin. In this way Stalin created for himself an abundant fresh reservoir of patronage. Some of the new recruits made excellent careers for themselves, and became prominent figures in the 1930s. Many more were able to use the party ladder to escape from the working class, as the following figures from the 1927 party census suggests:

	'Social situation' %	Current occupation %
Workers	55.7	30.0
Peasants	19.0	9.9
Employees	25.3	42.8

Quite apart from the fact that the 'current occupation' rubric leaves 17.3 per cent unaccounted for, the figures suggest that nearly half of those members who had been peasants or workers on entry had moved up, mostly in a very short time, into the 'white-collar' category. The party, in fact, was now *the* major channel of social mobility in Soviet society. Education and other factors counted for very little. It is scarcely surprising that domination of party patronage had become such a powerful weapon in politics.

A comment is necessary on the term 'bureaucracy'. When Trotsky – and indeed Lenin in his last years – used it, they intended to imply that petty officials from the old regime were creeping back into the new regime and restoring their 'petty bourgeois' practices. As applied to the state machinery, that reproach may have been partly correct, but it certainly did not apply to the party. Nor is the term 'bureaucracy', in the sociological sense, very appropriate to the emerging party apparatus. In the Weberian usage, the term implies a compartmentalized and specialized body of administrators, obeying the law and written instructions, and operating on rational criteria. Party secretaries did not behave in that manner at all: they would have been sacked if they had. They were expected to be generalists, to obey 'revolutionary consciousness' rather than law, to cope with emergencies at all hours of the day and night, to use violence where they thought it necessary, and ingeneral to get on with the job at all costs. Stalin described them as 'an order of Teutonic Knights at the centre of the Soviet state', and this image certainly conveys far better their conviction, their devotion to duty, their often brutal methods, and even their frequent sense of being an occupying force among a sullen and suspicious population.

At any rate, Stalin was able to utilize his tightening grip on appointments to weaken his potential rivals. In January 1925 a conference of political commissars called for and obtained Trotsky's resignation from the post of people's commissar for war. Zinoviev and Kamenev, alarmed by Stalin's growing power and his policy (short-lived, as it turned out) of concessions to the peasantry, went into opposition, and they too soon found themselves deprived of their power bases in the Leningrad and Moscow party organizations. Yet they found it difficult to work together with Trotsky to concert their opposition to Stalin. Years of personal differences impeded their rapprochement. Trotsky was, in any case, a difficult person to work with. A towering figure in revolutionary upheavals, he seemed incapable of stooping to the daily infighting of ordinary politics. With the mixed arrogance and humility of those who believe history is on their side, he disdained the conciliatory gestures and the menial bonhomie of the politician who needs allies. It was not until 1926–7 that he, Zinoviev and Kamenev managed to form a United Opposition. They were joined by other members of earlier groups, such as the Democratic Centralists and the Workers' Opposition. Many of the great names of the revolution were in the United Opposition, but now they lacked any local or institutional power base, and any organized mass support. Their moral authority had been weakened by their inconsistencies and their mutual quarrels of the past. As Anastasy Mikoyan tellingly remarked at the Fourteenth Party Congress, 'When Zinoviev is in the majority, he is for iron discipline. . . . When he is in the minority, he is against it.' All of them had acquiesced in the crushing of the other parties, so that now there was nowhere for anyone to go who wanted to resist Stalin and his 'secretarial regime'. Besides, most of them felt, like Trotsky, that 'history offers no way of being right but through the party.'

Stalin exploited their weaknesses, their doubts and their potential divisions very skilfully. Defeated at a Central Committee meeting in April 1926, the Opposition tried to present their case at the Fifteenth Party Conference in October, but were denied the right to speak. When they tried to appeal direct to the mass of the party by addressing meetings of workers in factories, party militants turned up, tried to rouse those present against the Opposition, and if they failed, broke up the meetings in disorder. This was the first time violence had been used by the party against its own members. Workers who tried to attend clandestine gatherings of the Opposition found themselves under investigation by the GPU.

More research needs to be done in this area, but it is difficult to avoid the impression that working-class support for the Opposition was at a low level. This may have been partly a result of party and police repression, but at the same time, as we have seen, there was ample reason for workers to feel alienated from all wings of the party. Some of the members of the Opposition, notably Trotsky himself, had been among the most forthright in their schemes for depriving the workers of political and economic rights.

When the Opposition tried to prepare a statement for the Fifteenth Party Congress in December 1927, they had to work in secret, for under the provisions of the Tenth Congress they now constituted an illegitimate 'fraction'. Their clandestine printing press was discovered by the GPU, and this associated them with 'criminal' activity. Stalin was thus able to obtain the expulsion of all the leading members of the Opposition from the Central Committee, and in the case of Trotsky and Zinoviev from the party itself. To compound their political defeat with a moral one, Stalin offered to readmit them if they would repudiate their oppositional activities and confess their mistakes before the party. This early example of a subsequently familiar Stalinist ritual did split the Opposition. Zinoviev and Kamenev agreed to recant and to denounce 'Trotskyism', while Trotsky and some of his closest associates refused to do so and were deported to Central Asia the day after the Congress. Pseudo-religious politics had already taken its grip. Crushed by the party whose monopoly position and internal rigidity they had enthusiastically helped to build up, the Opposition left the stage unsupported and unlamented by the workers whom they had disdained in their days of power.

Of those who remained, some, such as Zinoviev and Kamenev, made the required self-abasement, in order not to be left without a role. As I. N. Smirnov put it, 'I can't stand inactivity. I want to build! In its own barbaric and sometimes stupid way, the Central Committee is building for the future. Our ideological differences are of small importance before the construction of great new industries.' Others refused to compromise their consciences before brute power, and sat helplessly in their apartments, drinking glasses of tea and discussing politics and literature, while their comrades were arrested one by one. There was not the slightest chance of doing anything, for they were under the closest surveillance. Victor Serge reckoned that in his Leningrad apartment where about thirty people lived, three were reporting regularly on him to the GPU.

The desperate nature of their plight was well summed up by a man who was not a member of the Opposition, indeed had been thought of as a pillar of the regime, but who was nevertheless soon to share their fate: Bukharin. In 1928 he was secretly in touch with Kamenev, to see whether anything could still be done to halt the rise of Stalin. 'What can one do before an adversary of this kind?' he asked in bewilderment. 'A Gengis Khan, a debased product of the Central Committee. If the country perishes, we all perish. If the country manages to recover, he twists around in time, and we still perish.'

With Stalin's newcomers in the ascendant, and many of Lenin's once closest comrades in a mood of impotent foreboding, the party moved on to cope with the economic problems thrown up by NEP.

Lenin leaving the First
All-Russian Congress
on Education, August
1918 (*Keystone*)

Generalissimo Stalin,
1950 (*Keystone*)

Khrushchev (*third from right*) discussing his favorite crop—maize—with Walter Ulbricht (*far left*) during a visit to the German Democratic Republic in 1957 (*Keystone*)

(*from right to left*) Gromyko, Brezhnev, and Kosygin talking with Chancellor Schmidt of West Germany during his official visit to the USSR in 1980 (*Keystone*)

6

Revolution from Above

Communists had always assumed that a 'socialist' society meant a highly industrialized society, in which the means of production were nationalized and planned. Ever since 1917 the Soviet government had been developing institutions designed to plan and direct the economy as a whole: Vesenkha, GOELRO (the nationwide electrification plan launched by Lenin in 1920), and Gosplan, the state planning authority set up in 1921 'to work out a single general state economic plan and methods and means of implementing it'. By 1925 Gosplan had collected enough information to be in a position to begin publishing annual 'control figures', projecting economic development for a year ahead at a time, and soon after it began producing drafts for longer growth plans, spread over five years at a time.

The maturing of this long process coincided with a renewed crisis mood in the country. In 1927 the nation was reminded for the first time since 1920 of the possibility of intervention against it by capitalist powers. The crushing of the Chinese Communist rising in that year, together with the (temporary) rupture of diplomatic relations with the USSR by Britain revived fears of foreign encirclement and even invasion. People began to hoard food as before a war, and the leaders were reminded of the country's military vulnerability – with the army dependent for much of its equipment on secret agreements with the German Reichswehr.

In 1928 the party Central Committee had before it a Five Year Plan for economic development. This had been through a stormy history. During its elaboration, two main schools of thought competed for it. The first, whose main support was in Gosplan, favoured a strictly scientific plan, based on collating existing figures, and predicting future relationships between different sectors of the economy such as would serve to give an overall balance. The other, with its bastion in Vesenkha, might be called the 'teleological' school, in that they selected one crucial sector – heavy industry – recommended desirable figures for that alone, and then let all other sectors arrange themselves behind it, in accordance with its needs. As the statistician S. G. Strumilin said, 'Our task is not to study the economy, but to change it.'

Stalin told the Central Committee in November 1928 why industry had to occupy this central position. We have caught up and overhauled the capitalist countries, he claimed, in our political forms. 'But that is not enough. To achieve the final victory of socialism in our country we also need to catch up and overhaul those countries in the technical and economic sense. Either we do it, or we shall be crushed.' In a later speech (February 1931) he dramatized even more the stigma which so many Communists, including Lenin, had felt to be weighing upon Russia: 'One feature of the history of old Russia was the continual beatings she suffered because of her backwardness. . . . We are fifty or a hundred years behind the advanced countries. We must catch up this distance in ten years. Either we do it or we go under.' Heavy industry, he argued, had to be at the centre of this modernizing effort, because that alone could guarantee the needs of military defence, and because from heavy industry would in time come benefits for all the rest of the economy.

As will be apparent, Stalin had more or less taken over the arguments of the Opposition, which he had defeated less than a year before. And indeed, before long, he discovered a 'right deviation', consisting of those who contested his policy of putting increased pressure on the peasantry (see below, page 158) and who considered the draft Five Year Plan excessive and unbalanced in its economic indicators. The principal targets were Bukharin, Aleksei Rykov (chairman of the Council of People's Commissars) and Mikhail Tomsky (head of the trade unions). Stalin used his patronage system to undermine their strongholds, such as the Moscow party organization, the party cells in the universities and the trade unions, and by late 1929 had had them removed from most of their official positions. Like Kamenev and Zinoviev before them, they publicly recognized that 'our views ... have proved erroneous', and were permitted to stay in the party and keep some of their official positions.

The same kind of political pressure was operating on the planners. In Gosplan the whole notion of balance between different sectors of the economy began to be politically suspect. The former Menshevik, Groman, principal exponent of equilibrium planning for optimum economic development, was dismissed along with his working group. Several of them appeared in 1931 in a publicized trial, where they were accused of having tried 'criminally' to retard the country's industrial development.

At any rate, most planners preferred, as the statistician Strumilin put it, to 'stand for high growth rates rather than to sit [be imprisoned] for low ones'. Planning became a matter not of prediction, but of command. The effect was what Naum Jasny has called 'Bacchanalian planning', some results of which can be seen in the following table. The 'first version' represents the plan confirmed by the Sixteenth Party Conference in April 1929, but this was followed by two upward revisions, as well as a decision to 'fulfil the Five Year Plan in four years' (it actually began in October 1928 and ended in December 1932).

	Actual 1927–8	First version	Optimal 1932–3	Amended 1932	Actual 1932
Coal (m. tonnes)	35.4	68	75	95–105	64
Oil	11.7	19	22	40–55	21.4
Iron ore	5.7	15	19	24–32	12.1
Pig iron	3.3	8	10	15–16	6.2

As can be seen, even some of the original plan figures proved optimistic, let alone the subsequent wild flights of the imagination. What cannot be doubted, however, is that during the first Five Year Plan, considerable growth was in fact achieved in key sectors of heavy industry, especially the output of machine tools, and the foundation was laid for the creation of whole new industrial areas. Especially notable was the rapid construction of a giant hydroelectric scheme on the lower Dnieper, which attracted a cluster of later factories, the creation of new metallurgical combines at Magnitogorsk in the Urals and near Kuznetsk, in western Siberia, where it was linked to coal. This latter began the movement of industry away from the vulnerable western areas of the country into Siberia. Huge new tractor factories were set up at Stalingrad, Chelyabinsk and Kharkov, to provide for the needs of mechanized agriculture – though their output subsequently proved inadequate. Also, if some of the results of the first plan were disappointing, that was partly because some of its most ambitious projects only came on line during the second plan (1933–7).

All the same, the first Five Year Plan left conspicuous imbalances, some of which have become more or less permanent features of the Soviet economy. Even in heavy industry some branches were neglected, such as the chemical industry, whose lagging has posed persistent problems for other branches ever since. The textile industry actually declined during the first Five Year Plan, which meant that clothes were of poor quality and in very short supply. The railways were relatively neglected, with the result that goods once manufactured could not always be despatched to their destination before spoiling. Housing, consumer industry and services were almost totally neglected, and food supplies disrupted by collectivization (see below). Workers desperately needed on the job had to spend time queuing for essentials. According to Khrushchev, for example, in 1932 all factories and workshops in Moscow were instructed to raise rabbits to keep their canteens supplied. It must be remembered too that the collectivization almost destroyed cottage industry, on which much of the population relied for their clothes, furniture and tools.

Another lasting heritage of the first Five Year Plan was a structure and style of industrial management. Centralized ministries – or People's Commissariats, as they were still called – were set up to take over from Vesenkha the task of administering the proliferating branches of industry. In 1932 there were three of them; by 1939 their number had reached twenty, and by 1948 they numbered thirty-two. This luxuriant expansion offered abundant scope for Stalin's patronage, especially among the new 'Red specialists' being trained for the purpose. Party secretaries in the localities, moreover, now found that they were being judged by the output indicators of the major enterprises in their region. Success was not merely fulfilment of plan figures, but 'over-fulfilment', which they were exhorted to achieve at whatever cost. This meant that party secretaries spent much of their time using their influence to help industrial managers secure scarce supplies in competition with factories from other regions. Even the major projects of the Five Year Plans were allocated in fierce competition between party organizations anxious to boost their prestige.

Once such projects had been allocated, of course, then 'overfulfilment' of the planned targets became the number one priority, to which everything else had to be sacrificed, including health, safety and the interests of every other sector of the economy. The industrial scene became more like a battlefield, with its 'fronts', 'campaigns' and 'breakthroughs'. Scarce men and supplies were rushed in to deal with emergencies, and victories were reported with rhetorical flourishes in the press. The successful industrial manager was no bureaucrat, but more like a pioneer or even freebooter using rough and ready methods to open up new territory. Some were known to hijack lorries and ambush freight trains to commandeer supplies intended for a rival: provided they overfulfilled their plan, they would receive no more than a rebuke which cost them nothing. But if they failed, the penalty might be dismissal, disgrace, even arrest, on the charge of 'sabotage'.

The life of the working class was dramatically transformed by the Five Year Plans. First of all, their numbers rose very fast:

(in millions)	1928	1932	1937	1940
Industry	3.1	6.0	7.9	8.3
Construction	0.6	2.5	1.9	1.9
Transport	0.9	1.5	1.9	2.4
Total	4.6	10.0	11.7	12.6

Broadly speaking, working-class numbers doubled during the first Five Year Plan, and nearly trebled between 1928 and 1940. Unemployment disappeared, and the payment of unemployment benefit ceased. The majority of the newcomers flooded in from the countryside, some with handicraft skills, but mostly with little or no education and no experience of industrial processes or discipline. They had to crowd into the existing housing or else into hastily erected wooden barracks. At Moscow's Elektrozavod (electricity works) new arrivals were fitted into a long wooden hut, where beds without blankets or pillows were crowded side by side: these beds had to be shared in shifts, and even then there was often not enough space, so that some workers found themselves sleeping on the floor. Families were squeezed into cramped 'communal apartments' – usually single-family pre-war flats divided up so that a family occupied each room, sharing kitchen, bathroom and toilet. Sometimes there was not even a whole room to spare for a family. Harold Eekman, a Belgian diplomat, described the contrivances he glimpsed through windows in Moscow in the late 1930s as families tried to protect their privacy: 'They made pathetic efforts to isolate from their neighbours the few square feet of floor space allotted to their use. Every piece of furniture, every stick they owned, every ragged remnant saved from old curtains, was pressed into service to build up some sort of fence or stockade around their cramped refuge.' In Magnitogorsk, which had been no more than a village, workers even lived in tents until more permanent dwellings could be erected, while in a ravine overlooking the railway, Bashkirs and Tatars built themselves mud huts topped by scrap metal – a shanty town known to the locals as 'Shanghai'.

Working conditions and practices suffered enormously from the universal pressure to 'overfulfil', especially since so many workers had neither the training nor the experience to cope with the sometimes sophisticated machinery they were making. When the first director of the Stalingrad tractor factory asked a worker how he measured the sockets he was grinding, the worker demonstrated how he used his fingers for the purpose – there were no measuring instruments. Lathe operators used coarse cutting tools instead of fine ones, in order to get their jobs done faster. Drills were used without proper protection, and injuries resulted. Machines were not properly cleaned, oiled and maintained. Unpredictable shortages, sometimes of the most elementary tools or materials, held up whole production lines. At Elektrozavod, an American spindle lathe, imported for $25,000, lay unused and badly rusted because of a minor breakdown that would have cost $50 to repair in the USA. Safety levels were appalling. In Magnitogorsk in 1933 scaffolding on a building site at the metal works was so rickety and slippery that workers fell off and were seriously injured: one riveter fell into a pipe, got stuck there and froze to death overnight. In the Kharkov tractor factory in 1935 increased output capacity was not matched by improved ventilation, so that poisonous gases accumulated round the production line, though in this case it is only fair to add that the trade union publicized the matter and had it corrected.

Levels of pay were low, and differentials between skilled

and unskilled workers increased, following a deliberate policy decision: Stalin dubbed 'equalization of pay . . . a petty bourgeois prejudice'. Qualified engineers received four to eight times the pay of an unskilled worker, while administrators and managers earned anything between eight and thirty times that level, not counting the extensive non-monetary privileges they also received. To some extent the workers' material situation was eased by the Workers' Cooperative stores, to which they had access, and where they could buy standard essentials at moderate prices. Here they would buy their rations during the famine of 1932–4. Outside the factory, government stores offered better quality at higher prices to those who could afford it, while the peasant market (see below, page 170), grudgingly tolerated by the authorities after the early excesses of collectivization, provided a fall-back, with usually good quality food at very high prices. Actual starvation did not threaten the towns as it did the countryside, but the hunting and queueing for scarce food supplies were exhausting and certainly detracted from workers' productivity.

Not surprisingly, many workers felt very discontented at their way of life, and frequently left their jobs to look for something better. Since most enterprises were short of labour, they were usually able to obtain work somewhere else, only to find that conditions there were no improvement. The average period of employment in the coal and iron industries in 1930 was a mere four months. The government tried a number of measures to get a grip on this constantly migrating mass of humanity. In December 1932 the introduction of internal passports and dwelling permits (*propiska*) meant that anyone who lived in a town was registered with the police, and could not move to a new town without their permission. Since passports were withheld from peasants, the authorities were now also able to get more of a grip on migration from the villages into the towns.

From September 1930 the worker had a 'wage book' at his place of employment, and 'arbitrary termination of employment' was recorded in it. In 1938 this became a 'work book', which a worker had to carry with him all his working life: any infringement of discipline was entered in it. Absenteeism, defined in 1932 as one day of absence from work without good reason, was deemed to be sufficient grounds for dismissal – and dismissal at that time usually entailed eviction from home, loss of ration card and loss of access to the Workers' Cooperative. In 1939 absenteeism was redefined as being twenty minutes late for work without good reason, and in 1940 it was actually made a criminal offence, for which one could be sentenced to six months' 'corrective labour': this usually meant continuing in one's normal job, but with a 25 per cent cut in pay. 'Arbitrary termination of employment' also became a criminal offence, punishable by imprisonment.

The existence of these draconian provisions does not necessarily imply that they were invariably applied. Employers were short of labour and anxious to retain workers, especially those with skills or good work records. But the very existence of such legislation speaks volumes about the party's attitude towards the class in whose name it claimed to rule.

On the other hand, workers who stayed on the job, took extra training and observed labour discipline, could do very well in these years. Workers were encouraged to take part-time courses in apprenticeship schools (FZU), to increase their qualifications. As a result they would receive higher pay and possibly better housing or social security benefits. Outstanding (*udarny*) workers, who overfulfilled their norms, received decorations and honours which put them into a kind of workers' aristocracy (the word *znat*, a colloquial term for 'nobility', was officially applied to them): they received higher pay, better conditions and the promise of a better pension, as well as being celebrated on notice boards and in newspapers. Many of them were selected for special technical education and eventual promotion out of the working class to become administrators and party officials.

The apogee of the campaign for 'overfulfilment' was reached in 1935, when Alexei Stakhanov, a coalminer in the Donbass, hewed 102 tonnes of coal in a single shift, instead of the 7 tonnes prescribed. This was in fact done by halting all other work in his sector of the mine, and using a whole gang to perform the auxiliary work that normally had to be done by the man at the coal face. Similar feats were contrived elsewhere, and glorified in the newspapers, with the message that 'there are no fortresses Bolsheviks cannot storm.' The opportunity was taken to raise norms generally. Stakhanovites became the cream of the new znat, receiving huge pay rises and the pick of the few new apartments being built for workers. It seems, however, that some Stakhanovites were lynched by their fellow workers, and the campaign was eventually dropped in favour of a more sober alternative, that of the 'rationalizers': workers who could suggest better working methods and demonstrate their usefulness.

By 1940, then, the Soviet government combined a virtually military discipline on the shop floor with very attractive rewards for those who obeyed this discipline and overfulfilled their norms. Those who performed less well could expect a harassed and marginal existence, overshadowed by the threat of arrest and despatch to one of the fast-expanding labour camps.

The explosive growth of the towns naturally required a considerable increase in agricultural output and marketing. The first Five Year Plan simply assumed that this would take place, but even as it was being drafted, the signs were moving in the opposite direction. After reaching a peak in 1926, grain procurements began to decline, and in fact by January 1928 state purchases were running at less than three-quarters of the level of the previous year. The reason for the shortfall was partly that the prices the government offered were well below those on the free market, and partly that manufactured goods for the villages were in short supply. Besides, peasants were beginning to be wary of being too obviously productive and of getting themselves labelled as 'kulaks'.

In this incipient 'scissors crisis' the regime reacted in the opposite way from 1923. Instead of making the terms of trade more favourable to the peasants, it resorted to coercion. This was first tried out in the Urals and western Siberia, where there was known to have been a relatively good harvest. Peasant markets were closed down and private trade in food was banned. Better-off households were ordered to deliver grain, and prosecuted under article 107 of the criminal code ('speculation') if they failed to do so. The immediate results were quite encouraging: a good deal of surplus grain was discovered and brought into the towns. The longer-term effect of the operation, however, as during the civil war, was to discourage peasants from sowing more grain the next year than they needed for their own subsistence. The method, all the same, was extended to other areas, and the Central Committee sent prominent emissaries to see that it was properly executed: Stalin went to the Urals and Siberia, Zhdanov to the Volga, Kossior to the Ukraine, and Andreyev to the North Caucasus. Committees of Poor Peasants were once again formed, as in 1918, to compensate for the party's weakness in the countryside, to 'unleash class war', and to put inside knowledge of the villages at the disposal of the requisition teams. Village assemblies were ordered to hold meetings at which a classification of all households was carried out, each being labelled 'poor peasant', 'middle peasant' or 'kulak'. The last were then assigned very heavy delivery targets. In some cases whole villages were punished for shortfalls in procurement quotas. In the Crimea, for example *Pravda* reported in October 1929 that some settlements had been declared 'under boycott'. 'Nothing was sold in the cooperatives [village shops]; no post was issued or accepted; [villagers] were not allowed to travel anywhere; an inventory of property was taken, and some settlers were arrested.'

After an encouraging start, the yield of the new policy was disappointing, and in fact bread rationing had to be reintroduced in the towns during 1929. But by now the party had other solutions in mind. Already the Fifteenth Party Congress, in December 1927, had resolved that 'the task of uniting and transforming the small individual peasant holdings into large collectives must become the principal task of the party in the villages.' At that stage, what was envisaged was still a campaign of propaganda and persuasion, as a result of which the peasants would voluntarily join collectives. Indeed this aim was never explicitly dropped, and the voluntary creation of collectives did get under way during 1928–9, but in the autumn of 1929 it began to merge with the new-style grain collections into a single coercive campaign. The ostensible idea of the campaign was to create larger and more productive mechanized farms, but in the absence (yet) of an adequate tractor industry, the main practical aim was to simplify food procurement by reducing very sharply the number of collection points and bringing them under much stricter control. It was represented, however, as a decisive stage in the building of socialism, a return to the early, visionary days of the revolution, for which so many party members hankered after the uncertainties and compromises of NEP. The slogans of battle were gratefully revived: 'Those who do not join the *kolkhoz* [collective farm] are enemies of soviet power.' And Yury Pyatakov, a former member of the Opposition, proclaimed, 'The heroic period of our socialist construction has arrived.'

The first stage of the campaign was frankly designated as 'dekulakization'. Stalin put the issue in stark terms. In December 1929 he told a conference of agronomists: 'Either we go backward, to capitalism, or we go forward, to socialism. . . . What does that mean? It means that we have passed on from a policy of *limiting* the exploitative tendencies of the kulaks to a policy of *liquidating* the kulaks as a class.' Having decided that there was no certain way of extorting food supplies from the better-off peasants who were best able to provide it, the party had made up its mind simply to eliminate them from the village, and to put their property at the disposal of the new collective farms.

In effect the label 'kulak' was now applied to anyone suspected of resisting the grain deliveries or of being unwilling to join the collectives. Those who were quite obviously not in any sense 'wealthy' were called *podkulachniki*, or 'subsidiary kulaks'. Typically, the suspected 'kulak' was summoned to the village soviet and there interrogated by the chairman, or by a party emissary, or by the local GPU official, or by all of them successively, trying to get him to confess that he had hidden grain somewhere, or had sold it on the black market. A requisition team, guided by a local 'poor peasant', would visit his hut and search everything, breaking down doors, tearing up cushions, ripping up floorboards, and confiscating not only food, but often also furniture, clothes, tools, anything they considered potentially useful to the collective. Many households, in anticipation of such a visit, hastily sold belongings, slaughtered cattle for meat, and drank their supplies of home-brewed vodka in a bitter farewell celebration. Viktor Kravchenko, who was sent as a party emissary, observed one peasant woman set fire to her own home, shrieking, 'Infidels! Murderers! We've worked all our lives for our home. You won't have it. The flames shall have it!'

The next stage was to gather together kulak families marked for deportation. Some, forewarned, managed to escape or to commit suicide, sometimes in whole families. Some even contrived to go into hiding. Osip and Nadezhda Mandelstam, travelling in Voronezh oblast a few years later, saw one such family being finally evicted from a dugout and their improvised home being flattened. What struck the Mandelstams most was that the women still managed to dress decently and had kept spinning wheels and sewing machines – preserving a minimum of normality in a world turned upside down.

Those who did not elude the authorities were rounded up

and marched to the nearest railway station, where they were loaded into cattle trucks. In those trucks, crowded together without toilet facilities, and with irregular food and drink, they were transported thousands of miles to an unknown fate somewhere in Siberia, the Urals or the northern part of European Russia. The family of the later well-known poet, Alexander Tvardovsky, was taken along with five hundred or so others to the northern Urals, hauled down a frozen river on sledges, and dumped in the forest at a point where there was nothing but a hut for some twenty loggers. There they were ordered to start building a settlement. Many kulaks were sent to labour camps, where they formed the first really huge contingent of convicts. Others were exiled to remote regions where they had to report regularly to the police, and where the only work available was analogous to that in the labour camps. Those who could find no work starved. The novelist Vladimir Tendryakov described seeing them in a small town in the northern oblast of Vologda:

> In Vokhrovo . . . in the station square Ukrainian kulaks, expropriated and exiled from their homeland, lay down and died. One got used to seeing the dead there in the morning, and the hospital stable-boy, Abram, would come along with his cart and pile the corpses in.
>
> Not everyone died. Many wandered along the dusty, sordid alleyways, dragging dropsied legs, elephantine and bloodlessly blue, and plucked at every passer-by, begging with dog-like eyes. In Vokhrovo they had no luck: the inhabitants themselves, to receive their ration, had to stand in the bread queue all night.

There was some armed resistance to this campaign, though its nature and extent were carefully concealed by the Soviet authorities, and even today we know very little about it. Peasants were not as well armed or trained as they had been in 1920–1, and violence usually took the form of murdering individual party or GPU emissaries. Nevertheless, in the

Ukraine, the Caucasus, the Don region and Siberia, peasant resistance sometimes went further than this. These were areas where both grain requisitioning and 'dekulakization' were at their most ruthless. On some occasions units of the Red Army had to be sent in, including in at least one case aviation. In the North Caucasus, GPU troops under the direction of Kaganovich rounded up whole villages for deportation to the far north. The authorities saw the whole operation as a war: whether the 'kulaks' resisted or not, they had been identified as the 'enemy'. When the writer Mikhail Sholokhov protested to Stalin about the methods used, Stalin replied that the kulaks were quite prepared to let the towns and the army starve. 'This is a silent war against Soviet power – war by starvation, my dear comrade Sholokhov.' And as the writer Maxim Gorky reminded readers of *Pravda* and *Izvestiya* in November 1930, 'everyone is against us who has outlived the epoch allotted to him by history, so we are entitled to consider ourselves in a state of civil war. The logical consequence of this is that, if the enemy does not surrender, he is to be exterminated.'

It is far from clear how many people suffered 'dekulakization'. Soviet sources have more or less admitted a figure of 1 million households, or perhaps 5 million people, but the émigré historian Moshe Lewin, in a sober and thoroughly researched history of the subject, estimates that that figure should probably be doubled.

The fate of those who stayed behind in the villages was not always preferable. A Central Committee resolution of 5 January 1930 called for 'total collectivization' by the spring of 1932 at the latest, and for the Volga basin and North Caucasus by a year earlier. This was the language and spirit of the most extravagant versions of the first Five Year Plan. Special emissaries, usually young workers with a good party record (and many of them recruits of the Lenin Enrolment), were despatched to the villages to organize the collectives. Hastily trained at special two-week courses, they were generally known as 'twenty-five thousanders', because that was the number of the first contingent. They were told frankly that the immediate aim of the operation was to extract grain, at any price. Viktor Kravchenko was told, 'Pump it out of them, wherever it's hidden. . . . Don't be afraid of taking extreme measures. The party stands four-square behind you. Comrade Stalin expects it of you.' Lev Kopelev, another 'twenty-five thousander' later recalled the lofty and militant ideals which filled him at the time:

> The grain front! Stalin had said, 'The struggle for bread is the struggle for socialism.' I was convinced that we were soldiers on an invisible front, waging war on kulak sabotage for the sake of bread that the country needed for the Five Year Plan. For bread above all, but also for the souls of peasants whose attitudes had hardened through low political consciousness, and who succumbed to enemy propaganda, not grasping the great truth of communism . . .

Once they arrived in the village, the emissaries' first job was to call a meeting of the mir assembly, at which they had to persuade the peasants to set up and join a collective farm. They were able to offer inducements of credit or machinery (not always subsequently delivered), and to threaten heavy taxes, increased delivery quotas or even exile. In most cases they succeeded in obtaining the formal resolution they required, and were able to report it. The official campaign figures swelled impressively, reaching 80 per cent collectivization in some areas by March 1930. The reality did not match the paper. Most peasants were deeply distrustful of the new collectives. The Russian-born American journalist, Maurice Hindus, who talked with the peasants of his native village, commented: 'These peasants had never believed in anybody's words; they had always distrusted the whole world. . . . And now they were to give up their individual land, their horses, their cows, their farm buildings – the things that had given them bread, protection against starvation, the very security they needed to hold body and soul together – all on the mere promise of a youthful agitator that this would enrich their lives!' Extravagant rumours circulated: that the children would all be sent to China, that a special machine would burn up the old people so that they would eat no more grain, that the village women would become 'socialist property'. Sectarians warned that the Anti-Christ was coming, and the devil's seal would be affixed to the kolkhoz gates, heralding the end of the world. Colour was given to these dire warnings by the fact that collectivization was often accompanied by the arrest of the village priest and the closure and even destruction of the church.

Although instructions had been issued about the *pace* of collectivization, no one had indicated just what a kolkhoz should look like. In the early days the 'twenty-five thousanders' tended to extremes (as they had been instructed) and tried to make everything collective, including household furniture and clothes, which aroused enormous opposition. Many peasants slaughtered their cattle, rather than hand it over. *Kolkhozniki* (collective farmers) going out to the fields would sometimes be set upon by their non-collectivized neighbours with pitchforks, and had their tools and clothes stripped from them. Total chaos reigned, and, fearing for the fate of the spring sowing, the party decided to call for a pause. On 2 March 1930 Stalin published an article in *Pravda* entitled 'Dizzy with Success'. With unmatched aplomb he reproached local officials with 'excesses' and with not observing the 'voluntary principle' of the kolkhoz movement. Reluctant entrants were allowed to leave the new collectives. They did so in droves, and between March and June 1930 the reported proportion of collectivized households fell from more than half to less than a quarter.

The following autumn, however, once the harvest was safely in, the campaign was renewed. Now it was on a somewhat more sober and carefully planned basis, and it was generally agreed that the artel (which allowed each household a small private plot, a cow and some poultry) should be the basic model, but the compulsion was no less determined.

By the summer of 1931 more than half the households were once again in collectives, and by the summer of 1936 that figure had reached 90 per cent.

The immediate results of collectivization were disastrous. True, the grain harvest fell by only a relatively small amount (but it had been expected to double). The state procurements, however, increased considerably, depriving the rural population of the precarious surplus they had previously enjoyed. A Soviet scholar gives the following figures (in million tonnes):

	Grain harvest (barn yield)	State procurements
1928	73.3	10.8
1929	71.7	16.1
1930	83.5	22.1
1931	69.5	22.8
1932	69.9	18.8
1933	68.4	23.3
1934	67.6	26.1
1935	75.0	29.6

The figures for meat and dairy products were far worse. Cattle fell from 70.5 million head in 1928 to 38.4 in 1933; pigs from 26 million to 12 million; sheep and goats from 146.7 million to 50.2 million. The country did not recover from this disaster until the mid-1950s, so that for the next twenty years most of the population was desperately short of meat and milk.

Since state procurements were now taking a much greater proportion of the harvest than previously, the towns and the army continued to be fed, even if not abundantly. In fact, exports of grain were continued on a high level up to 1931, in order to earn foreign currency, and not abandoned altogether, even thereafter. But in the countryside a famine took hold which was even more serious than in 1921–2. In the western region, the Smolensk archives show that *all* grain was considered liable for procurement, even what was intended for next year's sowing. Armed 'troiki' (from soviets, party and GPU) were sent to the villages, and special controllers watched over the transport, milling, baking and sale of bread.

When Kravchenko entered a village in Dnepropetrovsk oblast, he was surprised by the deathly silence. 'All the dogs have been eaten,' he was told. 'We've eaten everything we could lay our hands on – cats, dogs, field mice, birds. When it's light tomorrow, you will see that the trees have been stripped of their bark, for that too has been eaten.' Conditions like this were widespread, especially in the fertile grain-growing regions: for this was a famine deliberately created by the state in order to keep up deliveries to the towns and the army. Consequently, in contrast to 1921, the government deliberately kept the famine secret, both from the foreign press, and as far as possible from townsfolk even at home. Special road blocks were set up on the roads leading into major cities to stop starving peasants from coming in and begging for bread. When an American worker in Samara saw an old woman and two children who had eluded the guards and were lying close to death in the street, a Red Army soldier warned him off, saying, 'These people do not want to work. They are kulaks. They are enemies of the Soviet Union.'

By contrast, the officials of the party, the GPU and the Commissariat of Agriculture lived apart from the village community, usually in houses commandeered from kulaks, and eating specially delivered rations. Kravchenko describes them as 'a caste apart, living in an intimate clique, supporting each other, banded together against the community'.

They were men under tremendous pressure. On the one hand the state procurement organs were constantly demanding deliveries. On the other the peasants were sullen, obstinate and quite obviously starving. This was a

circle that could not be squared. At one and the same time
Terekhov, first secretary of the Kharkov oblast party committee, insisted on confiscating grain which a village soviet
chairman was trying to save for next spring's sowing, and yet
he was also writing to Stalin, reporting the desperate plight of
the peasants and begging for emergency supplies. Stalin dis-
dainfully reprimanded him for inventing 'fables about famine' and advised him to become a writer of fiction.

Overall it is impossible to overstate the significance of the
collectivization campaign. It destroyed the structure of the
traditional Russian village in almost all areas save the re-
motest, removing the peasant households which had been the
most productive and often enjoyed the greatest respect. It was
also a trauma for the party. Collectivization renewed the
psychosis of wartime, only now in conditions of peace, and
accustomed party officials to regarding themselves as an
occupying force in a hostile country. Some cracked under the
strain. Isaac Deutscher once met a GPU colonel, who told
him, sobbing: 'I am an old Bolshevik. I worked in the underground against the tsar, and then I fought in the civil war.
Did I do all that in order that I should now surround villages
with machine guns and order my men to fire indiscriminately
into crowds of peasants? Oh no, no!'

Finally and less obviously, perhaps a casualty of the
campaign was truth. Pasternak speculated in *Doctor Zhivago*
that collectivization was such a disastrous mistake that it had
to be hidden at all costs, 'and so it was necessary to teach
people not to think and make judgements, to compel them to
see the non-existent, and to argue the opposite of what was
obvious to everyone.' Certainly the collectivization coincides
with the time when the party's public media parted completely from reality, and began to portray a beautiful im-
aginary world in which, as Stalin put it a few years later, 'life
has become better and more cheerful'.

The collective farms themselves slowly recovered from the
worst of the disaster, and by the late 1930s were regularly
achieving harvests better than those of ten years earlier.

They worked to delivery plans handed down from the Commissariat of Agriculture. Political and economic control over them was mediated through Machine Tractor Stations (MTS), each of which had a dozen or so farms to supervise. The main ostensible purpose of the MTS was to hire out machinery to kolkhozy (there not being enough to equip them individually): payments for this service were made in kind, so that the MTS acted as a procurement agency. In addition party cells centred on the MTS, whose deputy director was normally an employee of the GPU (or NKVD – People's Commissariat of Internal Affairs – after the renaming of 1934): he was responsible for tracking down 'subversive elements'. For a time the MTS was even assisted by a 'political department' on the model of the Red Army.

The payment of kolkhoz members depended on the amount of labour they put in on the collective fields. The unit of payment was the 'labour day' – the actual working day of a skilled worker being more highly valued than that of an unskilled one. Thus a tractor driver might receive four times as much as a night watchman. The real problem about the 'labour day', however, was that it had only a residual claim on the kolkhoz's funds: it was paid out of whatever was left over after the kolkhoz had discharged all its other obligations, to procurement agencies, the MTS, the banks, and so on. In bad years very little was left over. In fact, even in 1939, a relatively good year, the labour day was worth precisely nothing in 15,700 kolkhozy out of a total of 240,000.

It is little wonder that the peasants themselves regarded collective work as a reimposition of *barshchina* (corvée). Their feeling of having been reduced to serf status was intensified by the state's refusal to issue passports to them when these became compulsory for change of residence in 1932: by that means they were, indeed, more or less fixed to the land at the pleasure of the kolkhoz chairman.

Only in one respect did the party compromise with the peasants. The Model Kolkhoz Statute of 1935 did guarantee them the right to cultivate small plots of land of their own, and to keep one cow, a limited number of pigs or sheep, and unlimited poultry. The products of these private plots were used first of all for subsistence, but any surplus could be sold at specially licensed markets, on which, as we have seen, the towns became largely dependent for certain kinds of food supplies. These private plots thus became an essential resource, both for the peasant economy and for the urban diet, though the fact has only been reluctantly admitted by the party. Naturally enough, the time and energy the peasants devoted to private cultivation has detracted, at times quite seriously, from their work on the collective fields.

In short, the collectivization campaign, though it did eventually (after early disaster) solve the problem of grain deliveries for the towns, bequeathed a demoralized rural population and a permanently underproductive agricultural system.

Alongside the industrial and agricultural transformations there was to be a third which Lenin regarded as, if anything, even more important. That was in the field of 'culture'. The Russian word *kultura* has a much broader connotation than the English: in Lenin's usage, particularly, it referred also to technical skills, work discipline, efficiency, probity and public spirit. It was precisely these qualities that he felt, in the last years of his life, the new Russia lacked, and he had recognized that consequently the new regime would remain dependent for some time to come on foreign and 'bourgeois' specialists.

He had accepted the logic of this already during the civil war, by inviting the old managers back to run the factories and encouraging practices to their taste, such as piecework payment for workers, the ending of 'workers' control', and the adoption of Taylorist 'scientific' management. The early planning efforts of the Soviet state rested on proposals put forward by such specialists: thus GOELRO, the electrification plan of 1920, was based on a scheme put forward by Professor Grinevetsky, head of the Moscow Higher Technical Institute. Vesenkha and Gosplan, too, in their early days, were staffed by existing economists and administrators, most of whom had initially little sympathy for the Bolsheviks, but recognized the need to get the country going again somehow.

Relations between the new rulers and the old specialists were, naturally, uneasy and sometimes stormy, especially in the provinces, where the wider concerns of the top party leadership were not always appreciated. In March 1919, for example, Professor Dukelsky, an agronomist teaching at a college in Voronezh, wrote to Lenin complaining of harassment by the new local political bosses, who were mostly, he commented rather sniffily, 'from lower-middle-class elements, village policemen, small-time civil servants and shopkeepers':

> It is difficult to describe the full horror of the humiliations and sufferings caused at their hands. Constant, shameful denunciations and accusations, futile but extremely humiliating searches, threats of execution, requisitions and confiscations, meddling in the most intimate sides of personal life. (The head of a squad demanded that I, who am living in the school where I teach, absolutely must sleep in the same bed as my wife.)

Lenin himself, of course, disapproved of such behaviour, and published Dukelsky's letter in *Pravda* to encourage greater respect for men with skills which the country badly needed. The frictions did not cease, but all the same many specialists, and their professional unions, came round to the view that one could work with the Communists, since they had formed a government evidently determined to restore law and order, to give high priority to technical development, and even to keep the workers in their place. General Ipatiev, a leading chemical engineer under the tsarist government, and a man of very conservative views, agreed to become director of the State Scientific Technical Institute under the Communists, because, whatever else one might think about them, they had 'saved the country from anarchy and at least temporarily preserved its intelligentsia and material wealth'. Smenovekhovstvo, the idea that the Bolsheviks now embodied the Great Russian state, the tsarist regime having failed in that mission, became widespread among the specialists.

From the very beginning the new government kept careful track of the specialists, as a scarce resource. Already in December 1918 Sovnarkom opened a register of them, for potential employment in industry and the economic administration. At the Twelfth Party Congress in 1923, the Orgburo incorporated this register into the burgeoning system of files which Stalin was keeping for the 'registration and distribution of cadres'. In this way the party gained greater control over the reliability of technical specialists, though it was not yet in a position to do anything much about purging the less satisfactory, for lack of anyone with whom to replace them. As late as 1928 a survey showed that in the whole of Soviet industry only 138 engineers were party members. This was in marked contrast to the industrial managers, very few of whom had higher degree qualifications, but 70 per cent of whom were party members. The party had, in fact, by this time managed to move many of its own members into management jobs, where, as *praktiki* – practical men without special knowledge – they relied on the advice of the non-party specialists.

This split between management and specialist knowledge was not something the party was prepared to tolerate indefinitely. It wanted to set about the task of training its own specialist cadres. But this process encountered considerable difficulties during the 1920s. The colleges which were training the new cadres were, on the whole, required to favour applicants of working-class or peasant background, but of course these were often less well prepared for special and higher education than entrants of middle-class and professional background. To help overcome this gap, the less privileged students were usually first of all put through a *rabfak*, or 'workers' faculty'. Set up in 1919, the rabfaki were designed to give intending worker and peasant students without formal secondary education the basic grounding for study in their chosen speciality. Their success was very patchy, and many of their alumni failed to meet the expectations of the teachers in the technical colleges. Evidently quite a number – Soviet statistics do not say how many – failed to qualify at all. Resentment against the professors built up, especially in the Komsomol organizations of the universities and colleges.

In the end, the party decided to move against the 'bourgeois specialists' in industry and in the *vuzy* (higher educational institutions), as it was doing in the economic administration. In doing this it was able to draw, as we have seen, upon a good deal of worker resentment at the privileges accorded to the 'bourgeois'. From 1928 to 1931 there was a series of sensational and well publicized trials of such specialists. In the first, the Shakhty trial, in the Donbass in May 1928, fifty-three engineers, including three from Germany, were accused of wrecking equipment, organizing accidents, and maintaining links with the former capitalist owners of the coalmines. What in fact had happened was that some foreign equipment had been misused, probably owing to inexperience and haste, and fires and explosions had occurred in the mines. Such contretemps were not unusual, but this was the first time the regime had deliberately used them as a weapon against 'class enemies'. The case was brought to Moscow and tried in public in the Hall of Columns amid a press campaign calling for 'Death to the Wreckers!' Some of the accused confessed in court to the charges, some did so only partly or tried to retract what they had stated. By later standards it was a very imperfectly staged spectacle, but eleven death sentences were pronounced and five actually carried out.

Stalin followed up the trial with a warning. 'Shakhtyites

are now ensconced in every branch of our industry. . . . Wrecking by the bourgeois intelligentsia is one of the most dangerous forms of opposition to developing socialism.' Other trials accordingly followed. In one of them, as we have seen, Menshevik members of Gosplan were accused of 'criminally' trying to undermine industrial development by proposing low planning targets. In another, forty-eight leading officials of the food industry were charged with sabotaging food supplies – a convenient way of explaining away the current shortages. In yet another the well-known agronomists Chayanov and Kondratyev were accused of conspiring with kulaks to revive the Socialist Revolutionary Party and overthrow the Soviet system. In addition to all this, some thousands of engineers seem to have been dismissed and arrested. Then, in 1931, the spate more or less ended, for reasons we shall see below.

Purges of a less dramatic but far-reaching kind were going on in the educational system. Komsomol and party committees tried to weed out students who came from 'old regime' backgrounds, and the proportion of students from working-class backgrounds rose from 30 per cent in 1928–9 to 58 per cent in 1932–3. Non-party professors were hissed at their lectures, or even subjected to direct verbal attack. Many were dismissed by university councils now determinedly infiltrated by the party. At the Academy of Sciences, hitherto a haven for non-party scholars, more than a hundred research workers were arrested in 1929–30 and communists were firmly installed in its governing body. The Communist Academy and the Institute of Red Professors, both established by the party in 1919–21 to train Marxist scholars for social science teaching, were expanded (one of the Institute's graduates at this time was the future authoritative ideologist, M. A. Suslov).

As far as schools were concerned, Soviet educational theory in the 1920s was, broadly speaking, divided into two main tendencies. The first, supported by Lenin, held that schools should teach the same basics as in tsarist Russia.

Lenin believed it vital to ensure that *all* children should have access to such basic education, but he did not believe it was necessary to change its actual content very much, beyond giving it a somewhat more practical bent: working-class and peasant children needed to master the same elements as 'bourgeois' children. The second tendency, identified above all with the utopian educational theorist, V. N. Shulgin, aimed to adapt the *content* of school education to the new society, getting away from the academic emphasis of traditional pedagogy to learn practical and vocational subjects, if possible not at the schoolroom desk, but out at the factory bench and in the community. Shulgin believed that any system of formal education was inherently elitist, and he included in his strictures the school system set up by the Commissariat of Education (*Narkompros*) under Lunacharsky, whose educational views were close to Lenin's.

In practice, for most of the twenties, most schools taught by traditional methods, partly because no new training was available for teachers, and partly because there was no finance to launch ambitious experiments. Progress was slow, even towards the most basic goal of universal literacy for primary schoolchildren.

Then, in 1929, under the impact of the Shakhty campaign and with the active support of the Komsomol, Lunacharsky was dismissed, and a reform was launched in the Shulgin spirit. The upper forms of middle schools were reclassified as *tekhnikumy*, or vocational training colleges, and by the end of 1930 all schools were required to attach themselves to an enterprise, where their pupils could acquire introductory instruction in the productive process. There was now far less classroom teaching: children spent much of their time on 'projects' to be performed within the community (where possible linked with the Five Year Plan), and on social and political work. The proportion of political instruction was also increased. In the countryside, schoolchildren and students were mobilized to carry out a 'cultural campaign' to eliminate illiteracy. This was often accompanied by the dis-

missal of the existing schoolteachers, the closure of the
church and the arrest of the priest.

Almost before they were properly under way, however,
these experiments ran into trouble. Some children found they
were receiving a grotesquely narrow education: at one school
in Orel, for example, all the pupils in the upper forms were
trained to become 'poultry-breeding technicians'. Factory
directors were often reluctant to have untrained and undisciplined children on their premises, disrupting tight work
schedules. In Tula the children had to stage protest demonstrations, 'coming to the factory gates with slogans, banners
and songs, in order to gain access to production'. Or
alternatively, directors might pursue the very opposite policy
and exploit the children as unpaid menial labourers.
Schoolchildren apparently worked in the Donbass coalmines,
while at one point in Central Asia it was reported that the
fifth to seventh grades (ages eleven to thirteen) were occupied
for weeks on end with nothing but cotton-picking. Children
on project work would sometimes check in at school in the
morning, pick up their assignments, and then disappear for
the rest of the day. Shulgin's phrase, 'the withering away of
the schools', threatened to turn into an unpleasant reality.

This 'cultural revolution' in the schools, as we shall see, did
not last very long. But it did have lasting effects, driving out
many of the older, non-party teachers, and leaving the
schools with a heavily politicized atmosphere.

All this left the way open, both in education and in industry, for the posts recently vacated by 'bourgeois
specialists' to be filled by new 'Red specialists'. Recruits were
duly coming forward to do this. In the vuzy, for example, the
proportion of the teaching and research staff educated since
the revolution rose sharply from 40 per cent in 1928 to 75 per
cent in 1933: most of the new appointees had replaced purged 'bourgeois specialists'.

Apart from building up cadres of reliable specialists, the
party had also initiated a crash programme to train its own
future leaders, men who should have both proven party

experience and also higher technical qualifications. In July 1928, the Central Committee ordered the recruitment of a thousand party members to be sent to technical colleges to study for higher degrees.

This was the first of a series of mass recruitments of 'thousanders', as they came to be called. Nominated by party, Komsomol or trade union committees, or by political departments in the Red Army, they went for three to five years study, supported by special, preferential grants. Mostly young men in their twenties, who had proved themselves by their loyalty and energy at work and in the humble social tasks that party members were called on to fulfil, they were consciously being selected for the vital party and state posts of the coming Five Year Plans. Viktor Kravchenko, even in the bitterness of emigration, remembered his excitement when he, a skilled worker of twenty-five in the Petrovsky- Lenin metal works in Dnepropetrovsk, was summoned to the director's office in 1930. There he discovered, sitting behind a vast mahogany desk, Arkady Rosengolts, a member of the Central Committee, who asked him to give a brief summary of his biography (a frequent Soviet ritual), and then said to him: 'You're a young man, not yet twenty-five. The party needs industrial engineers. Would you like to study? We'll send you to a technical institute for a few years. You will repay the party by giving it your best efforts. The party needs its own technical intelligentsia, to carry on the task of industrialization in loyal conformity with its policy.' So young Kravchenko was sent to the Kharkov Technological Institute to study aircraft construction. He found himself there among a very motley assortment of students, most of them over twenty-three and a few in their thirties, from 'factories, blast furnaces, mines and offices, from state farms and army camps. . . .' There were solemn-faced Central Asians who had never before seen a western city, war veterans, former partisans from Siberia, as well as Communist functionaries wise in the ways of the new politics.' Even though some of them had privileged support grants, however, material life was hard:

Often, in the winter of 1930–1, the Gigant [their hostel] was so cold that the water in our washbasin was frozen. We picked up stray pieces of wood, fence slats, broken furniture, old newspapers to feed the tiny iron stove in our room, with its crazy, many-jointed chimney stuck out of a window. Thus we lived, studied, argued and dreamed of our country's industrialized future while fighting frost and hunger here and now.

The quality of the education they received may be doubted, partly because of the speed and relative lack of preparation with which they had to absorb it, partly because of the continued overlay of political propaganda. 'Those who could not digest Marx's *Das Kapital*, the dialectics of Engels, the works of Lenin and above all the dissertations of Stalin were thrown out of the Institute more quickly than those who merely had trouble with calculus or blueprints.' On the other hand, those who had confidence in their political standing were often truculently self-confident, and despised their 'bourgeois' teachers. A chemist who entered the Kiev Polytechnic Institute in 1930 recalled that certain students would interrupt tuition with insults and ridicule, turning lessons into 'guerrilla warfare', while one student, an ex-Red Army soldier, was in the habit, when presenting himself for an oral exam, of placing a loaded revolver on the table in front of the professor.

However imperfect their education, though, these students were to be a major social and political force. They were the only people who combined political and technical qualifications, and were therefore ideally suited to leadership at a time of planned economic growth. According to Sheila Fitzpatrick, during the first Five Year Plan some 110,000 Communist adult workers and some 40,000 non-party ones entered higher educational institutions in this way, and in 1932–3 they represented almost a third of all students in higher education. How many actually graduated with their qualifications we do not know, as the figures have never been published. One later celebrated student, N. I. Khrushchev, of the Moscow Industrial Academy, did not. However, the successful graduates – and even some of the unsuccessful ones – had extraordinarily good chances of rising fast. Their entry on the political scene coincided with Stalin's preparations for his great purges of 1936–9, in which the party's Leninist Old Guard, the 'bourgeois specialists' and the praktiki all suffered badly. The new graduates were waiting to take their places. That is not to say that none of the new 'Red specialists' was caught up in the purges: many of them certainly were. But those who survived were uncommonly well placed to enjoy what one might delicately refer to as 'upward social mobility' over the corpses of their predecessors. We shall follow their subsequent careers in a later chapter.

'Cultural revolution' was also the order of the day in the sphere which we in the West more normally think of as cultural. Let us take the example of literature, which was of especial importance to the Bolsheviks, since they rated verbal propaganda so highly. Writers generally, like other 'specialists', had not wholly welcomed the Bolshevik seizure of power. When the party tried to call an 'organizational meeting' of them in November 1917, it was attended only by Alexander Blok, Vladimir Mayakovsky and three or four others, while the best-known of all Russian writers, Maxim Gorky, himself a former Bolshevik, thundered against Lenin's and Trotsky's 'shameful attitude towards freedom of speech'. Many of the most prominent writers of the time in fact went into emigration rather than cooperate with the Bolsheviks.

Those who remained tended to form themselves into groups. This is characteristic of writers in a period of crisis, and certainly during the civil war belonging to an organization was the only way to secure a minimal existence. Even when physical conditions improved, writers still found it easiest if they had a journal or publishing house in whose building they could congregate, and in whose pages they could find a home for their writings. In addition they now found themselves needing to compete for party approval and patronage, which again could better be done collectively.

These literary groups were of all kinds. In the early utopian days some tried to promote a specifically 'proletarian culture', with the encouragement of Lunacharsky, establishing choirs, studios and theatre workshops in factories, staging performances, painting canvasses and singing anthems whose subject matter was drawn from working-class life. There were even symphonies of factory whistles and steamer hooters. Perhaps the high point of this *Proletkult* was in Petrograd on May Day 1920, when the 'Mystery of Emancipated Labour' was performed in the streets by two thousand Red Army soldiers and drama students, while more than thirty thousand spectators sang the 'Internationale'.

Most party leaders, however, rejected as absurd the notion that there could be any such thing as an inherently 'proletarian culture'. Taking the same view as they did on military and technical matters, both Lenin and Trotsky regarded it as the duty of proletarian writers first of all to master the inherited skills of aristocratic and bourgeois culture. Trotsky even wrote in *Literature and Revolution* (1923): 'In the sphere of art it is not the party's business to command. It can and should protect, encourage and merely offer indirect guidance.' In this spirit, the party for most of the 1920s tolerated and even encouraged a variety of literary approaches, as long as they could not be considered 'counterrevolutionary'. As late as 1925 the Central Committee pronounced itself 'in favour of free competition between the various groupings and streams', though it did call the 'proletarian writers' the 'future ideological leaders of Soviet literature'.

One group in particular emerged as the claimants of this 'future ideological leadership'. That was RAPP, the Russian Association of Proletarian Writers, with its journal *Na postu* (On Guard). Unlike the old Proletkult, RAPP, which was distantly descended from it, had very few worker members. Most of its writers in fact came from the professional classes, and their strength was in the party's youth movement, the

Komsomol. RAPP's most prominent figure, Lev Averbakh, had been a founder member of the Komsomol, in fact, and was at one time its Moscow secretary; he was also a relative of Sverdlov. They were a group of party activists, in effect, and when they claimed to be exercising 'proletarian hegemony' they were in fact, by a familiar semantic substitution, presuming to speak for the party in literature. The very name of their journal betrays their characteristic literary posture: 'We shall stand on guard in order to ensure a clear and firm Communist ideology.'

Not surprisingly, their strength was not so much literature itself as criticism. During the late twenties a number of 'fellow travellers' – tolerated 'non-party' writers – fell victim to their attacks. Mayakovsky tried to appease them by joining them, an experience which made him so miserable that it probably contributed to his suicide in 1930. Another *cause célèbre* was their attack on Zamyatin. His novel *We* had in the end been published abroad because its satire was too strong for any editor inside Russia. It depicted a future society in which men were deprived of their fantasy, in an operation incongruously called 'fantasiectomy', so that they would be able to enjoy an undisturbed 'mathematically certain happiness'. RAPP objected to the fact that it had been published abroad (though this had hitherto been a normal practice) and condemned Zamyatin's outlook. Under pressure from RAPP (backed up by a *Pravda* editorial confirming that RAPP was, of all literary groups, 'closest to the line of the party'), publishing houses refused to bring out any more of Zamyatin's work, his books were withdrawn from libraries, and his plays were taken off the stage. In 1931 Zamyatin wrote directly to Stalin, declaring that for him being deprived of the opportunity to write was equivalent to 'the death penalty'. He admitted 'that I have the very inconvenient habit of saying not what is expedient, but what seems to me the truth. In particular, I have never made a secret of my attitude towards literary servility, careerism and apostasy: I have always thought, and still think, that they are demeaning both for the writer and for the revolution.' He asked to be allowed to emigrate in order to continue writing. Stalin granted him an exit visa.

Therewith began the split between émigré and Soviet culture that has remained to the present day. But the triumph of RAPP was not long-lived. Here too the bearers of 'cultural revolution' soon succumbed to the imposers of order.

7

Stalin's Terror

In his ode to Lenin of 1924, Mayakovsky had written: 'I fear that these processions and mausoleums, this regulated rendering of homage, will drown Lenin's simplicity in sickly-sweet unction.' His fears were amply borne out – which may help to explain his suicide in 1930. For Stalin, by the time of his fiftieth birthday in December 1929, had defeated both the oppositions, of left and right, and had more or less completed the process of taking over and monopolizing Lenin's memory. On 21 December all Soviet newspapers were filled with eulogies to Stalin: indeed *Pravda* spent five days listing the thousands of organizations which had sent him greetings, many of which included the word *'vozhd'* (Leader with a capital 'l'). A joint message from the Central Committee and the Party Control Committee hailed him as 'the best Leninist and senior member of the Central Committee and its Politbuiro'. An official biography was issued for the occasion, glorifying Stalin as 'the most outstanding continuer of Lenin's cause and his most devoted disciple', as one who 'was always with Lenin, never departed from him, never betrayed him'. This was how Stalin wished to see himself, as the Peter of the Communist pseudo-church, more faithful than Peter had been to Christ, even though Lenin had been surrounded by turncoats and traitors.

These fiftieth birthday publications began the rewriting of history, what Mikhail Geller and Alexander Nekrich call the 'nationalization of the memory' which was to become such a devastating feature of Soviet intellectual life. Even former oppositionists joined in the choruses of praise. Especially this was the case at the Seventeenth Party Congress of 1934, the so-called 'Congress of Victors' (because it celebrated the 'victories' of collectivization and the first Five Year Plan). There Bukharin praised Stalin as 'the field marshal of the proletarian forces, the best of the best', and Kamenev prophesied that 'the era in which we live will be known to history as the era of Stalin, just as the preceding era entered history as the era of Lenin.' Such encomiums completed the opposition's self-abasement, their ritual recognition that Stalin had overcome them morally as well as physically.

Not surprisingly, there were few in the party or outside it who were prepared to stand against this tide of acclaim. All the same, there were many who were appalled at the human and economic cost the nation was being asked to pay for the upheavals in industry and agriculture. In the autumn of 1930, Syrtsov, prime minister of the RSFSR, and Lominadze, leading party secretary in the Transcaucasus, were expelled from the Central Committee and demoted to minor posts for having privately expressed to colleagues their doubts about the excessive growth targets and the regime's disregard of the livestock disaster. Potentially more serious, perhaps, was the programme of Ryutin, which circulated among members of the Central Committee in 1932. This called for a disbanding of the collective farms, and a reduction of investment in industry, in order to revive agriculture, the retail trade and the consumer goods industries. Ryutin's programme has never come to light, but he seems to have made a bitter personal attack on Stalin as the evil genius of the Russian revolution, who by his personal lust for power had brought the revolution to the brink of ruin. The GPU discovered that Ryutin had a group of supporters, perhaps fifteen to twenty strong, including former members of the Right Opposition and a number of Red professors; it reported that he was trying to stir up subversive activity in the Komsomol and among students and workers.

The Ryutin case became a test of opinion in the Politburo. The GPU recommended applying the death penalty against him. Since he was an official of the Central Committee apparatus, this would have meant the first execution of a high-ranking party member. Stalin was prepared to establish this precedent, and urged his colleagues to take the GPU's advice; but a majority, apparently headed by Sergei Kirov (first secretary in Leningrad), voted against it. Ryutin was merely exiled.

There have been suggestions that Kirov's opposition to Stalin went further than the Ryutin case, that he headed a group in the Politburo which favoured reconciliation, both with the former oppositions, and indeed with the people at large, now that the harshest battles of socialist construction were over. Gorky, who had some influence with the party leaders, is known to have been of this opinion. There is little evidence in Kirov's speeches of any disagreement with Stalin, but it is known that Kirov was very popular, and that his appearance at the Seventeenth Congress was greeted with loud ovations. Stalin may also have distrusted Kirov because his fief, Leningrad, had once before furnished a geographical base for an opposition movement, that of Zinoviev.

However that may be, Kirov's career was abruptly cut short on 1 December 1934, when he was murdered inside the party headquarters, the Smolny, in Leningrad. His assassin, one Leonid Nikolaev, was a romantic or embittered former Young Communist who imagined himself stimulating the appearance of a second Narodnaya Volya, a new re-volutionary terrorist movement dedicated to eliminating the new 'bureaucracy'. What is suspicious about the murder is that, on at least one previous occasion, he had been dis-covered by security guards trying to approach Kirov with a revolver. Instead of arresting him and charging him with attempted terrorism, as would have been natural, they had released him and allowed him to take his gun. In short, circumstantial evidence suggests strongly, though not con-clusively, that the NKVD (as the GPU was now called) de-liberately enabled Nikolaev to kill Kirov, probably acting on instructions from Stalin, who was anxious both to rid himself of a rival and to create a pretext for the elimination of other opponents.

What is quite certain is that Stalin promptly used the occasion for his own purposes. On the same day a decree was issued ordering speedy investigations (not more than ten days) in cases of 'terroristic organizations or acts'; such cases were to be heard *in absentia* by a special military court, no appeals were allowed, and an immediate death sentence was to be carried out. Thus Stalin created a machinery of summary justice which was to last twenty years. On 21 December it was announced that Nikolaev had acted on the instructions of a 'Leningrad opposition centre' having connections with Zinoviev, and on this basis Zinoviev, Kamenev and seventeen others were arrested. In spite of the new provisions, they were not dealt with summarily, but were brought to trial in January 1935. They accepted a general political responsibility for the murder, without the court being able, however, to establish any direct connection. Perhaps Stalin still hesitated at this stage to implicate so directly in terrorism, two individuals of such former standing. Or perhaps the NKVD had not yet fully perfected the techniques they deployed the following year. At any rate Zinoviev got ten years and Kamenev five. They remained, at least, available for further questioning.

During 1935 the NKVD finally arrested all those members of the Left Opposition who had hitherto remained at liberty, and set to work to try to induce them to sign testimony that they had been involved in a vast conspiracy, organized from abroad by Trotsky, aiming to assassinate not only Kirov but also Stalin and other members of the Politburo, to overthrow the Soviet system and re-establish capitalism in Russia. This mythical scenario would complement the now habitual flood of eulogies of Stalin by showing how treacherous were all Lenin's other colleagues, and how great was the danger from which Stalin had rescued the party and the country.

While these fabrications were being painfully strung together in the Lubyanka and other NKVD prisons, the shock waves were spreading throughout the party. An 'exchange of party cards' was started – euphemism for a purge –

as a result of which about half a million members were expelled. All over the country party meetings were being held at which members were exhorted both to recall and to confess their own earlier 'mistakes' (which now came to mean disagreeing with the official party line in any way) and to denounce their colleagues. New categories of 'hostile acts' emerged: links with those already denounced – which might mean no more than the most fleeting personal or official acquaintance; 'failure to denounce', which might mean not having reported a private conversation. At the Kazan Pedagogical Institute, Evgeniya Ginsburg was accused at such a meeting of not having denounced the 'Trotskyist contrabandist' Elvov (who had written an article on the 1905 revolution which incurred Stalin's displeasure). To her objection, 'But has it even been proved that he's a Trotskyist?' she received the reply, 'But he's been arrested! Surely you don't think anyone would be arrested unless there were something definite against him?'

> Great concert and lecture halls were turned into public confessionals. . . . People did penance for misunderstanding the theory of permanent revolution and for abstaining from voting on the opposition programme in 1923; for failing to purge themselves of great power chauvinism; for underrating the importance of the second Five Year Plan. . . . Beating their breasts, the 'guilty' would lament that they had 'shown political short-sightedness' and 'lack of vigilance', 'compromised with dubious elements', 'added grist' to this or that mill, and were full of 'rotten liberalism'.

When someone was expelled from the party or dismissed from his job, the only safe thing to do was to shun all further acquaintance with him, for fear of being tainted by the epithets which would be hurled at him. And if a friend or colleague was arrested, it was prudent to abjure any further contact with his family, no matter how much one might pity their plight. Wives whose husbands were arrested were advised to seek a divorce as soon as possible. Children were encouraged to denounce their parents. One thirteen-year-old daughter of an arrested NKVD operative was turned out into the street when both her parents were arrested, and was required to speak at a Young Pioneer meeting saying she approved of the shooting of her mother and father, as they were spies.

The culmination of this denunciatory frenzy was a series of three show trials in Moscow. At the first, in August 1936, Zinoviev, Kamenev and others confessed to being members of a 'Trotskyist–Zinovievite Centre', which on instructions from Trotsky had conspired to murder Stalin, Ordjonikidze, Kaganovich, Voroshilov and other top party leaders. They also confessed to having organized the murder of Kirov. They were sentenced to death and executed, probably immediately. Their confessions implicated Tomsky (who thereupon committed suicide), Bukharin and Rykov. The prosecutor, Vyshinsky, announced that these implications would be investigated.

In the second, in January-February 1937, Radek, Pyatakov and others confessed to links with Trotsky and foreign intelligence services, and to setting up terrorist groups for assassination, wrecking and sabotage of industry (the latter referred to some disasters which had taken place in the fever of the Five Year Plans). Pyatakov was sentenced to death and Radek to ten years' imprisonment (he died in a labour camp a few years later).

In the final trial, in March 1938, Bukharin, Rykov, Krestinsky and Yagoda (himself a former head of the NKVD) confessed to membership of a 'Trotskyist–Rightist Bloc', involved in wrecking, undermining Soviet military power and preparing, in collaboration with the intelligence services of Germany, Britain, Japan and Poland, for an imperialist attack on the USSR and dismemberment of the country. This trial did not go quite so well as the others: Bukharin and Rykov both admitted general complicity in a 'bloc', but denied specific responsibility for any of the criminal acts enumerated in the indictment. Bukharin even made the telling remark: 'The confession of the accused is a medieval principle of justice.' All the accused were sentenced to death, and Vyshinsky concluded his prosecution speech by saying, 'Over the road cleared of the last scum and filth of the past, we, our people, with our beloved teacher and leader, the great Stalin, at our head, will march ever onwards, towards communism.'

Few people wholly believed the testimony of the courtroom, even at the time, but many observers, both domestic and foreign, felt there must be some substance to these charges, however fantastic they might seem. For otherwise why did tried and long-standing Bolsheviks, who had withstood the pressures of tsarist oppression, revolution and civil war, now agree to slander themselves in this extravagant manner in public? And why did the government, which had never scrupled to order summary executions, insist on the cumbersome rigmarole of obtaining signed confessions and getting the accused to repeat them in the courtroom?

The answers to these questions take us to the very heart of the Stalinist system. First of all, on the narrow legal plane, the confessions, whether they were repeated in court or simply (as in the great majority of cases) existed on paper, were indispensable to the presentation of a prosecution case which rested on no other evidence whatever. No scrap of documentary or material evidence was produced at any of the trials, only the statements of supposed witnesses, and the confessions of the accused themselves. Furthermore, the confessions were useful in that they could be used to implicate others, as Tomsky and others were implicated in the Zinoviev trial. This extended the network of conspiracies, and thereby increased both the work-load and the standing of the NKVD; it also enabled them to pull in more working hands for its slave labour camps, and to free a plentiful supply of vacant posts for the upwardly mobile to occupy. Perhaps that is why

the arrests of 1936–9 affected the highly placed dispro-
portionately.

At any rate, even in the (much more numerous) cases
where no public trial was intended, prisoners and interrogators spent millions of unproductive and tormenting man-
hours in the fabrication of 'statements' which both parties
knew to be false from beginning to end.

Why then did the accused agree to make these
'statements'?

For them too the basic logic of the situation had been
created by the way in which the party had seized and held on
to power. They had all whole-heartedly supported the party's
ruthless monopoly of power while they had been among its
leading members; many of them had continued to recognize
its authority even when excluded from such power, perhaps
in the hope of regaining a measure of it. As Kamenev had
explained to the Fifteenth Party Congress, they had made 'a
full and complete surrender to the party' because 'nothing
could be done outside and despite the party'. Begging for
readmittance in 1933, Zinoviev had straightforwardly used
the language of the religious penitent: 'I ask you to restore me
to the ranks of the party and give me an opportunity of
working for the common cause. I give my word as a revolutionary that I will be the most devoted member of the
party, and will do all I possibly can to atone at least to some
extent for my guilt before the party and its Central Committee.'

These men had given their whole lives to the party, and
they still believed, in spite of everything, in its ultimate
victory. To ask them to do anything else would have been
asking them to abjure everything they had ever believed.
They had no alternative moral or religious foundation on
which they could take their stand and resist the pressures
directed against them. As Bukharin said at his trial: 'When
you ask yourself, "If you must die, what are you dying for?"
– an absolutely black emptiness suddenly rises before you
with startling vividness. There was nothing to die for. Nor

indeed was there anything to live for once one was 'isolated from everybody, an enemy of the people . . . , isolated from everything that constitutes the essence of life.'

However, not all party members reacted in this way, and even those who did usually capitulated only after weeks, sometimes months, of 'working over' by their interrogators. The basic NKVD method for breaking their prisoners was the 'conveyor', a system of continuous interrogation for days and nights on end by successive relays of interrogators. Exhausted, deprived of sleep, often cold and hungry, sometimes beaten, prisoners would sign what was required of them in order simply to be able to get some sleep, or sometimes perhaps because their physical weakness induced psychological doubts about reality, reinforced by the repetitive, 'mad' style of the questioning.

Many investigators seem to have used threats against the prisoners' families as a weapon. In a world where all other certainties had broken down, memories of wife or children were often the most precious part of a prisoner's personality, the only positive value he had left to hang on to, so that threats to arrest, torture or kill them were extremely powerful in their effect. This was especially the case with someone like Bukharin, who had married late, and had one baby son to whom he was devoted. Evgeniya Ginsburg recalls how in prison the thought that tormented her most was how she had spanked her son Vasya (now the well-known writer Vasily Aksenov) in a fit of temper because he had smashed a bottle of perfume. The promise that their families would remain unharmed if they duly recited their prepared confessions in court must have been a powerful incentive to comply.

To others, promises were made that their lives would be spared if they were cooperative. Some of them were visited in prison by former comrades of the Central Committee, who held out hopes, not only of survival, but even perhaps of ultimate readmittance to the party, and productive work, if only they would confess. Most, but not quite all, of these promises were unceremoniously broken.

Very few prisoners withstood all these pressures. Indeed, the former populist Ivanov-Razumnik in his memoirs reckons that of more than a thousand inmates with whom he shared prison cells, not more than a dozen resisted making the confessions demanded of them.

All the same, it is noteworthy that in the end only some seventy prisoners were subjected to public trial. Even some leading Oppositionists, such as Uglanov of the right, and Smilga and Preobrazhensky of the left, were convicted without public trial. Perhaps the prosecution did not feel sure they would play the roles written for them. And when it comes to the wider party and public, the fate of most of those arrested was either to appear before a special secret military court, or even simply to have their sentence read out to them in the cell.

For the arrests did not just affect Stalin's immediate political opponents. They cut into all levels of the party and into all walks of life. All social classes were affected, the elites dispro-portionately so. Out of 139 members of the party Central Committee elected at the Seventeenth Congress in 1934, 110 were arrested before the next congress met in 1939. And out of 1,966 delegates who attended the Seventeenth Congress, 1,108 were arrested and in fact only 59 took their places at the Eighteenth. Some geographical areas suffered more than others. Of Leningrad's 154 delegates to the Seventeenth Con-gress, only *two* were present at the Eighteenth, and neither of them actually worked in Leningrad. In the Ukraine, where Nikita Khrushchev took over as first secretary in January 1938, only 3 out of 86 members of the Central Committee survived from the beginning of 1937 to the end of 1938. In Bielorussia, as a combined result of the arrests and the ex-changes of party cards, total membership of the party fell by more than half between 1934 and 1938. In Georgia, out of 644 members who attended a party congress in May 1937, 425 were arrested in the following months. In Kazakhstan the entire party bureau was arrested. The same happened in Turkmenistan, where, as a result, there was no party bureau at all for several months.

Not all the deaths of leading Communists in this period followed on arrest. Tomsky, as we have seen, committed suicide in order to escape the fate of Bukharin and Rykov. Kuibyshev, head of Gosplan, died in January 1935, reportedly of a 'heart attack', but in circumstances which have remained mysterious: he is rumoured to have opposed the imminent purges. Ordjonikidze, commissar for heavy industry, died suddenly in February 1937, after a bitter row with Stalin: it is not known whether he committed suicide or was murdered, but it is said that he wrote a long memorandum before his death, and that this was seized by Stalin himself when he came to the flat. Its contents have never become known. Maxim Gorky, another opponent of the purges, and perhaps the most influential, died in August 1936, again suddenly, and again in circumstances which have led to persistent rumours of murder.

It seems superfluous to mention that virtually every member of every 'opposition' or 'fraction' there had ever been in the party was arrested – though, for some reason, this does not apply to Alexandra Kollontai. Stalin also disbanded the Society of Old Bolsheviks and the Society of Political Prisoners (of the tsarist regime), which up to 1935 had continued to serve as centres for Lenin's comrades and for the former revolutionaries of tsarist days. Stalin in fact succeeded beyond the wildest dreams of any tsarist police chief in destroying the Russian revolutionary movement.

At local levels the purges were often equally sweeping. Typically, since local people tended, at least at first, to cover up for one another, a central emissary would come down to carry out the purge, and would often finish by sacking and arresting the entire local leadership. Thus, in June 1937, Kaganovich announced to a specially convened meeting of the Smolensk *obkom* that their first secretary, Rumyantsev, his deputy, and most of the other local secretaries were 'traitors, spies of German and Japanese fascism and members of the Rightist–Trotskyist gang'. They all disappeared without trace. Further down, in the *raion* town of Bely, similar, if less extravagant, denunciations took place. At a mammoth meeting, which lasted for four whole days, the first secretary Kovalev was attacked from all sides: for having allegedly left the party in 1921 in protest against NEP, for having lived with a Trotskyist, for having deserted from the Red Army, for abusive and dictatorial conduct. A representative of the oblast, who presided over the meeting, actually had the nerve to accuse Kovalev of appointing and dismissing members of his raion party committee, instead of following the electoral procedures laid down in the party rules. Kovalev admitted his mistakes, and was dismissed. His successor fared no better, and underwent the same ordeal six months later.

Not only the party suffered. The purges bit deep into the country's leaders in every field. Perhaps most striking, in view of the fact that the fascist danger was frequently cited in justification for vigilance, was the carnage among the senior officers of the armed forces. Among those arrested and executed were Marshal Tukhachevsky, deputy commissar for defence and the principal strategic thinker in the Red Army; Marshal Egorov, chief of the General Staff; Marshal Blyukher, commander of the Special Far Eastern Army, who had defeated the Japanese in a major incident at Lake Khazan only two months before his arrest in October 1938; the commanders of the Kiev and Bielorussian Military Districts (closest to the ever-vulnerable western frontier); the commanders of the Black Sea and Pacific Fleets. By 1940, in fact, three out of five marshals, three out of three first-rank army commanders, twelve out of twelve second-rank army commanders, and sixty out of sixty-seven corps commanders had been arrested. More than 70 per cent of divisional and regimental commanders, and more than 60 per cent of the political commissars went the same way. This would have been a crippling blow to any army. It was the more so to one which had painfully built up its senior officer corps over a twenty-year period, starting from very unpromising beginnings, and was now consciously preparing to fight its biggest war. The expectations this massacre aroused in the potential enemy were succinctly summed up by Hitler at a conference of his generals in January 1941. 'They have no good military leaders,' he claimed. He was almost to be proved right.

A similar, if not quite so devastating hurricane swept through every profession and walk of life. Diplomats, writers, scholars, industrial managers, scientists, members of the Comintern – all of them lived through two or three years in unceasing terror of the midnight knock on the door, which would come without rhyme or reason, and many of them disappeared without trace.

Not least to suffer were the NKVD themselves. Yagoda joined Bukharin and others whose frame-ups he had devised in the same dock. Yezhov, his successor, simply disappeared in the early months of 1939. Most of their assistants in the monstrous interrogations of 1936–8 went the same way as those they had tormented. Some, who were working for the NKVD abroad and refused to return to Moscow to meet an obvious fate, were tracked down and murdered in the countries where they had sought refuge.

The very last act of the purges also took place abroad. On 20 August 1940, a Spanish Communist, Ramon Mercader, murdered Trotsky in Mexico with an ice-pick. He was jailed for twenty years by a Mexican court, but was decorated *in absentia* by Stalin.

It would be almost impossible to exaggerate the sufferings of the Soviet people during this period. For certain classes of the population other times may have been worse – for the peasantry the collectivization, for the inhabitants of the western regions the German occupation of 1941–4 – but for the totality of the population 1936–8 was a nightmare, during which no one, save Stalin himself, could be certain of not being woken in the small hours of the night by a knock at the door, dragged out of bed and snatched away from family and friends, usually for ever. Since there was neither rhyme nor reason to the process, no one could be sure of not attracting the next accusation in the capricious chain. Many people, in fact, lived with a small suitcase permanently packed with a few essentials, just in case.

Why did it all happen? To start with, no doubt, Stalin wished to destroy and humiliate all those who had ever opposed him or might conceivably oppose him (this probably accounts for the carnage in the NKVD and the officer corps, the only bodies able by any stretch of the imagination to mount a challenge to him). He could not bear the presence of those who had even merely been Lenin's comrades, those who might have known about Lenin's Testament.

If that had been all, however, then a hundredth of the victims would have been more than enough. But what Stalin set in motion had a dynamic of its own. In all societies, individuals have grievances against one another. A colleague occupies a prestigious post that one covets, or lives in a luxurious apartment that one hankers after. In Soviet society of the 1930s, as we have seen, the number of young, ambitious and upwardly mobile people was unusually high. Doubtless many of them were envious of their seniors. The purges opened for them dizzy opportunities. A simple *donos* (denunciation) sufficed, no matter how absurd, for no party or NKVD official would run the risk of being accused of 'lack of vigilance'. Besides, given the structure of their economic enterprises (see below, page 199), it seems probable that the NKVD had a 'plan' to fulfil for arrests. And once an investigator had a prisoner in his hands, he needed for the sake of his career (and perhaps his neck) to secure a confession from him, and if possible more denunciations, leading to yet more arrests. Everyone was driven ineluctably on, the interrogators as well as the interrogated.

Perhaps, then, a pertinent question is: why did the purges ever stop? One answer is: they never have, quite. The security police even today retain most of the powers they had under Stalin, at least as regards the non-party majority of the population, and sometimes they make use of them in a similar way. But there was a real change in their methods after 1939, and again after 1953. Probably one main reason for this was that Lavrenty Beria, who became head of the NKVD in 1938, was determined not to go the way of his predecessors. Besides, the stage had long ago been reached when the arrests had begun to affect the country's industrial, scientific and military potential. A few years more at the tempo of 1937–8, and half the Soviet population would be guarding the other half in labour camps. It was only reasonable, if belated, to try to get a grip on the situation and halt the ineluctable chain. This Beria did. A few people under investigation were released – though those already in labour camps stayed there. Thereafter terror became selective and sporadic, a system of rule rather than a hysterical campaign. The point had been made and did not need to be repeated every day.

The labour camps to which the arrested – those who were not executed, that is – were sent were direct descendants of the concentration camps opened on Lenin's orders in 1918. But their nature and function had changed a good deal since then. The greatest changes had come about as a result of the first Five Year Plan. For much of the 1920s, socialists in prisons and isolators had enjoyed the status of 'politicals', and had not been required to do forced labour. The same did not apply to criminals, 'former classes' and 'counterrevolutionary elements', who had to do manual work at least to maintain the camps and prisons themselves.

By the late twenties, however, faced with a desperate shortage of labour, especially in the harsher and more remote regions, the Soviet state naturally sought it in the camps. A decree of 26 March 1928 envisaged 'a series of economic projects with great savings in expenditure . . . by means of widespread use of the labour of individuals sentenced to measures of social protection'. And a conference of prison officials noted in October 1929: 'Local conditions sometimes present serious obstacles to the recruitment of labour. It is here that the places of confinement, having at their disposal excess labour in great quantities ... can come to the assistance of those economic enterprises which experience a labour shortage.' In 1930 Gosplan received instructions 'to incorporate the work performed by those deprived of liberty into the planned economy of the country'. A special department of the Commissariat of Internal Affairs, GULag, or the Chief Administration of Camps, was established to run the new convict enterprises. With that the aim of 'reform through work' finally ceased to be (if it ever had been) the aim of penal confinement in Soviet Russia – though the inscription 'Labour is a matter of honour, courage and heroism' continued to stand over the gates of many camps.

The first great project undertaken in this way was the White Sea-Baltic Canal, the 'Belomor Canal in the name of I. V. Stalin'. Construction was organized by Yagoda, then deputy head of the GPU. In order to save foreign currency, modern excavation technology was not used in the work: instead convicts were brought in in large numbers. Work started in November 1931, and completion was announced, with great fanfares, in May 1933. Maxim Gorky headed a team of writers who went to see the completed project. They spoke to some of the convicts under the watchful eye of their guards, and returned to extol the great work of 're-education' which they claimed had been done there. Solzhenitsyn has called their collective publication 'the first work in Russian literature to glorify slave labour'. Originally intended to provide an escape route by which the Baltic Fleet might, if necessary, be transferred to the White Sea, the canal proved too shallow for that purpose, perhaps because of the haste with which it had been built. According to Solzhenitsyn, who tramped along part of its length in 1966, it has almost ceased to be used.

The convicts who worked on Belomor were told that they were going to be amnestied if they completed it in good time. In fact, however, the great majority of them were transferred to other forced labour. Detainees – or to give them their pithier Russian name, *zeks* – were used for certain fundamental industries, timber felling and logging, the mining of gold, platinum and non-ferrous metals, coalmining, and construction work of all kinds, especially where these activities needed to be carried on in remote and inhospitable regions, to which it was difficult to attract free labour. The original geographical centre of the labour camps was in Karelia and along the White Sea coast, where timber was the principal industry. Other major centres which subsequently developed were around Vorkuta and the Pechora basin in the Arctic regions of European Russia, where there were substantial deposits of coal; in the new industrial areas of western Siberia, the Urals and Kazakhstan, where zeks laid the infrastructure of roads, railways, mines and factories; and, most notorious of all, around Magadan and the Kolyma River basin in the far east, where gold, platinum and various precious metals, as well as timber, were to be found. This last region was a whole frozen continent of its own, cut off from the rest of the country by hundreds of miles of trackless waste, and only reached by convict ships whose conditions recalled the Atlantic slave trade at its worst. But by the late 1930s labour camps were to be found everywhere in the Soviet Union: there were convict construction sites in every city, including Moscow itself, surrounded by watch towers and fences topped with barbed wire, where zeks toiled only a few yards from ordinary 'free' passers-by. Solzhenitsyn, in the most famous book on the subject, refers to the system as an 'archipelago', superimposed on the Soviet continent, and linked by a communications network hermetically sealed off from any possible contact with the outside 'normal' world.

It is a commonplace of economic theory that slave labour is normally very inefficient, as slaves have no interest in high productivity. That, during the Five Year Plans, was something the Soviet authorities were not prepared to accept. They were determined to achieve high production indices even with slave labour. Indeed, sometimes output targets were set higher inside the camps than in comparable enterprises employing free labour. The secret weapon used to induce the zeks to work hard was the threat of hunger. One's daily ration depended on norm-fulfilment. According to Yury Margolin, the daily ration for 100 per cent fulfilment was 700 grams of bread, together with a thin soup morning and evening, some *kasha* (gruel) in the evening and sometimes a little salt fish. This was during the war, and rates reported from elsewhere were sometimes a little higher. There was also a 'Stakhanovite' ration for 150 per cent norm-fulfilment: 900–1000 grams of bread plus soup and kasha, but with the addition of macaroni or even meat rissole in the evening. This was the only diet available which really met the needs of a manual labourer, according to Margolin. The 'punishment ration', for under-fulfilment, was grossly inadequate: a mere 500 grams of bread, with a thin soup morning and evening. Of course, everything needs to be put in perspective, and even these rations were generous compared with those that pre-vailed in Leningrad during the worst of the wartime siege, when even manual workers got no more than 250–350 grams of bread a day. And there are reports, during the war, of peasants in Karelia coming out of their huts to greet columns of ragged zeks and begging *them* for bread.

Extra pressure was put on the zek by the fact that the daily ration depended on the output, not of the individual, but of the work-team. Thus the nourishment of each man depended on the hard work of his colleagues. This arrangement saved the guards and overseers a good deal of effort in spurring reluctant workers: their own mates could be relied on to carry out that function in the interests of being adequately (or less inadequately) fed.

The basic fact, however, was that the standard ration was insufficient to sustain hard and continued manual labour for ten to fifteen hours a day in the freezing cold, especially for those unaccustomed to it, as most politicals were. One witty zek in Kolyma applied to the camp commandant to be re-classified as a horse, since in that capacity he would receive work and rations in accordance with his physical strength, and would be allotted his own stable and blanket! The commandant put him in the punishment cells for ten days, but then, with lordly good humour, relented and allowed him warmer clothing and a Stakhanovite ration.

More normal was the experience of Margolin: 'We were never in a condition to do what was demanded of us to have enough to eat. The hungrier we were, the worse we worked. The worse we worked, the hungrier we became. From that vicious circle there was no escape.' And Varlam Shalamov reports from Kolyma: 'The gold mines turned healthy people into invalids inside three weeks: hunger, lack of sleep, hour-long heavy labour, beatings. . . .' No slave-owner of the past would have squandered his capital in this wastrel fashion, but then the NKVD did not have to pay for their slaves, and if they died could easily replace them by arresting more. There is every justification for the term Solzhenitsyn applied to the camps: 'exterminatory labour camps'.

The only way to avoid the vicious circle of under-nourishment, exhaustion, disease and slow death was to land a 'cushy' job that did not entail manual labour. The best ones were in the administration, the infirmary, the kitchens, or the KVCh – the Cultural–Educational Section, a curious appendage to many camps, which combined political propaganda work with attempts to mount dramatic productions or concerts. Some camp commandants took pleasure in having a 'serf troupe' on hand to perform. These 'cushy' jobs literally saved people's lives. As Margolin says, 'Social inequality in the Soviet Union is nowhere more blatant than in the camp, where the difference between the kitchen supervisor – or any other supervisor – and the ordinary zek driven out into the forest every morning is greater than that between the millionaire and the boot-black in New York.'

In some camps the politicals actually had an advantage in competition for these jobs: most of them were at least literate, and many of them had administrative experience. Increasingly, however, the 'cushy' jobs were reserved for ordinary criminals, who only constituted about 15 per cent of the zek population, but came to occupy a dominant position in the hierarchy. In post-war Vorkuta, Edward Buca reports that criminals monopolized all the 'cushy' jobs, living in separate, more comfortable quarters and enjoying better food and clothing. They brought the customs of the Soviet criminal underworld to their functions: strict observance of the interests of their own kind, and murderous exploitation of everyone else. They pillaged the politicals mercilessly, and imposed a kind of Mafia rule in barracks and workplaces.

Even the wretched 'ordinary labourers' had some mechanisms for survival, if they were in a good work-team. The key concept was *tukhta*, which means fiddling the books or padding the figures. An economy which runs so much on reported figures is always liable to this kind of distortion. Solzhenitsyn gives a good example of tukhta in a lumber camp. The work-team leader, if possible in agreement with the norm-setter, who might well also be a zek, would inflate the figures for the timber his men had felled, in order to ensure them a reasonable day's ration. The loaders, transporters and river workers, responsible for floating the logs downstream, would have no interest in disclosing the non-existent surplus, since they too could fulfil their norms with the help of it. The officials at the saw-mill downstream would work on the same principle, as would the freight crews transporting the wood by rail to timber yards. Only the ultimate recipient of the wood – perhaps a furniture works – would have an interest in showing up the discrepancy, but even he would be unlikely to refuse the consignment – he would be desperately short of raw materials, and only too glad to take what he could get. If he did decide to reclaim the missing quantity, the legal process would last months, and then might not result in improved supplies. Only in extreme cases did commissions of inquiry descend upon the camp, and by then the 'guilty' parties might well have been transferred elsewhere.

The principle of tukhta clearly applies not only to camps but to the entire Soviet economy, owing to the paramount importance of plan implementation figures, and the general practice of piece-rate labour remuneration. Its existence throws an element of doubt on *all* Soviet production figures.

Obviously, however, cosy arrangements of this kind could not be fixed everywhere and at all times. And indeed, the death rate in the camps was very high. It is impossible to make precise estimates, and conditions differed greatly from one camp to another: Kolyma and the Vorkuta railway were notorious, and lumbering was generally dangerous. Robert Conquest has estimated a minimum death rate of 10 per cent per annum up to 1950 (when things improved somewhat), and perhaps as high as 30 per cent in the worst camps.

It is even more difficult to give an accurate idea of the overall labour camp population. Nearly all calculations are based on projections from scraps of data about one camp, or from overall figures for the Soviet labour force, in which it is impossible to distinguish zeks from other working hands. On these uncertain foundations estimates of the zek numbers in the late 1930s range from 3 to 15 million. For a higher figure speaks impressionistic evidence that, among the urban and professional strata who have left written records, nearly everyone had friends or relatives who had been arrested. On the other hand, we really do not know how far the arrests affected ordinary workers and peasants, who after all constituted the majority of the population. In his authoritative work on the subject Robert Conquest arrives at a figure of 8 million, *not* including criminals, for 1938. Taking this as an average for the period 1936–50, he estimates that there were some 12 million deaths. Even this does not take into account those executed, nor the victims of dekulakization, most of whom will have died before 1936. With them in mind, it may be that the casualties of the Stalin terror totalled 15–20 million.

The labour camps and the terror were an intrinsic part of Stalinist society. They resulted directly from the methods the party resolved to use to transform industry and agriculture, to eliminate 'bourgeois specialists' and to appoint its own promising young men, as well as from the methods Stalin used to defeat his opponents. But no nation can consume its own population in such a reckless manner without suffering incalculable damage. As a system of rule Stalin's terror could not persist indefinitely. Yet trying to end it was to bring his successors some very difficult dilemmas.

8

Stalinist Society

During Stalin's lifetime, contemporary Western observers sought an explanation for the bizarre and horrifying phenomena of the late thirties by concentrating on the situation of the leader. In the absence of a vigilant press or parliamentary opposition, they hypothesized that he needed to combat corruption, sloth and incipient independence among his subordinates by instituting a 'permanent purge' in their ranks, periodically removing those who had taken root too comfortably, and replacing them with fresh appointees totally dependent on him personally. This 'permanent purge' was held to be the cardinal feature of a new kind of political system, 'totalitarianism', whose principal characteristics were (i) central direction of the entire economy, (ii) a single mass party mobilizing the population, either to 'build socialism' or to fight against enemies; (iii) an official monopoly of mass communications; (iv) supervision of everyone by a ubiquitous and terroristic security police; (v) adulation of a single leader; (vi) a single official ideology projecting a perfect final state of mankind and claiming priority over both the legal order and the individual conscience. Nazi Germany and fascist Italy (from where indeed the word 'totalitarianism' originated) were considered to offer further examples of this type, as were, after the war, Communist China, and the new socialist states of Central and Eastern Europe.

In most respects this model seems to me convincing. Whether it really applied to Nazi Germany or fascist Italy is questionable, but it certainly appears appropriate to characterize the type of society whose emergence I have been tracing in the foregoing chapters. All the same, it did not describe the society as a whole: it assumed that workers, peasants and intelligentsia were passive objects of the terror and the mobilization. It did not even examine at all closely the kind of ruling stratum the leader would need to exercise his power. With the benefit of hindsight, and increasingly rich historical documentation, we can now see that these various social strata were not simply passive, and that indeed their input, their goals and aspirations, have profoundly influenced the evolution of the system.

Actually, amidst the turmoil of economic transformation and terror, not just a new political system but also a new kind of society was taking shape, and one which proved in the long run not to be 'permanently purgeable', which indeed has turned out hierarchical, deeply conservative and surprisingly stable over the long term.

At its core were the new technical graduates who already had the beginnings of a party career behind them and were thus well placed to take over from the 'bourgeois specialists' who had dominated the economy and the professions throughout the twenties. In a period of fast economic growth the combination of political and technical skills possessed by the new graduates rendered them indispensable. As Stalin said in February 1931, in a dig at the already old-fashioned *praktiki* (the party men without proper technical qualifications): 'It is time the Bolsheviks themselves became specialists. In a period of reconstruction technology decides everything. And an economic manager who doesn't want to study and master technology isn't a manager at all. He's a poor joke.'

That the technological graduates of the first Five Year Plan period – those who survived the purges, that is – could do very well for themselves, can be seen from consideration of the following careers.

V. A. Malyshev graduated from the Bauman Mechanical Engineering Institute in Moscow in 1932 at the age of thirty, and went to work as designer at the Kolomna locomotive works, of which he became the director in 1937; after only two years in that post he was appointed USSR people's commissar for heavy machine construction in 1939, at the age of thirty-seven. *A. N. Kosygin* graduated from the Leningrad Textile Institute in 1935, aged thirty-one, became director of a textile factory two years later, and in 1939 became USSR people's commissar for the textile industry. In 1934 *D. F. Ustinov* graduated from the Leningrad Military-Mechanical Institute; in 1940 he became director of the 'Bolshevik' armaments works in Leningrad, and in 1941, aged thirty-three, was appointed to the crucial post of USSR people's commissar for the armaments industry. Compared with them, *L. I. Brezhnev* moved relatively slowly and kept closer to the party ladder: he graduated from the Dneprodzerzhinsk Metallurgical Institute in 1935, at the age of twenty-nine, and worked as an engineer for a time, becoming deputy chairman of the Dneprod-zerzhinsk soviet in 1937, and deputy secretary of the Dnepropetrovsk obkom (oblast party committee) in 1939. Likewise, *N. S. Khrushchev*, having been sent to the Moscow Industrial Academy in 1929, aged thirty-five already, left it for some reason after only two years, became a *raikom* (raion party committee) secretary in Moscow, then first secretary in Moscow in 1935 and first secretary in the Ukraine in 1938.

It will be apparent from the names I have quoted that these *vydvizhentsy* (upwardly socially mobile) of the early to mid-1930s have played a key role in the subsequent leadership of the Communist Party, right up to the very recent past. In 1952, just before Stalin's death, they formed 50 per cent of the ministers and deputy ministers on whom biographical data is available (57 out of 115) – while a further 22 had been adult graduates of technological institutes during NEP and 65 per cent of them were of working-class origin or had been workers a while. As late as 1980 they still formed half of the Politburo: Brezhnev, Kosygin, Kirilenko, Ustinov, Gromyko, Kunaev and Pelshe – all of whom except Kunaev were of working-class or peasant background.

During the 1930s, then, the social and educational

background of the leading party cadres changed considerably. In the 1920s the party had been led mainly by people of
middle-class and professional background, with an education
in law or humanities; in the thirties their places were taken by
people of working-class and peasant background, with a
predominantly technological education. The great
changeover took place between the Seventeenth Party Congress in 1934 and the Eighteenth Congress in 1939: only 29
members of the 139-strong Central Committee at the former
were also present at the latter. Most of the remainder had
been arrested by the NKVD in the meantime, and a good
many of them shot.

The new men rose to power in three areas: industrial
administration, government and party. But these three areas
were very closely interconnected, and posts within them to
some extent interchangeable in function. A government post
was by definition likely to be concerned with some branch of
industry, since most of the People's Commissariats headed
some branch of industry. *Obkom* and *gorkom* (regional and
urban party committee) secretaries also, especially in the
industrial provinces, spent most of their time advancing the
economic reputation of their territory, and that quite often
meant intervening personally to sort out confusions and
bottlenecks, and to ensure the securing of vitally needed
supplies or fuel. Thus, for example, when the government
decided in November 1940 that a new type of motor was
urgently needed for heavy artillery, they entrusted the contract to the Rybinsk motor construction works, and ordered
N. S. Patolichev, first secretary of the local obkom, to take
over direction of the works temporarily, and oversee the
speedy retooling that would be required. For Patolichev, who
had trained as a military engineer in the early thirties, this
was a familiar kind of task, and while he was away he was
able to hand over the political direction of the oblast to his
second secretary.

Nevertheless, they remained above all *party* men.
Typically, they had first attracted notice by their work in

party or Komsomol, they viewed their technological training as a party assignment, and they were subsequently prepared to move away from the particular speciality they had studied when the party required it. Kendall Bailes has done a computerized study of 1100 members of the technical intelligentsia who were singled out for official honours of some kind between 1958 and 1965 – most of whom, that is to say, were young men in the 1920s and 1930s. He found that they tended to have two distinct career patterns: those who rose in the party–state hierarchy, and those who remained in strictly technological posts. The political group tended to be closer in age (most of them were born between 1900 and 1914), more proletarian in social background and more provincial in education; they were mostly educated between 1928 and 1941, especially in metallurgy and mechanical engineering, the great staples of the first three Five Year Plans; Slavs were overrepresented among them, especially Russians, also Armenians and Georgians, but there were almost no Jews, and very few Asiatics or women.

These were the men who moved into the centre of the nomenklatura network in the late 1930s. A similar process was taking place in other fields, especially in the army, where former 'political commissars' were retraining in military academies and returning to the forces as fully fledged officers. Also in education, health, law, the diplomatic service, the arts, individuals enjoying the trust of the party's card-indexers were obtaining a proper professional training and returning to take charge of trade unions, educational establishments and research institutes.

The life of this embryonic ruling class was a strange one. On the one hand they were moving into a comfortable and secure existence. As Nadezhda Mandelstam wrote, with the jaundiced eye of a literary outsider: 'The new Moscow was being built up and adopting the ways of the world – people were opening their first bank accounts, buying furniture, and writing novels. Everybody could hope for speedy advancement, because every day somebody was plucked from their midst and had to be replaced.' Those who rose well up the nomenklatura network enjoyed privileges which most of the population could only dream of: spacious housing, special health care, access through special stores and distributors to good food supplies and to consumer goods at cheap prices. There were free or subsidized holidays, and indeed, for the very top people, weekend dachas in secluded areas and chauffeured motor transport. One could extend the list, without even mentioning levels of pay, which were no longer even nominally bound by 'petty bourgeois' notions of equalization.

On the other hand, in other ways the lives of these new appointees were strikingly *in*secure. They did not *own* any of the benefits mentioned above: they enjoyed them by virtue of their official positions, and hence at the pleasure of Stalin, the NKVD, and the Cadres Department of the party Central Committee. The nomenklatura system, which was finally perfected now, determined the distribution of these official positions, and the benefits which went with them. The word 'nomenklatura' designates two separate lists: a list of posts, and a list of personnel available to fill them. At Central Committee level this list of posts probably included party secretaries at republic and oblast level; all-Union commissars (ministers) and republican prime ministers; senior diplomatic officials; senior members of the judicial system and the procuracy; senior officers of the armed forces; leading officials in the NKVD (these were probably in practice appointed by Stalin himself); editors of all-Union newspapers; heads of trade unions, creative unions, youth and women's organizations; rectors of universities and heads of major research institutes; directors of factories of all-Union significance. At republican, oblast and raion/town level, the local party committee had at its disposal a list of similar posts at a correspondingly lower level, together with lists of individuals who might fill them. All personnel lists were kept up to date by the NKVD and the Cadres Department at the appropriate level, and no one would receive an official appointment who had displeased a superior or strayed from the current party line. Taken together, the nomenklatura lists constituted by now a formidable machinery of patronage extending to every influential professional or political function in the entire country.

Those whom Stalin had made he could always unmake. And he frequently did. When an official was dismissed or arrested, furthermore, he and his family lost all the privileges to which they had become accustomed. In case of arrest, in fact, they might lose *all* property rights: that is one reason why so many wives divorced their recently convicted husbands. Officials had two ways of warding off this threat: they might insure against it *collectively*, by forming a 'family circle' whose members would cover up each other's inadequacies, or *individually*, by denouncing their rivals and gaining the favour of the local NKVD. When the arrests eased late in 1938, the latter method usually yielded to the former. This induced in every appointed official extreme caution and reluctance to take responsibility, as has been noted by many visitors to the USSR.

Those whom Stalin promoted, however, could enjoy meteoric careers. As an example of an abrupt and breathtaking promotion one may take the experience of A. S. Chuyanov, who graduated in 1934 at the age of twenty-nine from the Moscow Chemical-Technical Institute of the Meat Industry. After combining graduate studies with work as a plant engineer, he did a year in the Central Committee apparatus, and then in 1938 was summoned to see A. A. Andreyev, currently the Central Committee secretary for cadres. Andreyev told him he was to be recommended as first secretary of the Stalingrad oblast party committee ('recommended' meant, of course, 'appointed', but formally the post was an elective one).

Now, Stalingrad was a showpiece new industrial city of nearly half a million people, named moreover after the leader himself, and Chuyanov, a mere four years out of college, understandably demurred that he had very little experience of party work. Andreyev replied: 'You'll get the experience. You have recently graduated from a vuz. . . . , you know agriculture and the fishing industry, so your candidacy is quite appropriate.' Brushing further hesitations aside, he added: 'As a future obkom secretary, you can't wear your old student suit', and rang the Central Committee business manager in order that 'Chuyanov be clothed and shod as a future obkom secretary, at Central Committee expense'. So urgent was the new appointment that Chuyanov, after picking up his suit, was not even allowed to go home and tell his family all about their good fortune: he had to make straight for the station, instructing his wife to meet him there and collect his old clothes!

The combination of emergency procedures with due concern for old-fashioned bourgeois standards of dress is characteristic of the new elite. Perhaps because they were mostly of working-class and peasant origin, these 'new men' were unduly impressed with the outward symbols of bourgeois and aristocratic life, often in their most old-fashioned and least tasteful manifestations. In architecture, for example, Stalin ordered a departure from 'oversimplified architectural designs', and more emphasis on 'facade motifs' – which meant in practice the grandiose, overwrought forms of Stalinist baroque, seen in their purest, or impurest, aspect in the Moscow underground and the 1953 Moscow University building on Lenin Hills. In a remarkable book a few years ago, Vera Dunham used novels of the late Stalin era to show how the 'new class' surrounded itself with chintz curtains and polka-dotted teacups at home, and with thick pile carpets and red-plush hangings at work. A taste for the unimaginative, monumental, easily comprehensible and traditional likewise invaded all the arts, now controlled through the various 'creative unions' by professionals promoted by the party and steadfastly loyal to it.

The taste for order and old-fashioned standards began to extend into other areas of Soviet life. Take the field of family policy, for example. In the 1920s the regime had tried to weaken the family as a 'bourgeois institution', which exploited women and perpetuated a paternalistic notion of property. Under legislation passed at that time, any stable cohabitation, whether registered or not, could be considered a family, and the resultant children had the rights of any other citizen. Abortion was available on demand. A partner to a marriage could obtain divorce simply by requesting it: the other partner had to be informed, but not necessarily consulted, so that sometimes divorce was achieved simply by sending a postcard.

There is little doubt that these provisions, together with the social upheavals of the time, quite seriously weakened the family as a social institution. In 1934 thirty-seven divorces were reported for every hundred marriages; and in the hospitals and clinics of Moscow there were 57,000 live births, but 154,000 abortions. The birth rate remained low, to the alarm of authorities anxious to see plenty of recruits coming forward for the army and the labour force. The break-up of families also meant a huge increase in the number of orphans – though this problem was certainly aggravated as well by the deportations and arrests. Some of these displaced children were absorbed into state orphanages, but many simply roamed the streets and begged. Some became diseased and died, while others formed into gangs, who would attack and rob people in the street, or even invade and ransack apartment blocks.

In the face of such unwelcome social developments, the media began during 1934–5 for the first time to extol stable family life and devotion to the upbringing of children. 'The state cannot exist without the family. Marriage has a positive value for the Soviet socialist state only if the partners see in it a lifelong union. So-called "free love" is a bourgeois invention. . . . Moreover, marriage receives its full value for the state only if there is progeny, and the consorts experience the highest happiness of parenthood.'

A greater element of ceremony was restored to marriages. An order went out to brighten up civil registry offices, and the manufacture and sale of gold wedding rings was once more authorized – though this must have deprived the Soviet Union of a proportion of its foreign currency earnings.

Divorce was made both more expensive and more difficult, becoming from 1944 contingent on court proceedings. Abortion was prohibited, except in cases involving a very serious health risk. During the public discussion which preceded this enactment, some women wrote to the newspapers, complaining of the curtailment of their right to work and study which this step would entail. 'If I become pregnant,' wrote one young woman, 'I shall have to leave the Institute; one cannot live in a hostel with children.' The editors replied, however, that the answer was to improve the childcare services.

The family as an economic unit was also strengthened. After the revolution the inheritance of property had been abolished, except insofar as was necessary to ensure the subsistence of dependents. Now it was progressively restored, until in 1945 the upper limit on the amount of property that could be bequeathed was abolished. This was far from being a restoration of bourgeois property rights, since in Soviet circumstances property is very limited, and plays a far smaller role in determining an individual's or a family's status than in the West. However, it certainly increased the power of the head of the family: an urban apartment could now sometimes be passed on, also perhaps a dacha with a small plot of land – by no means negligible benefits in a country desperately short of living space. Since, moreover, children of unregistered marriages were excluded from these arrangements, in practice the legal concept of 'illegitimacy' was restored.

In education, too, the Soviet state was turning away from the excesses of the 'cultural revolution'. In August 1931 the Central Committee passed a resolution noting that schools were 'not imparting a sufficient amount of general knowledge, nor adequately solving the problem of training fully literate persons with a good grasp of the basic sciences'. This reflected the views of both parents and employers that children were coming to their first jobs without good work habits and without the fundamentals a school could be expected to have taught. Over the next two or three years the content and style of school education was tightened up markedly. A core curriculum in mathematics, the sciences, the native language, history and geography was laid down; teaching of the social sciences was curtailed, to be replaced by programmed instruction in Marxism–Leninism. The project method was formally condemned, and regular classroom instruction reimposed, while manual labour and vocational studies almost disappeared. Officially approved textbooks were prescribed, and a formal system of tests and examinations restored, with marks to be awarded by the teacher, and not, as sometimes earlier, by the pupils themselves.

Of the newly prescribed syllabi the one in history is especially interesting. Teachers of history were instructed to avoid 'abstract sociological schemes', and instead to employ a 'chronological historical sequence in the exposition of historical events, firmly fixing in the minds of the pupils important events, personages and dates'. Pokrovsky, the doyen of Marxist historians, whose word had been law in the twenties, was now disdained; kings, battles and dates were back in fashion, especially battles won by the Russians. Ivan the Terrible and Peter the Great were once again national heroes, even if the regimes they presided over had been oppressive: the foundation and consolidation of a strong Russian national state was now held to be a virtue outweighing the exploitation of the masses.

In the late thirties a major symbolic return to pre-revolutionary conditions was accomplished when school uniforms were restored, complete with compulsory pigtails for girls. Fees were reintroduced for the three upper forms of the secondary school: since they were the forms which prepared children for higher education, the effect was to segregate academic from vocational training, leaving the former for the more privileged strata.

By the same token, the systematic recruitment of workers from the factory floor for higher education was suspended. The rabfaki were cut back, and then closed altogether: from 1938 they were replaced by extra-mural departments (*zaochnye fakultety*), where ordinary workers could supplement their education either in the evening or by correspondence, but in any case on top of a day's work, and without any financial support. Positive discrimination in favour of worker and peasant entrants to vuzy stopped, and candidates were admitted strictly according to academic criteria. Fees of 300–500 rubles per annum were introduced in 1940, but reduced or waived for students who received the highest marks in the examinations.

By the late thirties, in fact, the entire educational system had been remodelled along traditional – almost pre-revolutionary – lines, for the needs of a society which had become hierarchical, imperial and conservative in its outlook. The only new element – but it was a major one – was the introduction of systematic and compulsory tuition in Marxism–Leninism for all pupils and students. This was part of the imposition of a rigid and unimaginative orthodoxy in all spheres of intellectual and cultural life, which requires further examination, since it became the legitimizing ideology both for Stalin and for his new ruling class.

This ideology was formed directly out of Leninism, but selectively, taking those aspects of Leninism which remained expedient and reforging them in a new, cruder and more monolithic form. Stalin drew out particularly Lenin's reflections on building 'socialism in one country', dating from the period when both world revolution and War Communism had for the moment failed. Stalin argued that the socialist revolution was different in nature from the bourgeois revolution. Since no socialist economy had matured inside bourgeois society (as a bourgeois economy was held to have matured inside feudal society), it followed that the creation of a socialist economy had to be undertaken by the post-revolutionary state. 'The bourgeois revolution usually *ends* with the seizure of power, whereas for the proletarian revolution the seizure of power is only the beginning, after which power is used as a lever for the reconstruction of the old economy and the organization of a new one.' This implicitly contradicted the Lenin of *Imperialism* and of *State and Revolution*, who had maintained that the centralized economy developing inside late bourgeois society would enable ordinary working people to take it over and run it as a ready-made, semi-socialist economy. Stalin's reformulation laid much more emphasis on the state, assigned to it in fact a positive and leading role. Clearly, there could no longer be any talk about the 'withering away of the state', at least until mature socialism was attained. On the contrary, Stalin asserted that as the Soviet Union approached socialism, so the efforts of its enemies, both internal and external, would become ever more frenzied; the Soviet state would accordingly have to become *stronger*, in order to resist and destroy the 'class enemy'.

Stalin's teachings – the latest link in what was now reclassified as Marxism–Leninism–Stalinism – were expounded systematically in the *Short Course on the History of the CPSU(b)*, which became the staple intellectual diet of every schoolchild and student in the country. There it was shown how the Bolshevik party, under the unfailingly perspicacious leadership of Lenin, with his disciple Stalin at his side, had carried out the October revolution, and then systematically set about constructing a socialist society in spite of all assaults from within and without. All the other Bolshevik leaders – unless they had had the good fortune to die before the purges – were characterized as splitters, saboteurs or traitors who had done their best to impede the course chosen by the two great men. This was a simple-minded, mythical account of Soviet history, with its straightforward heroes and villains, and it appealed to the men of humble background and rudimentary education who were by now moving into the extensive network of party posts as ideologists, propagandists and agitators. From the moment it was published, the *Short Course* became the obligatory and sufficient authority on all the subjects it touched. Others writing in the same field had to repeat the sacred words of the master. Every schoolchild and student had to study it diligently and reproduce whole passages of it as required in examinations. It became in fact the canonical text of Stalinism.

Did people actually believe it? This is one of the most difficult questions to answer for a past epoch, especially since we have all too few honest testimonies from those who were the pillars of the system. For young people, of course, the Stalinist world view had considerable attractions: it offered a mission, a purpose to which one could dedicate oneself together with others, a reason for believing that life could and should be lived to the full. Raisa Orlova, a late 1930s student at IFLI (the Institute of Philology, Literature and History, which had taken over the humanities faculties of Moscow University) recalls, 'I passionately wanted to be happy, and lived with my eyes tight closed. . . . Everything negative in our life simply bounced off us, extruded by our whole frame of mind.' She admits that if anyone had got up in their auditorium and spoken the truth about the famine, the show trials and the labour camps, he would not have been believed, and indeed would have been shouted down. Thus a natural mixture of self-interest, spontaneous optimism and altruistic dedication to the common cause led many into a lifetime's devoted service to the Stalinist state.

Another satisfaction which the ideology afforded was certainty, the right to banish doubts. Wolfgang Leonhard, the German Communist, who studied in Moscow from 1935 to 1940, later wrote: 'Marxism–Leninism was for us the only scientific world outlook. Everybody else in the world, the social democrats, the liberals, the conservatives, had their opinions, but we, the Marxist–Leninists, we had a scientific world outlook. . . . They might be good specialists in this or that, but we knew the fundamental answer to the riddle of the past, present and future, for all nations and for all countries.' In the face of such majestic certainty, personal doubts about the odd arrest or show trial seemed very trivial.

Yet it remains true that probably the majority of the population could not really believe the official ideology. So what did they do?

Here we come to a curious and paradoxical feature of Soviet society. People were required to mouth the ritual phrases of the ideology, but God forbid that they should take it all seriously and act upon it. Thus one had to state with all apparent conviction that the Soviet constitution of 1936 was 'the most democratic in the world', but to attempt to avail oneself of the democratic freedoms it proclaimed was to invite disaster. Or, to take an opposite example, the mass arrests and the labour camps were never mentioned in the public media; but everyone knew, and the regime intended them to know, that people suddenly disappeared, that terrible things happened to them, and that many of them died.

The result was that most people were compelled to live two intellectual and spiritual lives, a public one where they repeated grotesque falsehoods and kept silent about terrible truths, and a private one, shared only with absolutely trusted friends, where perhaps the truth was faced, if one had the courage to face it. And because of the ubiquity of NKVD informers (*stukachi* or 'knockers', as they were called) many people had no one whom they trusted completely.

State monopoly of information and mass communications, deployed in this manner and backed by the widespread practice of police denunciations, degraded the nation's intellectual and cultural life. The assimilation and public discussion of uncomfortable facts, which is what enables people in most societies to form opinions about political issues, became impossible. In their absence most people no longer knew quite *what* they thought, and fell back on cynicism and acceptance, or lived in the ambivalence and confusion which George Orwell aptly dubbed 'doublethink'.

The function of ideology, then, had changed considerably since Lenin's time. Lenin had proclaimed that 'Marxism is all-powerful because it is *true*', and he had insisted on his own version of it because he wanted to *get things done*; his colleagues followed him (in spite of periodic doubts) because they wanted to 'change the world'. But as the utopian dream faded, and the real world became more intractable, the party leaders split into those who wanted to return to utopia by ever more coercive means (Trotsky and the left) and those who were prepared to recognize reality and to try to accommodate themselves to it (Bukharin and the right). Stalin took a third course, which was to consolidate the hold on power which was the Bolsheviks' one tangible achievement, abandoning the utopian dreams in practice, while still using the utopian myths, only now as a means, not of changing society, but of bolstering the existing power structure and inducing the population to accept it.

The new-style ideology, then, was no longer a guide to action, but a system of stylized myths and fictions to which the population was required to render symbolic obeisance. Actual belief in the myths could now be subversive: what was demanded was the external acquiescence. The fiction that 'life had become better and more cheerful' required the people to accept low pay, long hours of work and atrocious housing without complaint. The myth of 'the scientific nature of Marxism–Leninism–Stalinism' was intended to induce everybody to accept the present regime, on the understanding that it had a scientific conception of history, and was certain to attain its ultimate goals. The myths of the 'deepening class struggle', of 'enemies of the people', 'imperialist agents', spies, diversionists and such like justified a general attitude of vigilance and suspicion of one's neighbour, as well as a vast and uncontrolled security apparatus and the need for huge armaments and universal military service.

Only one myth turned out not to be a myth: that was the 'imperialist threat'. In 1941 that became reality in no un-certain fashion: and significantly the realization of one of his myths caused Stalin something approaching a nervous breakdown before he could face up to it. Hitler's attack in fact conferred on the Communist regime a legitimacy which it had largely lost in the eyes of the masses.

In some respects the Stalinist ideology resembled a religion. It claimed to understand the whole of human nature and indeed, in the form of 'dialectical materialism', the whole of the universe. It was backed by rituals and ceremonials that were partially reminiscent of religious ones. Yet, because it was essentially a political and economic doctrine, it failed to fill some of the main functions of a religion. Man's beliefs and values were regarded as secondary: they could have no autonomous meaning, because they were merely derivative. This lacuna proved very unsatisfactory, and in the publicly projected ideology a certain recognition of autonomous subjectivity did re-emerge. Especially in literature and the arts, a cult arose of hero-worship, patriotism, family attachment and romantic love, all sentiments far removed from classical Marxism, but answering the needs of the new 'Red specialists' of modest social origin and meagre cultural background.

The man most closely identified with the new tendencies in literature was Maxim Gorky. He had very much disliked the despotic style of the early Bolsheviks, and he had lived in Italy for most of the twenties. But from 1928 the party went out of its way to attract him back home, feeling the need of the man who had made his name as 'the great proletarian writer'. Gorky, in the end, gave way. Perhaps he was getting old and homesick, perhaps he had become disillusioned with the other émigré writers, perhaps he wanted to believe that a real future was being built in his homeland. At any rate, he returned to great public acclaim: a mansion was placed at his disposal, as well as two country villas, one of them in the Crimea. His supplies and furnishings were managed by the same department of the NKVD which looked after Stalin and members of the Politburo, and he was protected by a similarly tight guard.

The members of RAPP were none too keen on his return, and, although for a time he worked with them (for example, on the Belomor volume mentioned above), they were right to have forebodings. The party had grown tired of RAPP, as of other participants in the 'cultural revolution'. On 23 April 1932 a Central Committee resolution declared that 'the framework of the existing proletarian literary and artistic organizations is becoming too narrow and is hindering the proper development of literary work.' It announced that, therefore, RAPP would be closed down. Instead a new Union of Soviet Writers would be established to 'unite all writers supporting the platform of Soviet power and aspiring to participate in the building of socialism.' This union held its first congress in 1934; Gorky played a key role in its inception, and in formulating the guidelines the union recommended for the new literature. The basic principle of literary creation was now claimed to be 'socialist realism'.

This doctrine was consciously framed in such a way as to exclude too narrow an interpretation. Terms like 'proletarian realism', 'Communist realism' or 'the dialectical materialist creative method' were rejected as being too closely identified with a particular political or literary current. Socialist realism was declared to be the culmination of *all* the best literary currents of the past, whether Russian or foreign. Indeed all the great writers of the past were seen as precursors, in some sense, of socialist realism: they had all been *narodny*, or 'popular, rooted in the people', they had all depicted reality, they had all reflected a progressive outlook, at least in the context of their times. So, at least, it could be argued. Some writers, of course – Stendhal, Balzac, Dickens, Tolstoy, Zola – were seen as being closer to the standard than others. Then, through Chernyshevsky and Gorky, the world literary heritage flowed on to reach its high point in a few selected post-revolutionary Russian novels, such as Gladkov's *Cement*, Furmanov's *Chapaev*, Fadeyev's *The Rout*, and the first part of Sholokhov's *The Quiet Don*, which were constantly evoked in early discussions of socialist realism. In each of them, a hero appears from among the people, he is guided and matured by the party, which tempers his 'spontaneity' with its 'consciousness', and then he leads his comrades and followers to great victories over enemies and natural obstacles in the name of the wonderful future which the party is building. This characteristic outline, fleshed out in different ways and embellished with various sub-plots, could not be deduced from any of the official definitions of socialist realism, but it was to become the archetypal plot of the 'high literature' of the Stalin period.

What was being emphasized, in fact, at the time of the proclamation of the doctrine of socialist realism was not so much its revolutionary or proletarian nature as its identification with the party, as the indwelling spirit of the established socialist state, and with the best literary traditions of all times and all nations. Former 'proletarian' writers did less well in the distribution of official posts in the Writers' Union than the supposedly apolitical 'fellow travellers'. The Stalinist state was trying now to project itself as a great empire – of a new and higher kind, to be sure, but still possessing the positive attributes of the great civilizations of the past. Despite the obvious differences, one might compare the cultural life of the new Soviet Russia with that of seventeenth-century France, where the state of the Sun King also endeavoured to lay the foundations of a great literary tradition, through the Académie Française by prescribing norms of taste derived from the classical past.

The Union of Soviet Writers was established in this monolithic imperial spirit, and under strict party control. Its structure and functions may be examined as a model for all professional and creative unions in the Soviet Union. Party control is exercised, as in other professions, through the nomenklatura system, by which writers acceptable to the party are appointed to positions of authority in the union. The union provides for writers a whole range of services which they cannot command elsewhere. It has constructed blocks of flats, country villas, holiday homes, hospitals and sanatoria. It secures the writer advances on his work, arranges journeys for him to 'collect material', assures him peace and quiet for writing in a 'creative retreat', and provides a secretary to prepare the final typescript. Regular seminars listen to readings and discuss work in progress. The union, in fact, integrates writers into the nation's elite – with the 'top' writers in the highest ranks of it – and surrounds them with both care and vigilance.

It also owns a large number of journals and publishing houses, so that it regulates access to the most important benefit of all, that of publication. Its senior officials and editors are in regular close touch with cultural officials of the party Central Committee, so that they know at any moment what are the current frontiers of the acceptable. These senior figures are usually second-rate writers themselves, and hence dependent on their official position for the status and authority they possess. Even more than Marxist–Leninist ideology, it has been their tastes and prejudices which have done most in practice to determine the nature of literary production. With some notable exceptions, they have mostly been men of mediocre education and uncertain culture, whose tastes have derived partly from folk culture and partly from the mass literature beginning to take root in Russia before the revolution: adventure stories, detective fiction, love romances. This mixture has helped to account for some of the characteristics of Soviet literature, and especially fiction. There is, as we have seen, a stratum of 'highbrow' literature (Gorky, A. Tolstoy, Sholokhov, N. Ostrovsky, Fadeyev), mostly heroic and hyperbolic, with its roots simultaneously and incongruously in both nineteenth-century realist fiction and heroic folk epics; then a much commoner 'middlebrow' stream, hovering uneasily between *partiinost* (party-mindedness) and railway bookstall literature: novels of war and adventure, historical novels with heroes from the Russian past, or detective fiction in which Cheka or police officials thwart the designs of the imperialists. Altogether, the 'literary bureaucrats' have been quite close to their readers in taste.

The problem is, of course, there have been quite a few writers who did not fit readily into this structure. Indeed, they were often the best ones, who found political control and collective mediocrity repugnant. They practised, particularly in the Stalin years, what Babel (who was one of them) called 'the genre of silence', or they turned to journalism, translation or children's literature as a substitute for writing works which they knew they had no hope of publishing. A few, like Bulgakov, went on writing anyway, in the belief that 'manuscripts do not burn', and that posterity would read them. Among those who fell silent were Babel, Mandelstam, Pasternak, Akhmatova. Olesha turned largely to journalism, Pilnyak and Zoshchenko tried to conform and changed the nature of their writing, with poor results; Zamyatin, as we have seen, emigrated, with better results. Some major writers – Babel, Pilnyak, Mandelstam – actually went to their deaths in the labour camps, and by the indiscriminate irony of Stalin's Russia their fate was shared by their former tormentor, Averbakh.

The operations of the Writers' Union throw a good deal of light on the way ideology and culture have been administered in the Soviet Union, from the early 1930s onwards. The 'cultural revolutionaries' were disinherited by monolithic professional unions set up by the state and run by a mixture of 'Old' and 'Red' specialists under strict party guidance. The result has not necessarily been the imposition of Marxist orthodoxy. In fact, often the 'old' specialists (like Gorky) had the commanding influence, and the professional guidelines combined much of their outlook with a modified Russian patriotism and a selective Marxism–Leninism. The result was an eclectic mixture of socialism and Russian nationalism acceptable to the men now moving into the top positions in the power structure and needing ideology as a means of staying there.

During the thirties, then, amidst all the upheavals of social change on an unprecedented scale, a new hierarchical social structure was taking shape, with its focus in the party's nomenklatura appointments system. The new ruling elite was far from being a stable or established social class as yet, but it held in its hands formidable political instruments with which it could eventually consolidate its power. In one sense, this new class's greatest enemy was its creator, Stalin, and the security police apparatus which he personally controlled. In another sense, however, the new class needed the security police for its own protection. Raw, inexperienced and often still very young, its members had overwhelming power, but they still lacked tradition and legitimacy. In 1941 an ordeal burst upon them which enabled them to gain elements of both.

9

Religion and Nationality
under the Soviet State

The Soviet state, with its all-embracing ideology, rapidly took on itself, as we have seen, many of the claims and attributes of an established church. It was prone, therefore, to regard religious movements, and particularly the formerly established Russian Orthodox Church, as its rivals. In theory this should not have been the case: Lenin held that religion was simply a product of social oppression and economic exploitation. 'The social oppression of the toiling masses, their apparent complete helplessness before the blind forces of capitalism . . . that is the deepest contemporary root of religion.' Theoretically it followed from this that the elimination of social and economic evils should lead to the disappearance of religious belief. In practice, however, the party has never shown any confidence that this would happen: it has not felt able to concede the churches toleration, and let them decline of their own accord. On the contrary, from the beginning it has aimed at the destruction of the churches and the forcible secularization of believers. With the exception of the years 1941–53, that has remained the case ever since.

The very first ecclesiastical legislation of the Soviet state in January 1918 was entitled 'the separation of church and state'. In fact, however, it was not so much a 'separation' as a subordination, of the church to the state. Churches and religious societies were deprived of the rights of juridical persons, and all church lands and properties were nationalized without compensation, though congregations were given the right to hire back their buildings and sacred objects free of charge for the purposes of divine service. Churches might, however, now also be used by local soviets for other functions, such as concerts, film shows or political meetings. All clergymen were reduced to the socially inferior status of *lishentsy* or 'deprivees', that is to say, they were deprived of the vote, paid higher taxes, and received ration cards at the lowest level, while their children were debarred from specialist or higher education. Although 'religious propaganda' was not explicitly forbidden, in practice all religious education outside the family was made impossible, and all religious publications were outlawed by the state censorship. Meanwhile the party proceeded actively to carry out its intention (as stated in the 1919 party programme) 'to liberate the toiling masses from religious prejudices and to organize the broadest scientific-educational and anti-religious propaganda'. The methods of 'liberation' did not only include 'propaganda': the Soviet state actively and brutally persecuted the churches. A large number of church buildings were desecrated and destroyed or turned over for secular use. More than half the monasteries were closed down, and twenty-eight bishops and more than a thousand priests were arrested or died in violent clashes by 1921. Some of them were simply executed by the Cheka as 'class enemies'.

These early repressive measures were supplemented by further legislation 'on religious associations' in 1929. This laid down that religious activity was only to be permitted to registered congregations, each of which must consist of at least twenty people over the age of eighteen. Only such groups would be authorized to hire church buildings and the accoutrements of divine service, and to engage a priest to perform the service. Priests were thus no longer seen as pastors, but as mere employees of their congregations, hired to render a service, as one would a plumber or an electrician. All religious activities outside church buildings and designated prayer houses were prohibited. This meant an end to public funeral processions, to charitable and voluntary social work, and to prayer groups and bible study sessions – or rather it meant that they had to be conducted in secret. The theoretically surviving freedom of religious propaganda was now formally abolished, and replaced by 'freedom of religious worship and anti-religious propaganda'. Evangelism was thus explicitly outlawed.

Churches were in this way reduced to officially monitored congregations permitted to do nothing but hold a weekly service. The Russian Orthodox Church still had a central organization, as we shall see, but this had no legal standing, and could be ignored by the state at will. Rather than a single 'church', there now existed a scattering of isolated and disparate 'twenties', or congregations, each registered, supervised and often infiltrated by the authorities.

The Russian Orthodox Church, as much the largest and most powerful organization to be affected by these measures, met the revolution of 1917 as a divided and in many respects demoralized body. There had been much pressure within the church both to reform it and to end its suffocating dependence on the state. The reformers wanted, for example, to democratize the liturgy by conducting it in modern Russian (rather than Old Church Slavonic) and allowing the laity to participate in the eucharist. They also wanted to democratize the governance of the church by removing it from the Holy Synod and entrusting it to a *Sobor* (church council) properly elected by clergy and laity. They wanted to abolish the distinction between the 'white' clergy (married parish priests) and the 'black' (unmarried monks); since only 'black' clerics could become prelates, the distinction created a caste-like hierarchical division right through the ranks of the clergy.

The Provisional Government had called a Sobor, and thus met one of the demands of the reformers, but for most of them the results of the council were nevertheless disappointing. It did end the domination of the state over the church (very briefly, as it turned out), but, instead of placing the governance of the church in the hands of an elected Sobor, it restored the pre-Petrine Patriarchate. The reformers walked out when the decision was announced. Not much was accomplished, either, it would appear, to end the division between 'black' and 'white' clergy, or to bring the liturgy closer to the people, as the reformers had long recommended.

The new church leadership reacted vehemently to the Bolsheviks' evident intention to destroy the church. In January 1918, Tikhon, the new Patriarch, pronounced an anathema on the Bolsheviks. The so-called 'champions of the people's welfare', he commented, in fact 'trample on the people's conscience'. He called on the faithful to join together and resist the Bolsheviks by all possible *spiritual* means. It should be noted, however, that Tikhon did not call for the violent overthrow of the Bolshevik regime: he never explicitly supported the Whites in the civil war, nor did he recommend the restoration of the monarchy. There is not much doubt, however, that many Orthodox clergymen did so. Some of them fled abroad and called a church Sobor at Karlovtsy, in Yugoslavia, in 1921: this body issued a declaration endorsing the anti-Bolshevik cause and calling for the return of the monarchy. This declaration was to cause grave embarrassment to Tikhon.

In addition to persecuting the church and conducting anti-religious propaganda, the Soviet regime worked to split the church from inside. The issue which it used to make this attempt was skilfully chosen. In view of the terrible famine in the Volga region, the state demanded in February 1922 that the church should surrender all its valuables to raise money for famine relief. Tikhon replied that the church was prepared to sell non-consecrated valuables, if it were permitted to conduct its own relief work, which current legislation prohibited, but it would not alienate consecrated vessels, nor would it allow its resources to be used for state relief work over which it had no control.

The party thereupon sent in its activitists to confiscate the treasures, a move which was often bitterly resisted by local priests and congregations. There was, for example, a riot in the village of Shuya, in Kostroma province, after which eight priests and three laymen were condemned to death. In Petrograd, Metropolitan Veniamin himself led the resistance to the seizures. As a result he and four others were arrested, sentenced to death and executed. Patriarch Tikhon, who had been summoned to testify at Veniamin's trial, was subjected to house arrest.

In fact, however, there were groups inside the church who felt that it *should* have put its resources at the disposal of the state for famine relief. Some leading church reformers had established a pressure group known as the Living Church. Its best-known figure was Father Alexander Vvedensky, an intellectual who had been a late convert to the faith, and a Christian socialist: after the October revolution he declared that Marxism was 'the Gospel printed in the atheist language'. He was a romantic, eloquent figure who was prepared to defend Christianity in sophisticated intellectual arguments with Marxists; reportedly, he used to chant the liturgy as if it were poetry, raising himself to a pitch of almost hysterical ecstasy, which caused offence to his more sober colleagues. It is said that he held talks with Zinoviev in 1919, in which the latter maintained that the Living Church would be the most appropriate ecclesiastical body to promote and sustain an eventual concordat with the Soviet state.

There were other elements, however, among the renovationists. Bishop Antonin Granovsky headed a group known as the League for the Regeneration of the Church, whose main aim was to bring the liturgy closer to the people by simplifying the vestments, bringing the eucharist out from behind the iconostasis, allowing the laity to participate, and conducting the service in modern Russian. Then there was the leading exponent of the rights of the 'white' or parish clergy, Archpriest Vladimir Krasnitsky, who had before the revolution been the vicar of the Petersburg Church of the Union of the Russian People, and thus associated with the extreme right-wing, anti-Semitic sector of politics. In some ways it is difficult to see what such disparate people can have had in common, and their cooperation (though short-lived) was perhaps a sign of the extreme disorientation of the church at the time.

What united them initially was that they *were* prepared to cooperate with the state, immediately over famine relief, and in the longer term to promote stable church–state relationships. In May 1922 Vvedensky and Krasnitsky went to see Tikhon in his confinement, and persuaded him to stand down temporarily, since he was unable to exercise the duties of his office; he appointed Metropolitan Agafangel of Yaroslavl as his deputy. At this stage, however, the renovationists in effect mounted a coup: they set up a Higher Church Administration, with Bishop Antonin at its head, claiming to have received full executive powers from the Patriarch.

In April 1923 the renovationists held their own Sobor, from which the supporters of Agafangel were as far as possible excluded. They stripped Tikhon of his titles and even his clerical status, and annulled his anathema of the Bolsheviks. They passed resolutions in favour of the socialist reconstruction of society, and called Lenin 'a great fighter for the truth'. Parish clergy were given more influence over the administration of the church, and married priests were made eligible to become bishops.

This action caused an immediate and bitter split inside the Russian Orthodox Church. At first most priests refused to accept the new Administration, but they soon found themselves being dismissed and replaced by new priests installed with the support of the state. Within a year or so, the Living Church had in this way won over a very large number of clergy and parishes, probably about two-thirds of the total, including, for example, all but four or five of those in Moscow. Among ordinary believers, however, the response was much cooler. Perhaps this was because of the renovationists' only too evident complicity with the GPU, or perhaps it was because believers under pressure naturally tend to retreat into a safe and conservative version of their faith, and therefore found the innovations of Antonin unattractive. At any rate, it seems clear that, after some early interest, congregations with any choice tended to desert the renovationist parishes, and to attend the churches which stuck to the familiar practices.

Quite apart from this, the splits within the Living Church were becoming painfully evident, especially the disagreements between Krasnitsky and Antonin. Antonin had reservations about the anointing of married bishops, and objected increasingly to Krasnitsky's servility towards the state; he wanted to concentrate on the reform of the liturgy and to de-emphasize the hierarchy in the church rather than squabble about who should head it. The high point in their split came one day, during the mutual celebration of the eucharist: as they were about to embrace, Antonin proclaimed, 'Christ is not among us!' and refused communion to his colleague.

Faced with such evidence of unpopularity and fractiousness, the state seems to have decided to withdraw its support from the Living Church. In any case, the main aim of splitting the Russian Orthodox Church internally had already been achieved. Moreover, Patriarch Tikhon had decided to soften his attitude to the Soviet state, perhaps because, as the émigré scholar Mikhail Agursky has suggested, he felt that the Bolsheviks now offered the best chance of preserving the integrity of Russia as a national territory. His recantation was a limited one, but he did issue a statement promising not to remain an enemy of the Soviet authorities, and dissociating the church inside Russia from the decisions of the Karlovtsy Sobor. On this basis, Tikhon was released from arrest, and the trial being prepared against him – which might have ended as had that of Metropolitan Veniamin – was dropped.

Tikhon's change of heart laid the basis for a period of uneasy and one-sided compromise between church and state. The terms of this compromise were worked out only after Tikhon's death in 1925, and then under the heaviest possible pressure from the state. A number of Tikhon's designated successors were arrested before one of them, Metropolitan Sergei, could be induced to sign a statement expressing a rather more positive commitment to the Soviet system than had been given by Tikhon. According to some reports, the GPU threatened that, unless Sergei complied with their demands, they would arrest and shoot more than a hundred bishops. Certainly, no one could doubt by now their readiness and willingness to destroy the entire hierarchy and external apparatus of the Russian Orthodox Church. It was probably in the face of overwhelming threats of this nature that Sergei gave way, for in Orthodox theology the existence of the church itself is a cardinal element: the concept of *sobornost* emphasizes the individual's need of the church if he is not to stray from faith and fall permanently a prey to sin. As Sergei himself said later to a supplicant for the priesthood, 'We must preserve the church for the people. After that, the Lord will show us what we must do.' At any rate, in August 1927 Sergei proclaimed, 'We wish to be Orthodox believers, and at the same time to claim the Soviet Union as our civil motherland, whose joys and successes are our joys and successes, and whose misfortunes are our misfortunes.'

As for the Living Church, it dragged on a twilight existence for nearly another twenty years, before it was finally abolished in 1946, but it never succeeded in regaining the confidence of the state, nor in attracting the masses to its services. The whole renovationist episode had a profound effect on the Russian Orthodox Church. By allowing themselves to be used in effect as police agents, the renovationists discredited not only themselves, but the whole drive towards reform inside the church. Their apostasy left a church that was static and conservative in outlook and in due course was compelled to embrace the sycophancy towards the state which had been the renovationists' own worst feature. In that respect little has changed between the late 1920s and the present.

Even the pledge of loyalty towards the state did not markedly change official ecclesiastical policy. The campaign of repression resumed along with the collectivization of agriculture. First of all the village church bells would be hauled down and taken away to be melted as scrap metal for industry. A foreign observer, Eugene Lyons, describes the kind of scene which followed: 'When brigades arrived to remove the bells and icons, they sometimes found believers armed with sticks and pitchforks to defend their church. Troops, in many instances, were summoned to crush these riots, and the ringleaders found themselves quickly enough in prison or before the firing squad.' Then, most often, as the collective farm was set up, the church would be finally closed and the building converted to become a store or village club, while the priest was arrested or driven into exile along with the 'kulaks'. A second wave of arrests and closures followed during the great purges of 1936–9. As a result, by 1939, out of 163 bishops still active in 1930, only 12 were still at liberty. Sergei had, moreover, been compelled to disband the 'synod', or administrative chancellery, by which he had tried to impart some coherence and permanence to the church's organization. In spite of all his concessions, it looked as if the Russian Orthodox Church was threatened with extinction.

What effect all this had on ordinary believers it is difficult to say, for sheer lack of evidence. Obviously the loss of their traditional place of worship and of their spiritual father was a shattering blow. For many the disappearance of habitual forms of worship probably meant the end of active faith. But for at least a significant minority the reverse was true. The overwhelming external repression drove them underground, to more intense and improvised expressions of their faith. Quite a number of clergymen sought refuge by abandoning their habits and taking up some secular pursuit, sharing in fact the life of their congregation more closely than before. Others took to the road: wandering priests would pass unannounced through villages, gathering secret services in the forest at night. Believers without regular access to a priest would experiment with collective confessions, improvised prayer meetings, mutual administration of the eucharist and mass baptism. Thus, like the Old Believers of the seventeenth century, the most conservative adherents of the faith found themselves compelled to innovate.

New and sometimes extremist sects emerged. Some priests and congregations refused to accept the compromises of Sergei, or even of Tikhon in his last years, and took their stance on Tikhon's original irreconcilable position. Their leader (albeit from prison) was Metropolitan Iosif of Leningrad, one of Tikhon's designated successors who had refused to make a retraction acceptable to the authorities. These and other underground movements received large numbers of new recruits with the repression of the 1930s. They usually espoused a fanatical rejection of all aspects of the Soviet system, which they regarded as the work of the Anti-Christ. Some of them retreated into distant forest settlements in Siberia and the far north, to avoid having any dealings with the Soviet authorities, and to await the Day of Judgement, which they believed to be imminent.

The outbreak of war in 1941 caused a sharp change in official ecclesiastical policy. Almost overnight the German invasion converted the Russian Orthodox Church into an ally of the Soviet regime. From the start the church issued statements supporting the Soviet war effort, and ordered prayers for the triumph of Soviet arms. Priests and congregations raised money for a tank column called after the medieval Russian prince, Dmitri Donskoi; it was handed over to the Red Army at a special ceremony, at which Metropolitan Nikolai spoke of 'sacred hatred of the fascist robbers' and referred to Stalin as 'our common father'.

Eventually Stalin decided to regularize his relationship with the church, perhaps because he anticipated that its help would be useful among the populations of Central and Eastern Europe after the war. At any rate, in September 1943, he allowed it to reestablish the Patriarchate. Sergei, the natural candidate, died in 1944, but the following year a full Sobor convened and elected Metropolitan Alexei of Leningrad as his successor. A proper ecclesiastical administration was revived, with state approval, while several seminaries and three theological academies were opened to train aspirants to the priesthood. A very large number of churches were permitted to reopen for services: according to some estimates, some 20,000 or about half the pre-1917 figure.

It would be wrong to interpret this new tolerance as a full concordat between church and state. The subordination of church to state remained in force, though more generously applied. The government appointed a special Council for Church Affairs, with offices in all areas of the country, to supervise the church, and keep an eye on diocesan and parish appointments. Its first chairman, G. G. Karpov, was jokingly known as Narkombog (People's Commissar for God) – or even Narkomopium! Perhaps the most significant fact about him was that all his previous experience had been in the NKVD. In effect, one might say that priests and bishops were being absorbed into the nomenklatura system of appointments. The religious dissenter Anatoly Levitin has aptly called the arrangement 'a conservative church in a conservative state'.

Unlike the Orthodox Church, the Baptists actually benefited initially from the coming of the Soviet regime. The discrimination practised against them by the tsars was lifted, and for a time the Soviets even tolerated religious collective farms set up by Baptists. The decree of 1929, with its prohibition of evangelism, was, however, a bitter blow, for proselytising is considered to be one of the principal duties of a Baptist, and they suffered numerous arrests for it. In spite of this, the Baptists were in many ways better suited to the pressures of Soviet society than was the Orthodox Church. They were accustomed to coping with state persecution. Their ministers were used to combining secular jobs with their pastoral work. Believers were already in the habit of improvising Sunday schools and prayer meetings in each others' homes. Their morality – hard work, self-discipline, sobriety, mutual aid – was close to the official morality which the Communists preached but did not practise. Baptists could appeal to young people brought up in the new system, but disillusioned by the failure of party folk to live up to their own principles. Above all, the Baptists were a *literate* church: they laid great emphasis on bible reading, as the Orthodox Church had never really done. This made their faith especially attractive to a newly literate working class. They became particularly strong in the industrial towns of the Ukraine, the Urals and Siberia, and among the Russian communities in the cities of the Caucasus and Central Asia: these were all areas to which the Russians had come relatively recently, and the Orthodox Church was not strong.

The Baptists took a strongly patriotic line during the war, and Stalin rewarded them by making the same kind of arrangements as he had for the Orthodox Church.

The combination of national with religious oppression brought new life to those churches which were closely identified with a specific nationality, such as the Georgian and Armenian churches, and, from 1940, the Ukrainian Uniate Church, the Lithuanian Catholic Church, and the Lutheran churches among the Estonians, Latvians and Germans.

Islam faced the Soviet regime with problems which were in many ways distinct from those posed by the Christian churches. In the early years, as we have seen, some Communists even hoped to work *with* Islam, on the basis of common anti-imperialism, but Sultan Galiev's experience led to disillusionment on both sides. It was much more difficult, however, for the Communists to *suppress* Islam, which is both more elusive than Christianity – not readily confined to a building, a clergyman, or a set ritual – and also more closely integrated with the community and with the texture of everyday life. Lenin was aware of these problems, and was cautious in his approach to Islam: in the early 1920s it was accorded far more tolerance than the main Christian churches. Public rituals were still permitted, the sharia

(Islamic law) courts and Muslim schools were still open, and the mullahs remained full citizens, not subject to negative discrimination.

In the mid-twenties that changed quite suddenly. Perhaps because the Basmachi had largely been brought under control, the party felt able to proceed more directly. The religious endowments known as waqf were closed down. Most of them were in the form of land which provided an income for the upkeep of mosques, schools and hospitals: this land was redistributed to peasants, while the schools were replaced with secular alternatives, and the hospitals were absorbed into the state network. Most mosques were closed: their number fell from 26,279 in 1912 to 1312 in 1942. The sharia courts were phased out, and their remaining cases brought before Soviet courts. To some extent these changes went through without too much friction, because the *Jadid* (Islamic reform) movement before the revolution had already cast some doubt on the validity of the traditional Muslim legal and educational systems.

The same, however, was not true of the direct persecution launched from 1928. I have mentioned elsewhere (page 163) the resistance to the collectivization of agriculture, which threatened many settled Islamic practices. This was often accompanied by meetings of citizens persuaded 'voluntarily' to approve the closure of local mosques and their conversion into schools, clubs, cinemas or reading rooms. As for the mullahs thus displaced from their functions, they were sometimes persuaded to resign their office, publicly denouncing themselves as 'deceivers of the people'; more often, however, they were arrested and charged under an article of the criminal code, adopted only in Muslim areas, with 'exploiting the religious prejudices of the masses with the aim of overthrowing the Workers' and Peasants' Government or of provoking resistance to its law and decrees'.

In the towns the regime began an attack on some traditional Islamic customs which conflicted with the ostensible Communist morality. The most sensational campaign was that against the veiling of women, which began in 1927. On International Women's Day huge women's meetings would be held, in which the participants demonstratively cast off their veils and committed them to the flames of a large bonfire. These theatrical effects aroused very strong feelings among the more traditionally minded: some of the pioneers of the anti-veiling movement were murdered, others were beaten up or raped. Locally recruited policemen were usually unwilling to protect unveiled women against such assaults.

Similar official campaigns were instituted against ritual prayers and Ramadan fasting, both of which interfered with the regular work discipline of a planned economy: 'degrading and reactionary customs, which prevent the workers from taking an active part in the building of socialism,' an official statement called them. Payment of *zakat* (the charity tax which devout Muslims discharged) was stopped. Polygamy and the paying of *kalym* (bride-money) were forbidden as inconsistent with the Soviet legislation on the family. The pilgrimage to Mecca, which each believer was supposed to carry out once in his lifetime, was severely hampered by the tighter control the regime imposed on the frontiers, and was formally prohibited in 1935, as part of the strategy of isolating Soviet Muslims from their co-believers abroad.

Violent resistance to these measures was usually sporadic and uncoordinated. There were, however, widespread revolts among the mountain peoples of the North Caucasus in 1928–9, which had to be quelled by Russian troops. Among the Chechen people several Imams appeared and proclaimed a Holy War against the enemies of Allah. In Central Asia the Basmachi movement revived, with outlawed mullahs, up-rooted villagers and fugitive nomads among their numbers.

Although the persecution clearly diminished the open practice of the Islamic faith, it is quite impossible to estimate its effect on private belief and the maintenance of Islamic family customs – except to say that these seem to have been very tenacious. Perhaps, in fact, the persecution had an effect similar to that on the Christian faith: to drive it partly underground and intensify it. If that is so, the effect among Muslims may have been even more profound. Scholars have become aware in recent years of the continued existence of *tariqat,* or secret brotherhoods, well adapted to sustaining the faith underground even in times of intense repression. The tariqat derive their traditions from the Sufi branch of Islam, which is mystical, militant and conservative in its orientation. The term *tariqa* strictly denotes the *way* or *path* by which the believer comes to God. Its adherents learn devotional practices from a master (usually called a *shaikh*), and form a brotherhood, around which are lay workers practising a secular trade. The brotherhoods can thus be concealed in a workshop, plantation or collective farm. They can carry on the Muslim education which is not available publicly, and they can perform the ceremonies – circumcision, marriage, burial – in forms no longer permitted in society at large.

The tariqat have a tradition of resistance to outside rule dating back many centuries. They are known to have been involved in the Basmachi rebellions, and they probably also played a part in the violent resistance to collectivization, especially in the North Caucasus, where Soviet sources have reported that more believers gravitate to the brotherhoods than to the official mosques, few of which in any case remain open. By driving so many Muslim believers underground in the late twenties and thirties the regime seems to have enormously strengthened the tariqat. The full consequences of this perhaps still remain to be seen.

Soviet nationality policy in the Muslim areas aimed above all at forestalling any attempt to create either pan-Islamic or pan-Turkic unity. That is why the Bashkirs, close relatives of the Tatars and almost assimilated by them, were given their own republic, where the Bashkir population was initially only 25 per cent, and were encouraged to develop their own literary language, distinct from that of the Tatars. Both

Bashkir and Tatar republics were given only autonomous status within the RSFSR (Russian Republic). At the same time, the Tatar diaspora in other parts of the Soviet Union (which had been a powerful force in the dissemination of Jadid and pan-Islamic ideas) were gradually deprived of the right to publish newspapers or conduct schooling in their own language. Tatar influence and Tatar national feeling were to be strictly confined within the Tatar Autonomous Republic itself.

In the mountain region of the Caucasus, political fragmentation was carried to an extreme. Numerous tiny national republics were set up, inside the RSFSR, each conferring national status on more or less tribal units. Sometimes the new administrative divisions were formed in such a way as to bring together peoples of very different languages, while dividing those whose tongues were related, as in the case of the Kabardin-Balkar Autonomous Republic, and the Karachai-Circassian Autonomous Region. Arabic, which had been the religious language of all of them, and the means of common communication, was prohibited. In the southern area beyond the Caucasus, by contrast, Azerbaidjani was selected as the language and culture to be adopted by a variety of disparate ethnic and linguistic groups. Perhaps the close relationship with Persian culture made it less likely that Azerbaidjani could ever function as a focus for pan-Turkism.

Turkestan in Central Asia, the other great area where a pan-Turkic movement might take root, was decreed to contain five principal distinct nations, the Kazakh, Kirgiz, Uzbek, Tadzhik and Turkmen, each of which by 1936 had its own Union Republic. The Kirgiz Republic was a completely artificial creation: its people spoke virtually the same language as the Kazakhs, and differed from them only in being mountain-dwellers rather than nomads of the plains – indeed, till the 1920s the Kazakhs were generally known to outsiders as Kirgiz.

The Tadzhiks were a mountain people speaking an Iranian

language and enjoying strong links with their co-nationals across the border in Afghanistan. Their communities were closely intermingled with the Uzbeks, which led to conflicts between the two: Tadzhiks living in Uzbekistan resented having to go to Uzbek schools. The Uzbeks, the most numerous and urbanized nationality of the area, also absorbed other small Turkic peoples, and the old lingua franca of the region, Chagatai, was definitively replaced by Uzbek, even though that was the tongue of only one people. The formation of the Turkmen nation, by contrast, was relatively unproblematic: the nomadic tribes of the huge desert area east of the Caspian adopted spontaneously a single written language and set of institutions.

All the official languages of the Caucasus and Central Asia, however, suffered from a double alphabet reform. In 1929 they were all required to abandon their local script and adopt the Latin one. Then, ten years later, there was a change of policy, and the Cyrillic script used by the Russians was imposed on them. This did much to disorient the first mass literate generation of these nations. It also cut off future generations from the past culture of their own peoples, except where the Soviet authorities saw fit to republish ancient works in the modern alphabet. This historic break has weighed heavily on the subsequent culture of the Muslim peoples. It was supplemented by efforts to Sovietize the local literatures. Native poets, disoriented by the sharp changes taking place in social life and culture, would be co-opted by officials from the Union of Soviet Writers, offered a contract to write an epic in the local language on Lenin or Stalin, or on the collectivization of agriculture. They would be provided with a translator who would produce a Russian version of their work. These local writers, bestowed with privileges and honours, would become members of a multinational cultural elite, with its headquarters in Moscow, losing their local roots and their feeling for their own people's experience.

The practice of 'divide and rule' was further implemented by sending in outsiders, usually Russians or Ukrainians, to carry out senior administrative functions. In theory, Communist policy was to encourage the emergence of native elites (*korenizatsiya*, or the putting down of roots), but in practice, rapid economic and administrative change, not always acceptable to local populations, had to be handled largely by outsiders. This was especially true of the agricultural collectivization, after which some republics were for a time completely deprived of local leaders (see page 192). Kazakhstan was particularly badly affected, since there collectivization, on top of everything else, meant the forcible imposition of settled arable farming on nomadic peoples. The party delegates sent to enforce this policy had even less idea of a pastoral economy than of an arable one, and they failed to make proper provision for the absorption of huge herds of livestock into the new collectives. Between 1929 and 1932 the cattle and especially sheep in Kazakhstan were literally decimated, falling from 36,000 to just over 3000, according to Soviet figures. The proportion of Kazakhs living by livestock-breeding fell from around 80 per cent to only just over a quarter. This was a crippling assault on the nation's economy and its traditions, and virtual civil war erupted. The Basmachi, who had declined in the late twenties, revived, their numbers fed by those who refused to enter the collectives: they would raid kolkhozy, killing all the officials and party workers. Hundreds of thousands of Kazakhs migrated with their herds across the border into Chinese Turkestan. Some 15–20 per cent of the entire population was lost, according to Soviet figures, from what must have been a mixture of emigration, disease and violence.

The Five Year Plans for industry also affected national feeling in the Central Asian republics, for they introduced an appreciable colonial element into the relationship with Moscow. In Uzbekistan, for example, the first Five Year Plan envisaged reducing cereal production, in order to concentrate on an enormous growth in the output of cotton, most of which would go as raw materials to the factories of European Russia. This trade pattern threatened to reduce Uzbekistan to the status of purveyor of cash crops to a monopolistic market – a 'banana republic' in disguise. There was much local resistance to this policy. Under the slogan, 'You cannot eat cotton', the prime minister of the Uzbek Republic, F. Khodzhaev, and the first party secretary, A. Ikramov, drew up alternative plans for economic development, which would ensure the republic much greater economic independence and diversity. These plans were turned down, and both men were arrested, tried and executed in 1938 for 'bourgeois nationalism'.

In general, where the nationalities were concerned, the revolution of 1917 left, as we saw in Chapter 4, an ambiguous heritage. On the one hand they had been freed from the overt Russification practised by the last tsars, and they had been given a promise of 'self-determination'. Some of them had actually known a brief period of national independence. On the other hand, they found themselves after 1921 reintegrated into a new kind of Russian Empire, ruled monopolistically by a party which was tightly centralized and dominated by Russians.

During the 1920s this dual heritage worked itself out in different ways in the different republics. In the Ukraine, for example, the ruling local Communists were convinced believers in Ukrainian autonomy, at least in the cultural and educational sense. They set about establishing the Ukrainian language in all government offices and law courts, and ensuring that every primary schoolchild on Ukrainian territory learnt it, and through it the literature and history of the Ukraine. The twenties became, in fact, the richest period that Ukrainian culture had ever experienced, with the encouragement of Ukrainian historical and ethnographic societies, and of abundant publication in the Ukrainian language. Such was the extent of this Ukrainization, that it aroused much resentment among the substantial minorities of Russians and Jews who lived in the republic, especially in the cities and the eastern parts. They tended to despise

Ukrainian as a 'peasant dialect', and were very bitter at having to learn it to conduct official business, or having to bring up their children speaking it. Something similar took place in Bielorussia, where the local language and culture had had even weaker roots in the cities before 1917. Altogether, the twenties were the decisive phase in creating modern Ukrainian and Bielorussian nations. Though the roots of their cultures were rural, these nations were by no means only peasant: they now had numerous urban dwellers, representatives in every social class, a written literature with its own traditions, a national history, and a language in which all the subjects on the regular school syllabus could be taught.

Furthermore, the intensive industrialization begun in the late twenties in some ways strengthened these nations. Most of the huge numbers of peasants who flooded into the towns throughout the thirties were Ukrainians and Bielorussians in their speech. Some of them were literate, and many others became so as they moved into industrial jobs; indeed, the whole process coincided with an intensive government programme to 'liquidate illiteracy'. Lev Kopelev, a Russian Jewish youth living in Kharkov (a rather Russianized city) at this time, describes in his memoirs how he identified with Ukrainian culture, and recalls that most of the new recruits in the factory where he worked were Ukrainians. A literate mass base was being created for the championship of Ukrainian and Bielorussian language and culture which had long been promoted by intellectuals and professional men: the full effects of this process were not to reveal themselves for a generation or more.

Stalin, of course, never approved of this exuberant flowering of local national cultures. He never ceased to remind his audiences that, 'in addition to the right of nations to self-determination, there is also the right of the working class to consolidate its power.' This was an ominous statement to many local nations, for their cities contained many workers who were Russians: this situation had produced strife in 1917, and could do so again. Besides, the so-called 'vanguard

of the working class', the Communist Party, was also dispro-
portionately Russian: whereas Russians formed 53 per cent
of the population, they made up 65 per cent of the party in
1927.

Stalin also made it clear that his evaluation of a national
movement depended on political factors. Thus, in a
fundamental lecture on the national question to the Sverdlov
University in 1924 he argued that the nineteenth- and
twentieth-century Egyptian national movement, though led
by members of the bourgeoisie, was 'progressive', while the
British attempts to suppress it were 'reactionary', even when
the British government was headed by socialists. When
applied to the Soviet Union, of course, such arguments naturally led to the conclusion that movements in favour of
national autonomy and diversity were directed against the
unity of the state, and hence were 'bourgeois' and
'reactionary', whatever their class composition. Already in
1926 he was reproaching Shumsky, Ukrainian commissar for
education, that his policies were taking the form of 'a struggle
for the alienation of Ukrainian culture and society from the
wider Soviet culture and society, the form of a struggle
against Moscow in general, against Russians in general,
against Russian culture and its highest achievement –
Leninism'.

During the 1930s Stalin set about reversing the flowering
of non-Russian national feeling. In its place a modified
Russian nationalism became the norm. The attitude to pre-
revolutionary history changed: the tsarist government, which
in the twenties historians like Pokrovsky had condemned as
backward and exploitative, now began to receive a more
favourable interpretation. The tsars had, after all, created the
territorial state which had made the Soviet Union possible,
and they had developed and spread the Russian language,
which now acted as the cement of the new socialist society.
Figures like Alexander Nevsky (celebrated in Eisenstein's film
of 1938) and Peter the Great (subject of Alexei Tolstoy's
laudatory novel, 1929–45) were rehabilitated as historically

'progressive', while those who had fought against incorporation into Russia were no longer considered 'progressive' but became 'agents of imperialism'. Bogdan Khmelnitsky, the seventeenth-century Cossack leader who had revolted against the Polish nobles and concluded an alliance submitting his country to Russia, was no longer to be seen as a 'traitor to the Ukrainian cause', but as a great and 'progressive' leader. Shamil, leader of the Islamic Caucasian mountain peoples in their resistance to tsarist Russia in the nineteenth century, underwent the opposite evolution, more complicated in his case, as he was briefly rehabilitated during the Second World War in an effort to win the support of the mountain peoples. A character from an Edward Radzinsky play of the 1960s, a historian, dramatizes the twists and turns of these national policies:

> 'My first work was about Shamil. Shamil was the leader of a national liberation movement. But views changed . . . and at the end of the 1930s he began to be considered an agent of imperialism. So I confessed my mistake. Then, during the war, he became the head of a liberation movement again. So I confessed that I had made a mistake in confessing my mistake. Later, in 1949, he once again became an agent, so I confessed that I had . . . well, you see how it was. I had been mistaken so often that I began to think I was just one great big mistake.'

These farcical tergiversations were well rooted in the ambiguities of Soviet national policy. On the whole, however, during the 1930s, a course was set against local nationalism. Compulsory use of local languages in government offices was stopped. In all primary and secondary schools the study of Russian as a second language became compulsory, while the number of schools offering instruction in Russian as a native language rose, partly to meet the influx of Russians into national republics, partly to enable parents ambitious for their children's advancement to place them in schools where they would imbibe the 'imperial' language and thus be available for promotion beyond the confines of their homeland. Russian became the generally accepted language of higher education, except in Georgia and Armenia, whose peoples adhered jealously to the primacy of their own languages.

It should not be supposed that this implantation of Russian necessarily meant Russification. The anti-religious campaign and the collectivization of agriculture had devastating effects on some national cultures, especially those which rested on a village culture and had a strong ecclesiastical component. In the Ukraine and Bielorussia, for example, most villages during the thirties lost their church, their priest, their leading farmers and their land tenure system, all of which had been important elements in the national culture. The Russians themselves scarcely suffered any less from this weakening of national culture, for much of what was characteristic about Russian culture was connected with the Orthodox Church and the peasant village. Those who regard Stalin's measures as amounting to Russification should remember the destructive effect they had on Russian culture itself. The Russian language was acting as the bearer of a new multinational party-dominated Soviet culture, not of Russian culture as that had been traditionally understood. Of course, it is not surprising that other nationalities sometimes confused Russification and Sovietization.

Those 'national Communists' who attempted to continue the policies of the twenties found themselves being purged by Stalin. The Ukraine actually underwent a double purge. The first was carried out by Pavel Postyshev – who did not even speak Ukrainian: he was an emissary sent by Stalin to eliminate local party officials who had proved reluctant to effect the brutal collectivization of agriculture or who had attempted to protect Ukrainian culture. Skrypnik, Shumsky's successor as Ukrainian commissar for education, committed suicide, as did the best known Ukrainian writer, Nicholas Khvylovy, whose funeral turned into an anti-Muscovite demonstration.

Even Postyshev, however, was not ruthless enough for Stalin: he disappeared, as did most of the members of his Central Committee, and the Ukraine was directly ruled from Moscow until Khrushchev took over as the new first secretary in Kiev in January 1938.

In Bielorussia in 1933 a three-man purge team appeared, all of them Russians, and headed by N. K. Antipov, chairman of the party's Central Control Commission. They purged the Commissariat of Education and the schools and colleges of the republic, and announced the discovery of a 'Bielorussian National Centre', allegedly receiving instructions from Poland and aiming to establish a Bielorussian Democratic Republic independent of the Soviet Union. Most of the leading party and state officials were replaced with Russians, and, according to one report, 'about 90 per cent of the Bielorussian writers and poets were arrested and most of them were shot or tortured to death in prisons.'

The two years 1937–8 saw, in fact, a replacement of virtually the entire leadership of the Communist Party in the non-Russian republics, along with their colleagues from the national Sovnarkoms and many leading writers, historians and educationalists. Many of those dismissed and arrested had been attempting in their own way to carry out the party's proclaimed national policy, that is, to encourage the development of national cultures and the emergence of local cadres to implement a limited form of self-government. They were replaced, sometimes by more docile local appointees, or more usually by the direct assignment of Russians from Moscow. The most extreme cases, apart from the Ukraine, were perhaps Kazakhstan and Turkmenistan, where at one stage the entire Politburo disappeared. From the imperfect figures we have, it also appears that the proportion of native members in non-Russian party organizations declined sharply during the purges (in Uzbekistan from 61 to 50 per cent in 1933–40; in Tadzhikistan from 53 to 45 per cent; in Kirgizia from 59 to 44 per cent in 1933–41). Overall, it cannot be doubted that the effect of the purges and arrests was to Russify party membership and bring the national party organizations under much closer control from Moscow.

From the point of view of socialization and political control another most important change was the abolition of national units inside the Red Army. Along with the primary schools, the army is probably the most important factor in modern societies when it comes to deciding the sense of national affiliation among young men. During the 1920s, with the adoption of universal military conscription, some attempt had been made, though not consistently, to form units locally, so that they were ethnically homogeneous, or at least dominated by the local nationalities. Even at that stage, commanders had usually been Russian or Ukrainian. In 1938, however, the policy of forming national units was stopped, and thereafter new recruits were often deliberately sent to do their training in ethnically mixed formations a long way from their homeland. Russian became the universal language of command and training, so that all non-Russian recruits now had to gain a minimal competence in the imperial language, if their primary schools had not already inculcated it. The Red Army became more than ever a melting pot for the multinational society – as Brezhnev was later to declare, 'Our army is a ... school of internationalism.'

Stalin's new nationalities policy was most directly and brutally manifested in the annexation of new territories during 1939–40. Under the Nazi–Soviet Pact of August 1939, the Soviet Union occupied Eastern Poland (or Western Bielorussia and Western Ukraine, according to your viewpoint), and was given the option to annex Estonia, Latvia and Lithuania, which it exercised in the summer of 1940. In all the three Baltic states very similar policies were pursued, and they unambiguously amounted not only to Russification, but also to Sovietization. Plenipotentiaries were sent in from Moscow to supervise the incorporation process: Zhdanov to Estonia, Vyshinsky to Latvia, and Dekanozov, deputy commissar for foreign affairs, to Lithuania.

They saw to the mass recruitment of agents from among the population, arresting those who refused to serve the NKVD. Under pressure from the Soviet government, new elections were held, during which opposition politicians were disqualified and had their meetings broken up; many were arrested. As a result, pro-Soviet governments were elected, which finally requested incorporation as Union republics into the Soviet state.

During the following year, the Soviet authorities effected a complete transformation of the social structure of the Baltic nations. All bank accounts above a very small figure were frozen. Businesses and manufactures were nationalized. A radical land reform expropriated all but very small private holdings to form a State Land Reserve. The universities and schools were purged, and standardized Soviet-style syllabuses were imposed; libraries were 'cleansed' of books which reflected favourably on national independence, or glorified the nation's past history. To forestall any conceivable opposition, systematic large-scale deportations were carried through: these aimed to remove from their homeland all known members of non-Communist political parties, all officials of the 'bourgeois' regime, landowners, businessmen, clergymen and leading intellectuals. In the course of a single night (14–15 June 1941) more than 60,000 Estonians were deported, along with 34,000 Latvians and 38,000 Lithuanians. Rounded up with no more than a few hours' notice to gather their possessions, they were herded to railway stations, loaded into cattle trucks without adequate food, water or sanitation, and transported to Siberia or Central Asia. Many perished on the way. Families were usually split up, men being sent to labour camps, women and children to exile settlements. In this way, some 4 per cent of the Estonian population, and some 1.5–2 per cent of the Latvian and Lithuanian – those most likely to head any opposition to the new regime – were simply removed, and Russians were sent in to take over their homes and jobs. At the same time, because of the relatively high standard of living of the Baltic republics, some factories were dismantled and their equipment taken to other republics, while cattle and grain were confiscated to feed townsfolk and the army elsewhere in the Soviet Union.

In Eastern Poland, the situation was if anything even worse. The Soviets carried out similar deportations there, and up to a million people were forcibly expelled before the outbreak of war in 1941. Most subsequent accounts of labour camp life mention at least one or two such Polish zeks, so it is probable that they were widely dispersed in the Gulag empire. In addition to this, a large number of Polish army officers and intellectuals simply disappeared. Despite persistent official Soviet denials, it is now generally assumed by historians that these Poles were killed in mass shootings by the NKVD in the Katyn forest west of Smolensk, where mass graves were discovered by the German occupiers in 1943. Certainly, such a measure would have been wholly compatible with the policies the Soviets were pursuing in the other territories they annexed in 1939–40.

With the outbreak of war, risings took place in all the Baltic nations, and indeed seem to have gained control briefly – as Soviet officials hastily decamped – before the Germans arrived. Since it was not German policy to recognize any kind of national government in their occupied territories, those who wished to uphold national independence had no choice but to go underground, to bring out clandestine newspapers or carry out acts of sabotage against the occupiers. A few armed partisan groups formed, especially in the forests of eastern Lithuania.

Following their reoccupation in 1944, the Soviet authorities continued their pre-war policies, rounding them off with a mass collectivization of agriculture in 1949. This was accompanied by the deportation of 'kulaks': between sixty and a hundred thousand people were transported to Siberia or Kazakhstan in the same way as their predecessors in 1940. Peasants who managed to elude the NKVD transport squads went into hiding in the forests. There they joined the partisans or 'forest brotherhoods', who had banded together to resist the renewed Soviet occupation and to prepare for what many hoped was an imminent Western–Soviet war. Living in outhouses and bunkers, supplied with food by the local population and equipped with abandoned German arms, these groups numbered at their height several tens of thousands: perhaps 0.5 per cent of the population. They would raid Soviet supply trains, attack and murder Soviet officials, and even occasionally take control of a small town for a few days, flying the national flag from the church tower. But in the long run, of course, they were overwhelmingly outnumbered, and they received no support from abroad, so that they could not replace or even sometimes repair their arms. They seem to have been finally crushed by about 1952, but their survival in some places for eight years against such odds testifies to the degree of support they enjoyed among the local population.

In the Ukraine too a guerrilla army survived the successive occupations by the Soviets and Germans, and lived on till the early fifties, hiding in the forests, carrying out lightning raids on Soviet installations and personnel, and relying on the support of most of the population. This war is one of the unknowns of modern European history: virtually no survivors have lived to tell of what they experienced. The leader of the Organization of Ukrainian Nationalists, Stepan Bandera, was murdered in West Germany by the Soviet security police in 1959.

The mistreatment of these western peoples of the Soviet Union is exceeded only by the deportation of certain *entire* small nations from the Crimea and Caucasus region. The first to whom this measure was applied were the Volga Germans, in 1941. Then, in the later stages of war, the same was done to the Crimean Tatars, to the Meskhetian people from Georgia, to the Kalmyks of the steppe, and to four Islamic mountain peoples, the Chechens, Ingushes, Balkars and Karachais. They were all accused of having collaborated with the Germans, but it is clear that this was not always the case.

The Volga Germans were deported before they had a chance to do so – though this, it could be argued, was a prophylactic measure – and only the Tatars and Kalmyks had known an appreciable period of German occupation. What probably *is* true is that these nations had all proved exceptionally resistant to Sovietization in the 1930s, and that Stalin was anxious to crush, before it could arise, any further possible resistance in the post-war transition period.

At any rate the operation was devised with inventive ruthlessness. In some cases, it is reported, the Soviet authorities, in deference to the warlike traditions of the peoples, invited the menfolk to celebrate Red Army Day at a banquet, which, as the traditions of hospitality required, they would attend unarmed. While they sat merrymaking in full dress uniform, the NKVD dragged the women and children out of their homes and loaded them on to cattle trucks bound eastwards. They then did the same to the replete and drunken men, who were in no condition to resist. Most of the mountain peoples were resettled in the plains of Kazakhstan, where to survive they had to take up a form of agriculture that was unfamiliar to them. Many of them abandoned it, and went off to live in shanty suburbs on the edges of the towns. Families sometimes survived together, but the children had to attend schools where the only language of tuition was Russian. It seems, in short, as if Stalin intended to eliminate these nations as separate entities by depriving them of their homeland, their economy, their customs, their religion and their language.

One nationality occupied a very distinctive position in the Soviet Union: that was the Jews. Discriminated against by the tsarist government, the Jews were natural recruits to the revolutionary movement, and in many respects beneficiaries of the events of 1917–21. They were numerous in the Communist Party, and included some of its best-known figures: Trotsky, Zinoviev, Kamenev, Sverdlov, Radek. Notoriously some of the most vehement opponents of communism identified it with the Jewish 'international conspiracy'.

As a result of the revolution, discrimination against Jews was abolished, and access was opened for them to every geographical area and to every kind of education and profession. Many Jews moved out of the Pale, the western area of Russia to which the tsarist government had confined them, and during the twenties set up in business or the professions, settling in the large cities. Many, however, did not leave the old Pale. There was now a major divide in Soviet Jewry, between those who moved to the big towns, spoke Russian and had assimilated to a kind of joint Russian–Soviet nationality, and those who remained behind in the *shtetl* (the little home town in the west of Russia), spoke Yiddish, kept up the Judaic religion and maintained a distinctively Jewish identity in customs and family life.

The Soviet state, however, insisted on equating both groups, and imposing the same national label on both of them. The national label arose as part of the internal passport legislation of 1932: for each passport carried within it the later notorious 'entry no. 5', where officials registered a citizen's nationality. A child was normally assigned the nationality of its mother: it did not, however, receive its own passport till the age of sixteen, and might at that stage, if its parents were of different nationality, opt instead for the father's nationality. After that, there was no possibility of further change – whereas in tsarist Russia, a Jew had been able to change to Russian nationality by being baptized. The Soviet national designation was thus, in direct contradiction to Marxist theory, essentially a racial one.

This national identification might not have mattered very much had it not been for certain other peculiarities of the Jews' situation. Their religious language, Hebrew, was banned. Unlike other nationalities, moreover, they had no territory of their own. It is true that in the late twenties the government declared the area of Birobidzhan, on the Manchurian border, to be 'a national Jewish unit, administratively and territorially'. But few Jews ever went there, for the climate was harsh, the soil swampy and mosquito-infested. For Jews, who had no tradition of agriculture, such a forbidding environment was wholly unsuitable as a national home, and the Jewish population of Birobidzhan never reached more than some 14,000.

So most of the Jews who left the shtetl went to the big cities. There they attained a level of education higher than that enjoyed by any other Soviet nationality. This was not because the government specifically favoured them, but the traditional demand among Jews, especially urban ones, for higher education was very strong, and the government in the twenties and early thirties was not discriminating *against* them. At any rate, around 1935 nearly a third of Jews of student age were receiving some form of higher or specialist education. They consequently performed very well in the competition for entry to the professions, constituting, for example, some 16 per cent of Soviet doctors and around 10 per cent of university teachers, cultural personnel and engineers – compared with a share of some 3 per cent in the Soviet population as a whole.

Hitler's invasion, of course, brought untold suffering and destruction to the Soviet Jews. Some were rounded up and murdered at mass graves on the edges of cities, like the notorious ravine of Baby Yar, just outside Kiev. Others were transported to the death camps of German-occupied Poland. From a figure of about 4.8 million in 1940 the Soviet Jewish population fell to 2.3 million by 1959, the next census. The destruction was, however, much greater among the more traditional Jews of the old Pale than among the more urbanized and assimilated ones. One might have thought, indeed, that Hitler's brutal surgery would have gone some way towards eradicating the separate Jewish identity, leaving behind those who were anyway gradually being absorbed into a general Soviet or Russian sense of nationhood.

Two things prevented this from happening. One was that the Soviet government began to play on the long-established tradition of popular anti-Semitism in Russia. The other was, of course, 'entry no. 5'.

Anti-Semitic prejudices among Russians and Ukrainians had flared up violently during the revolutionary years, resulting in sickening pogroms. They had never wholly abated afterwards. During the 1920s, for example, nepmen were often regarded as Jewish, an identification which some members of the party did nothing to discourage. Later on, there was much grumbling and resentment at the Jews' relative success in gaining university places and good jobs. It was not, however, till anti-Jewish discrimination became official policy, after 1945, that Jews began to feel themselves trapped by 'entry no. 5' on the passports they had to bring with them whenever they were seeking education, housing or employment. By 1947, for instance, Moscow University was reported to be applying a rigid quota to Jews among their entrants, and turning away Jewish 'medal-winners' – that is, those who had come out top in the all-Union entrance examinations. Viktor Perelman, later an editor in the newspaper *Literaturnaya gazeta*, recalls that when he graduated from the prestigious Institute of State and Law in 1951, no one would employ him as a lawyer, and he became first of all a book-keeper and then a journalist. And the dissenter Vladimir Bukovsky later remembered with shame that, during the hysteria over the Doctors' Plot (see below, page 316), one Jewish boy in his class at school was beaten up every day at break: the teachers did not intervene, but simply told the boy afterwards to go and clean off the blood and dirt.

The establishment of the state of Israel in 1948 made the Jews doubly unlike any other Soviet nationality. Not only had they no territory at home, but now they actually did have a potential one abroad. Given the post-war concern, even hysteria, about spies and subversion, that could have only one consequence. Official discrimination moved on from mere discrimination to active persecution. Stalin's campaign against 'cosmopolitans' was mainly directed against Jews, who were now far more likely than anyone else to lose their jobs and be arrested. Everyone was encouraged to sniff out

'Zionists' (those who allegedly wished to abandon the idea of a socialist homeland, and work instead for the national state of Israel). The trials of East European Communist leaders in 1949–52 constantly featured accusations of 'Zionism' against the defendants. The campaign of vilification created an atmosphere where it began to seem natural that a nationwide purge of Jews would follow. In 1948 the Jewish Anti-Fascist Committee, set up during the war to enlist Jewish support in the struggle against the Germans, was abruptly disbanded. Its chairman, the Yiddish dramatist, Solomon Mikhoels, was murdered on Stalin's orders, the Jewish theatre in Moscow was closed, and virtually every well-known Yiddish writer and cultural figure was arrested. Twenty-six of them were executed in 1952, accused of plotting to make the Crimea a Jewish territory and then hand it over to the British and Americans. Rumours began to abound that all Jews were to be rounded up and deported to Siberia.

It was in this atmosphere that Stalin launched his fabrication of the so-called Doctors' Plot, which formed part of the mysterious circumstances surrounding his death.

Overall, Stalin attempted to foreclose on the ambiguities of Lenin's nationalities policy by strengthening its centralizing tendencies at the expense of 'national self-determination'. This was not really Russification, but rather 'Sovietization' or 'Communization'. It involved subjecting all nationalities, including the Russians, to the centralized political control of the party and to the economic domination of the centralized planning apparatus. Even in Russian areas, this involved a weakening of the national identity in the religious, agrarian and cultural spheres. In non-Russian areas it entailed in addition a reduction in the use of the national language. Since the language and culture of Sovietization were in fact Russian, it was inevitable that this policy should seem like Russification, and should be resented as such by those who had to endure it. But in practice local languages continued throughout to be used as the medium of instruction in primary schools, and some publication in the local languages still survived; there was no attempt, as there had been under the tsars, to prevent a national culture from emerging at all. On the contrary, the liquidation of illiteracy, the establishment of universal primary education and the migration of millions of rural dwellers into the towns, all had the effect of intensifying local national consciousness in a very real sense, even as Stalin was draining political and economic power away from the national republics. New nations, in fact, were taking shape under extreme pressure, and old ones were struggling to keep their culture alive. The party was, furthermore, trying to encourage the emergence of native elites who could lead the national republics. This policy of korenizatsiya was rudely interrupted by the purges of the late thirties, but it was not terminated, so that, by Stalin's death, stable national Communist Party elites were forming, selected by the nomenklatura system and woven into it. These men later on became power-brokers between an authoritarian centre and national consciousness back at home.

If Stalin's policy was to move towards a single Soviet nation with a Russian language and culture, then he made some progress towards it. But at the same time, the heritage of the revolution, plus the unintended effects of Stalin's own policies, also generated opposite tendencies and left a paradoxical and potentially explosive situation for his successors.

A peasant woman returns to the ruins of her home in Bielorussia after the Germans were driven out in 1944 (*Keystone*)

Russian peasants being interrogated by a German occupation official during the war. Note the *starosta*, the German-appointed village headman, standing guard over the villagers (*Keystone*)

A family at the entrance to a dugout or air-raid shelter of the kind in which many had to live after the war (*Keystone*)

10

The Great Fatherland War

It is very difficult for a Westerner to write about the Soviet-German war of 1941–5. This is partly because of the sources. The war has produced a greater flood of prose than any other period of Soviet history – which is itself a significant fact – but much of it is written by officers in the armed forces, is concerned narrowly with the military side of the war, and insofar as what they write reflects on wider issues, it is usually stilted and ritualized. Universal heroism is the order of the day, and criticism of the higher leadership was by and large only attempted in the works written during the short-lived 'de-Stalinization' of 1956 to 1965 or so. Relatively few Soviet sources give a real sense of what life was like for the great majority of the population, in the rear, or (for some of them) in German-occupied territory.

Even more important than this, the sheer scale of the war, the extent of the sacrifices it demanded of the Soviet peoples daunts our imagination because we in the West have never experienced anything like it, even during that same war. This becomes clear even if we merely consider the stark fact that Soviet losses were probably some forty times those suffered by Britain or some seventy times those suffered by the United States. And this is without taking into account the immeasurably greater cruelty with which the Germans treated the Russians, the catastrophic shortages of housing, food and basic services with which the ordinary people had to cope. To understand what the Soviet peoples lived through, and how they achieved their victory, we have to make a special effort of the imagination, especially since the leadership which directed their efforts had only just inflicted horrifying sufferings on those same peoples.

When the Germans invaded at dawn on 22 June 1941, they achieved total surprise (for reasons considered below, page 269), and complete mastery of the air. This, together with the inept initial responses of the Soviet commanders, ensured them a lasting superiority. The early goals of the Barbarossa invasion plan were achieved in full. Smolensk, more than half way to Moscow, was captured by mid-July, and by the end of August Army Group North directly threatened Leningrad. The Germans encountered tougher resistance in the Ukraine, where the quality of the Soviet command was higher, but even there they were poised to take Kiev by the end of August. Thereafter, however, Hitler hesitated about his next objective, and failed to press home attacks on Leningrad and Moscow, in order instead to secure the greater industrial riches of the Ukraine and the ultimate goal, the oil wells of the Caspian. By the time Army Group Centre did move on Moscow, the autumn had set in, and the roads soon became ribbons of deep mud, which minimized the normal advantages enjoyed by motorized formations and blunted the impact of Blitzkrieg. A month later, the Germans were approaching Moscow, in spite of everything , but they were totally unprepared for winter combat and found themselves at the end of very long lines of communications passing through country where the inhabitants were rapidly becoming hostile to them.

This was the first turning point of the war. Stalin brought his most promising senior commander, Georgy Zhukov, to Moscow and gave him fresh divisions, tanks and aircraft withdrawn from Siberia – where the intelligence network of Richard Sorge had told him there was no danger from Japan. Zhukov organized the defence of the capital just in time – visitors to Moscow today can still see, on the way in from Sheremetevo Airport, an anti-tank obstacle marking the furthest point reached by the Germans. The Red Army stopped the Wehrmacht, and even threw it back some distance, but failed to encircle large numbers of troops, as Zhukov had initially hoped. Even so, this was the first time that the German Blitzkrieg strategy had ever met a serious setback, and Stalin ordered that it be exploited by a general offensive, along the whole length of the front. This proved quite beyond the capacity of the Red Army, and only weakened its strength and morale at a critical time, so that when the Wehrmacht resumed its offensive in spring 1942, it once more met with success.

The following period, up to the early autumn of 1942, was in some ways the most discouraging one of the whole war. The German army pressed ever onward across the steppes of the Ukraine, taking Kharkov, the Crimea and Rostov-on-Don. In private – though they did not voice their feelings in public – most Soviet citizens began to be haunted by the question, 'How much further can we retreat?' The end came in September 1942, when the Germans reached Stalingrad, on the Volga. Beyond lay only the Asiatic steppes, or – turning to the north – the deep rear, well behind Moscow. In Stalingrad the Red Army made a determined stand, while Hitler, mesmerized perhaps by the city's name, resolved to take it. The ferocious street fighting which ensued showed the Red Army at its best, with small, courageous and tough groups of infantry now reasonably well-equipped, while the German Panzer armies were hopelessly constricted, operating on greatly overstretched communications, and quite unable to display their true qualities.

Meanwhile the Soviet Command prepared a classical and highly effective counterattack across the River Don, launched on 19 November 1942, into the rear of the German Sixth Army, which Hitler ordered to stand fast in Stalingrad. The result was its encirclement and eventual capitulation. The Germans thereupon withdrew their advance troops, which had got as far as the peaks of the Caucasus, and commenced a long retreat across the Ukraine.

Thereafter the Red Army was able gradually to mobilize

the long-term advantages over Germany afforded by the much larger Soviet population, the country's richer resources, and the help of its allies, Britain, France and the United States. A relocated Soviet industry was now turning out in sufficient quantities the ammunition and equipment needed – including items like the T-34 tank and the Katyusha mortar, which were superior to anything the Wehrmacht possessed. More and more often the Red Army was able to achieve superiority in numbers, equipment and air cover. This was demonstrated in the huge tank battle around Kursk in July 1943, the first time the Germans had ever been defeated at their own speciality: mobile armoured warfare. All this did not go without setbacks – in spring 1943, for example, the Germans were able to recapture Kharkov for a few months. But in general it was clear that the Soviets could only win in the long run, especially if their Western allies opened a second front in France, as they finally did in June 1944.

The Soviet advance was slow and on the whole methodical. Unlike their German counterparts, the Soviet commanders did not seek a war of rapid movement, but preferred well-prepared, deliberate and massive offensives in areas of marked local superiority. Even when that is said, however, there was one peculiar feature about their strategy. In the summer of 1944 the Red Army halted its offensive on the northern front, only just outside Warsaw, and, instead of taking the direct route to Berlin, spent the autumn and much of the winter conquering the Balkans. Perhaps Stalin's reasoning was political. The Polish resistance movement, whose chief component, the Home Army, was anti-Communist, had just declared its hand in August 1944 by rising in Warsaw: it may well have suited Stalin to leave the Germans the onerous task of suppressing them, while he secured Romania and Hungary. Certainly he refused to allow American and British planes to land behind Soviet lines in order to drop supplies to the Home Army.

Only in mid-January 1945 did the offensive in Poland

resume – by which time the Polish insurgents had been annihilated – carrying the Red Army to Berlin by late April. Hitler's suicide followed, and the final capitulation of Germany came on 9 May.

The period before the outbreak of war and the early months of combat showed the Soviet system at its most rigid and cumbersome. It is true that serious preparations for war were being made – indeed, this had been the case ever since Hitler's accession to power in January 1933. But these preparations were often poorly conceived and executed, partly as a result of Stalin's purge of his best commanders in 1937–8, and partly because, after concluding the Nazi–Soviet Pact in August 1939, Stalin seems to have placed excessive faith in it, trusting it to guarantee Soviet security permanently, or at least for several years, while the shortcomings in the armed forces were remedied.

The Red Army, which took the full force of the German assault in June 1941, had experienced, ever since its creation, a paradoxical and sometimes tense relationship with the society of which it was a part, and with the political leadership to which it was subordinated. On the other hand, it was a formative institution in that society, and its customs profoundly influenced party and state during the twenties and thirties. We have seen above (page 86) how it provided cadres for the party, and in 1928 Voroshilov estimated that two-thirds of the chairmen of rural soviets in the RSFSR were former Red Army men. Yet, on the other hand, with the failure of the 'labour armies' in 1920–1, the army had never actually become a working model for the creation of a new society – as later happened in the socialist revolutions of China and Vietnam. While the Communist nucleus in the army was recognized and encouraged, the political leaders never forgot that the bulk of both officers and men were drawn from social classes – the *voenspetsy* (military specialists) and the peasants – who were at best indifferent, at worst hostile, to the regime. For especially tricky operations, like those against the Antonov insurgency in Tambov and against the Kronstadt soviet, special Cheka troops and party activists were in the vanguard, rather than ordinary soldiers. Furthermore, after the end of the civil war, the army was very speedily demobilized down to about a tenth of its strength in 1920. Voenspetsy were given early retirement as soon as they could be replaced by young officers from the Komsomol.

Above all, the party kept an eye on the 'commanders' (as officers were then called) – even those of proletarian background and Red training – through its network of 'political commissars', who were answerable to the party Central Committee, and not to the Commissariat of Defence or the Armed Forces Command. The relationship of the commissar to the commander of his unit was redefined several times between 1925 and 1941, and the result was confusion and a good deal of resentment. From 1925 the commissar's powers were theoretically limited where the commander was himself a party member; but, in practice, even in such units the commissar did not always confine himself to 'responsibility for the moral and political condition of the unit', as the regulations prescribed, but tended to behave as if he possessed the full authority of the commander. Thus, when Petro Grigorenko arrived in 1934 as a new and self-confident Red battalion chief of staff in Bielorussia, he was disconcerted and annoyed to discover the commissar giving orders directly to Grigorenko's own assistants, and commandeering battalion staff cars without permission in order to go off on fishing trips. Such behaviour, irksome for any commander, must have seemed especially outrageous to the new Red commanders, who felt that they deserved the party's trust, and that their status and experience should absolve them from such conflicts of authority.

Similar tensions no doubt underlay the particularly vicious treatment Stalin accorded to the armed forces in his purges, during which political commissars were once again given equal and, where necessary, countervailing powers to the commanders. All commanders, both those who survived the purges and those who were subsequently promoted, got the message that strict obedience to orders was the most sought-after quality, and that any personal initiative was to be avoided, lest it lead to a 'mistake'. This undermined the capacity of field commanders to respond to the unexpected: their rigidity was demonstrated in the army's poor performance in the Finnish campaign of the winter of 1939–40, and in the opening months of the German war.

The quality of the command at the very top was also vitiated by the purges. Marshal Tukhachevsky had been training a new generation attuned to the opportunities presented by the tank, the aircraft and the armoured car. At the time of his death, Tukhachevsky had just issued an updated set of field service regulations, which envisaged a new combined-operations type of warfare, with infantry being complemented by specialized armoured and motorized units, and acting with air support. This new generation of senior commanders was destroyed and replaced under the eye of Stalin's civil war cronies, Voroshilov and Budenny, who were sceptical about the value of all these new-fangled techniques and preferred to rely on the cavalry units that had defeated the Whites twenty years before. The motor transport service as a separate administration was wound up, and production of new tank models (including the later famous T-34) was conducted at a snail's pace. The same was true of fighter aircraft, since their principal designer, Tupolev, was in a labour camp (where, however, he was given special conditions and allowed to continue his work as a kind of privileged slave). Most inexplicable of all, the old fortifications on the pre-1939 western frontier were dismantled *before* new ones could be erected further forward.

The armed forces were thus not in a position to take full advantage of the benefits the country's new industry placed before them. Nevertheless, much *had* been done to improve the quality and standing of the armed forces – even if some of it was carried out in a desperate hurry after the disastrous Finnish war. The improvements in the secondary educational system meant that both commanders and men were better able to cope with the technical demands of modern warfare; pre-military training had been extended into the schools and often included technical instruction on the new weapons. The status and training of commanders were also improved considerably during the late thirties – at least for those who survived or profited from the purges. Military service was made into an attractive lifetime professional career: ranks were reintroduced, more or less as before 1917, with regular promotion procedures, based partly on seniority, partly on merit. Commanders were allotted superior housing, while a separate network of shops, *voentorg*, assured them of high-quality goods and services. Saluting between commanders and men was restored for the first time since 1917, and discipline was generally tightened up. The army newspaper *Krasnaya zvezda* (Red Star) explicitly condemned 'party and Komsomol interference in the functions of commanders', quoting with disapproval the case of a junior commander who said to his superior, 'Have you any right to give me directions? I am a Komsomol member, while you are a non-party person.' This kind of 'Communist arrogance', as Lenin had called it, was now consigned to the past.

As for ordinary recruits, universal conscription for two to three years, without exemption for higher education, ensured that a larger and better educated body of men was available. Reserve formations were converted into standing ones, so that by 1939 the Red Army had probably reattained its 1920 maximum of 5 million men under arms. They were, moreover, supplemented by at least a quarter of a million NKVD and special troops to deal with emergencies and prevent the kind of desertions that remained a horrific memory from the civil war.

On the eve of war, then, the Red Army was improving the calibre both of its officers and of its men, and was beginning to heal the bitter rifts between party and military. But it had not got very far with either process, and had not adapted itself to the German Blitzkrieg strategy. That adaptation now had to be accomplished on the battlefield.

As I have said, the German invasion on 22 June 1941 took the Soviet armed forces by surprise. That it did so is remarkable, for the Soviet leaders had received repeated warnings of the German preparations over the previous few months, from the British and Americans, from their own intelligence services, and indeed from their commanders on the western front. This unpreparedness shows a characteristic defect of the totalitarian system: it is very bad at assimilating and evaluating information unwelcome to the leadership. Because Stalin chose to dismiss the growing evidence of German intentions as 'provocation' or 'misinformation', none of his subordinates was able to take it seriously, and still less were the public allowed to hear about it and judge for themselves. The only statement in the Soviet press about the reports called them 'clumsily concocted propaganda by powers hostile to the USSR and Germany, who are interested in a further widening and unleashing of war'. When Colonel General Kirponos, commander of the Kiev military district, wrote to Stalin proposing the evacuation of 300,000 civilians from the frontier regions, the manning of defensive positions there, and the construction of anti-tank obstacles, he was told this would be a 'provocation', and that the Germans must not be given 'a pretext for the initiation of military action against us'. He was actually instructed to countermand orders he had already issued, and pull units back from the frontier.

Even when, a mere matter of hours before the attack, Stalin was at least sufficiently alarmed to issue orders to the frontier units, these spoke of nothing more than assuming a state of alert and manning frontier posts. In case of actual attack, the only order was 'not to give way to provocative actions of any kind which might produce major complications'. Given the inflexible obedience of most Soviet commanders, such an order was bound to generate chaos, especially since, once the attack was under way, many communications lines had been cut by saboteurs, further orders often did not get through, and each commander had to improvise on the basis of the information at his disposal. As a result the German assault troops were able to deal with the Soviet formations piecemeal, surrounding them and destroying or capturing them. More than a thousand Soviet aircraft were caught on their airfields, uncamouflaged and undefended, and were annihilated: this was a catastrophic loss in view of the slow tempo of aircraft construction up to that time.

Only on the evening of that fateful day did the General Staff issue an order which at least accepted the reality of the German attack. But its content showed how out of touch with the situation the leaders still were: it called for 'deep counterthrusts with the aim of destroying the enemy's main forces and carrying operations into his territory'. The only effect of such an order could be to impede the defence in depth which was strategically necessary, and encourage units to try to move forward into positions where they would be easily surrounded.

As for Stalin himself, he suffered some kind of nervous collapse as a result of seeing one of his favourite myths, that of the imperialist threat, come true. He apparently withdrew to his dacha in the woods outside Moscow and stayed there prostrate for more than a week, while his generals and his immediate subordinates tried desperately to sort out the mess.

In the invaded regions party and state authorities hurriedly burnt their papers, and fled eastwards, abandoning the population to their fate. The NKVD shot their political prisoners and those with sentences of ten years or more, and tried to evacuate the rest: where they were unable to, they shot the rest as well before pulling out. The population, in fact, often welcomed the Germans: General Guderian recalls in his memoirs that women would come out from the villages bringing wooden platters with bread, butter and eggs to the soldiers. Peasants, in particular, hoped the Germans would dissolve the collective farms and reopen the churches; Ukrainians, Bielorussians and the Baltic peoples hoped they would permit them to establish national states of their own; and everyone hoped that the Germans, as a 'cultured' nation, would at least allow them to lead a more secure and settled existence than they had known under Stalin's terror. They were to be disappointed, but that was not immediately apparent.

The panic of those early days had a long-term demoralizing effect on the Soviet army and population. Arguably, indeed, morale did not recover completely until after the battle of Stalingrad, more than eighteen months later. Certainly, throughout the autumn of 1941, despite some heroic rearguard actions (which were important because they delayed an offensive which had to be rapid to succeed), the encirclements and disorganized retreats continued. The atmosphere of the time is well evoked by Khrushchev in his memoirs. As the Germans advanced on Kiev, where he was in charge of the party apparatus, workers came from the factories to the Central Committee, volunteering to defend the city, and asking for weapons with which to do so. Khrushchev rang Moscow, where the only person he could raise was Malenkov.

> 'Tell me,' I said, 'where can we get rifles? We've got factory workers here who want to join the ranks of the Red Army and fight the Germans, and we don't have anything to arm them with.'
> 'You'd better give up any thought of getting rifles from us. The rifles in the civil defence organization have all been sent to Leningrad.'
> 'Then what are we supposed to fight with?'
> 'I don't know – pikes, swords, home-made weapons, anything you can make in your own factories.'
> 'You mean we should fight tanks with spears?'
> 'You'll have to do the best you can. You can make fire bombs out of bottles of gasoline or kerosene and throw them at the tanks.'

Khrushchev, not surprisingly, was dismayed and indignant at this conversation. He did not tell anyone about it, for fear of sparking off panic. Suffice it to add that Kiev, where Budenny was commander, was soon the scene of another rout: at least half a million men were encircled and either died or were captured.

Not long after, Moscow itself was in danger. As an offensive of Army Group Centre, begun on 30 September, approached the capital, the order went out to evacuate government offices, the diplomatic corps, and high party bodies to Kuibyshev on the Volga, and to other towns far in the rear. Factories were mined, ready to be blown up. All this was rational in the circumstances, but it naturally induced an atmosphere of fear and uncertainty in the capital. On 15 and 16 October there was a sudden panic rush to get out of the city. Those who could wangle an official pass or commandeer a lift in a car did so, and left with the columns of official transport, leaving behind a smell of burning papers. Others dragged themselves out of the city on foot, carrying children and a few possessions in a rucksack or on a handcart.

Yet in the end Moscow never fell. In the end, too, the Soviet Union won the war, in spite of the disastrous start. How was this possible?

First of all, there was Stalin himself. Having recovered from his inaction of the early days of the war, he went on Moscow radio on 3 July 1941 to broadcast to the people. His opening words were highly significant. As well as the now habitual terms, 'comrades' and 'citizens', he also addressed his listeners as 'brothers and sisters' and as 'my friends'. He was taking as his starting point an old and traditional form of human solidarity, based on the family, to which the party had never before appealed in its propaganda, which indeed in its early years it had tried to undermine.

Similarly, in October, the Moscow panic was stemmed at least partly because, on the morning of 17 October, Alexander Shcherbakov, first secretary of the Moscow town party committee, made a broadcast announcing that Stalin was still at his post in Moscow, that he would stay there, and that the city would be defended 'to the last drop of blood'.

And three weeks later, Stalin was at his accustomed place on Lenin's mausoleum to take the salute at the military parade celebrating the anniversary of the October revolution. The decision to hold this parade as usual, within the sound of the German guns, was taken at the last moment, and surprised nearly everyone. There was no time for preparations: the troops marched past in their battle kit, and many of them proceeded straight from Red Square to the front line. Stalin's speech on that occasion again sounded some unfamiliar notes. He reminded his listeners of the emergencies the newly founded Red Army had faced and overcome in 1918, but he also appealed to pre-revolutionary traditions, to the Russia of Alexander Nevsky, Dmitri Donskoi and Mikhail Kutuzov. His words evoked the warfare of nations, not of classes. 'The German invaders want a war of extermination against the peoples of the Soviet Union. Very well, then! If they want a war of extermination, they shall have it! Our task now . . . will be to destroy every German, to the very last man, who has come to occupy our country. No mercy for the German invaders! Death to the German invaders! The enemies were now 'Germans' rather than 'fascists'. This was Stalin's 1920s slogan of 'socialism in one country' with the emphasis on the 'one country' rather than on the 'socialism'.

Konstantin Simonov, in his novel *The Living and the Dead*, published at a time when Stalin was at the nadir of his post-war reputation, described the people's reactions to these speeches. 'They loved him in different ways, wholeheartedly, or with reservations; admiring him and yet fearing him; and some did not like him at all. But nobody doubted his courage and his iron will. And now was a time when these two qualities were needed more than anything else in the man who stood at the head of the country at war.' All this was absorbed into military symbolism: the war-cry of the Soviet soldier as he went into battle was 'For the motherland! For Stalin!'

Stalin also served well as an administrator and even (with considerably greater reservations) as a military leader. The

Soviet leadership solved at an early stage a dilemma which Russia's First World War leaders had never coped with, the coordination of the civilian and military sides of government. At the highest level, this was accomplished by the State Defence Committee (GKO) under Stalin's chairmanship. This was the supreme war-directing body, with the power to issue decrees binding on all organs of party, state and armed forces. It was small: five to eight members, all of whom were civilians, except Marshal Voroshilov, who in any case was swiftly removed from operational command once his incompetence had become plain. The other members were Molotov, as Stalin's deputy; Malenkov, as senior party secretary; Beria, as head of the security police; Kaganovich and Mikoyan, as members of the party Politburo; and Voznesensky, as head of Gosplan. The principle of strictly civilian control was thereby asserted.

Military power was vested in the *Stavka*, or Supreme Command, the head of which was also Stalin. It consisted of all marshals of the Soviet Union, the chief of the General Staff and the heads of the various services and their principal arms. Members of GKO could attend Stavka meetings, which was not true the other way round. Stalin's domination of Stavka was all but absolute: few generals had the courage or self-confidence to challenge his judgement. On the other hand, he usually conducted affairs by letting his military leaders each present their arguments for particular courses of action, listening to each of them attentively, and only taking a decision at the end of the discussion. On the whole, in fact, he preferred to lead by choosing competent senior commanders, and then let them do the conceiving and planning of operations, presenting alternatives for him to adjudicate. Probably Stalin's greatest ability as a war leader was his readiness to jettison the incompetent – no matter how senior and how close to him personally, like his cronies Budenny and Voroshilov – and to seek out and promote the young and promising. He was prepared to go even into the labour camps to find the latter, as the examples of Rokossovsky, Gorbatov and Meretskov testify. When he tried to exercise his own military judgement against that of senior generals, he was very fallible. The enormous losses at Kiev in September 1941 were due to his insistence that the armies fighting there should not retreat. Similarly, his decision to launch a counteroffensive right along the front in the winter of 1942 was based on a grossly optimistic notion of Soviet strength and a similar underestimate of the enemy's. The inbuilt tendency to disbelieve bad news persisted far into the war and percolated far down the command hierarchy. The air force officer who first reported the breakthrough of German tanks towards Moscow in October 1941 was branded a 'panic-monger' by Abakumov (in charge of the security apparatus), and was about to be dismissed and court-martialled before the story was confirmed.

Both Stalin and his senior commanders, however, displayed some capacity to learn from their mistakes. This was important because, given time, Soviet resources in manpower and materials were in the end superior to Germany's: prudent marshalling of them, rather than brilliant leadership, was what was required to achieve ultimate victory. The Soviet leaders nearly failed that test, but just managed to pull themselves together.

But why did the Soviet peoples, who had so many reasons to hate Stalin, the NKVD and the Communist Party in 1941, nevertheless rally round and fight so staunchly for the system?

The most obvious reason, of course, is that it was their homeland which had been invaded. The hope that the Germans might provide more 'cultured' leadership soon evaporated as it became clear that the Nazis – and indeed on the whole the German army – regarded the Slavs as *Untermenschen*, 'subhumans', potential slaves to be ruthlessly exploited in the interests of the Great German Empire. Himmler's declaration, from a speech of 1941, summed it up: 'If ten thousand Russian females die of exhaustion digging an anti-tank ditch, that interests me only insofar as the ditch is dug for Germany.' Under this philosophy millions of Soviet civilians left behind the lines were rounded up and deported to slave labour enterprises in Germany. An even more immediate danger faced Jews and Communist party officials: execution by the special SS Einsatzkommandos.

This German brutality was a powerful incentive to the Soviet population to give of their best for the war. As a Soviet colonel remarked to a British journalist, 'In such a hell . . . the thought that a comfortable bed and breakfast – the kind of thing British prisoners get – may be secured by the simple act of surrendering to the Germans might be bad for morale. . . . It's a horrible thing to say, but by ill-treating and starving our prisoners to death, the Germans are *helping* us.'

To defend the homeland against such invaders became a sacred duty, evoked in the party's new propaganda tone of military nationalism. Furthermore, in spite of the appalling bereavements and physical sufferings of the Soviet people, in some ways their spirit actually *improved* with the outbreak of war – or at least by the time Zhukov's defence of Moscow proved that the Germans were not invincible. Looking back afterwards, Pasternak wrote: 'When war flared up, its real horrors and real dangers, the threat of a real death, were a blessing compared to the inhuman reign of fantasy, and they brought relief by limiting the magic force of the dead letter.' Or, as a humble newspaper reader put it, 'Reading *Pravda* after the German invasion was a terrible shock. Up to then you could safely assume that everything you read was pure fiction, but now you were face to face with the awful truth. *Pravda* was describing the real world.' War correspondents shared something of the life of the troops, and wrote about it with a degree of frankness and accuracy that would have been unthinkable before the war. Vasily Grossman's accounts of the battle of Stalingrad, or Ilya Ehrenburg's tirades against the Germans, were probably more widely read and appreciated than any previous Soviet journalism. In this way a certain degree of trust between rulers and ruled was restored.

Complete freedom of information was, however, not the order of the day. Soon after the outbreak of war all citizens were required to hand in their private radio sets. Thereafter only relays from public loudspeakers were permitted: the Soviet leaders did not want the people to get their news from German radio or even the BBC.

Raised morale and a new sense of national unity were crucial, but were not the only factors which contributed to the ultimate Soviet victory. The fact was that the political system itself proved in some ways well adapted to the demands of war. As we have seen, the party tended to use the rhetoric of war even in peacetime, and certainly many of its officials seemed to flourish in an atmosphere of campaigns, offensives and emergencies. This point should not be exaggerated. The extreme authoritarianism which stifled initiative and flexibility was still present, especially in the armed forces; so too were the competing cliques, squabbling over slender resources.

Nevertheless, both the party and the state functioned reasonably well as a mechanism for mobilizing the nation's resources. This was by no means a foregone conclusion: adoption of the rhetoric of war should not be confused with capacity to fight. But, especially in the emergencies of the early part of the war, the party was in a strong position to effect the rapid mobilization of military and economic resources which alone could save the situation. As the Germans approached a town which till recently had been thought to be far in the rear, a town defence committee would be hastily formed, consisting of representatives of the local front command, the town soviet, the party and the NKVD. The committee would take over local factories to make military items in short supply (see Khrushchev's dilemma above), and it would raise volunteer and Home Guard units from the working population, while trying to ensure equipment for them, as well as preparing defence lines and fortifications. So serious was the position in the autumn of 1941 that such raw units, with no combat experience and no more than a fortnight's rifle practice, had to be sent to plug gaps in the front line.

Thus, for example, in the Lenin raion of Moscow, a Home Guard division of 16,000 volunteers was formed during the first week of July. Care had to be exercised to ensure that factories were not deprived of their key skilled workers, many of whom volunteered. Even some professors apparently offered their services, concealing their degrees, and were annoyed to be rejected and sent back to their work. One of them, the aged academician B. A. Keller, insisted that they requisition his car for use at the front. The new formation, many of whose members had never even held a rifle before, had a week's training at a camp (which they had to help build) just outside Moscow, and then were sent on to the forward defence line at Maloyaroslavets, about 100 kilometres to the south-west of the capital. They did further training there while helping to build fortifications. In mid-September they became part of the 33rd Reserve Army, and were moved into the front line, where they took part in action from the first day.

Their induction into service was almost leisurely compared with what happened in October, when some Home Guard battalions were sent into action almost without training. In this way a considerable proportion of Moscow's intelligentsia was lost in the Vyazma encirclement in mid-October, when the Germans took more than six hundred thousand prisoners and captured more than a thousand tanks.

The local defence committee was particularly successful in Tula, the armaments manufacturing town south of Moscow. Most of the armaments works were evacuated to the east, but many of the less skilled workers stayed on and formed a Tula Workers' Regiment, of five battalions, which took part in the staunch defence of the town once it had been encircled in December. Unlike Vyazma, Tula did not fall.

Further behind the front, in Yaroslavl, a similar defence committee was set up, and a Communist Division was formed, consisting entirely of party and Komsomol members, and equipped and clothed as far as possible from the resources of the oblast. The raikom party secretaries became regimental commissars in the new formation.

The most famous example of local defence initiative was that of Leningrad. Here a City Defence Council was established by Zhdanov and Voroshilov in August, with the help of party activists, approaching the city. It had its *troiki* – three-member directorates from the party, the Soviet and the NKVD – in each raion and in each factory. Their job was to mobilize workers' battalions, arm them with anything available (including pikes, daggers and Molotov cocktails), and get them constructing street barricades, fire points, machine-gun nests and anti-tank traps. Much of the digging was done by women and teenagers.

Significantly, Stalin seems to have been very suspicious of Leningrad's Defence Council. He insisted that the commanders of the workers' battalions should be appointed from Moscow, and in fact soon had the Defence Council closed down, claiming that it was duplicating the Leningrad Front Command. This certainly had something to do with internal Kremlin politics: Stalin had always been suspicious of Leningrad as an alternative power base. Now, with the German encirclement of the city, it developed an intense local patriotism of its own.

The siege of Leningrad is one of the most remarkable stories of endurance in a war which was full of them. Blockaded from the end of August 1941 to January 1944, and for most of that time cut off from overland communication with the rest of the country, the city was in a truly desperate situation. Especially that was true during the first winter. The siege had not been anticipated, and nothing had been done to lay in supplies for it: indeed, until shortly before, food was actually being taken *out* of Leningrad to provide for its evacuees resettling in remote and poorly supplied regions of the country. Although children and some essential workers were transferred out of the city to other centres, most of the population remained behind. The only supply line lay across thirty miles of Lake Ladoga, to the east of the city. The winter was very cold, and the ice formed early over the lake, so that from late November it was possible to mark out routes that could be taken by heavy lorries across the ice. In that way some supplies could be brought in.

They were not enough. In December 1941, 53,000 people died in Leningrad, as many as in the whole of 1940. It was to get worse. The city came more or less to a halt. Coal for the power stations ran out, so the trams stopped running, the water supply froze, and the houses were no longer heated or lit – this in a city where the temperature could drop to –40°C and which in mid-winter was dark for eighteen hours a day. People sat in frozen apartments, burning old furniture or even books to try to keep a little warmth in the stoves. The city authorities issued ration cards in an attempt to distribute the meagre food supply equitably. For much of the winter a manual worker's bread ration was 400 grams a day, with dependants getting half that; at the worst time, in December-January, the figures were 250 and 125 grams. This was not remotely enough to sustain physical activity, and from mid-December work simply stopped in many factories. People sat at home, and gradually starved. A city official later described their extremities:

> To fill their empty stomachs, to reduce the intense sufferings caused by hunger, people would look for incredible substitutes: they would try to catch crows or rooks, or any cat or dog that had still somehow survived; they would go through medicine chests in search of castor oil, hair oil, vaseline or glycerine; they would make soup or jelly out of carpenter's glue (scraped off wallpaper or broken-up furniture). But not everyone in the enormous city had such supplementary sources of 'food'.
>
> Death would overtake people in all kinds of circumstances; while they were in the streets, they would fall down and never rise again; or in their houses, where they would fall asleep and never awake; in factories, where they would collapse while doing a job of work. There was no

transport, and the dead body would usually be put on a hand-sleigh drawn by two or three members of the dead man's family; often, wholly exhausted during the long trek to the cemetery, they would abandon the body half-way, leaving it to the authorities to deal with.

In these circumstances, loss of a ration card was almost a death sentence, and any difficulty or dispute over food aroused the strongest feelings. The following incident, observed by a schoolteacher, Elizaveta Sharypina, encapsulates what most people were living through. One day, in a baker's, she saw a woman hitting and swearing at a boy of ten, who was sitting on the floor stuffing his mouth with a hunk of black bread. The woman had just received her day's bread ration from the sales assistant and left it for a moment on the counter. The youngster, who was desperately hungry, had snatched it and sat down to devour it, heedless of the blows showered on him.

> When Sharypina tried to calm the woman, she broke into tears and sobbed that she had taken her only child to the morgue a few weeks before. Finally, Sharypina got the people in the bread store to contribute bits of their ration to the woman who had lost hers. She then questioned the ten-year-old. His father, he thought, was at the front. His mother had died of hunger. Two children remained, he and a younger brother. They were living in the cellar of a house which had been destroyed by a bomb. She asked why they hadn't gone to a children's home. He said they had to wait for their father. If they went to a home, they would be sent out of Leningrad and never see him again.

That was the worst stage. During the second winter of the blockade supplies were better organized. But the experience of going through this together in isolation gave Leningraders, already aware of their special history and traditions, a very powerful sense of local solidarity. As a seventeen-year-old schoolgirl put it towards the end of the war, 'All of us Leningraders are one family, baptized by the monstrous blockade – one family, one in our grief, one in our experience, one in our hopes and expectations.'

Things were better in the rest of the country, but not so very much better. The German invasion had totally disrupted economic life. It is true that some contingency plans had been drawn up for converting industrial plants to military production, but they rested on the assumption of a short, offensive war conducted on enemy territory. Viktor Kravchenko, who was an official of the Ferrous Metals Commissariat, later recalled:

> I was in daily official touch with commissariats responsible for factories and stockpiles and workers in the area under attack. It soon became apparent to us that no one in the Kremlin had bothered, in the twenty-two months of grace [from the Nazi-Soviet Pact to the outbreak of war], to formulate a programme for the evacuation of people and property. The initiative, of course, could only have come from the top. For anyone else to raise the question would have opened him to charges of 'defeatism' and 'demoralizing rumours'. . . . Faced with a defensive war of immense weight, we were helpless. We had to improvise everything from scratch – evacuation, mobilization, guerrilla resistance in the enemy's rear.

However, as in the early thirties, it turned out that the planned economy was better at improvising than at planning. Within days of the outbreak of war, reconversion of factories had started. In Moscow a children's bicycle factory started making flamethrowers, at a die-stamping plant teaspoons and paperclips gave way to entrenching tools and parts for anti-tank grenades, and a typewriter works began to manufacture automatic rifles and ammunition. In Chelyabinsk the famous tractor factory was entirely converted to construct tanks, for which purpose equipment was brought from the Kharkov diesel engine works, and workers came from the Stalingrad tractor factory.

The mass evacuation of whole factories was the most impressive feat of these early months. GKO set up a special Evacuation Council under the trade union leader, Nikolai Shvernik. This received applications from enterprises to be evacuated to the rear (significantly, the initiative came from below), tried to assess their relative importance, and assigned a destination, together with locomotives and rolling stock to get them there. The council appointed plenipotentiaries to the industrial commissariats, to the local party committees, and to major railway junctions, to sort out priorities and keep the traffic moving. In spite of reports of trainloads going round in circles, and of precious machinery waiting in the rain for wagons to come and collect it, the process was effectively carried out. By the end of the year some 1500 enterprises had been bodily shifted eastwards, to locations in the Volga basin, the Urals and Siberia. Sometimes they had to restart in schools, theatres or even old watermills, till more suitable premises could be improvised. Remarkable feats were achieved: within a fortnight of the arrival of the last pieces of equipment at a new aircraft factory on the Volga, the first MiG plane was already assembled and coming off the production line; three weeks later more than thirty planes had been completed. The habit of 'campaigns' and 'shock working' certainly paid off here.

In this manner some 10 million people were transferred eastwards, and new industrial heartlands created beyond the Volga. By 1945 over half the metal output of the Soviet Union was produced in the Urals, compared with a fifth in 1940. This of course was a key factor for the war effort, and the authorities paid the closest attention to what was going on in the new industries. According to Nikolai Patolichev, first secretary in Chelyabinsk, 'members of GKO daily phoned direct to the directors of the Magnitogorsk metallurgical combine, the Chelyabinsk tractor factory and others.' When there was a hitch in the production of ferrous metal, Stalin would send a telegram warning that 'non-fulfilment of the daily plan' would be regarded as a 'crime of state importance' and punished accordingly; when a defect appeared in a tank engine, a special GKO commission headed by Malyshev (see above, page 206) flew out to investigate. The local party secretary, of course, was supposed to keep an even closer eye on all these things (which meant understanding something of the technical processes involved), and on the allocation of manpower, transport, fuel and other facilities needed to keep production going without interruption. As Patolichev says, 'The working day of the obkom secretary would begin with *Pravda* and with a study of the situation on the railways.'

Party secretaries in key positions like this played, if anything, an even more important role than before the war, since now the emergencies were even more pressing and the need for immediate decision-making by the men on the spot even greater. They were also very dependent on each other, and on their ministerial, police and military colleagues, to get the job done. The atmosphere of mutual suspicion, which had often vitiated relationships between these agencies before the war, was now muted, and personal connections – and for that matter feuds – forged then proved to be very durable after the war.

The results, at any rate, were impressive, at least as far as military production was concerned. After a terrible slump in output during the evacuation period, it shot up, and by 1943 the Red Army was receiving tanks, guns, ammunition and planes in very adequate quantities. But there remained considerable weaknesses. Soviet industry still showed itself inept at turning out certain kinds of items: thus many of the Red Army's boots, field telephones, jeeps and lorries had to be supplied by Britain and the USA under the Lend-Lease programme. Tinned spam and many medicines came from the same source. Furthermore, production in all fields not directly related to the war fell markedly: thus even steel production declined from 18.3 million tonnes in 1940 to 12.3 million in 1945. This meant that virtually none of the steel produced was being used for civilian purposes. And one can imagine what the enormous decline in tractor output – from 66,200 to 14,700 – meant for agriculture.

The drafting of workers into the armed forces generated, naturally, a desperate labour shortage. Numbers declined from 31.2 million hands in 1940 to 18.3 million in 1942. To help fill the gap the whole population of working age was made liable for compulsory labour mobilization, which was overseen by a GKO committee. Women, apprentices, teenagers and old men were drawn into branches of industry hitherto totally unknown to them, given a hasty training and installed at the factory bench. The share of women, in particular, in the industrial workforce rose from 38 per cent in 1940 to 53 per cent in 1942. For most of those women, of course, domestic work had become no less onerous, and had to be performed in addition to industrial tasks. There may have been fewer males at home to feed, but shopping and the carrying out of simple household chores had become much more difficult in the absence of consumer goods.

The war accentuated the differentiation of a worker aristocracy. Highly skilled workers in essential war industries, exempted from military service, were paid reasonable wages and guaranteed tolerable food rations and fixed prices. Average wages rose nominally by 75 per cent between 1938 and 1944, while the maximum published wages rose by three times.

In actual fact, anyone with regular manual employment in a factory was assured of survival through the network of ORS (Worker's Provisioning Department) shops at their place of work. It was those outside this category who had the greatest difficulties. In the ordinary shops, rations could not always be honoured, and in the kolkhoz markets prices were frighteningly high. Alexander Werth, arriving in Moscow in June 1942, found bread in the markets costing 150 rubles a kilo (about £3, more than an average week's wages). Dairy products and sugar were very scarce, potatoes and vegetables were unobtainable. Scurvy had become quite common, especially among those with class two (employee) or three (dependent) ration cards. Even the buffet in the Bolshoi Theatre had nothing on sale except glasses of water at three kopecks a time. (The foreign colony and privileged Russians, however, continued to be well catered for.)

Vladimir Bukovsky, whose parents were journalists, reports that in Moscow queues for flour would sometimes last for several days: one's place in it was recorded in indelible ink on the palm of one's hand, and one would return morning and evening to check on the current situation. In such circumstances, unofficial connections might play a vital role in survival. In the dark days of October 1941, Anatoly Fedoseev, a foreman in an arc-light factory in Novosibirsk, got 600 grams of black bread a day as rations, but managed to secure a contract for electrical wiring in an agricultural institute for pay in kind: for every Sunday he put in there, he would get half a sack of potatoes and cabbage.

The agricultural situation was, indeed, desperate. The German advance at its height deprived the country of land which before the war had yielded 38 per cent of its grain, half of its industrial crops, and as much as 87 per cent of its sugar beet. Cattle could to some extent be evacuated (though not without formidable losses), but crops could not, and there was neither the time nor the available machinery during the war to open up new arable acreage on any scale. Existing cultivated land had therefore to meet the nation's needs. But of course, most of the able-bodied men who had hitherto worked it were now at the front line: by 1943 only a third of those who had worked in the kolkhozy in 1940 were still active there. They were replaced by women, young people below conscription age, old men and to some extent even by those who had previously been considered invalids. Fyodor Abramov, one of the most honest and sober of rural novelists, described the results in a far northern forest village:

They drove out old men already clapped out by a lifetime's work, they dragged teenagers from their school desks, and set little snotty-nosed girls to work on the fir trees. And the women, the women with children, what they went through in those years! No one made any allowances for them, not for age or anything else. You could collapse and give up the ghost there in the forest, but you didn't dare to come back without fulfilling your norm! Not on your life! Come on, let's have your cubic metres! The Front needs them! And if they could even have eaten their rations in peace – but no, the children's hungry mouths must be stuffed first.

This reduced workforce had to manage with fewer machines – we have already seen what happened to tractor production – or with machines in poorer condition, and fewer mechanics to service and repair them.

It is scarcely surprising, then, that agricultural output fell catastrophically. From a level of 95.5 million tonnes in 1940, the grain harvest fell to 30 million tonnes in 1942 and 1943. The cattle stock was halved, while the number of pigs declined from 22.5 million at the end of 1940 to 6.1 million in 1942.

The state met this crisis with a mixture of compulsion and flexibility. Within the collective farms, the minimum labour-day requirements were raised by about 50 per cent. Compulsory deliveries to the state were not increased, but in view of the decline in output, they initially represented a heavier burden. In recognition of this, they were in due course actually allowed to fall. The state did realize that coercion alone was likely to prove counterproductive. It withdrew most restrictions on the cultivation of private plots and on the markets where the produce from them was sold. The result, as we have seen, was a flourishing but expensive private food market. Travelling by train from Murmansk to Moscow in the summer of 1942, Alexander Werth saw peasant women trading all kinds of food at every station along the line, usually for barter rather than money: their prices were so high that many of the passengers were quite bitter about them. This was the legalization of the civil war 'bagmen'. Of course the peasants worked very hard for their rewards: the private plot had to be taken care of in addition to the demanding collective obligations. Many urban work-men experienced the same double load, since the state en-couraged them to cultivate private allotments on evenings and days off. In this way some workers resumed peasants' occupations they had perhaps only recently abandoned.

The overall result of these processes was to weaken the structure of collective agriculture. The rewards to be gained on the private market were so much greater that many peasants worked only with the greatest reluctance on the collective fields. To meet this difficulty, some kolkhoz chairmen in practice allowed much of the collective work to be performed on the *zveno*, or 'link' system. The zveno was a group of a dozen or so peasants, usually with a family as its nucleus, taking complete responsibility for a stretch of land throughout the annual cycle, meeting compulsory delivery targets from it, and consuming the rest or selling it for private gain. Peasants who worked in this way were usually much more productive, partly because of the material incentive, and partly perhaps because they were no longer a small cog in an agricultural assembly line, but had responsibility for the whole work process. In addition to this, some farms tacitly permitted households to take over parts of the collective fields to work privately, and even put collective equipment, animals and fertilizer at their disposal. Provided the food was produced and marketed, no one was likely to ask questions.

Overall, then, peasants worked incredibly hard during the war. From the party's viewpoint, however, this had the dis-advantage that many of them became relatively wealthy and also developed expectations that the collective farm system would be run down and private agriculture resumed.

Perhaps the most unfortunate Soviet citizens of all were those soldiers and civilians who fell into German captivity.

The Germans regarded them as 'subhuman' and herded them together in what were essentially concentration camps where they slowly died of starvation and disease while performing manual labour. The Soviet government's attitude towards them was no more solicitous: it equated surrender with treason and had refused to sign the Geneva Convention on prisoners of war, which meant that the Red Cross could not forward letters or food parcels to them from their families at home. Furthermore, those who managed to escape – and this included those who made their way out of military en-circlement – were promptly subjected to intensive NKVD interrogation, and many of them were sent to labour camps, or even executed as spies. This was not just a matter of official attitudes. In February 1943 when Kharkov was briefly retaken by the Red Army, Alexander Werth saw emaciated Soviet prisoners of war, newly 'liberated' from German camps, but still living in them because there was nowhere else for them to go. No one was feeding them. The attitude of the local population was quite uncaring: they had enough problems of their own – and in any case who could be sure the prisoners had not been left as spies?

In the circumstances, it is not surprising that a good many Soviet prisoners sought release from such a hopeless existence by enlisting in the German army. They are referred to as 'traitors' in Soviet publications, but whether that term can be fairly applied to people who had already in effect been aban-doned by their own government must be dubious. Altogether, at various times, about a million of them served in various formations of the Axis armies, usually in very small groups, since Hitler was unwilling to tolerate any Slav national for-mations (though he did permit Cossack and Caucasian ones).

More surprising, perhaps, at first sight is that a fair number of Soviet officers (who relatively speaking were better treated by both sides) should have been prepared to fight on the German side, and indeed to try and raise an army to over-throw the Soviet regime. Their leader was General Andrei Vlasov, who had been one of the heroes of the Soviet winter counterattack before Moscow. The Germans captured him in the summer of 1942 when he was encircled on the northern front. Apart from the Moscow campaign, all his combat experience came from the early, demoralizing part of the war, when the Stalin regime seemed not only brutal, but also incompetent; and this impression must have been deepened by the circumstances of his capture, since his army was simply abandoned, with no attempt to supply it or help it to fight its way out.

Vlasov was typical of many who had worked their way to the top in the Red Army. A peasant by origin, he had fought in the Red Army during the civil war, and had subsequently trained as one of the new 'red commanders'. His father was 'dekulakised', but, as we have seen, this did not necessarily imply any family wealth. In any case, Vlasov became a party member about 1930. In the appeal he sent in 1943 to Russian soldiers and civilians behind the German lines, he outlined his reasons for deciding to fight for Hitler. He felt that the Bolsheviks had not given the people what they had promised them:

> I saw how hard the life of the Russian worker was, how the peasant was forced into the kolkhoz, how millions of Russian people disappeared, arrested without any investigation or trial. I saw everything Russian being trampled under foot, and sycophants being promoted to command posts in the Red Army, people who did not have the interests of the Russian people at heart.
>
> The system of commissars demoralized the Red Army. Irresponsible prying and denunciations made the commander a plaything in the hands of party bureaucrats.

Vlasov had some appeal even in the ranks of the Red Army. When his leaflets were dropped behind the Soviet lines near Smolensk in January 1943, apparently several thousand deserters came across, all of them asking about Vlasov and his 'liberation army'.

But there was no 'liberation army'. Until the very last months of the war, when it was far too late, Hitler would not allow Vlasov to set up his own Russian national formations, let alone to form a Russian government in exile, as Vlasov and his political advisers would have liked to do. This was what doomed his enterprise. Many other Soviet commanders captured by the Germans refused to join Vlasov, though not because they thought it treacherous. As a German historian of the Vlasov movement has remarked, 'They admitted that they would prefer to serve a government that did not constantly keep check on them, watch them, demand daily proofs of solidarity from them, and threaten them with professional, familial, physical or psychic annihilation. But they all wanted to have . . . assurances that would enable them to trust in the good will of the Germans.'

Only in September 1944 was Vlasov permitted to set up a Committee for the Liberation of the Peoples of Russia (KONR). In November it published a political programme, the Prague Manifesto. This was influenced by the émigré organization, the National Labour Union (NTS), which had been established in Belgrade in the 1930s to try to find a middle way between socialism and capitalism. Under the name of 'solidarism' the NTS tried to combine individual liberty with state welfare in a form that was to become familiar in Western Europe after the war. Vlasov's programme was rather more left-wing than that: it accepted the October revolution, and asserted that the Soviet regime had only subsequently become tyrannical. It offered civil liberties and guarantees of free economic activity together with restraint on unbridled capitalism and with state provision for essential public utilities. It proposed a 'national labour' system of social welfare, with free education and health care, old age pensions and the like. It promised self-determination for the nationalities of Russia. Remarkably for a programme published under the sponsorship of the Nazis, it contained no trace of anti-Semitism. It stood no chance of being adopted, but it is interesting as revealing something about the political aspirations of those who had grown up under the Soviet regime, once they were released from its tutelage and able publicly to reject its ideology.

Vlasov's Russian Liberation Army was formed only just in time to fight briefly and inconclusively on the eastern front in March 1945. Its commander, General Bunyachenko, then evacuated it to Czechoslovakia, where it saw action *against* the Germans, helping to liberate Prague from the SS. Vlasov himself was captured by the Americans and handed over to the Soviets, who shot him as a traitor, along with his leading associates, in 1946.

Those Red Army commanders who were not captured and who survived the war found themselves enjoying a much higher standing in society than had been the case before 1941. They were no longer called 'commanders', but 'officers', in accordance with the tsarist usage. Not only were their ranks restored (that had largely happened before the war), but so also were their full dress uniforms and insignia. Just before the battle of Stalingrad, when the Soviet predicament looked as grave as it could be, the British Embassy was astonished to receive a Soviet request for huge quantities of gold braid. Embassy officials considered the request 'absurdly frivolous' when the country was urgently in need of more elementary supplies, but nevertheless complied with it. As a result, Soviet officers were henceforth able to appear gorgeously attired at parades, some of them sporting decorations redolent of old Russian military tradition, such as the Order of Alexander Nevsky or of Mikhail Kutuzov.

To train officers for their elite status, special Suvorov Military Schools were set up, named after the famous eighteenth-century Russian general, on the model of the tsarist Cadet Corps. They took their entrants exclusively from the sons of serving officers or of other ranks who had died at the hands of the Germans. The schools provided a general secondary education along with military training which fitted its graduates for junior officer status, or for entry to a Military Acadamy. Symptomatically, one item on its curriculum was ballroom dancing, for social graces were now considered *de rigueur* for fledgling members of the new elite. As intended, the Suvorov schools have been much patronized by the sons of officers, so that military dynasties have begun to form since the war.

In some ways most important of all, *edinonachalie* (or single command) was finally restored in the autumn of 1942. The political commissars were downgraded to become 'assistant political officers' (*zampolity*), responsible for political education and the maintenance of morale in their units, but having no further right, even theoretically, to interfere in the officers' operational dispositions.

Altogether it could be said by the end of the war that the officers enjoyed a degree of autonomy and status given to no other group in Soviet society, before or since. They held that status because they had rescued both the regime and the people from a desperate situation. They have subsequently been prepared to go on ensuring the nation's defence but in return they have demanded that they be allowed to exercise their profession properly, and that they be afforded the resources they feel they require.

The Communist Party, by contrast, lost some of its pre-war power and influence. Its membership grew considerably, but this was in some ways a sign of the dilution of its standards. Membership was being conferred not so much for political reasons as to reward a distinguished combat record: thus the military, or at best the zampolity, were deciding who should become party members. By the end of 1944 (when admission rules were tightened up again) there were 3 million Communists in the armed forces, half the total membership of the party. Of these, 57 per cent were privates and NCOs, compared with 28 per cent before the war. The party had thus become both more democratic and more military.

Even in the rear, party recruitment was more generous at this time and drew more upon the lower strata: 27 per cent of new members were workers and 31 per cent peasants, compared with less than 20 per cent and 10 per cent respectively in

1939-41. The high peasant intake is especially striking, though it may in fact reflect the need to appoint new officials in the rural soviets and kolkhozy, to replace those who had left for the front.

The upper levels of the party yielded noticeably to the other organs of political power. The Central Committee scarcely met during the war, its normal functions being at least partly taken over by GKO or by military bodies; similarly, Politburo members met more often in their alternative incarnation as members of GKO. In the localities, so many party officials were mobilized for the front that party secretaries often seem to have ruled unencumbered by regular meetings of their committees and bureaux. As we have seen, they found themselves often having to intervene to sort out local economic difficulties and bottlenecks. Altogether, the war gave them experience of hard work, inventiveness and power such as they had not known before. In 1941 many of them had still been young, hastily trained and very raw in their jobs. By 1945 they had faced extremely testing emergencies, often with insufficient resources. This developed further in them what already existed, a highly authoritarian decision-making style, but also a reliance on their immediate colleagues, combined with varying degrees of fear and respect for their superiors, whom they sometimes *had* to deceive to get things done. These were the formative years of the party's medium and upper apparatus officials, years which they have looked back on with pride ever since, their 'test of maturity', as one of them, Patolichev, entitled his memoirs. The military cast of mind which they had picked up in the thirties was thereby confirmed and consolidated, and they emerged even less suited to the gentler but more sophisticated demands of running a peacetime economy.

All in all, the Soviet peoples displayed between 1941 and 1945 endurance, resourcefulness and determination which may well be beyond the capacities of economically more advanced nations. They won the war partly because of, partly in spite of, their leaders. The issue was well put by two colleagues of the economist Alec Nove. One of them asserted, 'The result of the battle of Stalingrad showed that Stalin's basic line had been correct.' The other retorted, 'If a different policy had been followed, the Germans would not have got as far as Stalingrad.' Both comments are quite persuasive. The war showed the Soviet system at its best and at its worst.

11

The Last Years of Stalin

In 1945 the Soviet Union was a country victorious, yet devastated. To win the greatest war in history it had lost far more people than its enemy – far more, indeed, than any other combatant nation has ever lost in any war. Recent research puts the military losses at about 7.5 million, the civilian deaths at 6–8 million. In late 1939 the Soviet population had been 194.1 million; in 1950 it was 178.5 million, in spite of the annexation of new territories in the Baltic, Transcarpathian Russia (taken from Czechoslovakia in 1945) and Moldavia (taken from Romania in 1940). To add to losses directly caused by the war, the labour camps had continued functioning throughout, carrying out emergency construction work, lumbering and mining on the colossal scale demanded by the war, with rations that were probably even less adequate than in peacetime. Altogether probably some 20–25 million Soviet citizens died premature deaths between 1941 and 1945.

Disproportionately, of course, the victims were men. The carnage among Soviet men born between approximately 1910 and 1925 was horrifying, and has left permanent scars on the demographic structure of the country. Very many women of similar age were left without husbands, often bringing up children single-handed while also working in a war-torn economy desperately short of labour. Thus in the 1959 census for 1000 women between the ages of thirty-five and forty-four there were only 633 men. As a result, there was a sharp drop in the birth rate during the 1940s, though the war was not the only cause of this, since the decline continued, at a gentler rate, right into the 1970s.

The Ukraine, Bielorussia and much of European Russia were devastated: some 25 million people were homeless, squatting with already overburdened relatives, or even living in chilly dugouts in ruined cities. The economy was both distorted and gravely depleted. Grain production was down by two thirds – at least that proportion of it recorded in the official figures. Industrial production had risen only in what had now become the superfluities of war, while the products most urgently needed for the people's welfare and for post-war reconstruction were at a very low level: steel 12.3 million tonnes (down from 18.3 million in 1940); oil 19.4 million (31.1 million); cement 1.8 million (5.7 million); wool fabrics 53.6 million metres (119.7 million); leather footwear 63 million pairs (211 million). Housing construction and repair had been almost wholly neglected, despite huge movements of population. Even in a city like Novosibirsk, well away from enemy action, the engineer Anatoly Fedoseyev found in the late 1940s many industrial workers living in a shanty town on the outskirts, in shacks built of rusty iron, planks, cardboard boxes, wire, glass and earth.

Apart from housing, what the people needed most of all was regular food supplies. As we have seen, the government had turned a blind eye to much private cultivation and marketing during the war, in order to avert mass starvation. Many peasants hoped, as a result, that the kolkhozy would be abolished, or at least considerably loosened, as under the 'link' system (see above, page 288). The Politburo member in charge of agriculture, A. A. Andreyev, was known to favour the widespread adoption of the 'link' as a basic unit in collective agriculture. So too did N. A. Voznesensky, chairman of Gosplan during the war years: he even recommended encouraging peasant cultivation of private plots and putting the state retail network at their disposal for marketing.

Such a policy would have amounted to a partial rehabilitation of NEP, with all the consequences many party members had found so distasteful then. Stalin, at least, was not prepared to contemplate it. On the contrary, a decree of September 1946 ordered that all land acquired by private persons should be returned to the kolkhozy. This meant that many peasants, whose private cultivation of collective fields had been tolerated during the war, now had to surrender what they had become used to exploiting for their own profit. The drift to privatization was halted, and emphasis once more returned to production plans and compulsory state deliveries. These were paid for at such ruinously low prices that, in the case of potatoes, the income did not even cover the cost of transporting them into town. For this reason, kolkhozy sometimes preferred to resort to the ludicrous practice of buying eggs, vegetables or milk on the private market and delivering them to the state at a loss, as the least expensive way of fulfilling their obligations. At the same time taxes on private plots were raised, and kolkhoz chairmen were instructed not to provide facilities (ploughs, tools, fodder) for peasants working privately. Even finding hay for the family cow became a time-consuming and exhausting problem.

Furthermore, in 1950 the 'link' system, having been practised intermittently alongside the more normal 'brigade' system ever since the late thirties, was suddenly condemned in *Pravda*, on the grounds that it impeded the mechanization of agriculture. Andreyev confessed that he had been at fault in recommending 'links', and disclaimed any intention of introducing them generally. Supervision over the production process was unambiguously restored to the Machine Tractor Station (MTS) and its party organization: the MTS once again handed out production plans, performed the mechanized work, and collected the compulsory deliveries as payment. Kolkhozy were, moreover, much enlarged, ostensibly to facilitate mechanization, and to profit from economies of scale – in practice probably to simplify control by the MTS and the rural party organizations. The number of kolkhozy dropped in two years from 250,000 to 97,000. In the industrial spirit which governed this change, some of them were converted to sovkhozy, or state farms, which usually specialized in particular crops, and paid their labourers a regular wage, like factory workers.

The results of this tightening of the screws were disastrous. At a time when food was desperately needed, agricultural production recovered only very slowly from its wartime trough; 1946 was a year of drought in the Ukraine, but there was no relaxation of state procurement targets. As in 1933, the state took away all the peasants' food reserves, using force if necessary. One kolkhoz chairman wrote to Khrushchev as first secretary of the Ukrainian Communist Party: 'We have delivered our quota to the state. But we have given everything away. Nothing is left for us. We are sure the state and party won't forget us, and that they will come to our aid.' Alas, his confidence was misplaced: the peasants were left to starve. Cases of cannibalism began to be reported from the villages – but not of course in the press, which kept the famine secret, and indeed entertained the public with fairy tales about collective farmers celebrating their affluence on suckling pig and red wine. When Khrushchev, with great misgivings, dared to report the real state of affairs to Stalin, the latter bluntly refused any help, and mocked him: 'You're being soft-bellied! They're deceiving you! They're counting on being able to appeal to your sentimentality when they report things like that.' Khrushchev was in fact replaced for a time by the 'tougher' Kaganovich.

The grain harvest recovered terribly slowly from the post-war trough. Even by 1952 – a relatively favourable year – it had still not reached 1940 levels, and productivity per acre was actually lower than in 1913. Malenkov's boast, at the Nineteenth Party Congress that year, that the country had solved the grain problem, was certainly ill-founded. In other branches of agricultural output, the situation was even worse. In 1953, indeed, the Soviet Union had fewer head of cattle than in 1916, to feed a population which had grown by 30 or 40 million, a much higher proportion of whom lived in the towns. Meat and dairy products were available only in the best-supplied cities, and then intermittently. Produce from the private plots, whatever the official objections, was the mainstay both of the urban diet and of the peasants' real incomes. In 1950 those plots, 1–2 per cent of the land, produced nearly half of the country's vegetables, more than two-thirds of its meat, milk and potatoes, and nearly nine-tenths of its eggs.

Both on the private and on the collective land, women formed the bulk of the labour force. So many of those men who had survived the war more or less able-bodied did their utmost not to return to the poverty-stricken and demoralized village. What they were avoiding can be seen in the income figures for collective farmers. In 1946 the average labour-day in 50 per cent of kolkhozy brought in one ruble or less – that is, less than one-third the price of a kilogram of black bread or of 100 grams of sugar at current market rates. Alec Nove has calculated that in 1948–50, to purchase a poor-quality suit would require well over a year's pay for the average collective farmer.

The low morale of the rural population and the political reflections which this penury engendered are well summarized in a novel by Fyodor Abramov about the far northern villages. A raion party secretary has come in 1951 to visit a kolkhoz chairman and his wife (who actually ran the farm for several years while her husband was at the front). She complains that six years after the war, people are still hungry, and the state is still demanding more. The party secretary reproaches the chairman with being a 'poor businessman'. The chairman retorts:

'Have you ever seen a businessman who would ask eleven kopecks for a pair of fur boots that cost him two rubles to make? Well, that's the price they pay for milk deliveries, and that milk costs me two rubles.'
'Who pays you? The state?'
'Aha, trying to catch me out saying the wrong thing! Yes, the state. Why shouldn't I say so? What did Lenin say

after the civil war? He said we must establish proper relationships with the countryside, we mustn't take absolutely everything away from the peasant. . . . And what sort of businessman am I, anyway? All I can do is to brandish my stick and shout at people. It's time we used the carrot rather the stick.'

The party secretary can only agree with him, though they both decide afterwards that they had better pretend not to have had this conversation. Though their voices were hushed, there were certainly many party officials and rural administrators who were similarly in favour of change, and prepared to welcome a leadership which would implement it.

Life in the cities was only a little better. Even those fortunate enough not to live in dugouts, barracks or makeshift shelters, still suffered from severe overcrowding. Apart from the upper levels of the elite, most people lived in communal apartments, with usually just one room for a family, and sharing kitchen, bathroom and lavatory. Quite often rooms had to be divided by partitions, or even just by blankets suspended from the ceiling, with a family each side. The historian Alexander Nekrich personally knew of a case where three families totalling thirteen people all inhabited a single room of twenty square metres, containing seven beds: the six 'extras' slept on the floor. This may have been exceptional, but their plight was not considered unacceptable: in spite of repeated applications to the local soviet, they were rehoused only in the early sixties. Stalin preferred erecting huge, flamboyant prestige buildings for the new and bloated government ministries (no longer called Commissariats from 1946 – another return to traditional usage).

Conditions were aggravated by the government decision in 1946 to abolish the multi-tiered pricing system which had existed during the war and had enabled workers to buy food at tolerable prices. Prices in all retail outlets were set at nearly the free market level: in other words, the government passed on to its citizens the full cost of the shortages caused by the war. As a result, a kilogram of black bread rose from 1 ruble to 3 rubles 40 kopecks, a kilogram of sugar from 5 rubles 50 kopecks to 15 rubles. Then, in 1947, rationing was abolished (earlier than in any other combatant state of the Second World War), and a currency reform was carried through. The aim of the latter was to mop up the excess of inflated money which had accumulated from black market dealings, and from peasants selling privately. All small savings in state banks, up to 3000 rubles, were converted into new rubles on a one-to-one basis; higher savings received a less favourable rate. Rubles held in cash were exchanged on a 10:1 basis, so that money stowed away under the bed by peasants, moonlighters and black marketeers was abruptly devalued. Even state war bonds were declared to be worth only a third of their nominal value, since, the decree stated, 'the fact cannot be overlooked that, during the war, loans were subscribed to in depreciated currency.' The state thus sharply reduced its own debt, and reduced the risk of inflation, at the cost of the living standards of most of the population.

Shortly afterwards, the price of bread was reduced slightly, from 3 rubles 40 kopecks to 3 rubles. This was the first of a series of gradual food price reductions which at last brought some improvements in urban living standards every year from 1948 to 1954. As we have seen, they were paid for by the poverty of the kolkhozy. Meanwhile real urban wages by 1952 were for the first time beginning to regain the level where they had stood in 1928.

The fourth Five Year Plan, launched in 1946 by N. A. Voznesensky, aimed at rapid growth in all sectors of the economy. Wartime labour legislation was not lifted, so that the workforce could be mobilized for whatever sector the planners thought desirable, while draconian penalties continued for lateness at work, absenteeism, drunkenness etc. In practice, it was only heavy industry which reached its targets. By 1950 pre-war output had already been surpassed in pig-iron, steel, coal, oil, electricity and cement. Indeed, three times as many tractors were being produced in 1950 as in

1940, an outstanding feat of post-war retooling, which may help to explain the agricultural revival which came a little later. Such figures were often achieved by rebuilding factories on their pre-1941 sites, while leaving their evacuated counterparts still turning out the goods in the Urals and Siberia – to the disappointment of transferred workers who had been looking forward to returning home.

In consumer goods, housing, services and, as we have seen, agriculture, the plan generally was not fulfilled. Much less investment was channelled into them, much less priority given to them. The shape of the recovery thus froze the Soviet economy back into the shape it had assumed in the thirties, even though the war had made clear its shortcomings. Wartime technical innovations, for example in plastics and synthetic chemicals, were not absorbed and developed. The already largest industrial ministries, having the greatest political influence, pulled in the greatest share of resources, crushing new initiatives at birth. Hostility to foreign influences after the ending of Lend-Lease in 1945 aggravated this unresponsiveness to innovation. It began to seem as if the planned economy had an unchangeable structure, which was insensitive both to the consumer and to technical advances, while performing excellently in the field of capital goods.

After the war those strata of society which had gained power and status during it were anxious to consolidate their position. For a man who liked to rule single-handed, Stalin had given some hefty hostages to fortune to rescue the country from the consequences of his ill-judged diplomacy. He had conferred considerable independent standing on the army officers, the security police and the state machinery, all at the expense of the party, which had found itself largely reduced to performing morale-raising and mobilizational tasks for the State Defence Committee, the Armed Forces Command, and the major industrial commissariats. True, certain party secretaries, particularly those in the unoccupied areas where industry was relocated, had developed a self-reliance and an *ésprit de corps* which was to stand them in good stead, but at its lower levels the party had been swamped by hastily selected and ill-prepared new recruits, who weakened its discipline and diluted its ideology. Ideology was in any case a delicate point after the war: it had been adulterated by an admixture of nationalist elements, which were repugnant to many propagandists. Besides, the experience of war had disturbed the precarious equilibrium of 'doublethink' in the minds of Soviet citizens. They had tested their imbibed ideals in practice, under ferocious conditions; they had also seen how their leaders had reacted under the same strains. Many of them had been abroad, and were able to compare Soviet reality with other kinds. How much the security services feared this can be seen from their treatment of those who returned from captivity or from a spell of living abroad. They were subjected to rigorous interrogations, and many were sent for long spells in labour camps. In some cases the NKVD even dispensed with such formalities, and simply had the repatriated shot as they disembarked at Soviet ports.

Those foreign journalists who saw Marshal Zhukov give a press conference in conquered Berlin in June 1945 remarked that he seemed to take most of the credit for the Red Army's victories on himself, adding a tribute to Stalin 'almost as an afterthought'. This presumption will not have escaped Stalin, and Zhukov was accordingly soon transferred to the relatively obscure Odessa military district. Everything was done, in fact, to reassert the weight and internal discipline of the party in its relations with the military. From June 1946 the right to 'elect' (i.e. appoint) party secretaries in military units was transferred from the Armed Forces Command back to the party hierarchy. And while the system of political commissars was not restored, officers were encouraged to improve their own political training by attending special party schools established for them in 1947. Accepting, in other words, that the higher standing of the military was now permanent, the party set about ensuring that officers would themselves become more 'party-minded'.

The party's whole recruitment and admission policy was considerably tightened up as early as October 1944: as before 1941, applicants were once again required to secure recommendation by long-standing party members and to undergo a period of probation, which had been waived during the war. The number of entrants began to decline immediately: as a result, party organizations were less under pressure from raw, untrained novices.

At its upper levels, the party now began to pay much more attention to formal qualifications as a prerequisite for promotion. A Central Committee decree of 2 August 1946 established a network of party high schools in all republican capitals, and in thirty-five Russian and Ukrainian oblast centres. These provided two-year courses for secretaries, instructors and propagandists at the raion level; to rise further, a promising graduate could proceed to the prestigious Party High School attached to the Central Committee in Moscow. At the very top, an Academy of Social Sciences, set up at the same time, filled the gap left by the Institute of Red Professors by conducting research and training personnel to teach in the party high schools. In this way the finely graded career structure of the party 'cadres' was finally consolidated: the leather-jacketed upstarts of the twenties would never have survived in this milieu of tight protocol and formal diplomas.

The party's governing bodies also took on renewed life after the war. GKO was abolished in September 1945, and thereafter the Politburo began to meet regularly, while the Central Committee re-emerged from its wartime semi-redundancy, and elected a new Secretariat and Orgburo. It did not, however, go so far as to convene a full Party Congress till 1952.

Literature and the arts had known a certain freedom from day-to-day party interference during the war, and most writers and artists naturally hoped that a victorious nation would be able to permit itself a continuation of this relative relaxation. The Central Committee, however, resumed its

strict tutelage with a decree of August 1946, attacking the
literary journals *Zvezda* (The Star) and *Leningrad* for
'servility towards everything foreign' – both, significantly,
published in the city Stalin most distrusted. Andrei Zhdanov,
the party's cultural chief, picked out two Leningrad authors
for particular criticism. One was the satirist Mikhail
Zoshchenko, who had published a story in which a little
monkey escaped from a zoo, spent a day observing Soviet life,
and found the experience so distasteful that he returned with
relief to captivity. Zhdanov accused Zoshchenko of
'preaching a rotten ideological nihilism [*bezideinost*],
vulgarity and apoliticism, designed to lead our youth astray
and to poison its consciousness'. 'Zoshchenko', he complained, 'is not interested in the labour of the Soviet people,
in their heroism and their high moral and social qualities'.
Zhdanov's other target was Anna Akhmatova, whose very
personal lyrical poetry, much of it concerned with love (and
hardly published during the thirties), he branded as 'imbued
with the spirit of pessimism, decadence . . . and bourgeois-
aristocratic aestheticism'.

All this signalled that the party was once more identifying
itself with a literature of high (however contrived) moral
principles, heroic attitudes, collectivism, and an idealized
view of Soviet reality, recast 'in the light of its revolutionary
development', that is to say, described as it *ought* to be rather
than as it was. Hence the mendacious depictions of rural
plenty noted above. Alongside this pompous optimism a new
theme was becoming ever more dominant: the superiority of
everything Soviet and/or Russian (even pre-revolutionary)
over everything foreign. All that was truly 'progressive' had,
it was asserted, orginated in Russia. This attitude coexisted
with a remarkable degree of apprehension about the
potential attractiveness of foreign, especially Western, ideas
for Soviet citizens.

In works dealing with Soviet society itself, the leading role
of the party now had to be stridently reiterated, perhaps
because it had been undermined during the war. In 1945,

Alexander Fadeyev, first secretary of the Writers' Union, and a loyalist in every sense, published a novel called *The Young Guard*, recounting the heroic resistance of young partisans to the German occupation in the Donbass. He was officially rebuked for not having demonstrated how the Communist Party had prepared and organized that resistance, and he had to rewrite the whole work in an even more stylized form. That second version, published in 1951, gives an interesting exposé of the values and symbols of late Stalinist society. It is a profoundly conservative, hierarchical and patriarchal work. Many of the scenes show how the heroic traditions of the Reds in the civil war are transmitted through the party to their successors in the Great Fatherland War. Yet the novel also evokes the supreme value of mother love and of dedication to the Russian soil. Although the Donbass is the setting, there are no descriptions of coalmining, or indeed of any other industrial processes; but many of the scenes take place against a natural background, which is depicted in pastoral terms. These were the values which the party leaders cherished after the war.

Similar attitudes were struck in the other arts, as well as in science and learning. The theatre was thoroughly combed, and plays by Western writers taken out of the repertoire for 'poisoning the consciousness of the Soviet people with hostile ideology'. The famous film director Sergei Eisenstein was condemned for an insufficiently heroic portrayal of Ivan the Terrible and his security police-cum-private army, the *Oprichnina*: the parallel with Stalin and the NKVD was all too clear, though unexpressed, as was the message that Russian tsars, especially the cruel, commanding ones, were now considered as 'good'. Music by Shostakovich, Prokofiev and other leading composers was attacked for containing nothing but dissonance – not a single melody which could be whistled by a worker.

The social sciences suffered the same kind of resubjection to the party. At the Institute of Law, Vyshinsky, master of ceremonies of the 1930s' show trials, came down in person to give a four-hour lecture on the dangers of underestimating the state as a weapon in the hands of the proletariat (in case there were any lingering notions about its 'withering away'). The director of the institute was dismissed, and special public meetings of its academic council were convened at which individuals were accused of 'rootless cosmopolitanism' and 'crawling on their bellies before bourgeois authorities'. Many of the victims were Jews, among them, Professor Gurvich, who had been one of the authors of the 1936 constitution. This was both a final campaign against surviving 'bourgeois specialists', and also a simple settling of personal scores. Any member of the institute could get up and make an accusation against a colleague: once that had happened, it was virtually impossible for anyone to defend the accused, and even if the victim exercised 'self-criticism' and expressed repentance it was often not enough to prevent his dismissal.

In linguistics, the theories of Academician Marr had held sway for many years. They fitted well with classical Marxism, for Marr proposed that all languages had a common root and, in the course of economic and political development, would one day amalgamate again into a common language, that of the international proletariat. This pristine internationalism did not, however, suit Stalin in his post-war mood. In 1950 Stalin decided that Russian, and only Russian, was worthy of being the ultimate proletarian language, and personally wrote an article condemning Marr's theory as 'unscientific and anti-Marxist'. Stalin's position was scarcely any more Marxist, since he asserted that language was a permanent feature of a nation's culture, and implied that it was impervious to social change. At any rate, the new authoritative doctrine soon became a lever for purges and dismissals engineered by the envious and covetous against their colleagues. Nadezhda Mandelstam, who was working at a provincial college of education at this time, was roused from bed one evening and summoned to a special meeting of her faculty. There she found her female colleagues dressed up in their best for the occasion. They denounced her for 'lack of attention to comrade Stalin's brilliant teachings on language, the dragging in of Marrist doctrine, the persecution of progressive younger elements among the staff, and the setting of excessively high standards in the award of examination marks'. She was given two weeks to round off her work and leave the college.

The party contributed its own unwanted cadres to these personnel changes. Its less successful senior members were no longer being arrested in the indiscriminate way of the late thirties: instead they were often eased out into the academic world, into fields where their rigidity and obtuseness would not impede the advance of science and technology — that is to say, into the humanities and social science faculties. Needless to say, they hastened there to implement the party line in whatever they conceived to be its latest form.

Recent trends in Western science and philosophy worried Zhdanov, since they appeared to pose a threat to the simple, ordered universe of materialist determinism which was officially espoused and taught in all the schools. At a special meeting of philosophers in June 1947, he warned: 'The Kantian vagaries of modern bourgeois atomic physicists lead them to inferences about the electron's possessing 'free will', to attempts to describe matter as only a certain conjunction of waves, and to other devilish tricks.' He also attacked G. F. Alexandrov, the leading expert on Hegel, for over-estimating the West European contribution (especially Hegel's, of course) to the formation of Marxism. Marx and Engels were about to be annexed as honorary Russians who had somehow had the misfortune to live abroad.

As the above reference to atomic physics shows, it was not only in the humanities and social sciences that the 'anti-cosmopolitan' campaign raged. Some of the natural sciences were also divided into 'bourgeois' and 'socialist' branches, and the former anathematized. The most far-fetched and destructive example of this kind was in the field of biology, in which the 'bourgeois pseudo-science' of genetics was outlawed and replaced by the 'progressive' agro-biology of Trofim Lysenko and his disciples.

The original rise of Lysenko dated well back before the war, and resulted from the atmosphere of 'myth-making' which characterized the late twenties. We have seen how, in economics and planning, serious empirical research and the elaboration of precise mathematical models yielded to planning by way of proclamation and willpower. Very much the same process occurred, though over a longer period of time, in agricultural science. Here too, encouraging but largely unsubstantiated hypotheses were prematurely seized upon by the party leadership and inflated into great truths because they promised quick advances in a difficult situation.

Lysenko had claimed to be able to shorten the ripening period and increase the yield of grains by a process he called 'vernalization': soaking the seeds at a certain temperature for a period of time before sowing. In this way winter crops, always vulnerable to Russia's severe climate, could, he asserted, be sown in the spring and still produce good yields. The background to this technique lay in his belief that heredity was determined not by discrete genes grouped in chromosomes inside an organism, but by the condition of all the cells in it, which implied that characteristics derived from the environment could be transmitted hereditarily. This amounted to a revival of scientifically largely discredited pre-Darwinist theories.

Lysenko's early experiments had some success, in the Ukraine in 1927–9, and they came in very handy to a party leadership worried about the wheat crop, and looking out for panaceas to accompany the mass collectivization on which they were about to embark. They were reluctant to waste time in further experiments to make sure the theory was correct. As Vilyams, a colleague of Lysenko, said: 'When Lenin was establishing the Soviet regime in Russia, he did not agree to leave the Ukraine to Hetman Skoropadsky in order to compare which regime is better.' Without further ado, therefore, vernalization was widely recommended, and through the nomenklatura system more and more agronomists and party officials willing to enforce it were appointed to rural areas.

The academic establishment, however, mostly resisted Lysenko's ideas as of dubious validity. Resistance to him was centred in the Institute of Plant Breeding, whose director, N. I. Vavilov, had spent most of his adult life assembling and studying an enormous variety of plant species for cross-fertilization and the development and selection of high-yield, disease-resistant hybrids. Vavilov himself, ironically, was an enthusiastic socialist, for he believed in large-scale meticulous experimentation, and held that only a socialist system could guarantee the resources and organization necessary to accomplish it. His work was based on the scientifically much better attested Mendelian system of genetics.

In 1938, however, thanks to the party's appointments system, Lysenko became president of the Lenin Academy of Agricultural Sciences, and thus the ultimate arbiter in these matters. He and his colleagues adopted the Stalinist labelling technique, and dubbed Vavilov and their other opponents 'wreckers', 'Trotskyites' and 'kulak hangers-on'. This had the desired effect. In 1940 Vavilov was arrested and convicted of spying for Britain and of agrarian sabotage. He died later in a labour camp.

The post-war atmosphere and the burgeoning 'anti-cosmopolitan' campaign provided the ideal background for Lysenko to complete the defeat of his opponents. He was able to portray himself as an authentic son of the people, building a truly Soviet – and Russian – agricultural science against the opposition of arrogant foreigners and gloomy, pedantic academics. At a meeting of the Agricultural Academy in August 1948 he forced through the election of his own protégés as new academics, and the outright condemnation of Mendelian genetics in favour of his own doctrine which, after an earlier Russian scientist, he called Michurinism. In his report he specifically divided science crudely into 'bourgeois' and 'socialist' camps:

The Weissmanist–Mendelist–Morganist current in bio-logy is an anti-popular [*antinarodny*], pseudo- scientific, pernicious tendency. It disarms practice and orientates man towards resignation to the allegedly eternal laws of nature, towards passivity, and an aimless search for hidden treasure and expectation of lucky accidents.

Thus science yielded to willpower, and the doctrine 'there are no fortresses Bolsheviks cannot storm' was taken to its ultimate extreme. A wholesale purge of the biological estab-lishment followed. Institutes and laboratories of genetics were disbanded. University syllabi were rewritten, textbooks destroyed and lecturers dismissed. When, at a party meeting, the well-known geneticist, I. A. Rapoport, declined to recant, but asked, 'Why do you think that Comrade Molotov knows genetics better than I?' he was both fired from his job and expelled from the party. By contrast, Lysenko's portrait was hung in scientific institutes, busts and plaques of him were put on sale, and the State Chorus incorporated an anthem on him into its repertoire.

In effect, this was the destruction of the science of genetics, and of large areas of botany, zoology and agronomy. A whole generation of scholars in these fields was paralysed and then routed by a bunch of 'barefoot scientists' who had nothing of permanent value to offer.

Stalin's last years marked the nadir of intellectual and cultural life in the USSR. Both Marxism and Russian nationalism were raided to produce a crude, reductionist and paranoid view of the world, which was made obligatory for every artist, scientist and scholar, indeed for anyone who wished to get into print. Yet, like all paranoid visions, it had its own internal consistency and its own compelling logic. This was acknowledged in a backhanded tribute by Vasily Aksenov, the novelist who ten years later was to symbolize the revolt against it. 'Even as we giggled over Zoshchenko's little monkey and wrote out Akhmatova's verses for our girls,' he wrote in his semi-autobiographical novel *Ozhog*

(The Scorch Mark, 1980), 'even then deep down – yes, deep down – we were convinced of the normality of Zhdanov's world and of the abnormality, sickliness and shamefulness of Zoshchenko's.'

Politics at the highest level in the post-war years is shrouded in a good deal of mystery, and it would be disingenuous to pretend to clarity about it. Even exhaustive 'Kremlinological' research has failed to penetrate the smokescreen thrown up by official secrecy, and to produce an indisputable version of the personal power struggles going on behind the pages of *Pravda*.

It seems clear that Zhdanov was, after Stalin, the dominant figure of the immediate post-war years, and that this ascendancy was associated with the party's recovery of influence. But in August 1948, Zhdanov suddenly died, and there followed a savage purge of the Leningrad party organization, with which he had been so closely associated during the blockade. The most prominent victim was Voznesensky, who had worked with Zhdanov in Leningrad before becoming chairman of Gosplan. All the leading party and Soviet officials in the city and in Leningrad oblast were arrested and executed, as were hundreds of their subordinates. Several explanations may be hazarded for this purge. It followed closely on the expulsion of Yugoslavia from the Cominform (see below). Now the Cominform had apparently been Zhdanov's brainchild, as a means of coordinating the work of the various European Communist parties, and in this it had conspicuously failed. A Yugoslav delegation had visited Leningrad in 1947 and been particularly impressed by the spirit they sensed in the city; one of its members, Milovan Djilas later wrote that the Leningraders' achievement in withstanding the German siege had 'surpassed the Yugoslav revolution, if not in heroism then in collective sacrifice'. Such links were sufficient to arouse Stalin's suspicion, especially since he had always distrusted the independence and *ésprit de corps* of the Leningraders. From other sources it appears possible, furthermore, that plans were being seriously discussed to make Leningrad the capital of the RSFSR and the headquarters of a Russian Communist Party (equivalent to the Ukrainian Communist Party etc., but much bigger). In the post-war Russian nationalist mood of many cadres, such a plan would probably have been popular, and it would have rectified a long-standing anomaly in the structure both of the party and of the Union. But there can be no doubt that a 'revived' Leningrad of that kind would have represented a powerful rival to Moscow: the imbalance which Stalin had helped to create in the institutions of the Soviet Union would have been turned against him. Arguably, therefore, Stalin moved to prevent any such plan being realized. Circumstantial evidence for this version is provided by the fact that one of the victims of the purge was M. I. Rodionov, who was unconnected with Leningrad, but was currently prime minister of the RSFSR.

At any rate, every effort was made to expunge Leningrad's heroic war record. The Museum of the Defence of Leningrad was closed, its director was arrested, and its archives were confiscated. Planned collections of materials on the blockade were withdrawn from publication, and Leningrad newspaper files from the war years were placed under restricted access in libraries.

The eclipse of Zhdanov (whether his death was natural or not) and the destruction of the Leningrad organization seemed to mark the revival of two figures who had risen to prominence in the late thirties: Beria, as head of the security police, and Malenkov, as the principal cadres secretary, and hence the man responsible for the nomenklatura network. Even this cannot, however, be asserted with absolute certainty. Beria's empire, for example, had been cut in two by the division into an MGB (Ministry of State Security), responsible for the security police and its auxiliaries, and an MVD (Ministry of Internal Affairs), responsible for the ordinary police, public order and the labour camps. Beria headed the latter, while the security services were taken over by men not thought to be closely associated with him: V. S. Abakumov till 1951, then S. D. Ignatiev. The latter even instituted a purge in Mingrelia, the part of Georgia which had been Beria's own homeland.

Purges, as can be seen, were now selective and sporadic, no longer all-pervasive as in the late thirties. They did not need to be: the nightmare memory of those years lurked in most people's minds, ready to be activated by the slightest threat. Most of the intellectuals victimized in Zhdanov's campaigns, for example, were not actually arrested as they would have been a decade earlier: they were 'permitted' to carry on a menial existence as laboratory assistants and nightwatchmen.

There is, however, considerable evidence that at the end of his life Stalin *was* contemplating another major purge. The leading cadres in both party and government were men who had occupied high positions for the best part of fifteen years. They had formed strong personal relationships and even a certain mutual solidarity. This meant they were a potential obstacle to Stalin's exercise of unlimited power. He may have concluded that the time had come to replace them with a younger generation, who would, initially at least, be more malleable.

In 1952 a full Party Congress was called, the nineteenth, and the first since 1939. In one sense it put the seal on the regularization of the party's affairs which had been proceeding ever since 1945. In another it might be seen as the first step towards Stalin's intended grand purge. Both the Politburo and Orgburo were abolished, and replaced by a new body, the Presidium, which consisted of thirty-six members: the ten members of the old Politburo (minus Andreyev) were swamped by relatively younger newcomers. Khrushchev's later interpretation of this reform was that Stalin 'aimed at the removal of the old Politburo members and the bringing in of less experienced persons so that these would extol him in all sorts of ways. We can assume that this was also a design for the future annihilation of the old Politburo members. . . .'

If Khrushchev was right, it would explain what happened shortly after the congress. In January 1953 it was announced that a group of doctors (mostly with Jewish-sounding surnames) were planning 'to wipe out the leading cadres of the USSR' by medical means. The accusations levelled against these doctors – wrecking, terrorism, acting as American spies – strongly recalled those of 1936–9. The security services were reproached with 'lack of vigilance', which suggested that the next person to be arrested might be Beria, and after that nobody knew who might follow.

The purge did not, however, take place, as Stalin died fairly suddenly on 5 March 1953. In view of his evident designs on his closest colleagues, one is bound to ask: was his death natural? There can be no clear answer to that question. On the one hand, Stalin was elderly and in poor health: he had suffered his first stroke some years before. On the other hand, his colleagues (if they can be called that) had such obvious motives for hastening his end. There were in fact one or two suspicious circumstances surrounding his death. During the months beforehand his personal secretary, Poskrebyshev, the head of his bodyguard, General Vlasik, and his personal physician, Dr Vinogradov, had all been dismissed and the last two arrested. Stalin had become convinced that they could not be trusted any more: his paranoia had reached the stage at which he was undermining his own safety. When he suffered a stroke on the night of 1–2 March, his dacha was sealed off by security troops, and he could have been deprived of medical aid, or indeed given some injection to help him on his way. His daughter, Svetlana, says that the last time she saw him, he was surrounded by 'unknown doctors'.

This is all conjecture. What is certain is that his successors all acted thereafter as if their first priority was to get the security services under their control, and prevent any purge being implemented. The Doctors' Plot was dropped immediately. Beria reamalgamated the MVD and the MGB under his own control. All the other leaders thereupon decided that *he* was now the principal danger to them all, and united against him. In July, at a combined meeting of the party Presidium, the Council of Ministers and some of the principal generals (whose cooperation was essential), Beria was arrested and accused of 'anti-party and anti-state activities'. According to Khrushchev, he was shot on the spot, to forestall any attempt by the security police to rescue him; other sources say that he was executed in December after a secret trial. The justification for his execution was that he was a 'British spy'.

Stalin's own methods were thus used to eliminate his most dangerous successor, after which the surviving leaders strove to bring the security services under collective control and prevent any one person from ever again using them as a private weapon.

After the war a new dimension entered Soviet politics. This was the condominium of nations lying under direct Soviet influence in Central and Eastern Europe. This grouping, soon to be generally known as the 'Soviet bloc', both raised the power and standing of the Soviet Union in the world, and also provided an arena where alternative models of socialism could be tried out – in ways not always welcome to the Soviet authorities. The Soviet bloc, in fact, brought its Soviet masters both new opportunities and new tensions.

During 1944–5 the Red Army conquered Poland, eastern and central Germany, Czechoslovakia, Hungary, Romania and Bulgaria, while Communist-led partisans seized power in Albania and Yugoslavia. At the international conferences of Yalta and Potsdam the Western powers recognized the dominant Soviet interest in these areas, while attempting to stipulate that the new regimes established there should be 'democratic'. It soon emerged that the Soviet interpretation of that word differed fundamentally from the Western one.

In the early stages, however, that was still not clear. There were plenty of reasons why the populations of Eastern and Central Europe might actually welcome left-wing governments in 1945. All except Czechoslovakia had ex-

perienced the breakdown of liberal democratic systems between the wars, as well as the malfunctioning of the
economy during the depression. The German occupation
had undermined or destroyed the traditional ruling classes
in both agriculture and industry. Moreover, after suffering
the horrors of Nazi rule, most of the peoples of the area
had some reason to welcome the Red Army when it came,
even where, as in Poland or Hungary, anti-Russian feeling
was traditionally very strong.

Stalin had therefore a basis of popular support from
which to work in creating regimes that would be friendly
and, in his terms, 'reliable'. He decided not to proceed as
he had done in the Baltic and Poland before the war – by
direct annexation of the new territories under his control
and by deportation of hostile elements. The Germans had
in any case already accomplished part of the latter task for
him. He had also come to the conclusion that the Soviet
Union's security for the foreseeable future depended on
continuing the alliance with the Western powers, and he
did not wish to offend them by a conspicuously brutal
show of force.

Soviet methods in Eastern and Central Europe were therefore somewhat different. Non-Communist political parties
were permitted to form and to some extent to organize themselves. Communists actually shared power with them for a
time in coalition governments. Then came a stage of what
Hugh Seton-Watson has termed 'bogus coalition'. By the use
of police powers, liberal and peasant parties were driven into
opposition, their ranks split by Communist stooges, their
leading politicians harassed or arrested, their meetings and
organizations broken up. At this stage the Social Democratic
Party was usually persuaded to merge with the Communist
Party to produce a 'United Workers' Party' (the name
differed slightly from one country to another) which then
exercised power single-handed, or with a few cowed
nominees from other parties in a 'Popular Front' (again with
slight variations in terminology). All this would be confirmed

in referenda or elections conducted under overwhelming police pressure and in the absence of serious opposition.

The tempo of these successive stages varied from one country to another: in Poland, Romania and Bulgaria the first stage was very short, whereas in Czechoslovakia it lasted till February 1948. In Czechoslovakia, in fact, the Communists enjoyed considerable popular support: in the freely conducted elections of May 1946 they polled 38 per cent of the vote and became the largest party in the National Assembly, the only time a Marxist party has ever achieved a relative majority in a democratic parliamentary election. Even there, however, the final stages of the Communist takeover could not be accomplished without the application of police power. In each country the presence of the Red Army, along with advisers (usually from the NKVD) from the Soviet Union, was a decisive factor in the post-war political constellation. Significantly, in Yugoslavia, which had achieved its own liberation from the Germans, things were to turn out rather differently, as we shall see.

The social and economic changes introduced by the new regimes were very similar to one another. Industry was nationalized, and in some cases its equipment transported to the Soviet Union to help reconstruction there. State planning became general, with post-war recovery plans succeeded by Five Year Plans on the Soviet model. All the countries refused American Marshall Aid, and integrated their economies more closely with the Soviet Union, often on terms favourable to the Soviet interest. Workers in the nationalized industries were put on piece-rate wages, at low rates, while their trade unions were centralized and brought under political control. Provision was made for broad social security, but the benefits of it went primarily to those employees who stayed in the same jobs and accepted the labour discipline.

Education systems were completely overhauled, all religious and private schools being abolished or brought within the state system. There was a new emphasis on practical and technical education, while in the humanities and social sciences Marxism–Leninism–Stalinism became a compulsory element, on the Soviet model. Admissions authorities practised discrimination against the children of formerly privileged social classes, priests, etc., with the aim of raising a new educated class to take positions of leadership.

A radical land reform was usually effected, expropriating the old landowners and finally destroying the aristocracy where it had survived hitherto; the land thus set free was redistributed to smallholders. These, however, suffered grave handicaps from the start. First, because of the food shortages, they were required to make certain compulsory deliveries to the state at low prices; then, around 1949–50, the better-off ones found themselves subjected to discriminatory taxes while the rest were exhorted to enter collective farms. This process was not completed by the time of Stalin's death in 1953, when the East European countries began to be permitted a degree of latitude in pursuing their 'own roads to socialism', but in general it may be said that these countries repeated the path the Soviet Union had traversed in the twenties. In their case, however, the process was both telescoped and cut short (by Stalin's death and subsequent events). Since, moreover, the changes were being imposed from outside, often against national traditions and interests, it will be evident that by the mid-fifties abundant material for conflict existed there.

After 1948 or so it would not be unreasonable to regard the Central and East European nations as constituting a Soviet Empire, such was the degree of control exercised by the Soviet regime over them. Now, when a country acquires an empire, it takes on more than it realizes. This is especially true when the 'colonies' have a more advanced economy and a more differentiated social structure than the metropolis. The metropolis then finds itself importing ideas, culture and social structures from the colonies – unless, that is, it is prepared to seal itself off from such influences and to rule the subject nations by brute force. This the Soviet Union, at least since Stalin's death, has not been prepared to do, except at periods of crisis. In fact, under Khrushchev and subsequently, it would no longer really still be correct to call the Eastern bloc an 'empire', for the nations do have a limited measure of sovereignty; but the very fact that they coexist in a 'brotherhood' or 'commonwealth' of socialist nations means that ideas can travel readily from one country to another and influence each other's development.

What this mutual influence has usually amounted to is that the nations of Central and Eastern Europe have tested out some of the latent possibilities in the socialist tradition – which had been buried in the Soviet Union itself because of that country's highly authoritarian evolution. Some of these possibilities have been allowed to develop gradually and to become realities, while others have been crushed more or less at birth because the Soviet authorities found their implications for internal Soviet developments much too worrying.

The most radical of these experiments has been the one that began before Stalin's death: Yugoslavia. It is no accident that this was, along with Albania, the only socialist system to have liberated itself from German occupation with minimal Soviet help. Tito, the Yugoslav leader, admired the Soviet Union very greatly, and wanted to follow its example faithfully, but he was not directly beholden to it for his position. His Communist Party enjoyed popular support because it had led the fight against the Germans: unlike other East European leaders, he had not been brought into the country in a Red Army truck, and he did not depend on support and advice from the NKVD. He was, therefore, in a position to resist some of the arrangements which other East Europeans found most objectionable. He was furious, for example, at Soviet attempts to recruit Yugoslav citizens as agents of the NKVD – a normal practice in Eastern Europe at the time. He resisted one-sided trading arrangements which would have given the Soviet Union an exploitative position inside the Yugoslav economy. He annoyed Stalin, too, by pressing ahead very fast with the country's political and economic development, refusing to conclude any serious coalition with 'bourgeois' parties, as Stalin thought advisable, and embarking forthwith on a very ambitious Five Year Plan of industrial development. According to Djilas, who went with a number of Yugoslav delegations to Moscow, Tito and his colleagues were, moreover, shocked and repelled by the duplicity and the arrogant power politics which they felt characterized the Soviet Union's attitude towards its allies and fraternal Communist parties.

In the end Stalin lost patience with Tito's recalcitrance, and expelled Yugoslavia from the Cominform, the organization currently coordinating the policies of the ruling European Communist parties. This confronted the Yugoslav leaders with a sudden and grave crisis. The abrupt withdrawal of Soviet trade and advisers necessitated at least drastic revision of the industrial growth plan, while the nation's new isolation on the international scene obliged Tito to strengthen defences, to look for new allies, and to seek for maximum political support from the Yugoslav peoples.

The crisis called into question everything the Yugoslav leaders had taken for granted, and to that extent it was like the emergency Lenin faced in the spring of 1921. Unlike Lenin, however, Tito did not merely institute a stop-gap retreat from socialist measures. What he did, partly under pressure from his political advisers, was to rethink completely what socialism should mean in practice, and to elaborate a whole new philosophy of socialist development. Significantly, in his speech to the Yugoslav National Assembly in June 1950, expounding the new approach, Tito took his stand on Lenin's most 'libertarian' work, *State and Revolution*, and pointed out how far the Soviet polity had diverged from the principles laid down by its founder. The 'dictatorship of the proletariat', he asserted, had not withered away as socialism developed and the class struggle eased: on the contrary, the Soviet apparatus of coercion had grown stronger and more violent, and was being used not against class enemies or external foes, but against allies, supporters and innocent citizens. In contrast, Tito announced, Yugoslavia would take its 'own road to socialism', following genuine Leninist principles, through the devolution of state power as far as possible to the working people.

To describe how this has worked in practice would require a separate study. But the most important respects in which the Yugoslav model of socialism differs from the Soviet one can be summed up:

1. The state structure is more genuinely federal. At the lowest level, popularly elected People's Councils, later called Communes, control most local functions, including economic enterprises, and influence, within broadly defined limits, their investment and production plans. This is close to what many soviet supporters *thought* they were steering towards in Russia in 1917.

2. Economic enterprises are answerable to their own employees. By the law of 2 July 1950, all the workers in a given enterprise were to elect by secret ballot a Workers' Council, responsible for supervising the overall management of the enterprise and for appointing a board of directors to effect day-to-day running. This is close in spirit to the Bolsheviks' decree on 'workers' control' of November 1917.

3. Agriculture is mostly private or cooperative rather than collective. Since March 1953 it has been legal for peasants to leave collective farms, and most have done so, reclaiming their private plots. In place of the collectives, so-called 'general cooperatives' help with the provision of credit, machinery and bulk purchasing, while they give agrarian advice and facilitate marketing. Such a structure would have been a likely outcome of developing NEP in the way Bukharin envisaged, or indeed Lenin at the very end of his life.

4. The various nationalities of Yugoslavia enjoy very real autonomous powers, embodied in their national republics, to

pursue their own policies in such fields as economics, education, culture and social welfare. This is what many people expected from the Bolshevik slogan of 'national self-determination'.

What is not clear is the way these serious modifications of the Soviet model have affected the structure and functions of the Yugoslav Communist Party. At its Sixth Congress in 1952 it changed its name to the League of Communists and declared that its role was now educative rather than administrative. Its leading body (now called the Executive Committee rather than Politburo) was specially reorganized to give all the nationalities proper representation on it. Edward Kardelj, Tito's deputy, even talked about the 'withering away of the party', while Djilas, in his book *The New Class*, warned that it was no historical accident if the Soviet Communist Party had raised up a new 'ruling class' of corrupt and power-seeking politicians: any party holding a monopoly of power was likely to generate a self-perpetuating oligarchy of such office-holders. In the event, Djilas's book was banned in Yugoslavia, he himself was imprisoned, and there has been little sign of the party 'withering away'. Perhaps this is *because* the reformed political system is so loose-limbed that it needs some kind of cement to hold it together at all. This at least seemed to be Tito's major concern in the last years of his life. At any rate, it seems most unlikely that the nomenklatura system can function in the same way as in the Soviet Union, since candidates put forward for election by popular bodies must require at least some talents other than ambition and deference to superiors.

Tito's position after 1948 was a palpable challenge to Stalin. For the first time since the death of Trotsky, a socialist of real standing and enjoying popular support had infringed Stalin's monopoly of the Marxist heritage. Even inside the Soviet Union, despite censorship, people began to realize that it was possible to propose alternative interpretations of socialism. Elsewhere in Eastern Europe the effect was even stronger, and Stalin hastened to reassert control there in a series of purges and show trials, on the Vyshinsky model, in which the accused were required to confess, among other things, to being guilty of 'Titoism'.

In view of more recent events in Eastern Europe, it may be asked why Stalin did not invade Yugoslavia and crush Tito. One cannot be certain of the reasons for his restraint, but two main considerations may be hypothesized. First, Stalin could not be sure that the West would not intervene. In a crude deal with Churchill back in 1944, Stalin had agreed that the West had a 50 per cent interest in Yugoslavia, and expulsion from the Cominform had made the country's status ambiguous again: Tito, indeed, had turned to the United States to replace the funding which the Soviet Union had withdrawn. One must remember, too, that the USA possessed a monopoly of nuclear weapons at this time, a factor which will certainly have figured in Stalin's calculations. Secondly, Stalin knew that Tito was no puppet, that by and large he had the support of a people accustomed and trained to guerrilla warfare against foreign occupiers. Doubtless the Red Army could have overcome such resistance in the end, but not before suffering considerable losses, and degrading the international reputation of the Soviet Union. It may be that Stalin placed his hopes in organizing an internal coup against Tito. If so, he miscalculated: Tito outlasted Stalin, and remained a living witness to the fact that it was possible to institute a different kind of socialism. This was to have profound consequences for the future.

12

Khrushchev and de-Stalinization

Since 1953 something historically unprecedented has been taking place in the Soviet Union. A totalitarian society has been evolving, not as a result of external pressure, but from its own internal contradictions, to a point where it becomes questionable whether the term is applicable any more. During Stalin's last years, it may be hypothesized, totalitarianism as a system reached its furthest limits, beyond which it could not go without undermining social cohesion altogether. We have already seen how the system had become intolerable to its own leaders; at the other end of society, in the labour camps, it was proving no less destructive.

The crisis was first of all a demographic one. The repressions of the 1930s, followed by the war, had taken a formidable toll of the population, above all of the men. The labour camps were now continuing this attrition at an alarming rate. If one takes Robert Conquest's rather sober estimate of 8 million as the average labour camp population from the late thirties onwards, then one is driven to the conclusion that between a tenth and a fifth of the entire adult male population were incarcerated after the war, working in conditions that were likely to lead to their premature death. This was not a situation that could be allowed to persist indefinitely without, at the very least, seriously weakening both industry and the armed forces – a prospect intolerable to the leaders of a Great Power.

In the late forties, it became apparent that the leaders *were* worried by the situation, and trying to do something about it. From about 1948, rather unevenly because of the famine, the Gulag administration began to improve the food supplies, raising rations slightly, and introducing more meat and fat. For the first time, zeks began to receive a tiny wage, and camp shops were opened, where they could buy items like jam, margarine and semolina to supplement their diet. At the same time, authorities in individual camps were instructed to produce a report whenever a zek died: perhaps as a result, they began to issue better clothing and take greater care over the provision of medicine. Zeks became slightly better fed, better clothed and a little healthier, which at the margin makes a lot of difference.

Not that these relaxations were intended to apply to all. In fact in 1948 it was decided to pick out the more serious political 'offenders' and isolate them in special 'strict regime' camps, with harsher discipline, and with no right of correspondence or visits. It was also intended that at the end of their sentences – typically by now twenty-five years – the inmates should not be permitted to return home, but should be detained in permanent exile near the camp.

On the face of it, that sounds like the most daunting form of imprisonment yet devised by Stalin. Yet in practice, as Solzhenitsyn testifies from his experience in these Special Camps, morale in them eventually improved. One reason was that the 'article 58s' (the politicals) were now no longer intimidated by the criminals, who had been left in the 'general regime' camps. But in any case the make-up of the political fraternity had changed considerably since the war: a good proportion of them were now Red Army officers (conscious of having done better than the MVD at defending the country), or nationalists from the Baltic, Bielorussia, the Ukraine and Poland (most of whom hated the Russians, and some of whom had experience of guerrilla warfare against them). Unlike the helpless peasants and frail intellectuals of the thirties, they were used to violence, had experience of fighting and something to fight for. As Solzhenitsyn says:

The whole system of oppression elaborated in [Stalin's] reign was based on keeping malcontents apart, preventing them from reading each other's eyes and discovering how many of them there were; instilling it into all of them, even into the most dissatisfied, that no one was dissatisfied except for a few doomed individuals, blindly vicious and spiritually bankrupt.

In the Special Camps, however, there were malcontents by the thousands. They knew their numerical strength. And they realized that they were not spiritual paupers, that they had a nobler conception of what life should be than their jailers, than their betrayers, than the theorists who tried to explain why they must rot in camps.

In some of these camps, it became quite common for stukachi (informers) to be murdered (a zek with a twenty-five-year sentence had little to lose by committing further crimes), which of course soon meant that the authorities lost their source of information about what the zeks were discussing and planning among themselves. Resistance groups formed in some camps, usually based on a particular national group, and sometimes they established ties with the outside world through ex-prisoners settled in the region. With the hardening of the Cold War, fantastic rumours spread through the camps that America and Russia were about to go to war, so that the time was ripe for insurrection. Even in the ordinary regime camps some of the criminals (known as *blatnye*) refused to serve the authorities any more and set up their own proud fraternities, living off the rest of the camp and in a state of permanent and bloody feud with those other criminals (the *suki*, or 'bitches') who preferred the less glorious but more comfortable role of 'trusties'. In certain camps at certain times this feud broke out into pitched warfare in which hundreds of lives were lost.

These changed conditions generated a mutinous spirit and in the end risings took place against the authorities in some of the camps. The politicals had less to lose, something to fight for and a greater sense of solidarity than in the thirties.

The first rising about which much is known took place

near Vorkuta, in the Arctic region of European Russia, in 1948. The kernel was an organization of Red Army officers, all graduates of the Frunze Military Academy. The rebels typified the independent spirit which had emerged in some parts of the Red Army: they admitted to their circle only fellow officers who had participated in the war against Germany and who had never been members of the Communist Party. They managed to disarm and massacre their guards, and then seized and liberated a neighbouring camp, before marching on Vorkuta. Paratroopers and dive-bombers had to be sent in to disperse them. There was also a strike at Ekibastuz, in Kazakhstan, in 1952. Here the zeks made the fatal mistake of declaring a hunger strike as well. This technique is only effective where the authorities scruple to let their prisoners die: but in Ekibastuz it only weakened the strikers' physical strength and facilitated repression.

What really shook the camps, however, was the death of Stalin, and, following that, the news of the arrest and execution of Beria. The major risings of which we have evidence were those in Norilsk (northern Siberia) in May 1953, in Vorkuta in July 1953, and in Kengir (Kazakhstan) in May 1954, though there were certainly a number of others. In Norilsk and Kengir the immediate trigger of revolt was the shooting of a prisoner for straying into a forbidden zone; in Vorkuta trouble was started by a trainload of zeks from Karaganda who had been promised better conditions and pay, but then been denied them. In other words, prisoners were refusing to accept basic violations of human dignity which they had felt compelled to tolerate for years.

In each case the insurgents were able to disarm their guards, take over the camp compound and refuse to go out to work. Their demands were similar from one area to another: a re-examination of all sentences; better rations; a shorter working day; the right to frequent correspondence and visits; elimination of numbers from prison clothes; removal of bars from windows and bolts from the doors of the huts inside the barbed wire; no reprisals (and in Kengir, the punishment of those responsible for shooting prisoners). In other words the re-establishment of *legality* and respect for human dignity. In each case the insurgents refused to negotiate with the local camp authorities, and demanded an emissary from Moscow.

These risings put the local MVD officials in a nasty quandary. On the one hand, the strikes interrupted planned output, which could not go unnoticed for long: Vorkuta, for example, provided coal for Leningrad. On the other hand, the very fact of having to report a prisoners' strike was a grave, even unprecedented humiliation, likely to fix a permanent blot on a promising officer's career. In Kengir the authorities reacted by opening fire on the strikers and killing a number of them before discovering that they could not cope without outside reinforcement, whereupon they withdrew, leaving the compound to the zeks. In Vorkuta, on the other hand, the authorities made immediate concessions: they removed bars from windows, left barracks unlocked, and announced that prisoners could send letters once a month and receive annual family visits. Similar concessions were made in Kengir once the local officials had contacted Moscow. Their aim was to gain time, and to divide the insurgents. The latter effect was sometimes achieved: in Vorkuta camp no. 7, the authorities sent an ultimatum warning that the concessions would be revoked unless the zeks left the compound in columns. The zeks complied, and as they did so, guards and stukachi picked out the ringleaders, loaded them into trucks and transported them off: in their absence the strike collapsed. In another of the Vorkuta camps, however, where the Pole Edward Buca was the strikeleader, the rebels held out for a commission to arrive from Moscow. In the meantime they comported themselves in a studiedly non-violent manner. Buca forbade the murder of stukachi, negotiated with the camp auth-orities to perform essential safety measures in the coalmines, and allowed the soldiers of the guard to draw rations from inside the camp. Banners appeared over the compound, bearing the words 'Coal for the fatherland, freedom for us' and 'There is nothing more precious in the world than man himself – Joseph Stalin'.

Generals, procurators and senior Gulag officials came down from Moscow – though no members of the party Presidium. They promised that if the rebels returned to work, then certain of their demands would be met. The zeks, however, held out for all of them. In the end even Moscow was able to suggest nothing but crude repression. In Kengir, sappers cut huge gaps in the barbed wire, and invited the strikers to come out and give themselves up. Almost nobody did. Then tanks went in, dragging huge rolls of barbed wire on trestles to isolate one hut from another: in some cases their enormous caterpillar tracks crushed corners and sides of huts, and the prisoners within them, while infantry came on behind to shoot and bayonet those who tried to escape.

> At that moment some Ukrainian women, dressed in embroidered blouses, which back at home they probably used to wear to church, linked arms and, holding their heads high, walked towards the tanks. We all thought the tanks would halt before the serried ranks of these defenceless women. But no, they only accelerated. Carrying out Moscow's orders, they drove straight on over the live bodies. There were no cries: all we heard was a horrible sound of bodies being crushed and cracking bones. Meanwhile soldiers went round the barracks shooting down everyone they came across. The massacre lasted from three in the morning till half past eight.

The account of this incident, from an underground Ukrainian source, gives some idea of the spirit of the insurgents, and of the ruthlessness of their assailants. Its essentials are confirmed in Solzhenitsyn's *Gulag Archipelago*.

In spite of the repression, the outcome of these strikes was a perceptible improvement in the zeks' living and working conditions. The hated numbers were removed from the prison clothes, bars taken off the windows and the barracks left unlocked at night. Restrictions on correspondence and visits were eased. Health care, clothing and nourishment were improved. One or two eye-witnesses even begin to report zeks *sending* money or clothes to their relatives living in some of the grimmer collective farms.

In the long run, too, these outbreaks were bound to give the post-Stalin leadership a lot to think about. The labour camps were effective, and cheap to run, only so long as the inmates were docile. If that condition no longer held, then they became prohibitively expensive, and indeed a threat to internal security. The great fear must have been that zeks would succeed in disarming the warders and taking over a whole complex of camps: in view of their huge numbers, the arms they would then possess, and the experience some of them had in partisan warfare, it would require a formidable military operation to put them down. The leaders would not, of course, hesitate to mount such an operation if necessary, but was it certain that, in the more sophisticated economic climate following post-war reconstruction, the massive unskilled labour power of the camps was still such an asset?

We have no direct evidence of such deliberations, and can only reconstruct them from conjecture. But the crisis of the labour camp system coincided with a wave of letters and petitions from all over the country following the execution of Beria: these were from people – party and non-party members – requesting that the charges against their imprisoned relatives be re-examined after the revelation that Beria, head of the security services, had been a traitor. The Procurator's office acted on a number of these requests, and by the end of 1955 some 10,000 people – a tiny proportion of those illegally confined – had been set free. Perhaps even more significant, the Procuracy began to rehabilitate some of those convicted under Stalin, recognizing that they had been the victims of 'legal distortions'. Many of these re-habilitations were, of course, posthumous, and one may ask why they were declared at all. Why not simply announce an amnesty and release those who had survived?

We cannot answer that question with certainty, but two motives suggest themselves. First, a person actually cleared of the charges against him, as well as his close relatives, had the right to reclaim property confiscated by the state, a job commensurate with his status and the attendant privileges, such as a residence permit for one of the major cities. This was an important reinsurance policy for the elite. Secondly, it seems quite likely that the procuracy and the courts wanted to reassert their independence of the security police, and re-establish some kind of legality: certainly the press began to talk a great deal at this time about 'socialist legality'. In the attempt to secure it, soon after Beria's death the Prosecuting Department of the MVD was abolished, and with it the Special Tribunals, or 'troiki', which had passed summary sentence on so many. This meant that in future, criminal investigation, prosecution and trial had to take place outside the security police, before the regular courts, under authorities formally answerable to the Supreme Soviet, and actually to the Central Committee of the party.

At the same time the security police was appreciably downgraded. It was once again detached from the MVD empire, renamed the KGB (Committee of State Security) and subordinated to the Council of Ministers – or again, in practice, the party Central Committee. No longer would it be at the disposal of one man and his private chancellery. Men who had made their career not in the police, but in the party, were appointed to run the KGB: many of its new senior staff were former Komsomol officials, such as A. N. Shelepin (who headed it in 1958–61) and V. E. Semichastny (1961–7). The number of paid agents and informers was drastically reduced. The effect of these measures was to render the security police more accountable to the party leadership as a whole, and ensured that, at least outwardly, they would have to observe certain minimal standards of legality. So much was necessary to guarantee the future safety of the party–state elite. Yet, as we shall see, observing even minimal legal standards was to cause them some dilemmas.

Systematic work on the rehabilitations also made it clear just how dangerous was the path the leadership was treading. In 1954 the Central Committee set up a special commission, under P. N. Pospelov, to collect evidence on Stalin's repressions of leading party cadres. As the commission did its work, the full horror of the arrests and executions, which few had been in a position to appreciate entirely, became clear. Khrushchev says in his memoirs that the extent of Stalin's crimes was a 'complete surprise' to him. This is certainly partly disingenuous, though there is something in his pleading that 'we were part of a regime in which you were told what you were supposed to know, and you kept your nose out of everything else'. Clearly, too, Khrushchev was *less* responsible than Beria or even Malenkov, who had been in charge of cadres at the time. But whatever the precise measure of responsibility of each man, the Pospelov report faced all the leaders with an agonizing dilemma. How much should they disclose about crimes in which they had been part-accomplices? And with people being rehabilitated and released from the camps, would not the full truth come out anyway and discredit them more than if they admitted it publicly?

Their dilemma was complicated by the fact that Stalin's succession was not yet fully resolved. With no established procedure for inheriting power, the leaders had divided the principal jobs in party and state among themselves and declared 'collective leadership'. Malenkov, who became prime minister at Stalin's death, was regarded by many as the principal figure, but, as after Lenin's death, the first secretaryship of the party proved in practice to be the more powerful post. Its incumbent, Khrushchev, did not look like an obvious successor to Stalin. He had never lost the earthiness of his 'peasant-worker' background, and his garrulity, impulsiveness and occasional burst of demotic idealism – he loved to get out and about, hob-nobbing with workers and collective farmers – made him seem completely out of place in the world of sealed dachas and discreetly curtained limousines which the elite had now created for itself.

Nevertheless, he used well the advantages which his party secretaryship bestowed on him. Like Stalin before him, he made many new appointments at the republican and oblast levels of the party apparatus. These new appointees were far more powerful than they had been under Stalin, for they now controlled the security police rather than being controlled by it. They became, in effect, little Stalins in their domains, secure in the power and privileges they enjoyed. Khrushchev also appealed to their idealism with his bold new agrarian policies (see below), which promised to do something effective at last about deep-seated economic problems.

Malenkov found himself eased out of the premiership in February 1955, though he remained in the party Presidium (the successor to the Politburo, now reduced to its pre-1952 numerical level). He was replaced by N. A. Bulganin, a political general, who had risen at the time of Zhukov's decline in 1946. Of Stalin's closest associates of the worst purge years, Molotov, Kaganovich, Mikoyan and Voroshilov also remained in the Presidium. We do not know exactly what discussions took place between them over the question of how much to reveal at the first post-Stalin Party Congress, the twentieth (1956), but the nightmare of being themselves tried for complicity in Stalin's crimes clearly hung over them. Khrushchev claims in his memoirs to have urged his colleagues to 'make a clean breast to the delegates about the conduct of the party leadership during the years in question'. That is possible, but far from certain. What does ring true is the objection he attributes to Voroshilov and Kaganovich: 'We'll be taken to task! The party has the right to hold us responsible for what happened under Stalin! We were in the leadership, and even if we didn't know what was happening, that's just too bad – we'll still be made to pay!'

What they actually did was to compromise. The party's formal report to the congress, delivered by Khrushchev, said nothing about Stalin's crimes. But immediately after the official end of the congress, a special closed session was convened, a procedure reminiscent of Lenin's method of dealing with the sensitive issue of party discipline at the Tenth Congress in 1921. At this closed session, to which delegates were admitted by special pass, Khrushchev made a long speech devoted to Stalin's crimes, and he also read out Lenin's Testament, which had been suppressed by his successors in 1924 (see above, page 131). Stalin's 'cult of personality', Khrushchev charged, had given rise to 'a whole series of exceedingly serious and grave perversions of party principles, of party democracy, of revolutionary legality'. The delegates listened to Khrushchev in awed silence, and then dispersed immediately afterwards, no discussion being permitted. The speech was not published in the Soviet Union. It soon became known abroad, however, apparently because Khrushchev had invited leaders of some foreign Communist Party delegations. It was also subsequently discussed at numerous party meetings throughout the Soviet Union; at some of these, for example in universities, non-party people were also present, and apparently had no difficulty in getting in. At least some party leaders, then, were anxious that it should not remain a 'Secret Speech' (the name by which it is usually known), even if they were not prepared to publish it.

The contents of the speech were also a compromise, as they needed to be, to fulfil the aims of the divided party leadership. Khrushchev began his account of Stalin's repressions only with 1934, implying that all his previous policies, the crushing of the various 'Oppositions', the Shakhty trial and its immediate successors directed against 'specialists', the brutal collectivization of the peasants, had been entirely justified. Furthermore, he limited his accusations to Stalin himself and his principal security chiefs, evading the question of his own responsibility for the repressions, as well as that of his colleagues in the Presidium. In this way, Khrushchev attempted to set well-defined limits to the permissible area of discussion. He explicitly reaffirmed the correctness of the super-fast industrialization programme, of the collective farm structure, of the rejection of the policies associated with both the Left and Right Oppositions.

The main focus of the Secret Speech, in fact, was the long series of repressions of leading figures in the party and state, and of well-known public figures. Nearly everyone whose fate Khrushchev mentioned had belonged to the highest reaches of the nomenklatura patronage network. Apart from some of the deported nationalities, he made no reference to the sufferings of ordinary workers, peasants and employees. It was unequivocally a speech of the elite defending itself against Stalin's ghost and against any possible aspiring successor. Khrushchev implied that somehow the Communist Party and in particular its Central Committee had managed to lead a kind of separate and precarious existence, continuing to observe 'Leninist norms of party life', even as the tyrant was exterminating them. He appealed to this tradition at the close of his speech as a programme for the future: renunciation of the 'cult of personality' in favour of 'collective leadership', meticulous observation of the party statutes (holding regular congresses, frequent meetings of the Central Committee), the 'wide practice of criticism and self-criticism', observation of the Soviet consitution and the restoration of 'socialist legality'. As we shall see later, Khrushchev did attempt in his own way to carry out this programme.

The speech caused a veritable revolution (the word is not too strong) in people's attitudes throughout the Soviet Union and Eastern Europe. It was the greatest single factor in breaking down the mixture of fear, fanaticism, naivety and 'doublethink' with which everyone, according to temperament, intelligence and status, had reacted to Communist rule.

Not surprisingly, the shock was registered most immediately and violently in Eastern Europe, where Stalinism had shallower roots. There indignation was expressed most vehemently by the workers, defrauded inheritors of the new 'People's Republics', and by the scientific and creative intelligentsia, restive under the crude and monolithic ideological orthodoxy. Tension had been building up since 1953, and especially since Khrushchev legitimized the notion of 'separate roads to socialism' by publicly ending the quarrel with Tito in 1955.

In Poland it was the intellectuals who responded first. They began to revive the clubs and discussion groups which had been a feature of pre-war literary life: especially well known was the Club of the Crooked Circle, formed around the youth journal *Po prostu* (Simply). At a meeting of the official Council of Culture and Art in March 1956, just after the Secret Speech, the poet Anton Slonimski declared, 'We must give back to words their meaning and integrity . . . we must clear the road . . . of the whole mythology of the era of fear.'

In June the workers joined them. At the ZISPO engineering works in Poznań, they went on strike at an increase in production norms which signified in effect a reduction in wages. As they marched into the centre of town with placards calling for 'bread and freedom' and 'lower prices, higher wages', their numbers were swelled by other citizens whose placards bore more general political demands: 'Down with the Soviet occupation!' and 'Free Cardinal Wyszynski [the head of the Catholic Church in Poland]!' They attacked the radio building (from where Western broadcasts were jammed) and the police station. Internal security troops were brought in, and fighting broke out, in which, according to official figures fifty-three were killed and about three hundred wounded.

This massacre not only unleashed strikes in other industrial cities but also provoked a grave crisis in the party leadership. There was a substantial faction which proclaimed that the strikes were not the result of 'imperialist provocation' (as the official press claimed), but of mistaken policies: they demanded the return of Wladyslaw Gomulka, who had been arrested as a 'Titoist' in 1951 and quietly released in 1954. After anxious comings and goings by high Soviet officials, the Soviet Union eventually accepted this solution as preferable to sending in tanks and crushing the unrest.

Gomulka's programme was 'national communism', which meant combining patriotism (up to and including restrained anti-Russianism) with the search for a 'separate road to socialism'. In Poland's case this had something in common with the Yugoslav road: peasants were given permission to leave the collective farms and re-establish their private smallholdings, while in the factories elected workers' councils were given the right to supervise management decisions. One factor, however, was peculiar to Poland: that was the degree of independence accorded to the Roman Catholic Church, which since 1939 had increasingly become the focus of the people's national and spiritual aspirations. One of Gomulka's first acts was to free Cardinal Wyszynski, and to conclude an agreement with him, whereby the state guaranteed the church's right to teach religion in schools wherever parents wished (which was just about everywhere), while the church agreed to uphold the legitimacy of the socialist state, and its overall social policy. A small group of Catholic deputies was allowed to sit in the *Sejm* (the Polish parliament) and became, under the name of *Znak*, the only deputies in any East European parliament not under the direct control of the Communist Party.

To begin with, Gomulka's Poland really did seem to offer an alternative model of socialism, but with the passage of time, under Soviet pressure, it gradually reverted to the norm of Communist systems. In particular the workers' councils were reabsorbed into the party nomenklatura system and rendered harmless, while censorship slowly tightened. But some of the hard-won achievements survived: private agriculture, trade and services, a relatively independent church. Poland remained a living witness to the fact that an NEP-type of society could, with constant vigilance and reassertion of rights, exist under a Communist government, and that social groups could win for themselves a limited measure of autonomy. This point should not be exaggerated, for it remained true, as we shall see, that the party–state hierarchy was profoundly unhappy with this situation, and was constantly striving to erode autonomy and restore party control over every aspect of social life.

Their efforts to do this were aided by what happened in 1956 in Hungary. There discontent was held under pressure even longer by the tardy survival in office of the Stalinist Rakosi. The party had become so alienated from the mass of people that *real* politics was a vacuum, ripe to be filled by any group which could claim a measure of genuine moral authority. As in Poland, that role was initially played by writers. It was a series of meetings of the Petöfi Circle (so-called after a well-known Hungarian romantic poet of the nineteenth century) which provided the initial fuel for the protest movement. Among the demands raised were the expulsion of Rakosi from the party, the trial of the security police chief, Farkas, and the rehabilitation of his victims; the revival of the Patriotic Popular Front (the post-war coalition of parties under Communist 'guidance') as a genuine political forum representing real parties; the establishment of 'workers' control' in the factories.

As we have seen from the example of Poland, such a programme might have been acceptable to the Soviet leadership. But student meetings and street demonstrations on 23 October, encouraged by the news from Poland, demanded much more than this: a free press, free elections with genuine opposition parties, the withdrawal of Soviet occupation troops. Symbolically, the statue of Stalin in Budapest was hauled down and smashed, while the Hungarian national flag was raised with the hammer and sickle cut out.

Imre Nagy, hastily brought in as prime minister and himself like Gomulka a Stalin victim restored to power on a wave of public acclaim, resisted these demands as long as possible. But – and here the situation differed from Poland – he soon found that he had no support on which to fall back, so tainted was the party and so dependent on its Soviet masters. He was faced by a general strike, in which the leading role was played by the workers of the big Budapest factories. So in the end he gave way, accepting that the party had no popular following at all, and espoused the demands of the opposition. He even denounced the Warsaw Pact (formed the previous year to coordinate the military policies of the East European states) and declared Hungary's neutrality, unilaterally claiming the status that Finland and Austria had gained with the consent of the Soviet Union.

Bearing in mind the Polish comparison, this latter step probably made all the difference. On the morning of 4 November, Soviet troops reinvaded Hungary and imposed a 'revolutionary workers' and peasants' government' under Janos Kadar, a former associate of Nagy, who could not accept the latest changes in his policy, and wished to remain loyal to the Soviet Union. He claimed that the rightful revolution of 23 October had been taken over by 'counterrevolutionary elements': in other words he pledged himself to a course of moderate de-Stalinization.

Kadar wanted to take the same path as Gomulka, but the stigma of the Soviet tanks made this impossible. The most determined opposition to his government came from the workers, and was based on the workers' councils which they had set up in their factories before the Soviet intervention. These councils banished the Communist Party committees from the factories, and only allowed the old trade union branches to function where they would hold new, free elections. The principles on which the councils operated were close to the Yugoslav model: they were elected by all the workers in a given factory or shop, they appointed a board of directors and supervised their activity, and they reserved the right of fundamental decision over contracts, wage rates, hiring and firing. Not that they were ever able to perform these functions in the deepening winter of Hungary in 1956–7. But they did manage to set up a Central Workers' Council of Greater Budapest on 14 November, ten days after the invasion. This called for the release of Nagy (currently in refuge in the Yugoslav Embassy under threat of arrest), the withdrawal of Soviet troops and the holding of free elections, and until these conditions were met it upheld the general strike which the individual workers' councils had already declared.

In the end, however, the rigours of winter combined with those of the general strike to create an intolerable situation, in which the Central Workers' Council decided after agonized debate to end the strike, in order that the workers' sheer physical survival could be ensured. Gradually thereafter the Kadar government broke down resistance, arresting leading workers' council members, reinstalling Communist Party committees, and in the end abolishing the councils altogether.

The course of the Hungarian revolution suggested that the staunchest opponents of single-party Communist rule were the workers in whose name that rule was exercised, and that they aspired to the restoration of the kind of workers' self-government which Lenin had first proclaimed and then destroyed in 1917–18. Faced with Soviet troops and isolated from other elements in society, however, they were powerless to sustain an alternative model of socialism on their own.

Inside the Soviet Union itself, society was slower to reconstitute itself as an independent force. The effects of monopolistic rule and the suppression of independent thought were far deeper. But even here the worrying implications of Khrushchev's semi-public speech combined with the private denunciations of the growing stream of those released from labour camps and (in some cases) restored to their rights. Returning to the towns and villages embittered, thirsty for revenge, and bursting with graphic accounts of a hell which had hitherto been veiled from public gaze, they gave the public a new – though dimly suspected – picture of the society in which they all lived. One man unable to withstand the impact of their return was Alexander Fadeyev, who as secretary to the Writers' Union had approved the lists of his colleagues about to be arrested. A longtime alcoholic, he tried drunkenly and clumsily to ingratiate himself with some of his former victims, then suddenly stopped drinking, wrote a long letter to the Central Committee, and shot himself. The letter was immediately confiscated by the KGB, and we do not know what it contained, but rumour has it that in his last days he said bitterly: 'I thought I was guarding a temple, and it turned out to be a latrine.'

A discussion at the Writers' Union in March 1956, whose records happen to have survived, gives some idea of the opinions beginning to be more or less publicly uttered up and down the country. Some people were searching their own consciences: 'How could I have voted to expel decent people and honest Communists?' Others looked at the structure of their professional association with new eyes – or dared to voice publicly for the first time what they had always seen: 'A patron system of the Maecenas type was implanted in literature and art. The personal tastes of prominent party officials decided everything.' Yet others went on to the observation that nothing in that power structure had, as yet, changed: 'To this day we have leadership by the phone-call method – some instructor from the Central Committee gives his opinion as if it were the opinion of the Central Committee itself.' Some even drew the conclusion that decisive action was needed, evoking Stalinist echoes even while they tried to exorcize Stalin: 'The personality cult still exists in regard to the Presidium of the Central Committee. . . . We must carry through a purge of the apparatus and a purge of the party.' The last possibility was the one that most alarmed the leaders: in the mid-1960s the dissenter Vladimir Bukovsky encountered in a special psychiatric hospital a man who had been there since 1956 for writing a letter to the Central Committee demanding a full inquiry into those responsible for complicity in Stalin's crimes.

Less publicly, in universities and colleges, students and young people drew even more radical conclusions from Khrushchev's revelations, and from the experiences of Yugoslavia, Poland and Hungary. Perhaps most worrying for the authorities was the group which gathered round the young Moscow University historian, L. N. Krasnopevtsev, who was actually secretary of the faculty's Komsomol organization, and therefore a potential member of the ruling class. He seems to have hoped initially that he could work through the party itself to promote a more democratic socialism, but became disillusioned by the suppression of the Hungarian movement and decided instead to set up an underground organization to study the true history of the Communist Party and elaborate an alternative programme. He established personal links with the Polish Communist youth movement, and with the journal *Po prostu*. The group's major 'action' came in the summer of 1957, when its members dropped leaflets in the letterboxes of houses in two working-class districts of Moscow. It called for socialist reforms 'in the spirit of the Twentieth Congress': for the formation of genuine 'workers' soviets', for strikes in the factories, and for public trials of those responsible for the crimes committed during the 'cult of personality'. An interesting feature of the leaflet was its disdain for Khrushchev, who was referred to as 'drunkard' and 'the maize nut' (*kukuruznik*) – for reasons that will become apparent below. Members of the group were arrested and sentenced to between six and ten years for 'anti-Soviet propaganda and agitation'. They thus 'sat' throughout the very years in which Khrushchev was fond of asserting that there were no political prisoners in the Soviet Union.

Similarly, in Leningrad a student named Trofimov made a speech after the Twentieth Congress demanding the rehabilitation of Bukharin. He set up an underground 'Union of Communists', which distributed leaflets condemning the occupation of Hungary as a 'Stalinist phenomenon'. The union's programme recommended the creation of 'workers' soviets', the reintroduction of certain elements of private property in the economy, and the withdrawal of occupation troops from socialist countries.

There is no evidence that any of these groups had arms, or planned anything more explosive than the dissemination of ideas not yet given house-room in the Soviet press.

Nevertheless, the KGB kept a close watch on them, through its slimmed-down but vigilant network of agents, and closed in on them as soon as they began to take even that limited action.

Alarmed by such signs of public discontent, and annoyed by what they considered Khrushchev's 'demagogy' in other fields, his opponents in the Presidium decided to move against him. They formed an alliance with the new foreign minister, Shepilov, and with the youngish economic managers, Pervukhin and Saburov: they were opposed to Khrushchev's economic reforms, which transferred economic administration away from the central ministries to regional bodies known as *Sovnarkhozy* (Councils of the National Economy). There can be no doubt, however, that the main issue was the speed and nature of de-Stalinization, and its concomitants, such as the resumption of relations with Tito, and the pursuit of 'peaceful coexistence' with the West.

In June 1957, this alliance, which now constituted a majority of the Presidium, launched an attack there on the whole range of Khrushchev's policies, and on his high-handed personal style. They demanded his resignation as first secretary (though there may have been a plan to make him minister of agriculture). Khrushchev, sticking by the party statutes, rejoined that he had been elected by the Central Committee, and would only lay down his post at their behest. Since his opponents did not wish, or were not able, to deal with Khrushchev as they had with Beria in 1953, they could not prevent the convening of the Central Committee, where they expected in any case to have a majority.

In the event, the Central Committee gave their backing to Khrushchev. We do not know much about what happened at the sessions, which went on for a week, but we may hypothesize that they supported him for a number of reasons. At this stage some 60 per cent of Central Committee delegates consisted of republican and oblast party secretaries. Khrushchev, as first secretary, was their natural patron, and had indeed appointed a good many of them. They may well have mistrusted Malenkov,

Molotov and Kaganovich, suspecting that they might jeopardize their newly won freedom from security police supervision. The new regional economic councils gave local party secretaries much greater influence than they had enjoyed under the previous system of centralized industrial ministries. Probably many of them also felt that Khrushchev's dramatic agricultural programme was at least a serious attempt to grapple with the country's most pressing problem. Above all, perhaps, they felt Khrushchev had raised the party to become the leading body in the power structure.

Whatever the chief reason may have been, the Central Committee overturned the Presidium resolution, and Khrushchev survived as first secretary. He proceeded to dismiss his main opponents, whom he termed the 'anti-party group', from the Presidium and the Central Committee. From the dismissed Bulganin he took over himself in 1958 as prime minister, combining that post with the first secretaryship of the party, as Stalin had done from 1941. Marshal Zhukov become a full member of the Presidium.

Khrushchev's subsequent treatment of his former opponents was something of an innovation. Instead of arresting them as 'enemies of the people' or 'imperialist spies', he appointed them to minor but not wholly dishonourable posts: Molotov was named Soviet ambassador to Mongolia, while Malenkov become director of a power station in Siberia. They were permitted to retain most of the privileges associated with high office, including the right eventually to a generous 'personal pension'. Perhaps Khrushchev saw this as a form of insurance against the same one day happening to himself. At any rate, it transformed the nature of the power struggle at the top from the murderous to the relatively gentlemanly. This was a key moment in the evolution of the insecure ruling elite which Stalin had created into a ruling class in the full sense of the word. From now on its members were sure that, even in the event of political disgrace, they would continue to enjoy a high standard of living, and would still be able to give their children appreciable advantages in the struggle for high social status.

The outcome of the 1957 crisis ensured that de-Stalinization would continue in some form, in spite of the risks it entailed. In fact it was deepened at the Twenty-second Party Congress in 1961, when the denunciations of Stalin were public; and at the end of the congress Stalin's body was removed from the Mausoleum, where it had lain alongside Lenin since 1953. The wave of public discontent had shown that the new party leadership badly needed a fresh source of legitimacy to replace the combination of terror and personality cult which it had undermined. As the American political scientist Carl Linden put it: 'Khrushchev faced the iconoclast's problem of finding a substitute for what he had destroyed. Having shaken the foundations on which Stalin built dictatorial power, he attempted to find a new basis for his own.'

In part this was a matter of leadership style, and Khrushchev had shown from the start that he had a very distinctive manner. As a matter of fact it was a misleading one, since many seasoned observers thought at the time that he talked too much, drank too much, and indeed was a bit of a clown. But this is because he was a man of immense zest and gregariousness. As the experienced British journalist Alexander Werth reported of him: 'He was a man of quite fantastic energy and vitality. He loved travelling about the country, talking endlessly to peasant meetings, and going, in the process, into no end of technical details on stock-breeding and the growing of various crops.' All this was very different from Stalin, who after the early thirties never came nearer to ordinary people than the reviewing stand on top of Lenin's Mausoleum. Khrushchev, in fact, loved contact with peasants and workers, and was attentive to what they said, even if he sometimes tried to harangue them in return. This 'populism' was reflected in his overall approach to politics: he tried to replace terror by mobilizing the masses to participate in political processes.

The new outlook was summed up most fully in the Party Programme which Khrushchev presented to the Twenty-second Party Congress in 1961. Its basis was what he called 'a return to Leninist norms'. It was natural that, having dethroned Stalin, his successors should create something of a cult of Lenin. But there was more to it than that. There were indeed some strongly Leninist features to Khrushchev's political style, notably the tendency to confuse the concepts 'party' and 'people', and to enforce his own personal views while professing a democratic manner. Khrushchev was, moreover, the first Soviet leader to revive, albeit in muted form, the utopian and even semi-anarchist spirit of Lenin's *State and Revolution*.

The new Party Programme started out from the premise that the Soviet Union had already built 'socialism', and was now on its way to creating 'the material prerequisites of communism', when each person, regardless of the amount of his work, would receive from society according to need. Unwisely perhaps – for it is rash to assign an exact date to utopia – the programme predicted that this stage would be reached by 1980. Already, with the achievement of 'socialism', the 'dictatorship of the proletariat' was over, and the working class was no longer the ruling class, but only a 'leading class'. Even this distinction would fade away as communism approached, and all classes would merge into one another.

All antagonistic class relationships had ended, according to this theory. The state therefore no longer represented any particular social class, but became a 'state of the whole people, an organ expressing the interests and will of the people as a whole'. The programme accordingly called for 'active participation of all citizens in the administration of the state, in the management of economic and cultural development, improvement of the government apparatus, and supervision over its activity by the people'. Ultimately, it was envisaged that, with progress to communism, 'the organs of state power will gradually be transformed into organs of public self-government.' Khrushchev and his advisers evidently intended that the vehicle for this last development should be the party, for the programme recommended 'further enhancement of the role and importance of the Communist Party as the leading and guiding force of Soviet society'. The withering away of the state would therefore presumably mean that the party would replace the state as an expression of the people's urge to rule their own lives.

These were not mere empty words to Khrushchev. Indeed, it should be noted that he tried to move away from Stalin's outright manipulation of ideology as a means of rule: he attempted to restore some of its real meaning. He did try to make the party a body more sensitive to the opinions of at least its own rank-and-file members, and he also tried to involve it more in the business of government, especially economic administration.

As for the party's internal structure, the Twenty-second Congress introduced a significant revision. This was the principle of regular rotation of office. It was laid down that members of the Central Committee should not serve more than four terms (sixteen years altogether under the current rules), unless their 'generally acknowledged prestige' was recognized by at least three-quarters of its voting members in a secret ballot. Members of the Presidium should not indeed serve for more than three terms. At lower levels of the party hierarchy terms of office were to be even shorter: three terms at republican and oblast level (which in the case of the oblast committee, elected every two years, meant six years) and two terms at raion and town level (four years). These terms of office may seem long enough, especially at higher levels, but they came as a shock to full-time party officials who, since Stalin's death, had felt much more secure and indeed had become accustomed to regard their offices as lifetime incumbencies. Nevertheless, the Twenty-second Congress passed the reform.

In order to involve the party more closely in production, Khrushchev also reorganized its committees (at oblast and raion level) according to the 'production principle', that is to say, dividing them into 'industrial' and 'agricultural' departments. In effect separate industrial and agricultural hierarchies were set up reaching right into the Central Committee apparatus itself. Many secretaries reacted to this as an affront, some because it meant being transferred from a city out into the provinces, some because they felt themselves specialists in personnel and ideological work and did not welcome being forced into the mould of economic administrators. For nearly all, the reform meant a concentration and limitation of functions.

It might be thought that the division would require the appointment of many more party officials, but in fact Khrushchev hoped to cut them down. He intended to replace many full-time salaried party *apparatchiki* with voluntary and/or part-time staff, in order to increase the involvement of ordinary party members in the higher responsibilities of the party. Again, this was viewed as an affront by most full-time officials, who regarded their jobs as a highly developed speciality, not to say a mystique, incomprehensible to outsiders.

The new conception of the relationship between party, state and people demanded a new conception, too, of the role of law in society. The legal reforms introduced during the late 1950s had above all two aims: to make law more settled and predictable, so as to avoid arbitrariness and terror, and to involve ordinary people more in judicial processes. Of course, these two aims were not always easy to harmonize: indeed, sometimes they conflicted directly. Furthermore, while the party leadership wished to prevent a resumption of rule by terror, it did not want to deprive itself of the judicial weapons necessary to maintain its monopoly of power. For those reasons, there were tensions and ambiguities in the legal reforms.

Most important was the new criminal code promulgated in December 1958. Its basic principle was that civilians could only be convicted by a properly constituted court, and only for contravening a specific article of the criminal code. This meant that military and emergency courts could not be used for ordinary legal purposes, and that vague concepts like 'enemy of the people' and 'counterrevolutionary activity' could not be used to gain a conviction. Nor could anybody be convicted any longer simply for belonging to a particular social group, or for being a relative of someone already convicted. Likewise, criminal 'intention', or doing something 'analogous' to a crime mentioned in the code, were insufficient grounds for conviction. Defendants were no longer to be convicted solely on the basis of their own confession (the customary 'evidence' adduced in Stalin's courts), but only if there was other convincing evidence, which had been examined in court. Sentences were sharply reduced, the longest normally admissible being ten years (instead of twenty-five). The death penalty remained only for treason.

In order to involve the ordinary people more closely in the law, an institution of the 1920s was revived, the so-called 'comrade courts'. Local soviets, trade unions and house committees (which administered affairs in large apartment blocks) were empowered to set up these courts to try minor offences. They consisted of three members from a panel of fifty elected for a year at a time. They were not given power to order custody, but could impose fines of up to fifty rubles, or corrective labour without custody, as well as recommend demotion or dismissal from work, or eviction from housing.

The publicity which accompanied the establishment of the comrade courts implied that gradually they might replace the ordinary courts as part of the move towards 'self-administration'. As the press said, 'Cannot the Soviet public deal with violators of socialist law and order? Of course it can. Our social organizations are no less able and equipped for this than are the militia, courts and procuracy! Preventive and educational work are the main thing.' A campaign of public awareness of legal issues was mounted, using the Znanie (Knowledge) Society to arrange public lectures and exhibitions. All this was accompanied by a campaign of pressure against absentees, pilferers, rowdies and drunks: billboards erected at factory gates or even in the streets carried photographs of offenders and pilloried them with slogans like 'They shame our city!'

Experience of the comrade courts' actual functioning suggested that they offered rich opportunities for intrigues and petty jealousies at the workplace or in the apartment block, and they came to be more and more distrusted by judicial officials. Far from replacing the ordinary courts, they came to be used less frequently.

In other respects, too, the authorities showed ambivalence about their own new laws. One example of this was the so-called 'parasite' law, introduced in some republics as early as 1957. The intention was to prosecute people not performing regular paid work as 'parasites'. Rather like the vagrancy laws of sixteenth-century England, this was a vaguely worded provision which could be used to proceed against anyone who caused trouble to the authorities: it was easy enough to dismiss an intended victim from his job and then block his attempts to find another. Lawyers, however, objected to such unclear and ambiguous phrases as 'living on non-labour income' or 'working for the sake of appearances only'. The wording was tightened up somewhat, but the law still went on the statute books. One celebrated case of its use was the conviction of the young Leningrad poet Joseph Brodsky in February 1964: since he was not a member of the Writers' Union, the judge refused to accept that the poetic translations he was doing constituted 'work'.

Khrushchev himself evidently had doubts about the elaborate formalization of the law taking place under his aegis. In 1961 he moved to restore the death penalty for large-scale economic crime – which could mean underground manufacture and trading, or dealing in large amounts of foreign currency. This was a sign of how much the leaders were concerned about the flowering of the black market at the time. Nearly all professional jurists opposed the restoration of the death penalty, but it went through all the same.

Khrushchev, moreover, actually wanted it applied retrospectively against two notorious gold and currency dealers, Rokotov and Faibishenko, who had amassed an illicit fortune of some 2 million rubles: they had already been tried and given long prison sentences. It is said that when the procurator-general, R. A. Rudenko, protested that such a retrospective sentence would 'violate socialist legality', Khrushchev retorted: 'Which is more important to you: your legality or your socialism?' The two were duly executed. There could not be a clearer indication of the continued primacy of the political over the legal.

All the same, the ordinary citizen probably became more aware of legal issues as a result of the campaign for 'socialist legality'. He was certainly much better protected by the law than under Stalin. Both law and custom were replacing outright terror as guarantors of social cohesion. All this made it more difficult for the leaders to circumvent the law when they found it inconvenient, as we shall see in Chapter 14.

Khrushchev's social policy was of a piece with what he tried to achieve in the political field. He was concerned to mobilize the people's energies for production, to ease the harsher forms of compulsion applied by Stalin, and to relieve the stark poverty in which so many lived before 1953. Workers, for example, were freed from the threat of criminal sanctions for absenteeism or quitting, which meant that they had much more liberty to choose conditions and pay that suited them. Social security benefits were considerably improved: this was very important in a nation which, as a result of the war, had so many permanent invalids and one-parent families.

The horrifying housing problem was at last seriously tackled. By the mid-1950s most Soviet towns were surrounded by a forest of cranes and a sea of muddy building sites, which offered people at least a hope of eventual escape from the fractious intimacy of the communal apartments. Between 1955 and 1964, the nation's housing stock nearly doubled, from 640 to 1182 million square metres. In addition to provision by local government and industry, individual citizens were now given the right to join housing cooperatives: they could put down 15–30 per cent of the price of an apartment on entry, and then pay the rest at the dream-like interest rate of 0.5 per cent. In practice, professional people were more likely than workers to have the deposit ready. Besides, cooperatives were often attached to professional associations of one sort and another. Cooperative housing thus tended to become a sign of intermediate status in society, between the highly privileged, who had no need of cooperatives, and the ordinary workers and employees, who depended either on their employers or on the local soviet to provide them with a home. Soviet social structure was beginning to differentiate and to take on new layers.

In education too the grosser forms of inequality were eased by the decision to abolish fees for college tuition and for the upper forms of secondary schools. This made it easier for worker and peasant children to rise up the social scale. Khrushchev wanted to go further than this and change the whole nature of secondary education by abolishing the upper classes of the schools, so that at the age of fifteen all children would enter the labour force for at least two years, and learn a trade. Those who wanted to continue to higher education would, as he saw it, prepare by evening and correspondence courses, and would be at liberty to apply for college at the end of their two years' practical experience. Khrushchev intended in this way to reduce the inbuilt advantages enjoyed by children from professional families, and to encourage more young people to take up skilled manual trades, which the economy desperately needed.

Interestingly enough, Khrushchev did not wholly get his way over this issue. This was perhaps the first time he came up against opposition from the vested interests who hitherto had supported him. In Soviet society, where personal property was minimal, much the most reliable way to pass on privileges and social status was by ensuring a good education for one's offspring. The proposed reforms threatened to make this more difficult, by disrupting academic progress and creating a social melting pot between secondary school and college. Besides, university teachers, especially in the more demanding scientific disciplines, were concerned that students would come to them underprepared, and having lost habits of regular study. Nor did enterprise directors welcome having unskilled and sometimes unruly extra hands on their premises.

A watered-down version of Khrushchev's proposals became law in 1958, but even that was never fully implemented, and was repealed in 1965 without having much raised the numbers of skilled workers or markedly changed the social composition of universities. Indeed the most significant educational development of the Khrushchev years tended in the opposite direction. This was the striking expansion of schools specializing in fields such as modern languages, certain sciences, mathematics, ballet and the arts. These subjects had been chosen because, to train specialists at the highest level, it was thought beneficial to start specialization very early. Entrance to the special schools was by examination at the age of ten or eleven. Since they offered good access to very promising careers, they became extremely popular. 'Cramming' for their entrance exams became part of the life of children in the professional stata, and string-pulling or bribery to get one's offspring admitted was soon a normal way for the elite to give their heirs a good start in life.

Overall, since the war, there is no doubt that Soviet education had improved dramatically, both quantitatively and qualitatively, and this constitutes one of the most remarkable achievements of Soviet society. The number of students enrolled in higher educational institutions rose from 1.25 million in 1950–1 to 2.4 million in 1960–1, and to 3.6 million in 1964–5. Steady progress was also made towards the goal of providing full ten or eleven year schooling for every child between the ages of seven and seventeen or eighteen, a goal which had substantially been reached by the mid-seventies. The thirst of ordinary people for education was intense, and, since many of the most talented men and women chose education as a career, the public demand was well met. Paradoxically, progress was perhaps most marked in areas where Khrushchev least intended it, in providing a traditional academic education in city schools and in colleges and universities. The best Soviet scientists and scholars were of the highest international standing, while hundreds of thousands of graduates were being turned out each year with good professional training. The political content of education did not diminish, but most students seemed to regard it as a form of compulsory intellectual square-bashing, while putting in their main efforts elsewhere.

The most glaring inequalities in Soviet life, and perhaps the worst economic underproductivity, were caused by the legacy of high-handedness and neglect which Stalin had left in the countryside. We have examined the state of the collective farms in an earlier chapter. Broadly speaking, one could classify the weaknesses of Soviet agriculture as being of two types: those associated with its authoritarian collective structure, and those resulting from the low priority accorded to agriculture in the regime's policies. Khrushchev tackled the latter problem energetically, but he was perhaps only partly aware of the seriousness of the former.

As soon as he became first secretary, Khrushchev decided to arouse public awareness of agriculture by announcing a spectacular campaign to develop the 'virgin lands'. These were areas of steppe in north Kazakhstan, western Siberia and the south-eastern part of European Russia. His idea was to transform the 'virgin lands' into the major bread-producing region of the country, while turning the Ukraine, which had traditionally filled this role, into a provider of maize, for cattle-feed: this in turn would stimulate the notoriously lagging meat and dairy sector.

The designated areas suffered from a serious disadvantage: their rainfall was low, and in some years they experienced drought conditions. The Kazakh steppes, indeed, were on the edge of the Central Asian desert. Without extensive irrigation, that meant output would be uncertain and soil erosion likely. The Kazakh party leaders opposed the plan, not only for that reason, but also because they suspected (rightly) that it would mean an enormous influx of Russians into their republic. Khrushchev sent in Leonid Brezhnev to overcome their misgivings.

Initially the project was a great success. Within three years, by 1956, the 'virgin lands' were producing three times as much grain as before 1953. Hundreds of thousands of young people were mobilized by the Komsomol to go out and help with the harvest. Some went just for a couple of months, others to settle more permanently. Thousands of tractors and combine harvesters were transferred there: the sight of them advancing in echelons through rippling grain in fields that stretched to the horizon became the staple of Soviet newsreels.

In the event, however, 1956 proved to be the peak year. The natural, and initially very high, fertility of the soil began to decline thereafter, and the drawbacks of haste began to make themselves felt. For quick results, Khrushchev had discouraged any proper kind of crop cycle, or the use of fallow, and had failed to provide fertilizers to replace soil nutrients, even though scientists had warned him of the dangers. Eventually soil erosion followed: in a series of wind-storms between 1960 and 1965 some 4 million hectares of land were ruined in Kazakhstan, and more than 12 million hectares were damaged. Altogether, this amounted to nearly half the 'virgin lands'.

The human and mechanical problems of massive resettlement were also underestimated. Young enthusiasts often arrived to find themselves living in tents or, at best, flimsy huts in temperatures that could be roasting by day and freezing by night. They might be cut off, dozens of miles from the nearest railway or good road, suffering from unpredictable food supplies and even from shortages of the machinery they had come specially trained to operate. Altogether, it is scarcely surprising that many who came with high hopes found the struggle for existence too burdensome, and decided to return to European Russia.

Whatever its failings, though, the 'virgin lands' campaign *did* raise grain production appreciably at a critical time, and thus won a breathing space for agricultural reforms elsewhere; and it certainly put agriculture for the first time at the centre of Soviet politics, as a prior claimant for scarce resources.

In the traditional agriculture regions, Khrushchev offered a better deal to collective farmers. For their collective produce he offered much higher procurement prices, so that they could be sure of some sort of regular income from their 'labour days'. As for the private plots, he reduced taxes and eased restrictions on their use, so that production there rose too. All this entailed higher state investment in agriculture, and it was forthcoming: Khrushchev roughly quadrupled it between 1953 and 1964. We have seen, too, that he tried to involve party cadres more closely in agriculture – often to their resentment.

It was unfortunate, but perhaps in the nature of the Soviet system, that Khrushchev did not feel able to make major advances without campaigns of one sort and another. For the traditional agricultural areas the principal campaigns were in maize and cattle-raising, which in Khrushchev's mind were linked. 'With fodder,' he proclaimed, stating the obvious with his customary naive enthusiasm, 'there is livestock, meat and milk. Without fodder, the livestock perishes, and there will be no meat or milk.'

The maize campaign reached its climax after Khrushchev returned from visiting the USA in 1959. He had been very impressed by the Iowa prairies rippling with ripe maize. Forgetting, perhaps, that Iowa is well to the south of anywhere in European Russia, he ordered that maize should be cultivated generally, to be harvested as a green crop for silage wherever it would not ripen fully. A special new Maize Research Institute was opened, issuing its own journal, *Kukuruza*, and the virtues of the 'queen of the fields' were trumpeted in all the newspapers, and through all the rural party organizations. Woe betide any farm chairman who was dubious about sowing maize, no matter how different his soil and climate might be from that of Iowa.

At the height of the campaign, in 1962, no less than 37 million hectares were under maize, of which only 7 million could be harvested ripe. Indeed, because of the cool, wet summer, some of it could not be harvested in *any* form. Meanwhile the production of prosaic but essential hay fell dismally, ordinary crop rotations were disrupted, meadows abandoned, the advice of kolkhoz chairmen and agronomists ignored.

The accompanying livestock campaign was, if anything, even more rashly handled. In 1957 Khrushchev announced that within four years the Soviet Union would overtake the USA in the production of meat, milk and butter. Taking up the initiative in the approved manner, one oblast party secretary, A. N. Larionov of Ryazan, promised to treble meat sales by 1959. Since the promise was blazoned in *Pravda*, there was no retreat, but in order to meet his self-imposed target, Larionov soon found himself having to order the slaughter of dairy as well as meat cattle, and thus mortgage the future prosperity of his farms. At one stage he was reduced to sending emissaries to neighbouring regions to buy up or even rustle cattle there.

In the end, by hook or by crook, Ryazan did fulfil its 1959 target. Larionov was lauded to the skies and made a Hero of Socialist Labour. But the next year the bubble burst. With its herds decimated and its finances crippled, the oblast fell back well below the modest 1958 level of meat deliveries. The Central Committee sent a special commission down from Moscow to investigate, and Larionov shot himself in his office.

All in all, Khrushchev did alleviate some of the poverty and demoralization of rural life, and he did restore agriculture to its proper place in the agenda of politics. But in the course of doing so he displayed in striking form a characteristic of

Soviet politicians: as if steering an out-of-control juggernaut on a winding road, they tend to overcorrect, taking up a neglected policy area with heavy overemphasis.

Certainly the cost of his mistakes was high. In 1962 the government felt it had to raise food prices, and the result was a series of riots in the cities on a scale unprecedented since the civil war (see below, page 389). In 1963, moreover, thanks to a dry summer and the depredations of the maize campaign, the grain harvest was very disappointing, a mere 107 million tonnes. (Up to 1953 such a figure would have been hailed as a triumph – and this is a measure of Khrushchev's genuine achievement; but, understandably, everyone compared it with his promises and with the planned target of 170–180 million tonnes.) Already by early autumn there were bread queues in the Ukraine, Russia's traditional granary. Soon housewives and black market traders began descending on Moscow and Leningrad from other towns where the bread supply was uncertain. Remembering the riots of the previous year, Khrushchev took the unprecedented and agonizing decision to use up precious gold and hard currency reserves to buy grain abroad. It was almost the first time Russia had ever entered world grain markets as a net importer, and it was a staggering humiliation for Khrushchev in a field he had made his own.

In his later years of rule, Khrushchev became an increasingly unpopular figure, both among his colleagues and with the public at large, though this did not become obvious till after his fall. His colleagues had become impatient at his constant reorganizations of the party and state apparatus, which unsettled their lives without bringing obvious benefits. They considered many of his agricultural policies had been counterproductive, and even when correct, vitiated by exaggeration; the very poor harvest of 1963 seemed to substantiate their misgivings. Even though the most determined Stalinists had been defeated in 1957, other party leaders had reason to feel that de-Stalinization had gone quite far enough, and was jeopardizing the 'leading role of the party', especially in culture, science and the professions. The military resented Khrushchev's reductions in military spending, and his dismissals of officers; they also felt that his policy had been refuted by the experience of the Cuba missile crisis, when the Soviet Union had been humiliated because she did not have the force to challenge a US naval blockade of Cuba.

Professional people, who had things much better than under Stalin, wanted to extend their autonomy even further, and resented the party's continued sporadic and unpredictable interferences in their special fields of experience. Workers were discontented that Khrushchev had ended the annual reductions in food prices, and then indeed reversed them. Peasants and those concerned with agriculture felt he was responsible for the continued poverty and demoralization of the countryside, and for the need to import foodstuffs the country ought to be able to produce for itself. And everyone, perhaps, felt that Khrushchev had in the end shown himself to be not quite the stuff of which statesmen are made: the incident in 1960 when in the United Nations General Assembly Khrushchev interrupted a speech of which he disapproved by taking off his shoe and banging it on the table created a very bad impression inside the Soviet Union (where people learned about it, not of course from the Soviet press, but from foreign radio stations). This was felt to be undignified, and to bring the country into international disrepute.

On 14 October 1964 a plenum of the Central Committee took place to which Khrushchev had been hurriedly brought back from a holiday in the Crimea. There was only one main speech, a report by Suslov, which was in essence an indictment of Khrushchev. All his failings were enumerated, unbalanced by any of his achievements. Suslov accused him of erecting his own 'cult of personality', of attempting to be a specialist in every sphere, of continual meaningless administrative reorganizations, and of imprudent and indiscreet conduct of the country's foreign affairs.

No one seems to have spoken in support of Khrushchev.

The solid phalanx of oblast party secretaries who had backed him in 1957 now turned against him. Having been at that time a guarantor of their security, he had now become a threat to it, through his experiments and reorganizations, and because of the forces in society which he had, sometimes unknowingly and unwillingly, set free.

Yet in fact Khrushchev had been in some ways an outstanding statesman. More than any of his colleagues, he had sensed the seriousness of the internal problems facing his country. His attempts to solve them had been wilful and sometimes clumsy. Furthermore, he had proved unable to free himself completely from the Stalinist mould in any major field of policy. Nevertheless he left the country much more prosperous, and in some respects permanently changed. The manner of his departure was a symbol of this latter effect. As a British journalist commented at the time: 'Ten years earlier no one would have imagined that Stalin's successor would be removed by so simple and gentle a process as a vote.'

13

Soviet Society under 'Developed Socialism'

If the brutality of Stalinist politics had passed, its secretiveness had not. Khrushchev's departure was never properly explained in the press – it was attributed to 'advanced age and poor health' – and indeed Khrushchev himself was never again mentioned, except for a brief announcement of his death in 1971. Leading articles did, however, accuse persons unknown of 'hare-brained scheming', 'obsession with administrative solutions' and 'failure to take advantage of scientific knowledge'. From these hints the informed reader could conclude that the new leadership was going to restore administrative stability and adopt a more deliberate and pragmatic style.

The major internal problem that Khrushchev's successors faced was the legacy of directive planning in the economy, inherited from the 1930s and reinstated, as we have seen, after the war. A confidential report delivered in June 1965 by Abel Aganbegyan, director of the Novosibirsk Institute of Economics, highlighted the difficulties. Aganbegyan noted that the growth rate of the Soviet economy was beginning to decline, just when the rival US economy seemed particularly buoyant; at the same time, some sectors of the Soviet economy – housing, agriculture, services, retail trade – remained very backward, and were failing to develop at an adequate rate. The root causes of this poor performance he saw in the enormous commitment of resources to defence (in human terms, 30–40 million people out of a working population of 100 million, he reckoned), and the 'extreme centralism and lack of democracy in economic matters' which had survived from the past. In a complex modern society, he argued, not everything could be planned, since it was impossible to foresee all possible contingencies and their potential effects. So the plan amounted to central command, and even that could not be properly implemented for lack of information and of modern data-processing equipment. 'The Central Statistical Administration . . . does not have a single computer, and is not planning to acquire any,' he commented acidly. Economic administration was also impeded by excessive secrecy: 'We obtain many figures . . . from American journals sooner than they are released by the Central Statistical Administration.' Hence the economy suffered from inbuilt distortions: the hoarding of goods and labour to provide for unforeseen contingencies, the production of shoddy goods to fulfil planning targets expressed in crude quantitative terms, the accumulation of unused money by a public reluctant to buy substandard products, with resultant inflation and a flourishing black market.

Already in 1953, Malenkov had proposed reversing traditional priorities by putting more investment into consumer industry (sector B, as it is called) than into capital industry (sector A). Little had come of this idea, partly because consumer industries enjoy lower status in the nomenklatura hierarchy, partly because the customers for its products are more numerous, scattered and heterogeneous: their requirements are not easily captured in the form of gross output plans. Khrushchev's decentralization of economic administration was intended to make the system more responsive to the needs of the customer, but in practice merely succeeded in making it more complicated.

In 1965, the new prime minister, Kosygin, tried a different approach, absorbing some of the lessons of economists such as Aganbegyan. He restored the centralized industrial ministries which Khrushchev had broken up, but at the same time tried to render their planning mechanism more responsive by recouching targets in the form of 'gross realized output', that is, goods not only produced but actually sold. Henceforth a small interest charge was to be made for capital equipment, to discourage enterprises from hoarding unneeded resources, and managers were to have greater freedom to decide how to use their profits – as incentive payments to workers, for reinvestment, for payment into amenities funds, and so forth.

Kosygin's reform foundered, just like its predecessors, for a number of reasons. First, to make full use of the opportunities it afforded, enterprises would have needed the right to set the prices at which their products sold, and this they were never given. They would also have required much greater freedom to determine levels of employment, in particular to dismiss workers who were surplus to needs, or whose work was unsatisfactory. This freedom they were given to a limited extent, at least in theory, but resistance to dismissals, through the trade unions and some sections of the party apparatus, proved extremely stubborn, and the leaders, after the Novocherkassk experience (see below), were so sensitive to working-class discontent that they failed to support managers who dismissed workers.

Besides, successful implementation of the Kosygin reform meant innovation, the introduction of new technology into industry. But this is always difficult to accomplish in an economy where success is measured in terms of annual plan fulfilment. New equipment and work methods always take time to assimilate, and are bound to cause temporary reductions in output in the process. If by the end of the planning year the savings thereby generated do not outweigh the losses, then enterprise managers are unlikely to risk innovation.

There is some evidence, too, that serious implementation of the reform would have threatened the priority accorded to military production. Perhaps the overwhelming factor that crushed Kosygin's plans, however, was the resistance of party secretaries and ministerial officials to new practices which would have reduced their power to control the operation of the economy. The Czechoslovak experience of 1968 (see below) crystallized this opposition, and probably effectively doomed the reform.

During the late 1960s and early 1970s, the leaders chose an alternative way to try to revive the economy. On the one hand, they tightened the planning system and made it somewhat more responsive to the unforeseen by computerizing it; on the other, they tried to make up for the lack of innovation by buying new technology from the West. In many ways, this was a return to a traditional policy which the Soviet leaders had often adopted under pressure. Stalin had used it during the industrialization drive of the thirties, and again during the war. Khrushchev had sought chemical fertilizers abroad, because he attributed great importance to them, and realized Soviet fertilizers were very primitive. The post-Khrushchev leaders extended the practice into a much broader range of industries where Soviet technology was backward, including shipping and automobile construction, synthetic chemicals, food and drink processing, and oil and gas extraction. Western firms often welcomed joint development projects, as the Soviet Union could offer a huge potential market, as well as a cheap and docile labour force. The largest scheme of this kind was the 1966 contract with the Italian automobile concern Fiat to launch a huge factory at Stavropol on the Volga, now renamed Togliatti, in honour of the recently deceased Italian Communist leader. This factory opened the prospect – though not for many years the reality – of a family motor car on the Soviet market. One important result of the deal was to open up Western contacts for quite a number of Soviet citizens who would otherwise never have experienced them. Some 2500 Western specialists went to Togliatti at one time or another, and a similar number of Soviet engineers and technicians went to Italy to train.

This meant a broadening of something which had been going on, at first in a small way, since the mid-fifties: the partial opening of the Soviet frontiers to international exchanges, not only in technology, but also in science, culture and tourism. It remained true that, in order to travel abroad – and especially to the West – Soviet citizens had to undergo a cumbersome and in some respects humiliating 'security clearance' at the hands of the party and the KGB. Many of them failed it, sometimes at the last moment: hence the familiar spectacle, at international conferences, of a well-known Soviet scholar being unexpectedly replaced by a nonentity. All the same, with that proviso, the Soviet Union had by the early 1980s been a member of the international community again for a generation or so – something which was not true of the years of Stalin's domination. The resultant influx of Western, or 'bourgeois', ideas and practices was a source of constant worry to the authorities.

The men who overthrew Khrushchev included not only economic reformers, but also one or two ideological purists, like Mikhail Suslov, regarded as the chief authority on ideological matters, and Alexander Shelepin, the former head of the KGB. It was rumoured that Shelepin had plans to arrest a thousand or so intellectuals, those most closely connected with the cultural 'thaw', and thus eliminate ideological waverings once and for all. The arrests of Sinyavsky and Daniel in September 1965 (see below) may have been intended as the first step in such a campaign. But for most members of the Politburo (as the party Presidium was now renamed) memories of Stalin and Beria were still too vivid to risk letting terror get out of hand again. Shelepin, in fact, as the 'danger man', was eventually eased out of his key post in the party Secretariat into the comparatively harmless job of running the trade unions.

Leonid Brezhnev, who took over from Khrushchev as first secretary, was perhaps initially seen by his colleagues as an interim appointment, but he turned out to be the leader most suited to the current mood of the Politburo and the Central Committee. He speedily reversed the most disturbing of Khrushchev's reforms in agriculture, education, economic administration and the party apparatus, and he adopted as his watchword 'stability of cadres', which meant a more comfortable life for the medium- and upper-level party–state apparatus. Good-humoured and patient, he was very much a 'consensus' leader, content to blunt the differences between opposing factions, even when that meant adopting no clear policy line. Over the years he proved able to isolate his possible rivals and to manoeuvre his own supporters and protégés into top jobs. He did all this with majestic slowness: it was some twelve to fifteen years before he really stood out as *the* leader, with his own 'cult'. In 1977, he added to the post of General Secretary (as he renamed the first secretary, following Stalin's example) that of president, becoming head of state as well as head of the party. He also had himself promoted to the rank of Marshal of the Soviet Union and appointed supreme commander of the armed forces, as well as chairman of the Defence Council. He even published his memoirs, in recognition of which he was awarded the Lenin Prize for literature. Conferring it on him, the president of the Writers' Union, Georgy Markov, declared, 'For their popularity and their educative influence on the mass of readers, the books of Leonid Ilyich are unrivalled.'

The most serious test of the new leaders' consensus came not from within the Soviet Union, but as often happens in empires, from one of the dependencies, Czechoslovakia. Slow to 'de-Stalinize' in 1956, the party leadership there did so later on with greater determination and consistency than perhaps any other East European leadership. The process culminated in the dismissal of the Stalinist first secretary, Novotny, at a Central Committee meeting in January 1968, and his replacement by Alexander Dubček, a Slovak Communist who had been in Moscow during the war and who, initially at least, enjoyed Brezhnev's trust as the man most likely to provide responsible guidance for the completion of the reforms.

Unlike Hungary in 1956, the impetus for reform came not only from intellectuals, but from within the party apparatus itself. For some years a department of the Central Committee had been drawing up a report on the kind of political structure best suited to a modern society and economy. In a sense

its authors were trying to do more systematically and deliberately what Khrushchev had attempted in his impulsive
way, to find a new basis for party rule in an era when mass
terror was no longer acceptable, and society and the economy
were far more complex than they had been in the early years
of the socialist state.

The main result of their report was the Action Programme
of the Czechoslovak Communist Party, issued in April 1968.
This started from the same premise as the Yugoslav reforms
of the 1950s: that each nation has its 'own separate road to
socialism'. It also recognized that in a developed socialist
society contradictory interests can and do exist, but maintained that, with the major class struggle already won, these
interests could be allowed to form themselves into social
institutions and to compete in the political forum without
threatening the unity of society. This incipient pluralism
differed from Khrushchev's vision of democracy, which was
that the masses were essentially *united*, and that their common interest should be expressed through the party. Insofar
as the Czechoslovak reformers had precursors, they were to
be found among some of the Yugoslav theorists of the fifties,
and in occasional undeveloped insights of Bukharin back in
the twenties. They also considered that for the economy to
perform efficiently it was necessary to decentralize
decision-making and offer more effective material stimuli to
producers: this was very close to what Kosygin was trying to
do.

The Action Programme made a number of policy proposals, which lay at the centre of the ensuing debate. It recommended consistently promoting 'socialist legality', and providing guarantees against lawlessness and undue con-
centrations of power; to this end, it suggested, people should
have the right to organize themselves in groups and express
their opinions. Specifically, it was envisaged that the People's
Front (the 'bogus coalition' of 1948) should be revived, with
each constituent party enjoying a certain autonomous existence. How this was to be reconciled with the 'leading role of

the party' – also emphasized – was never resolved. Censorship should be abolished, and conditions created in which science, culture and education could flourish, both in order to ensure economic development, and because they were fundamental human needs.

During the spring of 1968 a number of 'social groups', with political implications, were set up to exercise the promised freedoms. The official Communist youth movement was more or less deprived of its base in the universities by mass defection to an autonomous Union of University Students, based in the Philosophy Faculty of Prague University. This union published its own Action Programme, based on the UN Declaration of Human Rights. A so-called 'Club K–231' was set up, consisting of former political prisoners (and named after the article of the criminal code under which they had been convicted): its primary aim was to consolidate 'socialist legality' by pressing for a full investigation of the repressions of the Stalin period. KAN, or the Club of the Politically Non-aligned, announced that it would put up candidates in the next elections to the National Assembly and campaign for the re-establishment of an independent Social Democratic Party (which had been forcibly merged with the Communists in 1948).

The most striking of all the independent political statements was the '2000 Words' of the writer Ludvik Vaculik, issued in June 1968. He warned that the party had so far only made *promises*. If people wanted things *done*, then it was not enough to wait passively for action from above: they must act themselves. 'It is simple: a few people convene, they elect a chairman, keep regular minutes, publish their findings, demand a solution, and do not let themselves be intimidated.' It was almost a direct restatement of Edmund Burke's classical argument for the existence of political parties.

Of course, this vision of political life aroused deep misgivings in Moscow. These must have been intensified when the Czechoslovak Communist Party issued its draft statutes on 10 August 1968, for these revealed that even the party itself was about to loosen and democratize its internal structure. Its officials were to be elected by secret ballot, and would hold office for no longer than eight or, exceptionally, twelve years: this would undermine the whole basis of the nomenklatura system. Furthermore the new statutes breached a principle laid down in Lenin's resolution of 1921 'On Party Unity' by permitting groups within the party to formulate and publish minority views, and to continue doing so even after a majority decision had gone against them. Neither Khrushchev, nor even Tito, had countenanced such a weakening of discipline. Not only the state, but also the party, was to be federalized, so that Czechs and Slovaks would have equal rights.

Unlike Nagy in 1956, Dubček stressed that Czechoslovakia had no intention of leaving the Warsaw Pact, or of ending the socialist system. All the same, on 21 August 1968, Soviet troops, supported by a few contingents from other Warsaw Pact states, invaded Czechoslovakia. Because of bungled political management, the intervention did not immediately achieve its aim: no Kadar emerged to take over power with Moscow's blessing. The Soviet leadership had to allow Dubček and his reformers to return, but saddled with an agreement which required them to 'normalize' Czechoslovak political life – which meant the restoration of absolute rule by the nomenklatura elite. The main reasons for the intervention were probably by and large those which were reiterated in numerous official statements, both before and after the invasion.

Chief among these were fears that the relaxation of censorship and of political life in general was opening the way for 'counterrevolutionary forces' to gain a permanent foothold. The Soviet leaders were perplexed and outraged by the uncontrolled existence of groups with their own political programmes, by the possible revival of non-Communist political parties (and they did not see how the party's 'leading role' was to be upheld), by the publication in the

Czechoslovak press of statements like '2000 Words'. They could see that their own emerging 'dissenters' were inspired by the developments in Czechoslovakia. They feared the example that would be set by a democratized and federalized Czechoslovak Communist Party. Petr Shelest, leader of the Ukrainian Communist Party, may have been prepared to make some concessions to the nationalists in his own republic, but he was not willing to loosen the ties with Moscow, to which he owed his power: he was one of the most vehement supporters of intervention.

The actual timing of the intervention leaves little doubt that it was intended to forestall personnel changes expected at the forthcoming congress of the Czechoslovak Communist Party, due in September. Many of the 'old guard' trusted by Moscow would undoubtedly have lost their posts, and been replaced by men committed to reform, who might have made the whole process irreversible.

In September *Pravda* issued a statement justifying the invasion. It accepted the principle enunciated by Khrushchev that each nation may take its 'own separate road to socialism', but added the crucial reservation that the freedom to do this 'must damage neither socialism in their own country nor the fundamental interests of the other socialist countries, nor the worldwide workers' movement, which is waging a struggle for socialism.' The implication was that, if such 'damage' did occur, then other socialist countries had both a right and a duty to intervene and curtail it. 'The Soviet Union and other socialist states, in fulfilling their internationalist duty to the fraternal peoples of Czechoslovakia and defending their gains, had to act and did act in resolute opposition to the anti-socialist forces in Czechoslovakia.' This declaration, soon nicknamed the 'Brezhnev doctrine', immediately established itself as the fundamental text underlying relationships between the Soviet Union and its allies. It meant that the Soviet Union felt able to step in and reimpose its own interpretation of 'socialism' whenever this seemed to be under serious attack.

Much criticism in the Soviet media was directed at the Czechoslovak deputy prime minister, Ota Šik. He was the architect of the economic reforms, which were intended to decentralize decision-making, establish profit as an important planning indicator, and withdraw automatic state support from inefficient firms. The idea was both to raise productivity and to make firms more responsive to the needs of their customers. They were similar to the reforms Kosygin had announced in the Soviet Union in 1965, though they went somewhat further. What worried the Soviet leaders, however, most of all were the political implications of Šik's proposed reforms, for the Czechoslovak Communist Party, unlike the CPSU, had no inhibitions about exploring these. Experiments were under way in factories to give the workers more access to decision-making: since an enterprise could now be closed down if it performed badly, the employees had a direct interest in ensuring that that did not happen.

It is certainly the case that the Kosygin reforms, never a robust growth, quietly wilted during and after 1968, though they were never officially withdrawn.

As in Hungary in 1956, it was the workers who eventually put up the strongest resistance to the Soviet occupation. The workers of the ČKD factory in the Vysočany suburb of Prague invited the Fourteenth Party Congress (forestalled by the invasion) to assemble on their premises: it did so, in secret – a considerable feat of improvisation – passed a resolution condemning the invasion, confirmed Dubček as first secretary, and elected a completely reformist Central Committee to back him. Under the terms of his agreement with the Soviet leaders, however, Dubček had to disavow this congress.

The creation of elected workers' councils with, formally at least, considerable supervisory powers over management continued, however, for some months after the invasion. Indeed, a full-scale draft law on the self-managed socialist enterprise was issued as late as January 1969. In practice, though, the powers of workers' councils were gradually screwed back by the reimposition of unreformed party authority within the factories. Finally the councils were banned in July 1970, on the grounds that they had sought to 'eliminate central planning and the influence of the Communist Party, the socialist state and the trade unions over management of the national economy'.

As for the rest of society, the 'normalization', or reimposition of nomenklatura control, went forward slowly but ineluctably. Dubček was replaced by Gustav Husak, more pliable to Moscow, in April 1969, and the reformers were eased one by one out of the top jobs in party and state, demoted to lesser posts, and then finally consigned to menial jobs somewhere in the provinces (Dubček, for example, eventually became a forestry inspector in Slovakia). There were no show trials of the major figures, but selective ones for some of the less prominent. The party was thoroughly purged: every member was interviewed by a screening committee, and questioned closely on his attitudes and activities in 1968. As a result, perhaps one-third of its 1.5 million members left or were expelled. Similar interviews and dismissals went on in many fields of employment, especially those connected with education, culture or the media. Organizations too deeply affected by the 'rot', such as the Writers' Union or the Institute of Philosophy of the Academy of Sciences, were simply closed down, or merged with other bodies, until such time as they could be reconstituted under reliable stooges.

The whole Czechoslovak affair left the Soviet leaders with a profound distrust of intellectuals, especially in the humanities and social sciences, as well as of all economic reformers. This coloured the subsequent policies of the Brezhnev regime, though perhaps it would be fair to say that it confirmed an existing trend rather than stimulating a new one.

By the mid-1960s the society which Stalin had created in embryo had become fully formed. It was a very hierarchical, stable and conservative society, especially now that the upheavals occasioned by purges, war, urbanization and rapid social mobility were receding into the past. It was also, to use the clumsy but apt epithet of the political scientist T. H. Rigby, a 'mono-organizational' society: that is to say, it was in effect one single vast organization, directed by the cadres of the party–state apparatus, with their own headquarters in the Central Committee of the Communist Party and its permanent departments, all situated in one building on Old Square (*Staraya Ploshchad*) in Moscow. Through the by now highly developed and sophisticated nomenklatura system of patronage, this Central Committee supervised in principle every single appointment of any importance in any walk of life, delegating these powers to lower-tier party organizations for appointments lower down the hierarchy.

Every factory, enterprise, educational institution, transport undertaking, farm, commercial network – in short, every place of employment – has its rank in this hierarchy, according to whether its work is considered to be of 'all-Union significance', or of republican, oblast, raion or town significance. Remuneration of its staff and employees is measured accordingly, as are the perks and privileges of its directors, and the urgency accorded to its requests for personnel and equipment.

The population is ranked in the same way, through the internal passport and the propiska (dwelling permit) system introduced by Stalin. Highest status belongs to those who live in Moscow, where the best jobs are to be had, the best education, the easiest access to food, consumer goods and services, the possibility of contact with foreigners, or with Soviet employees able to obtain goods from the West. Next on the hierarchy of towns are Leningrad and the republican capitals, then, one rank lower, the remaining towns of 500,000 inhabitants or more, especially those with military, space or other high-technology industry of 'all-Union significance'. Citizens in these towns enjoy some of the advantages of Moscow, but to a lesser extent. To all these cities access is restricted: the police registration department will only grant a propiska when an employer of some standing can put up a good case. A propiska can come in two forms, temporary or permanent, adding an extra rung to the ladder: the struggle to convert the former to the latter can take many years. 'Entry no. 5' on one's passport can make any of these processes more difficult, especially if it reads 'Jewish'. To circumvent these obstacles, one can always contract a marriage with someone holding a 'superior' propiska: such marriages appear to have become as regular a part of Soviet society as financial matches were in Balzac's France.

To live in a smaller town or village somewhere in the provinces is automatically to enjoy lower status. To move from such a place to Alma-Ata, Kiev or Riga is very difficult and depends on official favour; to move to Moscow is virtually impossible. Worst situated of all are the collective farmers. They do not even have a passport, and hence are debarred from all but the briefest stay in any town without official permission. The only occasion when a collective farmer can demand a passport is when he is about to undergo compulsory military service – this of course applies only to men – or when embarking on some form of specialized or higher education. Not surprisingly, most of the young people who leave the village in this way hang on to their passports afterwards, and try to get a job in a town, rather than return home. A law passed in 1974 appeared to promise the right to a passport to any collective farmer, but its wording was ambiguous, and in practice it seems that not many have received them. The 'second serfdom' remains in force, at least in the sense that the kolkhoznik is fixed to the land.

At the peak of the social pyramid are the 'cadres' of the party–state apparatus. It tends to be forgotten now in examining Soviet politics, but of course the origin of the term is military, and military also is the spirit which animates the 'cadres', at least in the sense that hierarchy and command are the air they breathe. To some extent this is even more the case since Khrushchev relieved them of the fear of arrest. Nevertheless even Khrushchev caused them some discomfort and alarm by his constant reorganizations: between 1956 and 1961 he replaced more than two-thirds of the members of the Council of Ministers, the party Presidium (Politburo) and oblast party secretaries, and half of the Central Committee.

His successors have eliminated even this source of insecurity. Brezhnev's watchword was 'trust in cadres', and he put it into practice by making as few changes as possible at the highest levels of party and state. Forty-four per cent of the 1966 Central Committee were still in place in 1981; indeed, by that time the average full member of that key body had held his mandate for thirteen years, more than would have been permitted as a maximum under Khrushchev's plans for rotation of office. For the same reason, the average age of the Central Committee rose from fifty-six to sixty-three between 1966 and 1982, that of the Council of Ministers from fifty-eight to sixty-five, and that of the Politburo from fifty-five to sixty-eight. By the late 1970s, a standard term for describing the Soviet leadership was 'gerontocracy', and Western journalistic speculation constantly dwelt on the health of its principal figures, noting their every temporary absence from public life.

The result of Brezhnev's policy was to give new stability and confidence to the men at the centre of the nomenklatura network, the members of the Central Committee, and the leading officials of its departments. Three-quarters of the Central Committee of 1981 came from senior positions in party and state: 35 per cent were oblast and republican party secretaries, 9 per cent came from the Central Committee departments, and 31 per cent came from the ministries. Other sections of the polity provided, by comparison, much less significant representation: the military 7 per cent, the diplomatic service 4 per cent, cultural and scientific personnel 3 per cent, KGB and trade unions 2 per cent each, and the rest negligible. Some further salient characteristics of Central Committee members are worth mentioning. Nearly three-quarters of them joined the party before 1950, and thus gained their early, and often decisive, experience of party life

under Stalin. 82 per cent of them were peasants or workers
by origin, but 78 per cent of them had higher education,
which means that many of them had risen a long way in the
world: they were the beneficiaries of a rapid social mobility
which had by then more or less ceased. 97 per cent of them
were men, which confirms one's impression that, for all the
'emancipation' of women, they had not succeeded in penet-
rating the top echelons of power. Slavs constituted 86 per
cent – and Russians 67 per cent – of the membership, far in
excess of their proportion of the population. 55 per cent of
them had worked at one time or another, perhaps during the
war, in the military, or in a defence-related branch of
industry. So the 'identikit' Central Committee member was
an elderly male Russian who had risen in the world and had
extensive experience of government and/or party leadership,
as well as some experience of the 'military-industrial complex'.

It was this composite figure who had decisive influence, at
least indirectly, on every appointment made in every walk of
life. Perhaps for that reason, by the 1970s Soviet society was
far more militarized than it had been in the twenties and
thirties. The rise in social standing gained by officers of the
armed services during the Second World War had proved to
be permanent. So also had their integration, through thorough political training, into the party. The military probably
were, and had reason to be, the most satisfied professional
group in Soviet society. True, there was a period when
Khrushchev cut defence expenditure and prematurely retired
a proportion of the officer corps. But, then, that may have
been one of the reasons for his fall. Apart from him, all the
leaders, from Stalin to Chernenko, granted the military – army,
navy, air and missile forces – more or less whatever they
requested in the interests of projecting Soviet power all over
the world, and attaining parity with the USA. Defence contracts
continued to have unquestioned priority in economic planning.
Civil defence and paramilitary training in schools, colleges
and universities became a routine part of life.

As for the party cadres themselves, Mikhail Voslensky, formerly a professor at the Lumumba University in Moscow, and a man with connections to the Central Committee apparatus, has given an account since his emigration in 1972 of how the selection process is managed. The young man (or much less likely woman) who wants to make a career for himself will begin by becoming a party activist at his workplace, taking on numerous unpaid and unglamorous jobs to do with propaganda and agitation, social security, trade union activities, and so on. He will assiduously attend party meetings and make his presence felt, without saying anything too controversial. In due course he may be elected to the party bureau at his workplace, and thence rise to become one of its secretaries, or even in the end *the* secretary – which in a large enterprise is a full-time, paid post. At each stage in his rise a testimonial will be written on him – the higher the rise the more detailed the testimonial – signed by the enterprise director, the chairman of the trade union, and by a leading figure in the party committee of the local raion: this will be sent to the raion party committee (or higher, if the enterprise is an important one), and will attest to the candidate's political maturity and reliability, to his specialist knowledge and to his administrative capacities. The local branch of the KGB, which has intimate links to the personnel department of the enterprise and plants informers among the workforce and staff, also writes a report on him, which must say that he presents no security risk – a much wider concept than in Western societies.

If he is successful as a full-time secretary, then the way is open for upward promotion into the medium and upper ranks of the party apparatus, a promotion often accompanied by a spell of study at a party high school.

Naturally, this method of promotion tends to generate cliques or 'clientele groups'. Each candidate for promotion has in effect to be sponsored by a leading figure in the party's next level above, and this sponsorship can be continued at a later stage, if the sponsor has in the meantime been promoted further. This tendency has been noted by most close students of Soviet personnel politics – the so-called 'Kremlinologists'. Brezhnev was a patient and adept practitioner of clientele politics, promoting to his side, especially in his later years, men who had served with him in the metal works at Dneprodzerzhinsk, or in the party committee of Dnepropetrovsk oblast (the 'Dnepropetrovsk mafia', as Western journalists call it), or later in the republican party organizations of Moldavia and Kazakhstan.

If there is a 'ruling class' in the Soviet Union, then its kernel is to be found in the nomenklatura posts at the disposal of each party committee, and in the people selected to fill them. Not all of them are equally powerful, of course: in fact, their degree of authority is painstakingly graded according to the origin of their appointment, and is reflected in the privileges available to each appointee. Incidentally, the party provenance of the appointment is never made public – indeed, many of the posts are in theory elective – and the whole system remains confidential. For that reason it is impossible to make an accurate estimate of the size of this 'ruling class'. If Voslensky's figures are correct, then down to raion level the nomenklatura appointees number about three-quarters of a million – together with families (given the low birth rate among the dominant Slavs) perhaps 2½–3 million people, or 1 per cent of the population. However, Voslensky appears to omit posts not directly attributable to party, government or economic enterprises. Another estimate, by Rigby, is more than twice as large – just over 2 million, or 1½–2 per cent of the labour force, even without families. But his figures are based on two relatively small republics, Bashkiria (an Autonomous Republic) and Georgia (a Union Republic), which may well be untypically densely provided with nomenklatura appointees. My own estimate would lie between the two – but any pretension to accuracy must be spurious.

The term 'ruling class', applied to a Western society, implies ownership of the means of production and the ability to bequeath it to one's heirs. In the strict sense the Soviet elite cannot claim such ownership. Nevertheless, through the central planning system, the nomenklatura appointees certainly *control* the means of production throughout the country. And although they cannot directly pass on this control to their heirs, they can use personal connections, and the educational system, to ensure that their offspring are well-placed in the struggle for similar nomenklatura posts in the future. Some family members of Soviet leaders have in fact made excellent careers for themselves. Thus, A. I. Adzhubei, Khrushchev's son-in-law, was editor of the daily newspaper *Izvestiya* and a member of the Central Committee – though, significantly, he lost both positions when his father-in-law was ousted. Brezhnev's son Yury became a deputy minister of foreign trade, while his son-in-law Yury Churbanov was a deputy minister of the interior until scandal broke out in 1982 concerning his wife's fondness for diamonds. Kosygin's son-in-law, O. O. Gvishiani, was head of the State Committee for Science and Technology, entrusted with the vital task of grafting new technology on to Soviet industry. Andropov's son, Igor, worked at the Institute for United States Studies, and later became a leading Soviet delegate at the European Security Conference in Madrid.

Nevertheless, on the whole it cannot be said that nepotism has yet become the rule throughout the Soviet apparatus as much as in some other societies. It may be that the family as such is less important to Soviet power-holders than is the case in most political systems (certainly the families are rigidly shielded from public view or comment), and that the Soviet equivalent of 'heir' is to be found in the clientele system described above. Under that hypothesis, it does appear that the Soviet elite has learnt to do very systematically and successfully what ruling classes have always done: to bequeath its dominant position to its heirs. Parallels with other societies, bourgeois, feudal or oriental, are all partly misleading: Soviet society is a new historical type, and it is right and proper that we should adjust our terminology to describe it adequately.

It will be seen from this argument that the centralized planning system exists for political rather than economic reasons. It is very doubtful – even to those who work within it – whether the system produces good economic results. Evidence by the late 1970s certainly was that a system which had once promoted very high economic growth rates was now failing to do so even in heavy industry. Rates of 5–6 per cent per annum throughout the fifties and sixties had fallen to 3.7 per cent in 1971–5 and 2.7 per cent in 1976–80. This, of course, still looked moderately impressive compared with the stagnation most Western economies were entering at the time; yet in view of the inbuilt interest everyone in the Soviet system has in reporting at least a modest growth each year, one may doubt whether a reported growth rate of 2.7 per cent does not in reality conceal levelling off or even a slight decline. Certainly, the perceptions of the population by the late seventies were that economic conditions were actually becoming more difficult, and scarcities getting worse.

The shortcomings of the centrally planned economy are such that a thriving and ramified 'second economy' has grown up to meet the population's needs for consumer goods, transport, repairs and services. In agriculture, of course, as described elsewhere, the 'second economy' is legalized in the form of the private plot and the kolkhoz market. In other sectors, however, it is strictly illegal. It flourishes, though, for quite simple reasons. The Soviet motorist who needs a windscreen wiper or a fan-belt may well find that official suppliers are unable to help him, at least not without long delay; so, rather than stop using his car, he asks around among his friends till he locates an unofficial supplier, who will charge much higher prices but will oblige immediately.

Where will the unofficial supplier get hold of the goods he sells? Sometimes he will be an employee at an automobile works or repair depot, who will quite simply have pilfered the required item, reporting it damaged or lost in transit. Or he may have acquired it from an auxiliary or even 'underground' workshop, manufacturing 'deficit' (scarce) commodities on the side, either unknown to the authorities, or for some reason protected by them. Factories and collective farms have been known to provide a façade for the operation of clandestine enterprises producing clothes, footwear, household gadgets, or processed food normally unobtainable on the state-controlled market. Thus, in August 1976 *Pravda* reported that in a certain village in the Caucasus most of the inhabitants were privately knitting woollen wear for the black market. The proceeds from these operations, usually considerable, went to the workers themselves, to the managers of the façade enterprise, and to any party or ministerial officials who had to be in the know.

Another much-coveted source for 'deficit' goods is the West. Western goods are sold for foreign currency or 'certificate' rubles at special shops in large cities (all in the 'limited access' category), which is why people who receive part of their pay in that form, or who are allowed occasionally to travel to the West, enjoy an especially revered status among their colleagues and subordinates. They are the source of Japanese cameras, German tape-recorders, Italian suits or Scotch whisky, which they can offer as favours in return for services, or on which they can make a huge profit. For the same purpose, there is a brisk black market in foreign currency.

Services can also be obtained on the 'second economy'. A flat-dweller who wants his plumbing repaired – which may of course be a very urgent matter – will usually find it quicker and simpler, though not cheaper, to turn to the services of a *shabashnik*, or 'moonlighter', who will do the job at evenings or weekends, often using tools and materials diverted from his regular place of employment.

Similarly, a hard-pressed enterprise director, unable to obtain urgently needed goods or services from the official supply agency, may well have recourse to the 'second economy' in order to meet his output target. If he is found out, he may receive a reprimand; but, if he does not fulfil his target, he and all his employees will suffer a drop in income, and his job itself may be at stake.

The party and state do not of course simply tolerate these transactions. They are a threat to the economic monopoly which justifies the offices held by many nomenklatura appointees. A whole army of supervisory organs in fact exists to curb the 'second economy'. Apart from the militia, the procuracy and the courts, there is a party–state network of Committees of People's Control, which works by trying to mobilize public vigilance against economic crime, and a state-run economic police, OBKhSS (the Department for Combatting the Theft of Socialist Property), which specializes in the complex investigatory methods sometimes needed to track down clandestine operators.

All the same, there are good reasons why the state should not take a wholly repressive line towards the unofficial economy. Firstly, the spare capacity it generates builds some flexibility into what would be otherwise an intolerably rigid system, and enables the economy as a whole to go on functioning. Furthermore, as the 'second economy' is parasitic on the official one, its operators are burdened with an additional form of personal dependence on the office-holders of state and party. They know that their illegal activities may be found out at any time, or perhaps already have been, and that they are therefore dependent on the personal favour of those officials who are in the know. The shabashnik who makes use of tools and timber from the building site where he works is in a real sense a 'vassal' of the foreman or site inspector who lets him get away with it.

In certain areas of the country the unofficial economy has developed to such an extent as to become apparently tightly enmeshed with the power-holders at the highest level. A sociologist, I. Zemtsov, who worked as a personal assistant for G. Aliev, first secretary of the Azerbaidjan party organization in the 1970s, has reported that under his predecessor, V. Akhundov, the illegal economy had spread its tentacles into every branch of public life. Anything could be had for money: cars, alcohol, drugs, foreign clothes, sex, entry into college, learned degrees – even, he asserts, public office. According to his figures, the post of raion procurator costs 30,000 rubles, that of police chief 50,000 and that of first raion party secretary 200,000 rubles. These figures sound extraordinarily high, only financially explicable if a very high and consistent level of bribery obtains. They have not been confirmed from elsewhere – and public sale of office would certainly be a new principle in a socialist society.

What is much more credible is that Akhundov maintained himself in office by keeping up friendly ties with some of the highest office-holders in Moscow – including Andrei Kirilenko in the party Politburo and Nikolai Baibakov, chairman of Gosplan – by offering them expensive gifts and luxurious holidays in secluded dachas within his fief. However that may be, Akhundov was dismissed in 1969, and replaced by Aliev, the previous KGB chief in the republic, with a brief to clean up political life there. He immediately criticized 'intrigues, slander, backbiting, in-fighting and bribery' among top republican officials, as well as appointments made through 'personal attachment, friendly relations, family or neighbourhood ties'.

A similar example was offered by the dismissal in 1972 of V. Mzhavanadze, first secretary of the Georgian Communist Party. His successor, E. Shevardnadze, was the former minister of the interior in the republic (and thus responsible for the militia, or ordinary police): he celebrated his assumption of office by arresting Mzhavanadze's wife for accepting bribes from the brothers Lazishvili, proprietors of a network of underground factories turning out 'deficit goods'. At one time the Lazishvilis' influence was said to be so strong that they influenced the appointment of party secretaries in Tbilisi. Shevardnadze, however, had them arrested as part of his drive against corruption of all kinds in the republic. It does not appear, in the long run, that he has been particularly successful in this: presumably the 'second economy' is too deeply rooted in Georgia. At any rate, for several years he had to travel everywhere in a bullet-proof car and with an armed guard, such were the fears of an attempt on his life. There was a wave of violence and terrorism in Georgia following his appointment, including the burning down of the Tbilisi Opera House in 1973, and an explosion outside the Council of Ministers building in 1976.

With the accession of Andropov to power in Moscow in 1982, the purgers of the 'second economy' came into the ascendant. Indeed, Aliev was called from Baku to Moscow as a first deputy prime minister of the USSR.

For the factory worker the centralized planning system means, on the whole, a poorly paid but secure and fairly undemanding life. It is very difficult for management to dismiss workers for laziness, incompetence, absenteeism or even drunkenness, as Kosygin's reformers discovered. In this respect, at least, Soviet trade unions have proved able to defend the interests of their members. Since compulsory mobilization of workers was abolished in 1956, in fact, coercion of the workforce has been replaced by a kind of tacit bargain with them. In return for low pay and a *de facto* prohibition of strikes, the workers are permitted quite low standards of work discipline. Save for glaring abuses, it is on the whole accepted that they will often arrive late, take leisurely tea breaks, go shopping during working hours (to secure scarce products in crowded shops) and sometimes even sleep off the effects of the night's 'moonlighting'. True, towards the end of each month, and especially of each year, they will be called on to undertake a *shturm*, a period of very hard work, with compulsory overtime, needed to complete the plan target for the immediate stage. But as soon as that is over a gentler work-rhythm resumes. A popular joke sums up the situation. A political instructor asks a worker: 'What is the basis of the Soviet economic system?' Answer: 'You pretend to pay us, and we pretend to work.'

As a social system, this, in a sense, works well enough. But it has its obvious frustrations, many of them rooted in the underproductivity it causes. Labour turnover is high, some 25–30 per cent per annum, and is the subject of continual worried press comment. Workers move on in search of a variety of benefits: higher pay, better working conditions, better housing, more reliable food supplies, more favourable arrangements for 'moonlighting', and so on. In the absence of a collective right to strike, this individual right to move on, though restricted by the propiska system, may be the Soviet worker's most valuable freedom. This is especially true since the alternative method of escaping frustration – individual promotion – is becoming much more difficult to achieve. From the end of the war till the mid-1960s or so, promotion was probably the best hope for the worker: there was still plenty of scope for the able, ambitious or obsequious to become an 'innovator', 'rationalizer' (suggesting improved work methods) or 'shock worker', to gain party membership and hope for promotion into the white-collar bracket. Now the white-collar ranks are already overfull; indeed it seems there are quite a number of ordinary workers who have a full ten or eleven years' schooling behind them, plus a special skill, and perhaps a failed application for higher education. In fact they are overqualified for the jobs they are doing.

Occasionally, in spite of everything, workers' discontents do crystallize in collective action, in the form of a strike or demonstration. It is impossible to tell how often this happens. Reports reach the West infrequently, but fairly regularly, and in view of the difficulty and delay with which they come out it seems reasonable to assume that they represent only a sample, of unknown size, of the labour conflicts that actually occur.

What is most striking about these reported conflicts is that the workers' grievances appear to range over the whole of their life. Whereas in the West, labour conflict usually focuses on pay or conditions of employment, in the Soviet Union it concerns housing conditions, food supplies, relations with the local police, and a whole variety of other issues. In other words, Soviet workers see themselves as being in a total relationship with their employers, one covering the whole of their life. And, indeed, it is usually the case that the enterprise owns the workers' housing, and that, through the party organization, the management can influence food supplies, community relations, and so on, in a way which is not open to Western managers. It is rather like working in a 'company town' in nineteenth-century America.

The earliest reported incident of serious labour unrest exemplifies the wide range of grievances presented. This was in September 1959, in the new industrial town of Temirtau, in Kazakhstan. Young workers and Komsomol volunteers had come from all over the country to help build a metal works. When they got to Temirtau, they found they had to live in tents (in country exposed to sand-storms), that the water supply was only intermittent, and the food very poor. To cap it all, they learnt that Young Communist brigades from East Germany and Poland working alongside them were being much better paid. A group of workers set fire to the canteen on the building site, and then marched on the police station, where, according to some reports, they hanged the police chief. The army was called in, but apparently some of the soldiers fraternized with the protesters, so that in the end special KGB troops were used. Several dozen people may have been killed and several hundred injured before order could be restored. Those held to be the ringleaders were arrested, and several of them were reportedly executed. If these reports are only partly true, they still suggest an enormous degree of frustration on the workers' side, and very poor riot control on the part of the authorities, who were presumably totally unaccustomed to civil unrest.

Food supplies and prices have always figured prominently among the most deeply felt issues, and they provoked the wave of unrest which affected a number of towns in the summer of 1962, when the government raised meat and dairy prices by about a third. In one town, Novocherkassk, this unrest took a violent course. At the Budenny electric locomotive works the management – by fortuitous bad timing, one presumes – simultaneously raised the piecework norms, that is, effectively lowered wages. The workers from two shops asked to see the director to complain about the new norms, but he either refused to see them or flatly rejected their protest. Thereupon all the workers in the factory downed tools, and draped the building with posters reading 'Down with Khrushchev!' and 'Cut up Khrushchev for sausages!' – an indication of the extent to which the price rises were identified with the first secretary. Some of the workers ripped up the track of the Moscow-Rostov main railway line, which passed right by the premises. When the police arrested about thirty workers whom they considered to be ringleaders, nearly all the factories in Novocherkassk went on strike, and huge crowds, including women (affected very directly by food prices), converged on police headquarters, and then on the gorkom (city party committee) building, showing clearly where they thought the centres of influence lay. Another maladroit piece of crowd control followed: special KGB troops guarding the party building fired warning shots into the air, but apparently hit some small boys who had clambered up into the trees. One army officer present is reported then to have refused to give an order to open fire in earnest at the furious crowd, but to have torn up his party card and shot himself. Others had no such scruples. The troops continued shooting, moreover, even when the crowd had turned in order to flee. At least seventy people were killed – far more, according to some accounts – and many were wounded.

A high-level delegation headed by Mikoyan and Kozlov (members of the party Presidium) flew into the Don region to supervise the aftermath of the affair and to undertake an investigation. They ordered special supplies to be rushed in, so that the food shops in the Don were well stocked for a while. In the meantime numerous workers were arrested, and some soldiers and officers court-martialled. According to

Solzhenitsyn, those wounded in the unrest were exiled to Siberia along with their families to keep them quiet.

The incidents at Temirtau and Novocherkassk seem to have been the bloodiest, and it may be that the authorities learnt something from them, both about how to avoid trouble, and how to cope with it when it arises. Since then their immediate reaction to workers' protests has usually been to satisfy any demands forthwith, then subsequently at leisure to arrest those whom they identify as ringleaders, and try them for presenting a 'threat to public order' or have them committed to mental hospitals.

Various incidents, not remotely on the same scale, have taken place since, over poor housing (Kiev 1969, Dnepropetrovsk 1972), food shortages (Sverdlovsk 1969, Dnepropetrovsk 1972, Gorky 1980), excessive work norms (Vitebsk 1973, Kiev 1981), and low pay (Sverdlovsk 1969, Dnepropetrovsk 1972, Togliatti 1981). Unnecessary violence used by the police against ordinary citizens has provoked mass demonstrations in Alexandrov (Vladimir oblast) 1969, Dneprodzerzhinsk 1972 and Ordzhonikidze 1981.

All these demonstrations and work stoppages were relatively spontaneous, that is to say, there was no more than the most improvised organization behind them. The trade unions are part of the nomenklatura network – at least those who run them are – and although they have been effective, as I have suggested, in defending certain workers' interests, there is no question of their ever undertaking collective action against the wishes of the authorities. To counter this situation, at least a couple of attempts have been made in recent years to set up independent trade unions. These have differed considerably from the official ones, and also from what we would recognize as trade unions in the West. They were strongly influenced by the human rights movement which had arisen in the 1960s (see next chapter). The founders of the first, the Free Trade Union Association of 1977, were minor officials as well as workers. What they had in common with each other was not so much social background as the fact that they ran across each other in the waiting rooms of the AUCCTU (the official trade union council), the procuracy and the Supreme Soviet, where they were endeavouring to obtain redress for various illegalities they had suffered at the workplace. Reading their case histories gives a lurid and necessarily rather one-sided picture of relations between management and employees in Soviet enterprises. As they said in the Free Trade Union Association's first official statement, issued to the Western press (the Soviet press, of course, would not publish it), '*Everywhere* we are refused even a hearing, and our complaints are sent to the very organs against whom we are complaining.'

The founder of this union, Vladimir Klebanov, is very much a case in point. A mining engineer in the Donbass, already from the late fifties he had complained about managers who stole materials for their own use, accepted bribes, diverted funds to their own purposes, and so forth. When his face was injured at work, his superiors declined to pay him compensation, and he had to apply to the courts for it: they duly found in his favour. Thereafter, however, Klebanov was refused work, evicted with his family from their flat, and committed for spells in psychiatric hospitals, where eventually he was diagnosed as suffering from 'paranoia' and a 'pathological development of the personality'. His case illustrates the weapons employers could use against workers, and yet also shows that justice could sometimes be attained through the Soviet courts against the wishes of local authorities. The required psychiatric diagnosis was also not obtained without difficulty: not all Soviet psychiatrists were prepared under political pressure to contravene their professional judgement.

However, in the end the authorities got their way, and Klebanov found himself dismissed and unable to secure employment, which is why he, like many others, was struggling for what he felt to be his rights in 1977. In its statutes, significantly, the Free Trade Union Association talked, not of the defence of material interests, but of the 'protection of rights and the search for justice', while the enemy was identified as 'bureaucratism and mystification, bad management, extravagance, and careless attitudes to national property'.

Most of the members of the Association were arrested soon after its foundation, and it was never able to operate in the way intended. Klebanov himself was soon sent yet again to a mental hospital. For that reason, the second independent trade union to be set up, the Free Interprofessional Association of Labourers (SMOT – 1978), soon ceased to publish its members' names. As a result, some of them at least remained at liberty, and SMOT continued to publish reports on violations of civil rights, especially but not exclusively in industrial and employment relations. This marked the first step of the civil rights movement towards the underground, in the late Brezhnev years.

As we saw in the last chapter, Khrushchev, though he did not fundamentally alter the structure of collective agriculture, did improve somewhat the material conditions of the village, and placed agriculture for the first time high on the party's agenda. His successors criticized him for his inconsistencies, and ended his maize and livestock campaigns, but continued trying to achieve his aims in a quieter and more consistent way.

At the Central Committee plenum of March 1965, Brezhnev announced that collective and state farms would henceforth receive their procurement plans for several years in advance, with higher prices paid for their produce, so that they could plan production and budgeting on a more stable basis. He also promised a more generous premium for above-plan deliveries. Restrictions on private plots, reimposed by Khrushchev in his later years, were once again lifted, taxes on them were reduced, and farm chairmen were instructed to make pasture-land or hay available for private cattle. Brezhnev also promised a high and growing level of state investment, for fertilizers, for land improvement, for building roads, schools, housing and other facilities in the countryside.

By and large, the government has adhered to these promises. Agricultural investment has been running at 20–25 per cent of all investment (compared with 4 per cent in the USA), a level which demonstrates indubitable commitment, though also inefficient use of resources. Prices paid to farms for their produce have remained much higher; moreover, they have not been passed on in full to the (mainly urban) consumer, presumably for fear of provoking anything like the Novocherkassk riots. To cover the difference, the state was by 1977 paying annual subsidies that totalled 19,000 million rubles – more than 70 rubles for every man, woman and child in the country, and what Alec Nove has called 'the most gigantic agricultural subsidy known in human history'. And this on top of regular grain imports.

All this has relieved the poverty of the countryside to a considerable extent. Since 1966 Kolkhozniki have, like the workers on the sovkhoz, been paid a regular wage, rather than 'labour days' calculated as a share of the farm's income. Consequently, by the mid-1970s, rural wages were running only about 10 per cent lower than average urban wages – while the villager is much more likely to have a private plot of some kind with which to supplement his pay.

Nevertheless, the rural population has been falling fast. Material incentives have proved insufficient, and people are still anxious to get away from the village if they can. In a way, this might have made possible a solution to Russia's age-old problem, surplus underemployed population to feed in the countryside. But unfortunately the rural exodus has not taken place in the right way for that. Because of the way the passport system works, it is mainly the young and the trained who have been leaving, while the old and the unskilled remain behind. According to Alexander Yanov, a journalist who travelled widely in the countryside in the 1960s, many parents are most anxious for their children to go into the town at fifteen or sixteen (just before they receive their passport), to take a course at a technical or vocational school of some kind: 'If only our children can have it a bit different,' was a sentiment he often heard. And of course, after their period of study, they do not return to the village.

During the sixties the controversy over the 'link' system revived, in the context of trying to provide more work satisfaction for kolkhoz workers. Under the standard 'brigade' system of work organization, a collectivity of anywhere between twenty and one hundred people will perform items of work on the collective as instructed by the chairman. Rates of pay are based on these items, not on the output eventually generated, so that, for example, it may be in the interest of a kolkhoznik to weed a field carelessly and fast, because it will bring in more income. Under the 'link' system, on the other hand (described in Chapter 8), a small group of workers would be responsible for the entire work cycle, and would receive their income according to what they were able to deliver to the state and to market at the end.

In one much-quoted experiment of this kind, in Krasnodar oblast, Vladimir Pervitsky and his ten-man 'link' tripled the yield of a plot of land normally cultivated intermittently by a brigade of eighty. An even more remarkable case was that of Ivan Khudenko, a veteran Communist living in Kazakhstan. In 1972 he and sixty chosen colleagues were given permission to take over a tract of marginal, hitherto uncultivated land, to work it on the 'link' principle. In the first harvest, the productivity per man achieved was reported as being up to twenty times the rate prevailing on adjacent farms. Even making allowances for the high fertility of virgin soil, this was an impressive performance. The locals were so pleased that they wrote a play about Khudenko, but the day after its preview, attended by numerous reformist journalists and economists, Khudenko was suddenly arrested and charged with obtaining state funds under false pretences. His farm was closed down. In spite of efforts to save him, he was sentenced to six years' imprisonment, and died in jail two years later.

As with the abortive efforts at reform in the industrial field, it seems there must be some overwhelming political reason why the 'link' idea has been crushed so many times. According to Yanov, the 'link' aroused resentment among farmers not attached to one: they might have similar qualifications and work just as hard, yet receive only a quarter of the income of a 'link' member. Total reorganization in 'links' also threatened to render superfluous much of the work done by rural party organizations and chairmen of collective farms. It would revive a system of agriculture somewhat reminiscent of that which existed before the revolution, when the basic production unit was the household (*dvor*), working within the legal framework of the village commune (mir). In practice, it might work rather like the Yugoslav system (see above, page 323), with the kolkhoz functioning as a 'general cooperative'.

At any rate, the collective sector remained underproductive, though to a lesser extent than twenty years earlier, because much had been achieved through higher investment. But the private plot remained vital. Rural families satisfied about 70 per cent of their own nutritional needs from it. And it played a major part in feeding the towns. As late as 1965 about two-thirds of the potatoes and eggs, and about 40 per cent of meat, milk and vegetables came from this source (which only constitutes 1–2 per cent of cultivable land). Since then, these levels have sunk somewhat, partly because collective productivity has improved a little, partly because rural incomes have risen to the point where many farmers, particularly the younger ones, are no longer prepared to put in long hours of extra work on their own plot. All the same, the 'kolkhoz market' remains important. Anyone who has seen a Soviet housewife preparing for a special occasion knows that she will for preference buy food at the kolkhoz market rather than at a state shop: the goods may be three of four times as expensive, but there will be a good choice, and they will be fresh and of high quality.

At all social levels, the smallest unit of Soviet society, the family, has been under considerable strain – and this in spite of the efforts of the governments, both under Stalin and subsequently, to render it more stable. In part this is the long-term effect of the old anti-family policies, as well as of the cataclysmic changes promoted by the government between the 1920s and the 1950s, which all involved uprooting millions of people from their families. Most damaging of all, perhaps, was the war, which killed so many men, mostly young, leaving millions of women without husbands, and children without fathers.

In a 1965 novel about young workers in Rostov-on-Don, Vitaly Semin has one character ask six of his colleagues how many of them have fathers: only one raises his hand. Everyone accepts that this situation is typical. Fyodor Abramov called one of his novels about the post-war village *Bezotsovshchina*, which means 'fatherlessness'. And so millions of children grew up without a model on which to base their own understanding of the paternal role in the family, a lack which may well have laid the foundation for marital difficulties in the following generation. Meanwhile, the women coped courageously with their single-parent families, usually holding down a job as well for financial reasons. The network of childcare centres, though far better developed than in the West, was not usually adequate to meet demand on this scale. The only counterbalancing factor was the presence of many middle-aged and elderly women, also often widowed, the famous *babushki* (grandmothers) of Soviet folklore, pitched willy-nilly, whatever their age or health, into a kind of second motherhood in order to ease the burdens of their daughters and daughters-in-law.

Of course, the post-war situation eventually eased considerably, especially since an enormous increase in social welfare benefits has taken place since Stalin's death. Between 1950 and 1980, state welfare expenditure increased fivefold: the improved provision of pensions, family allowances and housing subsidies was particularly marked, and this helped to relieve the previously terrible poverty of many rural dwellers, old people, invalids and one-parent families. With the passing years, moreover, the problem of the missing men has gradually eased, as a post-war generation has grown up and entered married life. But this problem seems to have been replaced by others. Since divorce was simplified once again in 1965, it has become more common at an alarming rate. From just over 100 per 1000 marriages in 1965, the rate rose to 340 per 1000 in 1979: in other words, for every three marriages, there was one divorce. This level rivals that of the USA, traditionally a high-divorce country, and runs completely counter to Russian traditions.

What are the reasons for this change? Among the causes cited in court for marital breakdown, the husband's drunkenness is mentioned most often, occurring in almost half the cases. I shall return to that important theme in a moment. Among the other causes mentioned are adultery, violence and 'incompatibility', whatever the last may mean. One gets a general picture of families living in conditions which put pressure on both partners, but particularly on the women.

First of all, there is the housing situation. Although this has improved enormously since the mid-fifties, it is still unusual for a couple, unless they belong to the privileged elite, to occupy a home of their own as soon as they marry. Most live with the parents of one of the partners – a notoriously tense and difficult arrangement. Some young couples still have to live in hostels, where they have no privacy.

Then there is the fact that most women have a paid job. The 1970 census showed that 86 per cent of women of working age have a full- or part-time job. They constitute, in fact, 51 per cent of the workforce. When asked *why* they work, 91 per cent of women respondents in Moscow replied that they did so above all for financial reasons, though 86 per cent also said that they wanted some kind of group activity, or valued the chance to do socially useful work. Most women seem to be motivated by both kinds of consideration.

The trouble is that social customs have not adjusted to the fact that working women are now the norm. A woman's pay is on average about 65 per cent of a man's. Sometimes this is because she tends to occupy the lower ranks of the same profession. But sometimes it is because a whole profession, in which women are strongly represented, receives lower pay. A dramatic example is the medical profession, in which about 70 per cent of employees are women: even quite highly qualified doctors may earn less than a skilled manual worker. Teachers and skilled office staff, overwhelmingly women, are among the lowest paid occupations in the whole employment field.

So women are not commensurately paid for the work they do. Nor have husbands' work patterns adjusted to the fact of near-universal female employment. Surveys indicate that the wife normally does 60–70 per cent of the housework, some of the rest often being performed by the resident babushka. Patterns are, however, slowly changing here, with better educated husbands apparently showing greater willingness to contribute their share to the domestic chores.

All the same, the 'double load' borne by the typical wife and mother is now recognized as a serious social problem. Her daily round, rushing from kindergarten to packed trolleybus to underground station to office to food queue, and then back to underground, trolleybus, kindergarten and finally home to an evening of cooking, cleaning, mending, ironing and putting the children to bed – all this is graphically described in a novel by Natalya Baranskaya, *A Week Like Any Other*, which struck a deep chord when it appeared in 1969. The feelings of many highly trained women are summed up in the heroine's outburst when her husband suggests she should give up work to devote herself to home and children:

> 'Don't you think I'd love to do what's good for the children? Of course I would! But what you suggest would . . . be the end of me. What about my five years' studying? My degree? My work experience? My dissertation? You think it's easy to chuck it all up – just like that?

And what sort of person would I be, living at home? I'd be sore as hell, nagging you the whole time. Anyway how can we seriously discuss it? We'd never manage on your salary alone . . .'

One result of the strain under which so many families suffer is a low birth rate. At the 1970 census (no figures seem to have been made generally available for 1979), the average number of children per family was 2.4 (it had been 2.9 in 1959). There were enormous and significant variations between one republic and another. Thus the rate was 1.94 in Latvia, 1.97 in the RSFSR, 2.04 in the Ukraine – but in Azerbaidjan 4.63, in Uzbekistan 5.64, in Turkmenistan 5.95. This seems to be connected, perhaps partly with Islam, and partly with the fact that in the high-birth areas a greater proportion of the population lives in the countryside and in extended families. Since 1970 the birth rate in Russia, the Ukraine, Bielorussia and the Baltic republics has been too low for generations to reproduce themselves, so that demographic decline is now setting in there, at least among the natives. This causes much concern to economic planners, since in the areas of developed industry insufficient young people will soon be coming forward to replenish the labour force, while the surplus population stays in the Central Asian villages, where the planned economy is much less strong, and on the whole they refuse to be lured to the towns of European Russia.

As a result, some Soviet demographers have been conducting a campaign recently to change family policy drastically. They argue that all mothers should stay at home, at least for several years, to look after their children, and, if necessary, should be financially encouraged by the state to do so. They would also like the state to invest far more in the service and retail sectors, so that shopping, repairs and maintenance become much simpler and less exhausting. All this, they argue, would encourage families to have more children, which in its turn would benefit the economy (and of course, though this is not usually stated, the armed forces). Not much has been done in these directions so far: services and retail trade remain neglected offspring in the planned economy. It is only fair to mention, however, that women do now have the right to a year's leave before and after childbirth, of which 112 days are on full pay, the rest unpaid.

In spite of everything, the family has actually survived in the Soviet Union, which might not altogether have been expected, given the intentions of early Soviet legislators, and the tremendous social upheavals. It seems, moreover, to be a rather conservative force, resisting the efforts of party and state to mobilize individuals, and involve them in collective action. The great majority of marriages are contracted between two individuals of the same social class, the same nationality and similar educational background: inherited patterns thus tend to be perpetuated, including those connected with religion or nationality. Furthermore, with the mass movement during the sixties and seventies out of communal apartments into individual family ones, the sense of belonging to a collective (albeit an infuriating one) has declined sharply. Surveys have shown that most people prefer to spend their leisure hours at home – doing household tasks, reading, helping the children or watching television – rather than attend public occasions and meetings. In some cases, the family is also a counterforce to the ideological pressures prevailing at school and work: children often grow up having imbibed values which at least partly contradict those officially propagated. The state seems reluctant today, except in extreme cases (usually involving sectarian religion), to interfere in this development of diversity.

There could be no better indication of the state's ambivalence about social problems than its policy on alcohol. Between 1970 and 1980 alcohol sales rose by 77 per cent, and a professor advising the Ministry of the Interior reported that 37 per cent of working men 'abuse' alcohol to one degree or another. Although no official figures were issued, estimates suggested that the USSR headed the world in the per capita consumption of distilled spirits. Yet official policy was to support the production and sale of alcohol, because it raised so much revenue. Desperate seekers after food and consumer goods in Russian provincial towns would note, with annoyance, that, whatever else might be out of stock, there were always plenty of bottles of vodka on the shelves, waiting to be bought. This was the one sector of consumer industry that seemed to work well in the planned economy.

Perhaps significantly, alcohol abuse was worst in the RFSFR, followed closely by the Ukraine and Bielorussia, while it was least prevalent among Jews and (naturally perhaps) the Muslim peoples of Central Asia.

Comment in the Soviet press then connected a variety of social ills with alcohol abuse. Alcoholism was itself the third commonest cause of death – and probably contributed towards the commonest, which was heart disease. It was responsible for huge losses to the economy through absenteeism and poor work. It was, as we have seen, a frequent cause of divorce. It was also closely connected with suicide – rumoured to be a very serious problem, though official figures were not issued until 1988. Many crimes were, of course, committed under the influence of drink: nearly all acts of 'hooliganism' and 80 per cent of robberies were committed by the intoxicated. The armed forces were also widely believed to have a drink problem.

In the end, only the Gorbachev leadership was prepared to tackle the problem head on by sharply reducing the production and sale of liquor. In doing so, predictably, he stimulated a lucrative branch of the 'second economy' in illegal distilleries and caused a crisis in official revenues. Alcohol abuse was just one among a whole complex of intractable social problems – including corruption, pilfering, poor work discipline and unstable family life – which by the mid-1980s was undermining the economic and military strength of the Soviet Union, and helping to make necessary the 'new thinking' which came with Gorbachev's accession to power.

14

Religion, Nationality and Dissent

The Soviet Union is now a highly educated society. One of the most striking developments since the war has been the increase in the number of people with higher education, while in the younger generation completed secondary education is now almost universal. The proportions of the working population involved have changed as follows over the years:

	Higher	Secondary
1939	1.3%	11.0%
1959	3.3%	40.0%
1970	6.5%	58.8%
1979	10.0%	70.5%

This influx of the qualified has completely changed the nature of stratification in Soviet society. In the 1930s, as we saw in Chapter 7, higher education was rare and gave its holder good chances of a swift rise in society. The same was true, at least in some degree, for some twenty years after the war, because of the manpower losses and the long educational backlog. But, by the 1970s, it was becoming clear that higher education, while now indispensable to success, was no longer a golden passport, as it had once been. Graduates were beginning to find it difficult to secure jobs commensurate with their qualifications, were having to content themselves with less demanding employment, or sometimes even manual jobs. On the other hand, pretenders to influential positions in the party, who had once been able to quote their Red Army

A contrast in architectural styles: (*above*) the bare, rectangular functionality of the Kharkov Palace of Industry, 1929 (*Keystone*); (*below*) the exuberant baroque murals of the Kiev station on the Moscow Underground (*Keystone*)

The central kolkhoz market in Moscow, where peasants sell the produce of their private plots (*John Massey Stewart*). This woman (*below*) travelling home on a Leningrad bus may have been to just such a market. She is carrying an *avoska*—an 'on the off-chance' stringbag—which town-dwellers keep permanently by them in case 'deficit' goods suddenly appear in the shops (*Keystone*)

service, their conscientious trade union work, their unflagging devotion to the Komsomol, now had to present a diploma of some kind as well if they wanted to be taken seriously: by 1970 such a higher diploma was a precondition of entry to one of the central party high schools.

It was also becoming more difficult to gain access to higher education: by the late 1970s university admissions were only two thirds of their level of the late 1960s. In practice, because of the advantages enjoyed by the children of professional families, this meant the avenues of upward social mobility were being closed off for workers and peasants. The social hierarchy was becoming more rigid.

In an earlier era, one might have referred to the college graduates as an 'intelligentsia' – and that is still the term Soviet sociologists use for them. It is misleading, all the same, because the word implies a distinctive, cultured lifestyle, and independent, even oppositional, political views. These implications were quite out of place for the majority of Soviet college graduates of the 1970s. Indeed, Solzhenitsyn proposed for them the term *obrazovanshchina*, implying something like 'educated rabble', to register the fact that they had satisfied external criteria without in any way absorbing the ethos of an educated person. Soviet students were among the most docile in the world, not least because they knew that their future careers depended on decisions taken by educational bodies under the supervision of the party. After graduation, moreover, they were far more likely than non-graduates to staff official positions. For this they were prepared by a curriculum which included instruction and examination in compulsory political subjects such as the History of the CPSU, Dialectical Materialism and Scientific Atheism. True, Stalin's *Short Course* was no longer on the syllabus, but the textbooks which had replaced it were only slightly less crude and were much longer. The political lectures were notoriously boring, and many students professed to take their knitting to them, or even to sleep through them. But examinations had to be passed, and so the students were compelled to some extent to internalize the ideology, especially as the stereotypes were daily reinforced in newspapers, on placards and at public meetings. A dissenting member of the educated strata, Alexander Zinoviev, has described the effect:

> It doesn't matter what attitude people take towards it' all in private or in conversation with friends. What is important is that people are in constant contact with the powerful magnetic field of ideological influence . . . they are willy-nilly particles in that field, and absorb from it a certain electric charge, standpoint, orientation, etc. There is physically no way they can escape from it.

As Vladimir Bukovsky has said, 'Whether he wants it or not, a Soviet citizen is in a state of permanent inner dialogue with the official propaganda.'

The graduates formed the most 'ideologized' stratum of Soviet society: their education and in most cases their career imposed the ideology constantly on them, even if only as an external ritual whose inner meaning they rejected or were indifferent to. According to surveys, most Soviet workers and peasants identified 'intellectuals' and 'officials' with one another, and were suspicious of both.

All the same, a few intellectuals – the so-called 'dissenters' – became the most discontented and 'de-ideologized' of all Soviet citizens. There were good reasons for this, in their outlook, expectations and lifestyle. Many of them were members of what we in the West would call the 'free professions', dependent on the nomenklatura for their appointment, but free of direct party interference in their daily working life. Two groups in particular tended to develop openly dissenting views: scientists and writers.

What both groups had in common was that they were accorded very high status in society, and were to a considerable extent encouraged to develop independent ways of thinking, in order to exercise their calling at a high level of achievement for the good of society as a whole. At the same time, they frequently encountered restrictions, usually political or ideological in nature, which impeded them from developing their full potential. If they wanted promotion, they also had to participate in political manoeuvring which some of them, at least, felt to be in contradiction with the inherent morality and probity of their calling.

The career of Andrei Sakharov exemplifies these tendencies. As a young nuclear physicist in the late 1940s, he moved into one of the most sought-after specialities in Soviet society. Anxious to match the American atom bomb exploded at Hiroshima in 1945, Stalin had invited Academician Igor Kurchatov to gather a team of nuclear physicists and establish a special institute just outside Moscow, with unlimited finances and the slave labour of the MVD at their disposal. Sakharov entered this institute in 1948 and, together with Igor Tamm, carried out the vital research which led to the explosion of a Soviet hydrogen bomb in 1953. The same year he was elected as a full member of the Academy of Sciences, at thirty-two the youngest man ever to achieve this honour. Looking back later on this work and on its results, he said:

> Every day I saw the huge material, intellectual and nervous resources of thousands of people being poured into the creation of a means of total destruction, something potentially capable of annihilating all human civilization. I noticed that the control levers were in the hands of people who, though talented in their own way, were cynical . . . Beginning in the late fifties, one got an increasingly clear picture of the collective might of the military-industrial complex and of its vigorous, unprincipled leaders, blind to everything except their 'job'.

In 1958 and 1961 he wrote personally to Khrushchev, warning of the unpredictable and probably highly malignant genetic effects of hydrogen bomb explosions, and appealed to him to halt all tests of it in the atmosphere. Recalling this stage later, he said, 'I had an awful sense of powerlessness. I could not stop something I knew was wrong and unnecessary. After that I felt myself another man. I broke with my surroundings.' His scientific power made his political impotence especially galling.

Scientists and scholars less prestigious than Sakharov also had grounds for frustration. Working in fields where rapid international exchange of ideas is vital, most of them resented the obstacles put in the way of meeting foreign colleagues, reading foreign periodicals and ordering foreign equipment. Those who became members of the party – which was almost *de rigueur* for a promising career – had to spend much time on their 'social' functions: when he was a member of the party committee in the Institute of History, Alexander Nekrich reckoned he spent some 40 per cent of his time on this kind of work, to the detriment of research and publication. Perhaps most irksome of all was the semi-feudal submission to a department or institute chief, on whom one depended for equipment, publication or promotion. These were of course nomenklatura appointees, installed as much for political as for professional reasons: some of them, indeed, were 'failed' politicians who in the post-Stalin era were no longer shot, but put out to grass in a not too demanding job. The moral implications of this relationship were explored by two Moscow biologists in an unpublished paper:

> If a scientist has good reason to know that he occupies his post by right and deserves the recognition of his colleagues, this gives him a sense of stability, independence, inner freedom and equilibrium: that is to say, it creates conditions in which it is easy to hear the voice of conscience ... Things are quite different, however, if a man occupies a place for which he is unfitted ... In this case, he has no inner confidence in himself or his own judgement. He lacks independence both inwardly and

outwardly, as he owes his position to someone else. He has to seem other than he is, to play a part instead of living, obtain recognition by fair means or foul, and select staff who depend on his favour. A man in the wrong place inevitably breeds others like himself, as they are the only kind on whom he can rely.

This contrast explains many of the conflicts that arose inside scientific and academic establishments. Those who asserted professional and moral concerns often did so in a vehement and uncompromising way which kindled personal friction and saddled them with the reputation of being 'unreliable'.

Some scientific fields, especially the humanities and social sciences, because of their subject matter, are particularly vulnerable to direct political interference. But, as we saw in Chapter 10, some natural sciences have also suffered in this way, notably biology. Since Khrushchev had a soft spot for 'village scientists', the adherents of Lysenko made something of a comeback under his aegis, and old battles were fought over again. This was one of the main reasons why the geneticist Zhores Medvedev became a dissenter.

Those scientists capable of rising beyond the boundaries of their own discipline and looking at the relationship of science to society as a whole were very worried at the tendencies apparent by the late 1960s. Only ten years earlier the Soviet Union had launched the first man-made satellite – or *sputnik* – into space, and had seemed to head the world in technology. Now the country was not only *not* overtaking the United States, as Khrushchev had promised so recently, but was actually falling further behind in all fields of advanced technology, especially automation and computer science.

In March 1970 Sakharov, along with the physicist Valentin Turchin and the historian Roy Medvedev (brother of Zhores), addressed an open letter to Brezhnev, Kosygin and Podgorny, explaining the underlying reasons for this backwardness. They did not criticize the socialist system as such, but the 'peculiarities and conditions of our life that run counter to socialism', and 'the anti-democratic traditions and norms of public life established in the Stalin era, which have not been decisively eliminated to this day'. They had in mind particularly the denial of information and basic human rights to the scientists, intellectuals and specialists who needed these rights to continue their work successfully. 'Freedom of information and creative work are necessary for the intelligentsia because of the nature of its activity and its social function. The intelligentsia's attempts to increase these freedoms are legitimate and natural. The state, however, suppresses these attempts by employing all kinds of restrictions – administrative pressures, dismissals from employment and even trials.'

The letter proposed a broad, though initially cautious, programme of democratization – meaning 'exchange of information' and 'participation' in decision-making – sponsored by party and government. Among the measures suggested to achieve this were the abolition of all preliminary censorship, amnesty for political prisoners, elimination of passport restrictions, much wider publication of social data, more expert training of leadership cadres, reinforcement of the independence of the judiciary, and introduction of a choice of candidates in party and soviet elections.

The other great source of dissent was literature. Like scientists, writers had both the moral and the social standing to make their opinions felt even in a highly repressive system. The tradition of the writer as an 'alternative government' had been established already in tsarist Russia. The Soviet government had tried to prevent the resurgence of any such 'alternative' by creating its own literary monopoly through the Writers' Union. But even this was, paradoxically, a tribute to the power of the word. As Osip Mandelstam once explained to his long-suffering wife: 'Why do you complain? Poetry is respected only in this country – people are killed for it.'

Besides all this, literature was the only force capable of doing battle with the most threatening weapon of the Soviet state, its capacity to paralyse people's constructive thinking through an induced mixture of terror, apathy, confusion and 'doublethink' (see Chapter 7). To overcome these inhibitions, it was necessary, first of all, to restore to words their direct relation with reality – that is, to say what one really meant, not what one felt constrained to say. But even to be sure what one really means is difficult in a society where free discussion is impossible. Ideas exist only in an embryonic state if they cannot be contested, modified, refined in the exchange of information, impressions and further ideas with colleagues. This was the truly inhibiting effect of the party monopoly of the media, where, as Raisa Orlova put it, 'The only alternative to the party seemed to be isolation.'

As Roy Medvedev once said, explaining why he edited, and indeed mostly wrote, an underground political journal for several years: 'It helped me to clarify my own views on a wide variety of events, to express my thoughts and opinions without looking over my shoulder at any "internal" censor or other editor.'

During the 1950s and early 1960s some writers, in different ways, began to find a way out of the vicious circle of propaganda, confusion and 'doublethink'. The period after Stalin's death, and especially after the Twentieth Congress, was one of uncertainty, when the party's ideological and cultural authorities were less sure what line they wanted to put over, and what they wanted to suppress at all costs. In this situation, some journals were able once again (for the first time since the early thirties) to publish articles attacking the 'varnishing of reality' – meaning, for example, the presentation of kolkhoz life as harmonious and prosperous. Instead they appealed for frankness and sincerity. In 1956 the novelist V. Dudintsev published *Not by Bread Alone*, in many respects an orthodox socialist realist work, but with the significant difference that the hero fighting for a better future was a lone scientist, while his enemies were established scholars, factory managers and party officials, seen, moreover, not as exceptional but as typical of their milieu. Socialist realism, it appeared, could be used *against* the party–state hierarchy.

Journals were important in another way too. Their staff and editorial offices functioned as a kind of centre for people to meet and share ideas and reactions to events along with the latest literature. All the major journals published articles on politics, economics, science, philosophy etc., along with artistic literature, so that the scope for mutual self-education was considerable. Especially this was the case with *Novyi mir* (New World), under its editors Konstantin Simonov and (particularly) Alexander Tvardovsky. As an Israeli scholar who made a special study of this journal has said: 'One must imagine the *Novyi mir* editorial offices – at least under Tvardovsky – as not merely the offices and desks of editors and their staff, but also as the meeting place for a fringe of active, interested writers and intellectuals who would drop in to talk, to discuss matters of mutual interest, to bring manuscripts which they considered worthwhile, or just to share the camaraderie.' With the curtailment of the security police, moreover, people could be slightly more confident that what they were saying, no matter how unacceptable to the authorities, was not being reported and filed for future action. People began, in fact, to trust each other more.

However, while conversation might be uncensored, there was still a limit, even in periods of the greatest uncertainty, to what might appear in print. Before real intellectual freedom could be attained, writers had to overcome this limitation too. The man who first adumbrated a way of doing this was Boris Pasternak, almost the last surviving representative of the pre-revolutionary flowering of literature and philosophy. During Stalin's years he had not been arrested, though he had seen the disappearance and death of valued friends and colleagues, and had himself been compelled to practise the 'genre of silence', while preparing translations of foreign poets. He also, however, wrote 'for the desk drawer' a novel in which he fundamentally reassessed the revolution from the viewpoint of a man educated in the pre-revolutionary era. This novel, *Doctor Zhivago*, he submitted to *Novyi mir* in 1956, hoping that in the aftermath of the Secret Speech it might prove publishable. *Novyi mir*, however, rejected it. The editors were in favour of an improved and democratized socialism: but they were in no way prepared for Pasternak's rejection of the revolution as a renewal of pre-Christian pagan power politics which failed to answer man's spiritual needs and, as a result, enslaved him.

Without really thinking very deeply about it, and no doubt annoyed by this rebuff, Pasternak offered the typescript to an Italian left-wing publisher, Feltrinelli, whose agent happened to be visiting Moscow. He subsequently tried to retract the implicit permission to publish, but Feltrinelli was determined to press ahead, and in 1957 the book appeared. A year later Pasternak was awarded the Nobel Prize, not least for *Doctor Zhivago*. This international recognition of a Russian literature not authorized by the Soviet state brought upon his head the wrath of the whole literary and political establishment. *Literaturnaya gazeta* called him a 'literary Judas, who betrayed his people for thirty pieces of silver, the Nobel Prize', while Semichastny, the KGB chief, referred to him in more demotic spirit, as 'a pig who has fouled his own sty'.

Under this pressure Pasternak declined the Nobel Prize. Nevertheless the attacks on him continued, and certainly played a part in undermining his health and perhaps bringing about his death in May 1960. His funeral became the first occasion when the emerging independent intelligentsia mounted an (albeit tacit) demonstration of protest against the regime's repressive policies. Ignoring official arrangements for the burial, individual pall-bearers, surrounded by a crowd of supporters, carried the coffin across the fields to the cemetery half a mile away.

Pasternak had used a technique which had not been applied since Zamyatin in the twenties: evading the Soviet censors by publishing abroad. Since by the late fifties a good many Soviet citizens possessed radio sets with short-wave reception, the effect was much more powerful than it had been then. Over the radio, and through copies smuggled into the country, many educated people with an interest in literature became acquainted with *Doctor Zhivago*.

Meanwhile some young poets in Moscow were experimenting with another technique, using carbon paper to type out multiple copies of their pointed, irreverent poems, and passing them round to their friends. This was the origin of what later became known as *samizdat*, or 'self-publishing'. Of course these carbon copies reached very few people: their full potential was only realized if they got outside the country and were rebroadcast. Some of the young poets gathered from time to time at the monument of Mayakovsky – the most irreverent of all Russia's twentieth-century poets – and read their verses aloud. These practices were not exactly forbidden – as long as the poems were not what could be called 'anti-Soviet' – but they were not exactly permitted either. They reflected the growing readiness of the educated public to trust each other, to act *as if* they were free, and see what happened.

After some hesitation, the authorities decided to take action. The Mayakovsky Square meetings were broken up by 'hooligans'; participants underwent house searches. One of them, Vladimir Bukovsky, was arrested, beaten up at a police station, and warned, 'Don't turn up at Mayakovsky Square again.' Of the young samizdat poets, Alexander Ginsburg was later arrested and given two years on an unrelated charge, while Valery Tarsis was committed to a psychiatric hospital. These hesitant official reactions indicated considerable embarrassment about how to proceed in the new era of 'socialist legality', while also providing some sinister precedents for the future.

The height of official tolerance was reached in the autumn of 1962, when the unknown Ryazan schoolmaster Alexander Solzhenitsyn was able to publish with *Novyi mir* 'A Day in the Life of Ivan Denisovich'. This was a depiction of an ordinary day in the life of an ordinary zek, an inmate of a typical Stalinist concentration camp, seen through his own eyes and recounted in his own language; its mood was resigned, stoic and without a trace of hope that the party could or would uproot the evils he was enduring. A much more radical challenge to established literary canons and to political taboos than *Not by Bread Alone*, it had to be submitted to Khrushchev himself before permission could be given for publication. Khruschev authorized it because he was in the midst of his second 'de-Stalinization' campaign, around the Twenty-second Congress, but even he had no idea of the response the work would evoke. It would be no exaggeration to say that overnight Solzhenitsyn became the best-known Russian writer. It was like the bursting of a dam. He received thousands of letters, a few of them hostile ('Why don't you show how the party was fighting these evils?') but the overwhelming majority relieved that at last the great dark secret was out, that what people had repressed within themselves could be made known publicly. Journals and publishing houses began to receive floods of labour camp memoirs. Solzhenitsyn himself made use of many of these in his subsequent great chronicle of the 'zek nation', *Gulag Archipelago*.

Quite taken aback, the authorities hastened to try to restore what they conceived of as order. At two meetings to which hundreds of writers were summoned, in December 1962 and March 1963, Khrushchev and Ilyichev (chairman of the Central Committee's newly formed Ideological Commission) warned that the party had itself exposed and dealt with the abuses of the past, and that further efforts in this direction were superfluous. They warned of the dangers of 'bourgeois influences' and reaffirmed the central pillars of socialist realism: party-mindedness, ideological maturity and a popular outlook (*partiinost, ideinost, narodnost*).

The cultural relaxation, and especially the Solzhenitsyn affair, were certainly among the motives that induced Khrushchev's colleagues to depose him. In February 1966 his successors tried to re-establish the borders of the permissible by means of a show trial. The victims were Andrei Sinyavsky and Yuly Daniel, two writers who under pseudonyms had published satirical short stories in the West. Sinyavsky was already widely known as the author of an excellent critical article which prefaced the official edition of Pasternak's poems; and both men had been pall-bearers at Pasternak's funeral.

The problem for the authorities was how, without Stalin's secret courts and vaguely worded criminal laws, to make sure that an accusation would stick. It was decided to prosecute the two writers under Article 70 of the criminal code for spreading 'anti-Soviet propaganda'. This was juridically a very risky step. Even Stalin, though he had killed writers, had never openly encroached on their professional autonomy so far as to make a literary text itself the basis for a criminal prosecution: his charges had always been much vaguer, and had not needed to withstand even formal scrutiny in open court.

In this case the authorities were only able to gain the conviction they needed by dissuading qualified defence counsel from acting for the accused, by refusing to admit most of the defence witnesses, and by having the prosecutor interpret the texts with flat-footed literalness, quoting opinions voiced by the characters in the stories as if they were the authors' own. As a result Sinyavsky was sentenced to seven years in a labour camp, Daniel to five.

This blatant infringement of the professional autonomy which writers thought they had just regained for themselves hit public opinion in a very sensitive spot. I say 'public opinion' because there had by now clearly emerged a very definite trend of opinion among professional men, and especially writers and scientists, who were determined, according to their professional judgement and conscience, to resist official attempts to confine their freedom of action. That this had happened became very clear in the response to the Sinyavsky-Daniel trial. Sixty-three members of the

Moscow branch of the Writers' Union wrote to the forthcoming Party Congress and to the Supreme Soviet. While accepting that the two writers had shown 'lack of political prudence and tact', they warned, 'The condemnation of writers for the writing of satirical works creates an extremely dangerous precedent and could impede the progress of Soviet culture.' When Mikhail Sholokhov, the famous Cossack writer, applauded the verdict and even hinted it was too mild, Lidiya Chukovskaya (daughter of the country's best-known children's writer) wrote an open letter to him saying: 'Literature does not come under the jurisdiction of the criminal court. Ideas should be fought with ideas, not with camps and prisons.' Protests at the procedural irregularities of the trial came in from a variety of individuals and groups, writers and scholars. Comment in the foreign press, even in Western Communist papers, was uniformly hostile. Soviet justice was made to seem a travesty, which indeed it had been in this case.

Not the least significant development following the trial was the compilation of a record of the court proceedings together with the letters and press comment surrounding it. The compiler was Alexander Ginsburg, earlier imprisoned for his samizdat activities (significantly the evidence brought against him then had *not* been the texts of his poems). This assembling of bald documentary evidence was an important step forward. The Soviet press had never published a transcript of the trial, perhaps because it was ashamed to expose the travesty. This non-publication of important historical evidence, in effect the creation of 'memory holes', had for decades been one of the ways in which the regime annexed and monopolized the country's history. By putting together his 'White Book' of documents, Ginsburg combated this monopoly. Furthermore, he acted openly, sending copies of it to the authorities and then making sure that some reached the West. In the end, he was arrested in January 1967, along with Yury Galanskov, editor of the samizdat journal *Phoenix*.

These arrests led to further protests. By now something of a chain reaction had come into effect, a movement of public opinion based on the principles that (i) facts must be recognized and made public, (ii) the authorities should observe their own laws. The adherence to these two principles grew out of long experience of the Stalinist regime, which had (i) suppressed facts and (ii) persistently acted with gross lawlessness. This time round, people could see what was happening, and they had sufficient mutual trust and confidence to fight against it.

The technique of calling on the authorities to observe their own laws had been conceived first of all by Alexander Esenin-Volpin, a mathematician (and son of the famous poet Sergei Esenin) at the time of the Mayakovsky Square trial, in 1962. Volpin's friends treated his obsession with the laws with good-humoured tolerance, as a personal foible, but he insisted, 'It's our own fault if we don't demand that the laws be observed.' He appeared at the court room with an open copy of the criminal code in his hands, and demanded admittance, on the grounds that the sentence must be pronounced publicly: the sentries, taken aback, let him in, turning what was supposed to be a closed hearing into an open one.

This technique exploited perfectly the regime's post-Stalin embarrassment over 'socialist legality'. It also made it possible for the individual to see his relationship with the state in a completely different light; and that also meant that he gained a different sense of his own identity. As Bukovsky comments, from the standpoint of one who was gradually converted to Volpin's technique:

The inspiration in this idea consisted in eliminating the split in our personalities by shattering the internal excuses with which we justified our complicity in all the crimes. It presupposed a small core of freedom in each individual, his 'subjective sense of right', as Volpin put it.

Of course, against a completely terrorist state, such a strategy would merely have been suicidal, but since the post-Stalin, and post-Khrushchev, leadership was not prepared, for its own reasons, to let terror get out of hand once more, the strategy now made a good deal of sense. The first public demonstration to adopt it took place on 5 December 1965 (appropriately on Soviet Constitution Day), when about two hundred people gathered on Pushkin Square in Moscow, and Volpin held up a sign reading 'Respect the Constitution'. He and several other participants were detained and questioned for a few hours, and then released. Their treatment was thus relatively lenient, but this did not detract from the incongruity of the spectacle of the Soviet police arresting citizens demonstrating peacefully in favour of the Soviet constitution. While he was at the police station, Volpin was asked if his message was addressed to government leaders. He replied, 'If you feel they need the advice, let them have it.'

A similar demonstration on 22 January 1968 against the arrest of Ginsburg and Galanskov was more harshly treated: this time some of the participants, including Bukovsky, were arrested and brought to trial. Meanwhile the Ginsburg-Galanskov trial itself generated a crop of documents and protests, sent to the authorities. In this case Larisa Bogaraz and Pavel Litvinov (grandson of Stalin's foreign minister) added the final item to the dissenters' repertoire of techniques by drawing up a protest addressed 'to world public opinion!', and sending it to Western correspondents stationed in Moscow. This was an expression of the futility of sending protests to the Soviet authorities: they were never answered, nor was any action taken on them. But far more than that, it was a way of ensuring that the protests were known to a far wider circle of people than the protesters themselves: many of them were now published in Western newspapers, and from there rebroadcast to the Soviet Union over the Voice of America, the BBC, Radio Liberty and other Western Russian-language services. This was to become the most effective way of breaching the official monopoly of the public media and disseminating facts the Soviet authorities were not willing to recognize. It put the Soviet leaders 'on trial' before Western public opinion and Western governments, with whom they were currently trying to conclude commercial and technological agreements, to which they assigned great importance in overcoming the persistent backwardness of the planned economy. On the other hand, the technique was a double-edged one, in that it laid dissenters open to the charge of deliberately allowing their activities to be exploited by 'bourgeois propaganda services', in other words of committing 'subversion'.

At any rate, by the spring of 1968 all the elements were in place for the protest movement to receive a new focus. This was the issue of the first number of a samizdat journal, named, with the neutral baldness characteristic of the movement, the *Chronicle of Current Events*. Its front cover blazoned its concern with legality and information by quoting article 19 of the UN Declaration on Human Rights (ratified by the Soviet government): 'Each man has the right to free expression of his opinions; this right includes the freedom to adhere to these opinions unmolested and to seek, receive and circulate information and ideas by all means of communication regardless of frontiers.' The journal set out to collate and present, without comment, instances of the Soviet authorities violating their own laws in dealing with the citizens of the country. Its editors remained anonymous, for, as the fifth number said, 'Although the *Chronicle* is not an illegal publication, working conditions are hampered by a peculiar conception of legality and of freedom of information held by certain Soviet organs.' Its channels of information-collection were also its channels of distribution. It advised its readers: 'Let the person from whom you received this paper know of information available to you; he will pass it on to the person from whom he received his copy, and the process will be repeated. It would be unwise, however, to pursue the chain yourself, for in that way you might be taken for an informer.' The organization, in fact, was remarkably similar to that which Lenin had recommended for an underground Social Democratic newspaper back in 1902, only now it was no longer a matter of preparing a revolution for an unknown future, but of ensuring immediate publicity for hidden illegalities. It has proved highly effective: apart from an eighteen-month gap in 1972–4, the *Chronicle* has survived to the present day, and still presents, every couple of months or so, a compilation of cases of human rights violations, drawn from the most diverse geographical regions of the Soviet Union.

Having a central organ of this kind enabled the dissenting or 'human rights' movement (as it became widely, and correctly, known) to take up and publicize citizens' grievances from many parts of the Soviet Union and over a wide range of issues. National and religious groups began to make known the acts of discrimination applied against them: some of them' even began to issue journals on the model of the *Chronicle*, typed on carbon paper and smuggled out to the West. Later on, other specialized groups arose: concerned with women's rights, invalids' rights, the rights of religious believers and of those compulsorily detained in mental hospitals. Workers' and employees' rights were taken up by free trade unions, as we saw in the last chapter. Furthermore, when the Brezhnev regime reached in 1975 its long-cherished goal of a European Security Agreement with the United States and the West European powers, the human rights movement set up special monitoring groups inside the Soviet Union to report on violations of the agreement's provisions relating to 'human contacts' across frontiers, and to 'respect for human rights and fundamental freedoms, including the freedom of thought, conscience, religion or belief'. The first of these Helsinki Watch Groups (as they were known from the location of the European Security Conference) was founded by Yury Orlov, a physicist who had first signalled his dissent back in 1956, when, at a meeting called to discuss Khrushchev's 'Secret Speech', he had spoken 'of the general loss of honesty and morality' and of the 'need for democratic changes'.

420 The First Socialist Society

In its early days, the human rights movement had no particular political ideology beyond that of urging the Soviet government to observe its own constitution. However, naturally enough, in the course of time distinctions in outlook did make themselves felt, and a few dissenters circulated actual political programmes. Broadly speaking, three trends emerged. The first might be styled 'pure Leninism', in that its proponents claimed to be returning to the original democratic practices of Lenin, later perverted by Stalin and never properly restored. The leading theorist of this trend, Roy Medvedev, proposed in his book *On Socialist Democracy* that elements of genuine competition should be permitted in political life, such as allowing factions to operate within the party and to put up candidates for election to party and Soviet posts. Even an opposition party, Medvedev felt, was not contrary to Communist principles. As a condition of this political competition, of course, genuine freedom of speech and association would have to be guaranteed. Medvedev envisaged a mixed economy, with state, cooperative and private sectors. He advocated a return to the Leninist nationalities policy, with much greater autonomy for individual Soviet nations, and the right in practice as well as in theory to secede from the Union.

Actually the view of most of these policies as 'Leninist' was an illusion: they tended towards social democracy, as that is understood in Western Europe, or even radical liberalism. All the same, Medvedev, although warned several times by the procuracy about his publications, was never arrested, perhaps because there were still sufficiently powerful elements in the party leadership who favoured policies of that kind, or at least thought they might one day be necessary.

The second broad trend, in which most human rights activists might be included, was liberalism. Paradoxically, it drew some of its texts from the Soviet constitution of 1936, which, as we have seen, possessed an elaborate liberal façade. The principal figure among the liberals was and still is Andrei Sakharov. Like Medvedev, he evolved from a kind of 'pure

Leninism', but went further, and was more conscious of the direction in which his thought was moving. The 'liberals' were on the whole very un-ideological, and not given to programmatic statements. They did however proceed from the assumption that political forms guaranteeing civil liberties were as appropriate for Russia as for any other nation.

The third dissenting current was that of the Russian nationalists or neo-Slavophiles, referred to by John Dunlop, the leading American student of the subject, as *vozrozhdentsy*, or 'revivalists'. They wished to see a revival of Russian national identity based on a return to the Russian Orthodox Church, and to the old Russian culture destroyed or distorted by the (originally) internationalist Bolsheviks. Their principal spokesman was Alexander Solzhenitsyn, whose 'Letter to the Soviet Leaders', published in the West in 1974, summed up their main concerns. He believed that the Russians had suffered demographically, culturally and spiritually from super-industrialization, agricultural collectivization, official atheism and over-involvement in international affairs. He recommended that the Russians withdraw from such involvement – which if necessary would mean letting the other nations of the Soviet Union go their own way – and devote their own energies to national revival. This revival would use the undeveloped resources available in Siberia, and would derive its greatest strength from private and cooperative agriculture, and from small-scale manufacture of the kind which the high technology of the seventies was making possible. Solzhenitsyn was sceptical whether liberal or parliamentary forms were appropriate for Russia, and envisaged, at least initially, an authoritarian state, with a major role for the Russian Orthodox Church as guarantor of the nation's spiritual health. The great weakness of his programme was that he did not explain how authoritarianism was to be made compatible with the civil liberties, especially freedom of speech and conscience, in which he also believed passionately.

In the West this dissenting Russian nationalism is often

confused with another kind, much more acceptable in official Soviet circles, which may be termed 'national Bolshevism'. This is non-religious in spirit (though not necessarily deeply hostile to the churches), and regards the Russians as a great nation in the political and military sense, with a natural right to dominate smaller and weaker nations. Its adherents naturally therefore wish to sustain Russia's heavy industry, and to continue the traditional priority for military affairs. They regard Marxism-Leninism as an acceptable ideology, because it has helped Russia to Great Power status, but they play down its internationalist features, and would probably jettison it altogether if it became incompatible with Russia's standing. This outlook is sometimes tinged to a greater or lesser extent with anti-Semitism, and is perhaps most frequently found in the armed forces and among Russian oblast party secretaries. At certain times, it has gained a strong foothold in certain officially published journals.

But the Russian national tendency has never become dominant in the party, and seems unlikely to do so. Inside the party leadership and probably in the KGB there is always a counterbalancing tendency, committed to a multinational imperial outlook, and to the international interests of the Soviet Union as a Great Power resting on an ethnically, economically and culturally very diverse population. One may presume that this tendency receives strong support from the party secretaries of the non-Russian republics.

Of course, the authorities were not content simply to let dissent, in all its various forms, be expressed. But the Sinyavsky-Daniel case showed clearly the difficulties of repression under the new legal system. In 1967 Semichastny, who had been ultimately responsible for the prosecution of that case, was replaced as head of the KGB by Yu. V. Andropov, former head of the Central Committee International Affairs Department, responsible for relations with other socialist countries. This was the first time a senior party official had been brought in to run the security police, and it marked the completion of an evolution which had been going on since Stalin's death:

the rapprochement of party and KGB to the point where they functioned almost as two branches of the same organization.

Already in 1966 new articles had been introduced in the criminal code, intended to make it easier to deal with dissenters. One mentioned 'violations of public order', which could be stretched to include any public demonstration, while the other specified 'the dissemination of falsehoods derogatory to the Soviet political and social system': this made it unnecessary to prove anti-Soviet *intent*, as the prosecution had had to try to do in the Sinyavsky-Daniel trial, but the new article still presented difficulties where the defence was able to show that the 'falsehoods' were in fact true. This was certainly one of the factors determining the bald factual tone of many dissenting statements in the coming years.

In general, however, it was easier for the authorities to avoid trials wherever possible, and use a simpler and wider repertoire of sanctions, or even just threats, against protestors. Since many of the latter were writers, scholars or students, it was easy enough to withhold promotion or an academic degree from them, to deny permission to defend a dissertation, or to publish a book. Those who were party members or belonged to professional associations or creative unions could be reprimanded with varying degrees of severity, or even expelled. Job dismissal might follow. Thus following the protests over the Ginsburg-Galanskov trial, we find the secretariat of the Moscow branch of the Writers' Union announcing that 'in view of the political irresponsibility manifested in the signing of declarations and letters, which, by their form and content, discredited Soviet laws and the authority of Soviet judicial organs, and for ignoring the fact that these documents might be exploited by bourgeois propaganda for purposes damaging to the Soviet Union and Soviet literature, the following measures have been taken' — and there followed a minutely graded list of warnings and reprimands.

If this kind of sanction proved insufficient to deter a

would-be dissenter from further activity, he might be summoned to the prosecutor's office for a 'prophylactic' chat, in the course of which he would be warned to desist. If this failed, he might be arrested and charged, on planted evidence, with hooliganism, possession of drugs, speculating in foreign currency, or some such offence.

Some especially well-known dissenters were 'encouraged' to emigrate, whether or not they were Jews, following the change in policy over this in 1970–1 (see below). This had the effect of disrupting the communications network and the tightly knit friendships of the dissenters. No doubt, too, the KGB hoped that the Western media would lose interest in dissenters once they had been outside the Soviet Union for some time. This hope was only partially justified in reality, and in fact exiled dissenters have given the West a much fuller picture of Soviet life than we possessed before the early seventies. (The present book would have been impossible to write without such testimony.) Furthermore, much of what they write has been rebroadcast to the Soviet Union.

A bizarre variant of this tactic was the exile of Sakharov to the town of Gorky in January 1980. This showed up very clearly the 'hierarchy' of places of residence mentioned in the last chapter (imagine, by contrast, exiling someone to Liverpool or Leeds!). Gorky is a city closed to foreigners. Cut off there from all Western visitors, Sakharov could much more easily be blockaded by the local police and KGB, and thus isolated from his Soviet friends as well. In this way it became immeasurably more difficult for him to function as a centre of communications for dissenters.

The grimmest of all forms of sanction against dissenters was compulsory confinement in mental hospitals. Occasionally used by Stalin, this tactic came into its own once the criminal code became more difficult to apply to dissenters. It had many attractive features for the authorities: once the necessary diagnosis had been obtained, no further 'evidence' was needed, such as might be contested in court, the sentence was indefinite, and the certified insane did not enjoy even the meagre civil rights (correspondence, visits) that remained to prisoners. If it seemed desirable, furthermore, the 'patient' could be treated with drugs that made him ill or depressed, or caused great pain. The only difficulty, therefore, was the diagnosis. In practice, it turned out that a good many Soviet psychiatrists were not prepared to further their careers by distorting their professional judgement for political reasons – indeed under this pressure one or two actually became dissenters themselves. Increasingly, therefore, the KGB had to resort to psychiatrists known to be pliable, such as Dr D.R. Lunts of the Serbsky Institute for Forensic Psychiatry in Moscow. Such men were willing to return diagnoses of 'creeping schizophrenia', characterized by such features as 'poor adaptation to the social environment', 'moralizing', and 'paranoid reformist delusions'.

This practice eventually became known in the West, though it took a long time to persuade psychiatrists here of what some of their Soviet colleagues were doing. The resultant indignation was such that in 1983, Soviet psychiatrists withdrew from the World Psychiatric Association rather than face almost certain expulsion for systematic professional abuse. As a result of this growing international pressure, the Soviet authorities became more circumspect about subjecting well-known dissenters to psychiatric confinement, and thereafter restricted the technique to obscurer figures.

A combination of all these techniques, applied with especial ruthlessness and consistency in the late seventies and early eighties (during a period when Andropov seemed to be securing himself a power base in the upper echelons of the party), gradually eroded the dissenters' capacity to appeal, through samizdat and Western broadcasts (now often jammed), to public opinion inside their own country. Open dissent became virtually impossible: its symbolic end was reached in September 1982, when Elena Bonner, wife of Sakharov, declared the last of the Helsinki Watch Groups disbanded, since nearly all its members had been arrested or exiled.

The dissenters who survived were those who, like the editors of the *Chronicle of Current Events*, chose to remain anonymous. For this reason in 1981 the surviving free trade union, SMOT (see previous chapter) created a parallel underground network of cells, to continue the work of issuing its *Information Bulletin* even if all its known members were arrested.

Stalin's successors did not differ from Stalin himself on the ultimate aim of their nationalities policy: to create a supranational socialist community, in which Russian would be used as the main language, and in which national consciousness (Russian or any other) would be a thing of the past. At the Twenty-second Congress Khrushchev suggested that the nations of the USSR had already drawn closer to one another (a process which he called *sblizhenie*, or rapprochement) and would eventually merge with one another (*sliyanie*, or fusion). However, the post-Stalin leaders were much more sensitive than Stalin had been to the susceptibilities of the individual nationalities: they were prepared to make concessions to them on the basis that national consciousness must be allowed to develop at its own pace. For this reason they dropped all mention of Russia as the 'elder brother', de-emphasized Russian-language teaching in primary schools, and tolerated more publication in local languages, as well as more research into the history, culture and past traditions of the various nations. For a time, under the sovnarkhoz principle, some nations actually became an economic entity once more, under much looser control from the centre.

All this meant that the national Communist Party leaders changed the emphasis of their policies too. Brokers as ever between Moscow and the pressure of their national elites at home, they now felt able to be much more tolerant of the latter. With the influx of former villagers into the cities, a formidable reserve of 'national consciousness' was building up during the late fifties and sixties: workers, employees, students, exposed to their own national culture in the intense form in which it is mediated by an urban environment. To a greater or lesser extent this was happening in the Baltic republics, Bielorussia, the Ukraine, Moldavia, Georgia, Armenia and Azerbaidjan. In the Muslim and Asian areas it was less clear, as the migration into the towns was much less marked: the patriarchal extended family, rural industry and village culture remained much stronger. It should be noted too that in some cities, especially those in Estonia, Latvia, Kazakhstan and the eastern Ukraine, the influx of Russians was greater than that of locals. This aroused resentment (rumours of Russians getting priority for scarce housing) as well as fears of creeping Russification. There were also complaints that Russians were not being required to learn the languages of their adopted homelands, while natives had increasingly to use Russian for their everyday business.

The outstanding example of a national first secretary using his position to attempt to strengthen the culture, economy and general political standing of 'his' republic was Petr Shelest, first secretary of the Ukrainian Communist Party from 1963 to 1972. The centrepiece of his policy was increasing the size of the Ukrainian Communist Party: between 1961 and 1971 it grew from 1.6 million to 2.5 million, a much larger growth proportionately than for the CPSU as a whole over the same period. This meant that more Ukrainians were available for promotion, in any walk of life, both within the Ukrainian Republic, and indeed beyond its borders. Shelest persistently argued for more economic investment in the Ukraine, where, he maintained, it would earn a better return than elsewhere: at the Twenty-fourth Party Congress in 1971, for example, he told delegates bluntly that it was 'incorrect' to divert funds from the coalmines of the Donbass to the production of oil and natural gas in Siberia. He is said to have insisted privately that the Ukraine was in effect being exploited economically by the rest of the Soviet Union. He tried, but failed, to introduce tuition in Ukrainian in the higher education establishments that came under the jurisdiction of the Ukrainian Ministry of Higher Education. He did, however, succeed in fostering much more publication in Ukrainian, including a remarkable multivolume *History of the Towns and Villages of the Ukrainian SSR*, no equivalent of which exists for any other republic. In a sense, Shelest continued the policies of Skrypnik (see above, page 249), whom, indeed, he attempted to rehabilitate. In May 1972 Shelest was dismissed, and replaced by V. V. Shcherbitsky, an associate of Brezhnev's, and a man content to follow a more 'Muscovite' policy. Interestingly enough, however, in recent years there have been signs that he, too, has felt constrained, presumably by pressures from within the republic, to pursue a more autonomous line.

In some other republics, similar semi-autonomous policies have been pursued, with a greater or lesser degree of success, according to circumstance. Akhundov and Mzhavanadze, in Azerbaidjan and Georgia (see previous chapter), clearly promoted the distinctive economic life of their own republics: Mzhavanadze also did much to protect the Georgian language and culture. In the Baltic, Johannes Käbin, first secretary in Estonia, and Anton Snieckus, in Lithuania, seem to have consolidated their power-base partly by cultivating support among local national elites, rather than simply relying on the security police. Under their leadership the proportion of natives within the local Communist parties has risen quite sharply, perhaps in part because many of the Russians who came more or less as occupiers in the late 1940s have been eased out again. Cultural life became more varied: writers, painters and musicians felt freer to emphasize national themes in their work. Many of them ignored 'socialist realism', and got away with it. While Khrushchev in Moscow was denouncing abstract art as 'daubing with a donkey's tail', Käbin in Tallinn quietly commented, 'I am not an art specialist.' For a time Estonia became a kind of haven for abstract art and serial music – which may indeed have been more genuinely popular there than anywhere else in

Europe, as a symbol of defiance to Muscovite rule. In Lithuania, the Roman Catholic Church became a focus of national self-assertion (see below).

The results of the 1970 census were reportedly rather a shock to the leaders in Moscow, for they showed that, on most indices, the hoped-for sblizhenie was advancing very slowly, or indeed not happening at all. Figures on national intermarriage, on migration from one republic to another, on the use of Russian by non-Russians were all disappointing, while the demographic stagnation of the Russians, contrasted with a rapid population growth among especially the Asiatic Muslim peoples, suggested that the Russians were losing their grip as the leading nation. The Brezhnev regime ceased to use the term sliyanie to describe its aim in nationalities policy, but continued to insist on sblizhenie, in a way which suggests they no longer expected nationalities eventually to lose their separate identity, but simply to work more closely together and to be more aware of, and sympathetic towards, each other's culture.

The 1979 census suggested that some advance had been made in this direction. The Russian language had gained steadily in its role as a second language for all Soviet citizens, of whatever nationality. The 1958 Education Act guaranteed all parents the right to choose which language their children should be educated in. In non-Russian republics, since Stalin's time, Russian-language schools have been provided in increasing numbers, and many parents send their children there, intending them to become fluent in the 'imperial' language, and thus available for employment and promotion anywhere in the Soviet Union. This has, however, taken place to a different extent in the different republics. In the Asian republics, use of Russian as a second language is low, but rose quite fast during the 1970s. Steady progress was made in the Ukraine (36.3 to 49.8 per cent) and in Bielorussia (49.0 to 57.0 per cent), in the Caucasus and, on the whole, in the Baltic, where, however, Estonia constituted a remarkable exception: there the use of Russian declined from 29 to 24.2

per cent. Popular rumour persistently identified Estonia as the republic in which the Russians were most hated: the census figures confirmed that impression. In Georgia, however, there was also conspicuous opposition to the growing use of Russian. At the Georgian Writers' Congress in 1976, the writer Dzhaparidze protested against the increasing use of Russian-language textbooks both in schools and universities. And in April 1978 several thousand people took to the streets of Tbilisi to protest against the proposal to introduce a new clause in the Georgian constitution, giving Russian equal rights with Georgian as the official language of the republic. The authorities stepped down, and left Georgian in its undisputed supremacy.

Of course, use of Russian as a second language does not necessarily imply any greater identification with Russian culture. It merely indicates a greater readiness to see one's life in an all-Soviet context.

In one sphere sblizhenie had definitely not taken place: that was in power relationships. Communist Party membership gives a certain indication of this: Great Russians and Georgians were somewhat over-represented in it compared to their proportion in the population, at the expense of every other national group, but especially of the Baltic peoples, the Moldavians and the Azerbaidjanis and (most of all) the Central Asian peoples. The disproportion was much more marked, however, in the party's central organs. The 1976 Central Committee was 82 per cent Slav (Russian, Ukrainian or Bielorussian), compared with a 73 per cent Slav share in the population. As for the Politburo, it has consisted almost entirely of Russians and Ukrainians, with token representation for a few other republics: Bielorussia, Latvia, Kazakhstan, Uzbekistan.

Even more important than the Politburo, the Secretariat consisted *entirely* of Russians and Ukrainians. Now it is the Secretariat which makes the leading personnel appointments, and in fact oversees the whole nomenklatura network. Its appointments in the national republics at this time seemed designed to ensure a high degree of Russian political dominance. The pattern which had stabilized by the 1970s was for the first secretary in each Union republic to be a member of the local nationality, while the second secretary and the head of the KGB were outsiders, almost invariably a Russian or Ukrainian. The second secretary is apparently in charge of cadres, so that he presumably exercised locally the nomenklatura patronage delegated from the Secretariat in Moscow.

The officer corps' representation in the top political bodies was likewise heavily skewed towards the Slavs. Of 101 officers elected to the Central Committee from 1952 to 1976, no less than 97 were Slavs (78 of them Russian): 1 was Armenian, and 3 probably Jewish. The Georgians, the Baltic nations and the Muslims were unrepresented in the upper echelons of the armed forces.

The Slav-dominated political system has naturally given many non-Russians a sense of having their destinies controlled from outside, by foreigners. In some cases this feeling cannot be accommodated within the system, and bursts out into open dissent. Especially this has been the case since the mid-1960s, when the channels have existed for dissent to make itself felt.

This dissent has been stronger among some nations than others. The Ukraine, freed from the constraints of Stalinism but benefiting from the advances in popular education achieved during Stalin's rule, saw a remarkable cultural flowering during the late fifties and sixties, especially in poetry, much of which had to circulate in samizdat, or be read in private gatherings. This caused some alarm to the authorities, who tried to prevent mass celebrations of the 150th anniversary of the national poet Taras Shevchenko in 1964. About the same time a mysterious fire at the Ukrainian Academy of Sciences in Kiev destroyed the records of the independent Ukrainian governments of 1917–20. In 1965 and 1972 there were waves of arrests of Ukrainian cultural figures, historians, journalists and those who had tried to protest against what they saw as repression of their nation. A television reporter, V. Chornovil, who, like Ginsburg in Moscow, assembled the materials bearing on their arrest and trial, and sent them to the Ukrainian chief procurator, was himself arrested and sent to a labour camp.

The indictment against Moscow was drawn up on Leninist lines by a literary critic, Ivan Dzyuba, in a samizdat text entitled *Internationalism or Russification?* Starting from a restatement of Lenin's national policy, in which he emphasized 'self-determination'; Dzyuba chronicled the violations of it practised by Stalin and continued in many respects by his successors. The Ukraine was economically exploited, its industrial and agricultural wealth expropriated for the use of other Soviet regions. Its literature, history and culture had difficulty in finding publishing outlets, while Russian books flooded into the republic. Ukrainian was forced into a position of being *de facto* a subsidiary language, while in law courts, government offices, colleges and factories anyone who demanded that the collective use Russian usually got his way, on the grounds that not everyone understood Ukrainian. In this way, often without deliberate acts of policy, creeping Russification was taking place, so Dzyuba argued. He issued an appeal to 'return to Lenin' and to 'overcome the psychological inertia deriving from chauvinism, Great Power ideology, national liquidationism, national boorishness and bureaucratic standardization'.

Of course Dzyuba's interpretation of Lenin was one-sided. (At certain periods Lenin himself might have been accused of 'national liquidationism'.) But he was pointing to an important truth: that the national policy Lenin had adopted in 1921–2 (see above, page 116) had provided the base on which the first great flowering of Ukrainian culture had taken place. Perhaps the use of Lenin's name provided protection for Dzyuba, or possibly his benefactor was Shelest. At any rate, shortly before the latter's fall in 1972, Dzyuba was arrested.

In 1970 an underground journal, *Ukrainsky visnik* (Ukrainian Herald) started to appear, on the model of the *Chronicle of Current Events*, recording violations of human rights in the Ukraine, as well as the pressures on the Ukraine's national identity. Copies were smuggled out to the West and published by Ukrainian émigrés. In November 1976, the poet M. Rudenko established a Ukrainian Helsinki Watch Group; one of its members, General P. Grigorenko, provided a link with Moscow dissenters until his emigration. By 1981 thirty of its thirty-six members had been arrested, and the other six had been allowed to emigrate. The Ukrainian KGB under Fedorchuk (subsequently Andropov's successor in charge of the all-Union KGB) was particularly determined in its efforts to eliminate dissent.

In the Baltic, too, the 1960s and 1970s saw a flowering of national culture, and for rather similar reasons. What till the late nineteenth century had been largely peasant languages, with a tiny intelligentsia, had by now, through a period of political independence (longer than the Ukraine's) and then violent confrontation with both Russia and Germany, forged its own strong national consciousness. In part this was 'protected' by the local first secretaries, as we have seen. Nevertheless, underground organizations were formed to protest against Russification and against the generally undemocratic style of political life. Indeed there seem to have been quite a number of them, some of only fleeting duration.

In 1974 several Lithuanian groups came together in Vilnius, the capital of their republic, to form a National Popular Front. Among their 'minimum' demands were the use of Lithuanian as the republic's primary language, respect for human rights, an amnesty for political prisoners, and the 'abolition of colonialism, including that practised by the USSR'. The 'maximum' programme envisaged a plebiscite on the question of national independence, the abolition of NATO and the Warsaw Pact, and the establishment of a 'free family of the United States of Europe'.

There seemed to be popular support for such a programme. In 1972 a student named Roman Kalanta, following the example of Jan Palach in Prague in 1969, set fire to himself in a public square in Kaunas, under a poster calling for 'Freedom for Lithuania!' His funeral sparked off riots in the city: people swarmed through the streets chanting 'Freedom', defacing Russian street names, and setting fire to party and police buildings.

The Roman Catholic Church was at the centre of Lithuanian national feeling, even though its hierarchy did not commit itself to a nationalist programme – which indeed would have been contrary to their own beliefs. Nevertheless, the underground *Chronicle of the Lithuanian Catholic Church*, smuggled out and published in the West, was the most constant source of information about violations of human rights and of national feeling in the republic. There were also numerous other samizdat cultural and political journals in Lithuania, and one petition in 1979 on behalf of the church carried 150,000 signatures (4 per cent of the republic's population).

An Estonian National Front, set up in 1971, issued a programme rather similar to the later Lithuanian one, and an underground journal, the *Estonian Democrat*, circulated for a time. In general, however, the Estonians seemed to feel less need for underground publishing, perhaps because they still enjoyed some measure of freedom in their official Estonian-language organs (which can be understood by virtually nobody outside their republic). In 1980, however, students and schoolchildren conducted mass demonstrations against Russification of their republic. There was also some working-class unrest at this time in Tallinn and Tartu, which may have owed something to contemporary events in Poland, with whom the Baltic nations naturally feel an affinity.

In Georgia, an Initiative Group for the Defence of Human Rights chronicled from 1974 the illegalities of the Shevard-nadze regime, including the use of torture in Georgian prisons, and what was seen as accompanying Russification. The writer Zviad Gamsakhurdia founded a journal called the *Golden Fleece*, to publish Georgian-language works refused by the censorship, and also a *Georgian Messenger*, to record human rights violations and the efforts of Georgian intellectuals in defence of their culture. That these had popular support was seen in the riots of April 1978 (see above, page 430). Gamsakhurdia was sentenced in May 1978 to three years' imprisonment for 'anti-Soviet agitation and propaganda'.

Less is known about Armenian nationalism, though it was brought rudely to the world's attention in January 1979 when three Armenian nationalists were executed, allegedly for organizing an explosion in the Moscow underground railway two years earlier.

Among the Muslims, discontent tended to take different forms, as we shall see below. One national movement, however, has taken its place in the general movement for human rights: that is the campaign of the Crimean Tatars to be allowed to return to their homeland. Whereas most of the other nationalities deported by Stalin were not only rehabilitated after 1956, but also readmitted to their former national territories, the Tatars were never allowed to return to the Crimea. This may have something to do with the strategic importance of the Crimea as headquarters of the Black Sea Fleet, or it may be due to the fact that many members of the elite, from all over the Soviet Union, have their sanatoria and holiday homes there. At any rate, the Tatars, mostly still in exile in Uzbekistan, had been appealing peacefully but in vain for some time when, in 1968, General Grigorenko took up their cause, and made it part of the human rights campaign regularly recorded in the pages of the *Chronicle of Current Events*. He advised them not merely to petition peacefully (their accumulated petitions to the authorities by that time carried a total of 3 million signatures – or ten signatures for every member of the nation!), but to make full use of their rights under the Soviet constitution. This they did, at a mass demonstration in April 1968 at Chirchik, in Uzbekistan, which was followed by some three hundred arrests. In an open letter, addressed to 'world public opinion', they accused the Soviet government of 'genocide', and appealed for help to return to 'the land of our fathers'. On and off, in the years since then, the appeals have been renewed, but the Soviet government has remained deaf to them, evicting those few families who have tried to return without permission to the Crimea.

The Jewish national movement took on very distinctive forms. After Stalin's death and the halting of the Doctors' Plot investigations, official encouragement for anti-Semitism diminished considerably – though it never entirely disappeared – and the assimilation of Jews, at least many of those in the cities, resumed. It was cut short by the Arab-Israeli war in 1967, when the Soviet government took a strongly pro-Arab line, which reminded many Jews of the 'entry no. 5' on their passports. Jews once more found themselves being actively discriminated against. Many of them decided that, in view of their peculiar national situation, the best way to campaign for their rights was to demand the right to emigrate and go to live in the national homeland, Israel.

In a sense this happened because the third possible alternative, the maintenance of a distinctive Jewish way of life inside the Soviet Union, did not seem to be viable. The Jews were, in effect, being given the choice of sliyanie as Stalin had understood it, or emigration. Hebrew was a forbidden language, while Yiddish had only one journal and one newspaper in the whole country, and was not taught at all in schools. Religious practice centred on the synagogue became more and more difficult. There was no central Jewish religious organization, so that each synagogue had to fend for itself: of these there were only sixty-two in the early 1970s, and only some thirty of these were in European Russia, where 90 per cent of Jews live. Matzo-baking and kosher slaughtering of cattle were subject to widespread and unpredictable bans. Most serious of all, the existing rabbis were ageing, and the Soviet authorities would not permit the opening of any higher institute of Jewish religious or legal learning to train successors. More than any other faith, in fact, the Jewish religion was being slowly stifled by administrative action.

But even emigration was a strictly rationed option. The authorities were not disposed to allow it to happen freely: they were afraid that to do so might provoke a flood of applications from people of all nationalities. Besides, as Sakharov pointed out, 'The freedom to emigrate is an essential condition of spiritual freedom for all.'

In 1968–9, encouraged by the growing 'human rights' movement, Jews themselves began to protest against this situation, sending their letters to foreign journalists and to the *Chronicle of Current Events*. In 1970 a Jewish samizdat journal began to appear, significantly called *Exodus*. The whole problem became an international one in December 1970, when two Leningrad Jews were sentenced to death for attempting to emigrate by hijacking a plane. In view of the universal indignation in the West, the sentences were later commuted.

Perhaps encouraged by this, discontented Jews organized a mass sit-in at the Supreme Soviet building in Moscow in February 1971, as a result of which, unexpectedly, many of the participants were granted exit visas to Israel. This concession evidently resulted from a policy decision reached at the highest level. One presumes that it represented a calculated concession to Western public opinion at a time when the Soviet leadership was seeking détente and increased international trade. The US Congress was known to be especially concerned about Jewish rights. Furthermore, by granting permission to emigrate *ad hoc* and unpredictably, the authorities gained an extra power over Jews: they must have reckoned (not always correctly) that those who wished to emigrate would remain docile pending the outcome of their application.

At any rate, the number of authorized emigrants increased dramatically in 1971–2. It later reached two peaks, 33,500 in 1973, and some 50,000 in 1979, but declined thereafter as relations with the USA deteriorated. Even at its height the grant of a visa was by no means automatic. Official identification of emigration with disloyalty and even treason persisted. Applicants could easily receive no answer to their applications, but be dismissed from their jobs, be subjected to searches and interrogations, and arrested for 'parasitism' or worse. A new word entered the vocabulary of the international mass media to describe them: refuseniks. Most serious of all was the case of Anatoly Shcharansky, a member of the Moscow Helsinki Watch Group, and an energetic organizer who helped to keep refuseniks in touch with one another and with Western correspondents. He was tried in July 1978 for 'treason' (links with US intelligence services) and sentenced to ten years in a labour camp plus three years' imprisonment. The accompanying expulsion of an American correspondent, Robert Toth of the *Los Angeles Times*, raised fears that links between dissenters and Western journalists were to be considered as 'treason'.

One of the paradoxical aspects of 'de-Stalinization' was Khrushchev's rejection of the quiescent policy towards the churches and his return to active persecution. In this, as in other spheres, Khrushchev sought to revive Lenin's spirit of party activism and militant atheism. By doing this, he could appeal to *some* anti-clerical feeling, while also appeasing the ideological purists whom in other respects he infuriated.

The change in policy came around 1960. One of its chosen weapons was a change in the position of the parish priest. Under the arrangements worked out in 1943–5 the priest had been recognized once again as the legal administrator of the parish, responsible not only for the spiritual welfare of the congregation, but also for 'the preservation of the buildings and properties of the church'. In 1961, however, a hastily convened Synod of bishops issued new regulations revoking this function: it explicitly confined the priest to his spiritual vocation and transferred exclusive administrative authority to the parish council, of which the priest could *not* now be a member. Even the 1929 regulations had not gone so far.

During the next three or four years, over half of the existing parishes of the Orthodox Church were disbanded and some 10,000 churches closed. Since these closures were usually decided by the parish councils themselves, suspicion naturally arises that, in the absence of the priest, the councils had been infiltrated by local party activists. This was the charge made by two Orthodox priests, Fathers N. I. Eshliman and G. P. Yakunin, in a letter of December 1965 to the Presidium of the Supreme Soviet. They accused the Council for Affairs of the Russian Orthodox Church of illegally transferring or dismissing clergymen (often making derogatory reports about their behaviour), manipulating the membership of parish councils, and allowing local soviets to take over the financial affairs of congregations. Patriarch Alexei suspended both priests from the ministry, and no action was taken over their complaint.

A report from a church dissenter in Kirov oblast (in the north-east of European Russia) gives a detailed example of how closure was achieved in the village of Roi. In September 1960 the village priest was summoned to the village soviet building, where the party secretary, the chairman of the village soviet, and the chairman of the local kolkhoz warned him to leave the village, and threatened violence if he did not. This warning was later reinforced by anonymous letters, and the priest did leave. Thereupon the kolkhoz chairman is said to have sent 'agitators' to the parish council meetings, as a result of which the council minutes showed a unanimous decision to close the church, and offer the building to the kolkhoz as a club. In December the secretary of the raion soviet executive committee arrived with some workers and demanded the keys of the church from the warden, an eighty-year-old woman, threatening to confiscate her house if she refused to hand them over.

Having seized them, they entered the church, locked themselves in and began by drinking ten bottles of sacramental wine and eating the offering brought there for a requiem.

The church was destroyed by drunken machine-operators from the kolkhoz. Suslov [kolkhoz chairman] ordered dumplings and alcohol and paid them five rubles an hour from kolkhoz funds.

When the crosses were removed from the church, Suslov did all he could to insult the believers who were standing at a distance and weeping. All the icons, holy vessels, bells and other valuables were removed without a record being made and subsequently disappeared without trace.

Admittedly this is a partisan account, but it seems from a number of sources that anti-clerical prejudice was being mobilized all over the country.

Most surviving monasteries were closed, including the famous Monastery of the Caves, in Kiev, the Russian Orthodox Church's oldest place of worship. A document from the Pochaev monastery, in the western Ukraine, indicates that pressure was applied for many years to bring about its closure as well. Ancillary buildings were gradually requisitioned by the local soviet, the police and KGB began to harass visiting pilgrims, and to detain the monks for questioning, accusing them of violating the passport regulations and warning them that the monastery was to be closed. Some of them were beaten up, others sent to psychiatric hospitals. Perhaps because this pressure was documented in good time and information reached the West, the Pochaev monastery was in the end kept open.

After Khrushchev's fall, active persecution of the Orthodox Church eased somewhat, though it never ceased altogether, and the rigid mechanism of control has been maintained to the present. The methods used by the Council for Religious Affairs were shown up in one of its reports smuggled out to the West in 1979. As it made clear, 'No ordination or transfer takes place without careful monitoring by senior Council officials.' Clergy were classified according to the degree to which they were 'loyal to socialist society' or, on the contrary, tried to activate the religious life and strengthen the influence of the church among the population. What the Council valued in priests and bishops was inactivity, a purely formal attitude to divine services, readiness to preach Soviet patriotism, the party's social policy and participation in the international peace movement. The Soviet state, in other words, was no longer trying to destroy the church, but to use it as a pliant instrument.

Influenced by the methods of the civil rights movement, some dissenting Orthodox priests and laymen set up in 1976 a Christian Committee for the Defence of Believers' Rights, which documented and publicized (in samizdat and by Western publication) violations of believers' rights, as well as trying to advise and help the victims of such violations. In November 1979, Father Yakunin, one of its members, was arrested, and subsequently sentenced to five years in a labour camp and five years' exile for 'anti-Soviet agitation and propaganda'. Other members of the committee were also charged with criminal offences.

In its relations with the Evangelical Christians and Baptists the state also changed its policy around 1960. New rules governing their activities were apparently issued (though never published). These had the effect, as in the Orthodox Church, of strengthening state control over the registration of believers and the conduct of their religious life. Reaction among Baptists was much sharper than in the Orthodox Church. An action group was set up to protest to the official Baptist leadership about the way in which evangelism (which Baptists consider a sacred duty) was being explicitly discouraged, and children were not being brought up in the faith. The action group – who became generally known as Initsiativniki – accused the official leadership of servility towards an atheist state and of conniving at state persecution of believers who had done no more than their religious duty.

They reported instances of prayer meetings being forcibly broken up, believers being dismissed from their jobs or expelled from college, their homes being searched and children being separated from their parents.

Dissatisfied with their leaders' response, the Initsiativniki broke away, under the guidance of one Georgy Vins, a Baptist minister, and established a number of unregistered congregations all over the country. These even managed to run a series of underground printing presses producing prayer books and bibles, to provide for the severe shortage of religious literature. When Initsiativnik members were arrested for 'infringement of the separation of church and state', their colleagues set up a Council of Relatives to collect money and help both the imprisoned and their families. This was a new form of solidarity for Soviet conditions (soon to be imitated by the 'human rights movement' in the form of the Solzhenitsyn Fund for Political Prisoners). Another was tried out in 1966, when the Initsiativniki held a public demonstration in the courtyard of the Presidium of the Supreme Soviet, demanding the restoration of their constitutional right to freedom of worship. When policemen approached, they refused to budge, and had to be carried, singing hymns, into coaches brought up to remove them.

If one looks at the geographical areas where the Baptists – both official and unofficial – have been most successful, it seems likely that they have provided a sense of community for otherwise uprooted and displaced workers and employees, especially in the new industrial cities and in the raw suburbs of old ones. They appear to offer comfort, doctrinal certainty and the support of colleagues in a milieu where the Communist Party makes promises but does not fulfil them. Many of those who join the Baptists say that they do so out of disillusionment with the behaviour of their colleagues and superiors at work – bribery, pilfering, speculation, sycophancy and drunkenness. Wives of alcoholics are especially prone to become Baptists: a Baptist doctor once, in fact, suggested to a Soviet interviewer that the only effective way to combat drunkenness would be to spread the Baptist faith!

The evidence of Soviet surveys would suggest that Baptists demand very high moral standards from their adherents and particularly from their pastors and elders. A Handbook for Elders instructs them, 'Know all your flock! . . . Know each one individually! Know their spiritual condition, their gifts, their joys and trials, and their family life. Visit church members in their homes. Render personal love to the weak, the needy, the mournful and the afflicted.' Since most elders are in full-time employment, it can be imagined how much zeal and devotion is demanded from those who take on the vocation, especially since they receive little remuneration and no social standing for their work. The result, however, seems to be strongly knit communities, especially among the Initsiativniki, resistant to the pressures of the world around them.

In general, perhaps, it may be said that the religious policies of the Soviet state have had different effects on different types of believer. On the one hand, the persecution and closure of churches has certainly driven many away from any kind of faith. From a figure of about 80 per cent of adults in the 1920s, the proportion of believers today, insofar as this can be measured, is reckoned to be between a quarter and a third. On the other hand, the state's pressures seem to have strengthened and intensified the faith of that minority of believers who have retained it. This in its turn has tended to strengthen the influence of the more conservative adherents within any denomination: reform and modernization tend to become identified with support of the atheist regime, as we saw in the case of the Living Church (page 234). In return the state has selected certain churches for official recognition and a limited measure of support: these tend to be the older-established, large and more conservative ones. But there also exist numerous relatively small dissenting sects, fervent in their faith, strong in their mutual support for their own members, and intensely suspicious of everyone else.

They resemble the heretical movements of late medieval Europe more than they do churches in the West today. Where a church is strongly identified with a *nation* – as in Georgia, Armenia, Lithuania and the western Ukraine (Uniate Church) – then even 'official' churches take on certain 'sectarian' characteristics.

About the position of Islam today there exist different views, and we really have too little reliable, up-to-date information to judge between them. According to one thesis, the combination of rapid population growth with the revival of Islamic fundamentalism across the borders in Iran and other parts of Asia poses a very severe threat to the stability of Soviet rule. The opposing view is that, through their economic and social policies, the Soviets have assimilated Central Asia and have established a tolerably good relationship with official Islam, which has restrained Muslim sentiment from crystallizing into anti-Soviet national or religious feeling.

To take the demographic point first: in 1979 the peoples usually identified as Muslim totalled 44 million, or about one-sixth of the population. Twenty years earlier they had numbered less than one-eighth, and their continued higher birth rate meant they were certain to exceed a fifth of the population by 2000, with higher proportions among young people – and therefore in the armed forces. Since the Muslims are concentrated on the Asiatic borders of the USSR, that might present a potential danger, especially if they ever felt China was a more attractive homeland.

Until the 1950s, one could have said with confidence that Slavic immigration into the Muslim areas was proceeding apace, and would ensure the maintenance of firm central control. Nowadays that is no longer the case: since the late fifties there has been net emigration of Slavs from Azerbaidjan and Central Asia, and even from Kazakhstan, the most 'russified' republic. Furthermore, although knowledge of Russian as a second language has increased, evidence shows that Muslims remain overwhelmingly loyal to the native languages in their own homelands, and are reluctant to migrate outside their own republics or to marry people of other nationalities. Far from 'merging' with other nationalities, they do not even seem to be effecting much 'rapprochement'.

Islam, like the main Christian churches, has officially recognized but closely supervised status in the Soviet system. Today four main Spiritual Directorates exist: in Tashkent (for Kazakhstan and Central Asia), in Ufa (for the RSFSR), in Makhachkala (for the North Caucasus and Dagestan), and in Baku (partly Shiite, for Azerbaidjan and the Transcaucasus). Their resources seem meagre: 400–500 mosques, or one for every 90–100,000 Muslims, two *medresses* to train the *ulema* (religious and legal authorities), and only one religious periodical. On the other hand, they have succeeded in reopening some closed mosques, and in gaining for some of their students the right to study abroad, where Islamic higher education is more sophisticated.

If official Islam does not meet the needs of the population, then these *may* be satisfied instead by the underground Sufi brotherhoods (tariqat – see Chapter 9). One Soviet source in 1975 estimated that more than half the believers of the North Caucasus belonged to such brotherhoods, which would suggest a figure of a quarter of a million there alone. Originally much stronger in the North Caucasus than anywhere else, they probably spread their influence to Central Asia as an unforeseen result of Stalin's deportations: at any rate, repeated attacks in the Soviet press make it clear that they are feared rivals of official Islam there too. But this is mostly speculation: we remain largely ignorant about these brotherhoods. Not even the Soviet authorities appear to know much about them.

Recent interviews with emigrating Germans who used to live in the rural and small town regions of Kazakhstan – not the most fervent Muslim area by tradition – suggest that many of the old Islamic customs have survived strongly. Ritual prayer was reported to be widely performed, even in the street: 'The Russians often kicked them, but they did it nevertheless.' Religious holidays and the Ramadan fast are usually observed: 'The higher-ups can't do anything about it: the Kazakhs say, "I'm in my own country – I can live in my own way."' Circumcision is common, even amongst Communist and Soviet officials, while burial rites are faithfully observed: there were rumours in 1980 that the proposal to provide a secular burial for soldiers killed in Afghanistan provoked a riot in Alma-Ata, capital of the Kazakh Republic. Other Muslim practices, on the other hand, are in decline: pilgrimage, the payment of alms, and the prohibition on pork and alcohol. It seems, too, that women have improved their social position: polygamy is rare, the veil scarcely seen, and the paying of kalym (bride-price) has declined. In the large towns of Central Asia, in fact, there are few signs today of Islam.

Perhaps the truth is that under pressure Islam finds it easier than Christianity to adapt, to retreat into the home, the village, the secret brotherhood, to live underground without attracting the attention of the authorities or of foreign visitors. In the absence of better information, though, this remains largely conjecture.

It is certain that religion is not dying out any more in the Soviet Union. Indeed, even before Gorbachev came to power, there were signs of a revival, especially among the educated. This resulted partly from the vacuum opened up by the degeneration of the Communist Party's secular faith. Attempts from Khrushchev onwards to implant secular rituals to mark public holidays and the major rites of passage in an individual's life met with varying degrees of success, but in any case never entirely supplanted the old observances. In some cases religious revival was connected with the reassertion of national identity in a system which offered few other national symbols.

In the seventies and early eighties there were, moreover, indications that some official ideologists were aware of the value of religion in strengthening the moral and social life of a nation. At any rate, in some literary journals writers were being permitted to manifest a vague but unmistakable approval for the social outlook of Christianity, probably in the hope of increasing social solidarity and loyalty to the Soviet state. While this dilution of Marxism clearly aroused alarm in other official quarters, it pointed the direction in which the rulers were looking to combat the demoralization undermining the society over which they presided.

15

The Soviet Union in the 1980s:
an Impasse and Its Causes

In the early 1980s an elderly generation of leaders, born before the First World War and first promoted under Stalin, was not quite leaving the stage. Since there was no agreed provision for succession of power, no General Secretary had yet proved willing to resign his post voluntarily, suspecting perhaps that what awaited him – even after Khrushchev's humanization of the system – was not honourable retirement, but disgrace, or at best oblivion, and a demoralized, if materially cushioned, old age.

Hence, at least until 1985, the old men tended to hang on till an ever more advanced age, while the speculation of the world's press focused on their health rather than on their policies.

Furthermore, when a succession choice did force itself on the leaders, as when Brezhnev died in November 1982, or Andropov in February 1984, there was a tendency to play safe, by selecting an elderly man, who, if he proved intractable, was at least not likely to outlast most of his colleagues. That certainly seemed to be the main motive for choosing the rather faceless Chernenko in February 1984. Even Andropov, though by no means faceless, was already sixty-nine and in poor health when elected as General Secretary in November 1982, in preference to younger rivals. A key role in both appointments was probably played by Andrei Gromyko, the world's longest-serving foreign minister, and Marshal Dmitri Ustinov, Stalin's armaments commissar back in 1941 and perhaps the most remarkable survivor of all (he finally died in office in December 1984). Only in March 1985 was the grip of the old men finally broken, when the fifty-four-year-old Mikhail Gorbachev was appointed General Secretary.

Admittedly, Andropov might, for all anyone knew, not have turned out to be a mere interim choice. Since he had so recently been the longest-serving head of the KGB, it was in some ways a surprise that his colleagues chose him. That they did so is a measure of the extent to which the relationship between party and KGB had changed since 1953. The party had achieved secure dominance over the security police, but at the cost of absorbing much of its outlook on the world and giving top priority to the protection of the status quo – rather than to economic growth or the building of socialism. In the light of that change, Andropov's appointment was a natural one, and indeed during his brief term he performed rather as one would expect a security policeman to do. He talked a certain amount about economic reform, but the measures he actually proposed were half-hearted, even compared with Kosygin's of nearly twenty years earlier. The Novosibirsk Institute of Economics marked the occasion by issuing a confidential report on the economy remarkably similar to Aganbegyan's of 1965 (see above, page 363).

Andropov's solution for the nation's ills was discipline and the elimination of corruption. As he said to Moscow machine-tool workers in January 1983, 'Introducing good order doesn't require any capital investment whatever, but it can produce great results.' He demanded discipline not only of workers, but of administrators and indeed of the party-state apparatus. In short, he wanted to see the Soviet system working properly according to its own laws. While still head of the KGB he had sponsored an anti-corruption drive which reached as far as the Brezhnev family itself – in fact, it was probably partly launched as a weapon against the ageing General Secretary who refused to leave office. And once Andropov himself was in Brezhnev's post he carried through the exemplary dismissal of a number of ministers charged with protecting or even actually running hugely profitable underground manufactures and commercial concerns.

For ordinary workers and employees Andropov instituted a regime of stricter work discipline, with exemplary punishment of offenders. At one time the militia was even combing through queues in shops and outside cinemas to find people who should have been at work. Slightly better output figures were achieved in 1983, perhaps as a result of this campaign. But after a few months it slackened: after all, the reason many people take time off work is that otherwise they stand no chance of obtaining 'deficit' goods in the shops. Most Soviets assume that the right to do this is a kind of informal 'social contract': 'You pretend to pay us, and we pretend to work.' Certainly to withdraw the right without radically improving the supply of goods and services was to risk considerable popular discontent, and this no leader had been prepared to do since Novocherkassk.

In his cadres policy, Andropov caused a minor earthquake after the Brezhnev calm. In just over a year he replaced about 20 per cent of ministers and of oblast party secretaries. Some of the dismissals were part of the anti-corruption campaign. As for the rest, there is no clear evidence that they were intended to bring in new blood to replace the 'Brezhnev generation': on the contrary, the average age of the oblast secretaries actually went *up* slightly as a result of the changes.

In any case personnel changes were not enough. The pressure for serious change was mounting, not only inside the USSR itself, but also in its dependencies. Two crises in particular, in Poland and in Afghanistan, seemed insoluble without far-reaching change inside the heartland of Soviet power.

If the example of Czechoslovakia 1968 indicated the dangers of reform, then the Polish crisis of 1980–1 warned of the dangers of not reforming. During the 1970s Gierek had pursued, in exaggerated form, the same kind of economic policy as the Soviet Union itself: heavy industrial growth, fuelled by imports of high technology from the West. These had to be paid for by borrowing, and the country descended deeper into debt, especially since the oil-price rises of 1973–4 hit the programme in mid-stream. At the same time, the industrial growth rested on an underproductive agriculture – underproductive not because it was collective (in fact most of it remained private after the 1956 reforms), but because the whole rural sector, as in the Soviet Union, suffered from low status and underinvestment. To ensure that the defects of agriculture did not mean high food prices in the towns, the government – again as in the Soviet Union – shelled out enormous subsidies, which periodically threatened to become altogether intolerable to the exchequer.

The workers in Poland – and this is quite unlike the Soviet Union – had retained and even developed their traditions of 1956. They had not been allowed to retain their factory committees, which meant they had to press their interests in other, more direct ways, at moments of crisis. Such moments occurred whenever the government decided that the food subsidy was out of control and would have to be reduced by raising food prices. In 1970, when it did this, workers' protests and demonstrations brought to an end the reign of Gomulka. In 1976, once again, workers posed a formidable challenge: in Radom, for example, they marched from the engineering works to party headquarters and set fire to them; a section broke into the privileged nomenklatura canteen, and threw out cheap, high-quality meat to the crowd outside, yelling, 'Red bourgeoisie!' In accordance with the by now customary strategy for dealing with workers' disorders, the authorities first gave way to their demands, and revoked the price rises; they then arrested numerous workers, some of whom were beaten up in detention.

These arrests gave rise to a phenomenon hitherto unprecedented in socialist societies. A small group of intellectuals, among whom the leading figure was Jacek Kuroń, set up a Workers' Defence Committee (KOR) to provide legal and financial aid for the workers arrested and mistreated, to campaign for their release, and to demand an investigation of the injustices they had suffered. This was the first time in a socialist society that intellectuals and workers had actually got together in a joint political campaign. KOR in one sense followed the example of the Soviet dissenters of the late sixties: they acted *as if* Poland were a Rechtstaat of the kind claimed in its constitution. On that basis they issued appeals which could be subscribed to by socialists and liberals, Catholics and atheists, nationalists and internationalists. They dropped ideology as something which divides rather than unites. Where they went much further than the Soviet dissenters was in forging an effective alliance with the workers: that they were able to do so probably owed much to their common sense of Polish national identity and Roman Catholic religious background.

At any rate this cooperation proved crucial at the next political crisis, when the government once more raised food prices in the summer of 1980. When the workers of the Lenin Shipyard at Gdańsk went on strike against the new prices and against the dismissal of a popular workers' leader, they soon found themselves at the centre of a network of national protest, all of whose participants were informed through underground newspapers of what was going on elsewhere, and were advised by members of KOR on political aims and tactics. As a result, the aims of the strike soon broadened, and, by the time government representatives agreed to negotiate, fundamental political changes were being demanded: the right to set up trade unions free of party domination and to go on strike, abolition of press censorship and guaranteed access of all social groups and religious associations to the mass media. The agreement signed at Gdańsk between the government and the workers, led by the electrician Lech Walesa, acknowledged 'the leading role of the party', but all the same it effected a profound change in the Polish political system, for it conceded not only to workers, but to other social groups, the right to create their own organizations and to express their views publicly. The new free trade union, Solidarity, authorized by the agreement, had 3 million members within a fortnight, and rose to a peak of 9 million, while people left the Communist Party in droves. The peasants, too, revealed an unexpected capacity for organization, and demanded their own Solidarity, which the courts eventually conceded to them.

Such large and spirited organizations could not help playing a major role in politics. Yet they were constrained by the 'leading role of the party', and by the implied threat of Soviet occupation which bolstered it. This paradox put the leaders of Solidarity in a very tricky situation: they possessed enormous negative power, but not the positive power which would have been needed to bring about effective change. They faced, furthermore, a Communist Party and a security police still largely unreformed, uneasy with the new political atmosphere, and anxious to restore 'normality' as soon as possible. The economy, already in serious crisis before the summer, was now declining further as a result of the upheavals. To reverse the decline, the party and Solidarity needed to work closely together, but this was just what they were incapable of doing. The party would not even publish full and frank information about the economic situation, while Solidarity declined to ask sacrifices of the workers as long as they were not being drawn into a full partnership with the party, based on mutual trust. Instead the history of the Solidarity era was one of crises, often provoked by resentful local party or police officials, and causing strikes or demonstrations which the loose-limbed Solidarity organization could not prevent, even when it wished to.

In the circumstances, Solidarity soon became much more than a trade union: it was a kind of repository of people's hopes, what one Western journalist called a 'civil crusade for national revival'. Its economic role soon involved it inevitably in much more than economics. As the Solidarity programme, passed at its national congress in September 1981, declared:

What we had in mind was not only bread, butter and sausage, but also justice, democracy, truth, legality, human dignity, freedom of conviction and the repair of the republic. All elementary values had been too mistreated to believe that anything could improve without their rebirth. Thus the economic protest had to be simultaneously a social protest, and the social protest had to be simultaneously a moral protest.

The result was stalemate, frustration and continued economic decline. The Catholic Church, which considered that it above all was responsible for the nation's moral state, tried to bring the potential partners together in a Committee of National Salvation, but nothing came of it. As for the party, decades of exercising power without being answerable to anyone had rendered it incapable of dealing with real social forces uttering uncomfortable truths and in a position to make demands. In effect, the party too abdicated: it claimed a 'leading role', but proved incapable of exercising it.

Into this vacuum General Jaruzelski stepped, by declaring martial law on 13 December 1981, arresting the leading members of KOR and 'isolating' Lech Walesa. He claimed that the country was on the edge of civil war. For this there was no evidence whatsoever: all Solidarity's strikes and demonstrations had passed off virtually without violence, save what was applied by the regime. If Solidarity had a fault, it was excessive caution rather than reckless activity. Probably the immediate precipitant of the military coup was the call by some outspoken Solidarity members for national elections in which the people could choose between Solidarity and the party. This could indeed be interpreted as a challenge to the party's 'leading role', and General Jaruzelski, having proved ineffective as the party's first secretary, tried to reimpose his authority through his other arm, the military. Poland was returned to a condition reminiscent of the immediate post-war years, with politics largely suspended, and soldiers and police running the country. Only this time the occupying army was a Polish one.

As a military operation, Jaruzelski's coup was unexpectedly successful. Solidarity proved too disorganized, and perhaps also demoralized, by the months of uncertain waiting and by the shortages of winter, to mount any really effective resistance. But the martial law regime was quite unable to restore the economy or public morale. The nation lapsed into a condition of sullen stalemate.

In December 1979 the Soviet army invaded Afghanistan, renewing, after a break of almost exactly a century, the advance into Central Asia which the tsars had pursued. It was the first time the Soviet Union had intervened in a country not assigned to their sphere of influence by the Yalta and Potsdam agreements at the end of Second World War. For that reason, it provoked a wave of indignation and hostility both among the Western powers and from the Islamic world, with both of which the Soviets had previously seemed anxious to cultivate good relations.

What induced the Soviets to do it? We cannot say for certain on present evidence. Some observers believed it was the first step in a campaign of aggression in the Middle East, aimed eventually at the Persian Gulf; others were more ready to accept Brezhnev's explanation that the situation in Afghanistan 'posed a direct threat to our southern frontier'. These two explanations are not mutually exclusive, of course: the most aggressive regimes in the twentieth century have been those who started by feeling vulnerable. But perhaps the simplest explanation is that the invasion of Afghanistan was another invocation of the Brezhnev doctrine, that a state which has once become socialist shall not be permitted – especially if it lies adjacent to the Soviet Union – to relapse into non-socialist political forms.

In April 1978 a military coup brought to power in Kabul a pro-Soviet Marxist party bitterly divided internally by factions. The Khalq (or People) faction, which came out on top, tried to carry out major social transformations very rapidly, regardless of opposition. By implementing land reform without proper preparation they unleashed bitter village disputes and undermined traditional elites in the countryside. Their attempt to reform the marriage laws by abolishing the Kalym upset the generally accepted basis of family contracts and hence the relationships between families. Campaigns for primary education and universal literacy on Soviet Marxist lines affronted Islamic believers. Symbolically most objectionable of all, the new rulers replaced the Islamic green flag with a red one.

All these brusquely executed reforms encountered tremendous popular hostility. The situation was similar to that in the Islamic areas of Soviet Russia in the early twenties, with headstrong reformers cramming ill-prepared changes down the throats of a population mostly determined to stick to its old way of life. And the response was the same. To avoid having to pay heavy taxes, forfeit family plots of land, or put their children in 'godless' schools, villagers took to the hills with their horses and with weapons acquired on the black market. Regular bands of guerrilla fighters formed – the *mujahidin* – like the Basmachi of the twenties, devoted to Islam and to national independence. And if the latter had received many of their supplies and weapons from over the border in Afghanistan, the whole conflict now moved one stage further south, with Pakistan acting as the source.

By this time the Soviet Union had numerous military and civilian advisers in Afghanistan, and was linked to it by a friendship treaty, signed in December 1978. Eventually, the Soviets decided that the socialist regime in Kabul was in danger from the vehement popular resistance. In December 1979, some 100,000 troops invaded, bringing with them Babrak Karmal, leader of the alternative Parcham (or Flag) faction, to form a new government. His policies were more moderate than that of the Khalq regime, whose political prisoners he at first released. He promised to 'respect the sacred principles of Islam', including 'family unity' and 'lawful private ownership', and even restored the green flag.

But the Soviet troops behind him belied his words, and he soon found himself imprisoning political opponents no less indiscriminately than his predecessors, and moreover introducing a harsh conscription law to raise enough troops for an Afghan army to fight alongside the Soviets.

Thus by the 1980s the Soviets found themselves fighting a long anti-guerrilla campaign in Central Asia, as they did in the 1920s, only now under even less favourable circumstances, in a country not accustomed to Russian rule and with a formidable record of resistance to imperialist invaders (hitherto mostly British). In their initial optimism, the Soviet authorities sent in troops from their own Central Asian republics, many of them Uzbek, Tadzhik or Turkmen, and thus able to speak some of the languages of the Afghan population: the expectation evidently was that they would be able to rally the natives to the Soviet side. In the event, these Central Asian troops proved unreliable, and had to be withdrawn. Reportedly, all the personnel of at least one Soviet unit were executed for refusing to fight against fellow Muslims. Furthermore, the Afghan army itself turned out to be often unreliable, so that the Red Army found itself taking over the rural pacification campaigns which the Afghans themselves were supposed to perform.

The result, once again, was a grim stalemate. Limiting themselves to about 100,000 men – perhaps to sustain the pretence that they faced only a limited number of politically motivated rebels – the occupants never extended their control much beyond the cities and main roads, and sometimes it was shaky even there. In the attempt to do more, they sometimes drove the population out of their villages and made them uninhabitable. However, the Soviet army had not enough personnel to secure the areas thus cleared. Sometimes the peasants were able to return and rebuild their homes, sometimes they went to swell the numbers of the mujahidin. But very many – at least a fifth of the population – became refugees, mostly in Pakistan. Whatever their original aims, the Soviets were prepared to risk genocide in order to achieve them.

As for the mujahidin, they had neither the numbers, the weapons, nor the organisation necessary to defeat the Soviet occupants. The result, then, was a grim and brutal stalemate, which devastated Afghanistan.

Faced with stagnation at home and stalemate abroad, in March 1985 the Politburo took its courage in its hands, and for the first time elected a member of the younger generation as General Secretary. Mikhail Gorbachev, 54 at the time of his election, comes from the fertile southern region of Stavropol, an area of Cossack traditions and rich peasant farming. During his spell there as party secretary in the seventies, he sponsored experiments with the 'link' system in agriculture (see page 394), even as it was being abandoned elsewhere because the apparatus feared it would lead to the break-up of the collective farms. Even more important as a preparation for his future role, Gorbachev studied at Moscow University in the fifties, which for a Soviet politician is decidedly unusual. The jurisprudence of the late Stalin years was far from liberal in spirit, but even so he will have had to imbibe, among other things, the principles of Roman and Western constitutional law, and with them the makings of an outlook on society potentially very different from that of his colleagues.

The election of Gorbachev testified to the Politburo's recognition that the country was in a very serious long-term crisis which would eventually jeopardize its standing as a great power alongside the United States. He was the candidate of those who wanted change, or who realised at any rate that it could no longer be postponed. Prominent among them was the KGB, perhaps the least corrupt of the major political institutions under Brezhnev, and the one in the best position to appreciate the depth of the crisis. Gorbachev's patron and mentor in the party hierarchy had been Andropov, and during his first year or so in office he continued his policies. He launched the slogan of 'acceleration' and tightened labour discipline, invoking the legendary feats of Alexei Stakhanov, and establishing an official quality control inspectorate, *Gospriemka*, which had power to reject badly made goods and cut the pay of those deemed responsible. He intensified the drive to investigate, dismiss and prosecute corrupt officials. He initiated a campaign against 'non-labour income', that is, against any earnings not acquired in officially recognised employment. He sharply restricted the sale of alcoholic drinks and banned their consumption on official occasions, even at celebrations. Mineral water was substituted, an affront to Russian traditions of hospitality and conviviality which earned Gorbachev the prim and disapproving nickname of 'Mineral Secretary'.

This was, if you like, Perestroika Mark 1, the fruit of Gorbachev's long years in the party apparatus and of his association with the KGB. It was launched to the catchy accompaniment of *glasnost*, or 'publicity', which at this stage meant little more than a new and livelier style of presentation, encouraging the media to probe the deficiencies of corrupt officials in what was becoming known as the period of 'stagnation' under Brezhnev.

Then, during the summer and autumn of 1986, a real change took place, gradually but unmistakeably, not just in the style but in the substance of Gorbachev's policies. It is difficult to know whether this was a transition to more radical changes which he had always intended to carry out, but was unable to until he could bring his supporters into the Politburo and Central Committee; or whether he genuinely changed his intentions, having learned on the job just how deep was the crisis the country faced. At any rate, the emphasis shifted from merely tightening up the system to changing it radically.

It may be that the explosion in the nuclear power station at Chernobyl in April 1986 was a turning point, dramatizing as it did the mortally dangerous defects of a centrally administered economy which handled awesome technological power with such secretive and slovenly irresponsibility. Chernobyl certainly brought home the damage wrought by restricted *glasnost* in arousing both hostility abroad and panic at home. Foreigners were indignant that they should learn of an explosion affecting public health right round the world from a non-Soviet source (the Swedes were the first to call attention to the increased radiation). As for Soviet citizens, thousands of them besieged railway stations to escape unknown dangers of which they were not properly warned by their own media, and of which they could only learn from sometimes exaggerated foreign radio reports. Even the authorities in Moscow had difficulty at first in discovering what the true situation was.

If Gorbachev's legal studies had ever interested him in freedom of speech and the rule of law, then the Chernobyl explosion was calculated to reawaken that interest. An intriguing theme began to crop up in his speeches: that the absence of an opposition party obliged Soviet officials to behave with particular probity and to be especially searching in their self-criticism and acceptance of criticism from others. In June 1986 he met a delegation of writers and told them they had an important role to play in the struggle which the Central Committee was waging, with the support of the people, against an intermediate 'managerial stratum, the government and party apparatus, which does not . . . want to give up its privileges'. The writers responded with bitter attacks on censorship and on environmental pollution at their Eighth Congress, just after the meeting, and by reorganizing some of the major literary journals so as to bring in proponents of much broader *glasnost*, in the spirit of Tvardovsky. 1987 and 1988 saw a veritable festival of banned literature, as Zamyatin's *We*, Pasternak's *Doctor Zhivago* and Grossman's *Life and Fate* at last reached the Soviet reader, while works like Anna Akhmatova's *Requiem*, Anatoly Rybakov's *Children of the Arbat* and Vladimir Dudintsev's *White Garments* swept back the veil of semi-secrecy which had obscured the realities of Stalinism even during Khrushchev's 'thaw'. Now the truth was revealed about his vilification and hounding of the opposition, the

brutal collectivization of agriculture and the consequent famine, the arrests and executions, the deportations of whole
peoples, and the costly wartime mistakes. In 1989 even Solzhenitsyn's *Gulag Archipelago* was announced for publication.

Symbolic of the new mood was the release of Academician
Sakharov from exile in Gorky in December 1986. The letter
which he had written to Brezhnev in 1970 (see pages 407–8)
may be said to contain the first sketch of what was now
emerging as Gorbachev's Perestroika Mark 2, at the centre
of which was the notion of an alliance between the party
leadership and the country's scientific and cultural intelligentsia, including those who had hitherto been execrated as
'dissidents'. After his return to Moscow, Sakharov was not
restricted in any way in his comments, but was permitted to
make known his views on political issues, even where he was
critical of Gorbachev and the party leaders. His boldness was
gradually imitated by others, until journals like *Ogonek* and
Moskovskie novosti became forums for authentic and wide-
ranging public debate on all the issues facing Soviet society.

Of course this novel outspokenness did not please all of
those who had voted Gorbachev into power: they were all in
favour of perestroika, but not necessarily of the new variety
he was now elaborating. But he displayed considerable
determination and skill in removing or downgrading his
opponents, while manoeuvring his supporters into top
positions. Three and a half years into his new office, he had
ousted from the Politburo and the Secretariat almost all of
Brezhnev's former associates, such as Tikhonov, Romanov,
Kunaev, Aliev, even in the end Gromyko, while promoting
nominees of Andropov, like Egor Ligachev, Nikolai Ryzhkov
and Viktor Chebrikov, and men of his own choice, such as
Edvard Shevardnadze, who became Foreign Minister, and
Alexander Yakovlev, who became secretary for ideology.
One of his own protégés, Boris Eltsin, brought from
Sverdlovsk to run the party organization in Moscow,
embarrassed him by his forthright attacks on privilege and
corruption inside the apparatus, and was expelled from the

Politburo in October 1987.

The 27th Party Congress, in February 1986, came a little too early for Gorbachev to have worked out a thorough reform of the political system. For that purpose he called a special Party Conference in the summer of 1988. Often held in the early years of the Soviet regime to tackle important issues between full congresses, such conferences had not been held since 1941. This one, the 19th, actually took decisions far more important than anything resolved at the 27th Congress. It outlined a programme of democratization of the party, which, if fully implemented, will seriously weaken the nomenklatura system: party officials are to be elected by secret ballot, with multiple candidacies and proper discussion of their merits, and they are to hold office for no more than two sessions (ten years). The legislative system was also to be remodelled. A new Congress of People's Deputies of 2,250 members was to become the supreme legislative assembly: it was to be elected by the people, voting partly in territorial constituencies, partly in national-ethnic constituencies, and partly through established institutions such as the Communist Party, the Komsomol, the trade unions, the Council of Soviet Women, the Academy of Sciences and the creative unions. Multiple candidacies would be permitted, though not compulsory: where they existed, there would be guarantees of proper public discussion of competing programmes. The Congress of People's Deputies was entrusted with the task of electing the head of state, the President of the Soviet Union (a post for which the General Secretary of the Communist Party would normally be expected to stand), and the new-style Supreme Soviet, of some 450 members, to which it would delegate its day-to-day legislative activity.

These complicated arrangements were intended to endow Gorbachev with a new source of legitimacy, deriving from the people, while not unduly weakening the grip of the nomenklatura elite on political power. The new legislative assemblies were thus more or less bound to function in an ambiguous fashion. They faced an enormous workload.

Perestroika Mark 2 meant sweeping changes in all fields of Soviet life, starting with the establishment of the rule of law itself. 'The law', declared the 19th Party Conference, 'is paramount in all spheres of society's life ... It is necessary to give paramount attention to the legal protection of the individual and to consolidate guarantees of the Soviet people's political, economic and social rights and freedoms.' The Soviet state had already announced its intention of adhering to the principles of the UN Declaration on Human Rights, and had made a start by releasing most 'prisoners of conscience' during 1987, and by setting up its own Human Rights Commission under the reforming political scientist Fedor Burlatsky. Now it required laws defining and guaranteeing freedom from arbitrary arrest, inviolability of the home and of private correspondence, freedom of speech and publication and the right of access to information and freedom to associate with fellow-citizens in voluntary associations of all kinds, including those directed to economic and to political ends. Criminal law procedures needed redrafting, not least in order to ensure that judges would enjoy immunity from pressure by the authorities and that defence lawyers would be able to defend their clients effectively right through the investigation and trial.

A major new initiative undertaken by the party at this time was to seek a rapprochement with the Russian Orthodox Church and other established denominations. In April 1988 Gorbachev received Patriarch Pimen and five other senior bishops, and told them 'Believers are Soviet working people and patriots: they have every right to express their convictions in a fitting manner.' He wanted to turn a substantial number of the disaffected into loyal citizens, and at the same time to begin to tackle some of society's intractable moral problems in a new way. This entailed guaranteeing them freedom of conscience and worship, and so a joint church-state commission was set up to elaborate draft legislation to replace the draconian laws of 1918 and 1929, give legal recognition once again to the central administrations of official churches, return to the priest his authority over the parish, permit some degree of religious education, at least in private homes and church premises, and authorize charitable and pastoral work by religious organizations.

In foreign and military policy, Perestroika Mark 2 meant moving away from ideological rigidity and from security through armed strength. The cost of the arms race, the threat of nuclear war, and the prospect of ecological disasters acknowledging no boundaries all contributed to this radical reassessment. Gorbachev's 'new thinking' explicitly downgrades the class struggle and asserts 'the priority of all-human values, a world without violence and wars, diversity of social progress, dialogue and cooperation for the sake of development and the preservation of civilization, and movement towards a new world order.' In pursuit of these goals, the Soviet Union executed a carefully phased withdrawal during 1988–9 from its expensive and demoralizing war in Afghanistan. It reached agreement with the United States on the scrapping of intermediate-range nuclear missiles and the reduction of strategic arms, and it began unilaterally to withdraw some of its conventional forces from Europe and the Chinese frontier, reckoning that the presence of excessive Soviet troops and weapons there was itself creating tension which detracted from Soviet security. At the same time, travel procedures for Soviet citizens in the outside world were gradually simplified, so that personal, professional and commercial visits in both directions have become easier and more frequent. In a real sense the Soviet Union has joined the international community, of which it has never been a full member before.

In the face of these changes, one is bound to ask what has happened to the ideology which has hitherto underpinned the party's rule, and which used to assert primacy for the class struggle and the building of socialism, not for 'all-human values' and the rule of law. During a visit to Siberia in 1988, Gorbachev was confronted by an earnest young man who asked him 'What stage of socialism have we reached now?'

Gorbachev replied good-humouredly 'You've all got used to thinking like that: you're a young fellow, and all you're interested in is stages! (Laughter) I believe we are at the stage of restructuring that which we have so far created. That's the stage we're at.'

This cheerful renunciation of any tangible goal must be one of the most disconcerting aspects of Perestroika Mark 2 for the old-timers in the party. Yury Bondarev, secretary of the RFSFR Writers' Union, has asked the warning question: 'Could our perestroika not be compared to an aircraft which has taken off without knowing whether there is a landing strip at its destination?' It is true that the coordinates of the 'landing strip' are still identified in very general terms. Fedor Burlatsky, for example, asserts that 'socialism has one simple and obvious goal: the welfare and culture of the working man. Everything else – industry and socialization – is a means to that end.' Actually Lenin was no more explicit: as we have seen, he had no blueprint for the construction of a socialist society, beyond the vague nostrums outlined in *State and Revolution*. He did, however, have a very distinct sense of the forward march of history, and, when he was forced to compromise, was quite aware of what he was doing. Significantly it is the greatest of those compromises, the introduction of NEP in 1921, which Gorbachev is now projecting as an ideal. And he steadfastly ignores the fact that Lenin saw fit to counteract his concessions by an actual tightening of the political system (see Chapter 5).

What results is a style of socialism which the Soviet Union has never experienced before: pluralist and ready to learn from the experience of others. The terms in which it is discussed – decentralization, popular representation, freedom of speech, access to information – are more reminiscent of John Stuart Mill than of Karl Marx, and remind one that Marxism is the offspring (albeit illegitimate) of bourgeois liberalism. The philosopher A. Tsipko has recommended that, to avoid Stalinism, Marxism needs to return to its origins. 'The rule of law is a legacy of bourgeois culture.

Freedom of conscience was also born there.' And Vadim
Medvedev, currently head of the Central Committee Ideological Commission, rejects 'indiscriminately brushing aside the
experience accumulated by capitalism', envisaging instead 'a
serious reassessment of the practice of present-day social
democracy in defending the social and democratic attain-
ments of working people'.

No doubt such considerations underlie the new Soviet
readiness to tolerate radical political experiments among its
Warsaw Pact allies. In Hungary the Kadar leadership ever
since the late sixties had conducted decentralizing reforms in
the economy, which had allowed a good deal of private
enterprise to emerge in agriculture, services, retail trade and
consumer industry, and had thereby considerably raised the
overall prosperity of Hungarian society. It had, however,
upheld the party's tight control over political and cultural
life. The result by the mid-eighties was a crisis which
manifested itself on the one hand in high inflation, indebted-
ness and glaring social inequalities, on the other hand in
chronic disaffection among the professional classes, including
the party apparatus itself. In 1988 Kadar was at last ousted,
and the new party leadership, though divided in itself, groped
its way towards ending censorship and permitting the
creation of rival political parties. It is almost as if the scenario
of 1945–8 were being played backwards, with emasculated
political parties regaining their capacity for independent
action. There was even discussion of leaving the Warsaw
Pact.

In Poland the stalemate created by martial law persisted
long after it was lifted, especially since the outlawing of
Solidarity deprived the nation of any political organization
which could articulate constructively its resentment and
frustration. A series of workers' strikes in 1988 finally
demonstrated the Jaruzelski regime's impotence, and it
reluctantly relegalized Solidarity, to enlist it as a partner in
the political and economic revitalization of the nation. In the
end an agreement was reached establishing a freely elected

two-chamber legislature, in whose lower house, the Sejm, 65 per cent of seats would be guaranteed to the Communist bloc, while the upper house, the Senate, would be open to candidates of any political persuasion. The elections, held in June 1989, were devastating for the Communists: they were swept out of the Senate, and on the first round could not even muster the required 50 per cent of votes for many of their candidates in the Sejm. General Jaruzelski was barely elected as President. A new kind of political instability seemed to threaten, caused by the Communists' patent loss of any moral right to rule, while Solidarity hesitated to challenge them by taking due advantage of the success it had earned at the polls.

The Soviet press reported these Hungarian and Polish developments in a sober and matter-of-fact manner, as if it were the normal stuff of politics for Communists to face competing parties. There were no rumbling warnings about 'counter-revolution' or 'the integrity of the world socialist system', as there had been in 1968 and 1980–1. On the contrary, Gorbachev went out of his way to reaffirm the right of all nations to choose their own path of development.

Yet inside the Soviet Union itself the Communist Party has not renounced its leading role or its right to decide what in any given circumstance constitutes 'socialism'. Indeed, the 19th Party Conference explicitly reasserted these preroga-tives. This claim to exclusive political rights directly contra-dicts the pluralism and openness which the party leadership is at pains to project as a constituent element of perestroika. The resultant ambiguity casts a shadow of uncertainty over the political arrangements which are taking shape. As Andrei Sakharov has commented, Gorbachev is trying to 'achieve democracy by undemocratic means'. Perhaps there is no other way of going about it: a totalitarian regime has never been dismantled peacefully before, and it would be surprising if the process advanced without ambivalence, confusion and alarm.

It is in this equivocal milieu that, for the first time since 1921, political associations independent of the party have arisen to articulate the concerns and aspirations of ordinary Soviet citizens. Some of them had their origin in the sports clubs and pop groups of a youth which had come to feel thoroughly alienated from the Komsomol. Others grew out of the peace movement, or the dissenting groups of the sixties and seventies, described in Chapter 14, concerned with human rights, ethnic and religious issues. All of them bore witness to a lively alternative culture existing semi-underground throughout the Brezhnev years, able, as soon as *glasnost* opened the way, to spawn exceedingly diverse informal political movements, determined, resourceful and well-informed.

Very often defence of the environment or of historical monuments was the vital catalyst which brought together small groups of concerned individuals hitherto isolated from one another. In Leningrad a number of alternative groups linked up only when the City Soviet decided in 1987 to demolish the Hotel Angleterre, in which the poet Sergei Esenin had committed suicide. The groups collected signatures in the street for a petition to save the building. The authorities cleared them away and moved the demolition workers in, but the protesters did not simply yield: they learned from their defeat that they must organise themselves better and make contact with a broader public. They stationed an information kiosk on the square in front of St Isaac's Cathedral to hand out information to the public and answer questions, and they set up an umbrella organization, the Cultural Democratic Movement (also known as Epicentre), with its own journal, *Mercury*. An editorial in the first number well captured the aim of the movement. 'The activation of public opinion, its mobilization as an effective instrument of perestroika – this is the main road which leads to socialist democracy.'

In Moscow an analogous campaign to rescue the seventeenth-century Shcherbakov Palace from demolition was more successful: the palace was occupied for two months by students and schoolchildren, whose leader, Kirill Parfenov, appeared on television to explain their campaign to save historical Moscow. What perhaps encouraged conservatio-ists most of all, however, was the success of writers and scientists in the summer of 1986 in persuading the party leadership to abandon grandiose and expensive plans to divert rivers of Siberia and northern Russia to flow south-wards and provide water for the semi-arid regions of Central Asia and the Volga basin. Sergei Zalygin, new editor of *Novyi mir*, called it the first ever major triumph of 'public opinion' over the leviathans of Gosplan and the industrial ministries.

By the first half of 1987, in short, there was a mood abroad that citizens' initiatives could have tangible results. The environment and historical monuments were an appropriate battleground for the first campaigns, since they affected everybody, while appearing to be a relatively apolitical subject. Chernobyl had, moreover, heightened public aware-ness and indignation over the way in which potentially lethal technology was being installed and run by the central government, disdaining any consultation with the local authorities, let alone the people.

One of the first voluntary associations which tried syste-matically to capitalize on the new mood was the Club for Social Initiatives, founded in Moscow in the autumn of 1986 to 'involve broad strata of the population in the process of self-government'. It obtained the support of Tatyana Zaslavs-kaya, author of the Novosibirsk economic report of 1983 (see page 449), and of the Soviet Sociological Association. It sponsored a whole range of activities: help for the old and ill, preservation work on old buildings, workers' seminars on enterprise autonomy, agitation for a monument to Stalin's victims, and discussion meetings on draft legislation pub-lished in the Soviet press. Analogous organizations soon began to appear in provincial towns as well.

The sheer multiplicity of the tasks waiting to be done soon motivated division of the Club into smaller units: the Philanthropic Society, for example, Social Self-Administration, and Civil Dignity (giving legal advice to people who felt their rights had been infringed). Splits took place for political as well as functional reasons. The Club for Social Initiatives was definitely a 'within-system' organization, aiming to promote from below the vision of a reformed socialism as projected by Gorbachev from above. But not everyone agreed that 'socialism', however one defined it, was a suitable goal, or that cooperation was expedient with authorities who had over decades proved themselves to be so incompetent and so unresponsive to the public.

Those who favoured 'within-system' activity gathered in August 1987 at a conference convened in Moscow by the Club for Social Initiatives, and established a Union-wide Federation of Socialist Clubs (FSOK). These groups were of a general 'broad left' persuasion, acknowledging an intellectual debt to Marx, but interpreting him through Gramsci, Marcuse, the Yugoslav revisionists and the theorists of the 1968 Prague Spring. Some of them were attracted by Scandinavian Social Democracy. They repudiated Soviet 'real socialism' as it had developed under Stalin and Brezhnev, but rejected the methods of the human rights movement of the sixties and seventies as too elitist, too remote from the interests of the masses. Instead they hoped to respond to Gorbachev's calls for 'initiative from below' by developing links with ordinary people in their workplaces and encouraging them to take advantage of their new rights under the 1987 enterprise law to participate in and monitor management decisions.

The more democratic electoral law announced by the 19th Party Conference gave the members of FSOK the opportunity to put their message before a wider public. In many towns they set about bringing together like-minded groups in so-called Popular Fronts for the Support of Perestroika to agitate for reform-minded candidates. Local party and Komsomol organizations were divided in their response to this unsolicited 'help': some tried to work with their unfamiliar and sometimes disconcerting allies, others disrupted their meetings and denied them space in the local press.

Those informal political activists who felt that cooperation, however critical, with the authorities was likely to prove self-defeating joined forces at a meeting in Moscow in May 1988 to form the Democratic Union. The new Union disavowed forthwith the nebulous status of 'informal association' and roundly declared itself 'a political party standing in opposition to the totalitarian peculiarities of the existing social order in our country'. It looked back to the February rather than the October revolution as its ideal, and stated that its ultimate goal was the establishment of a parliamentary democracy with a multi-party system, a free press and a market economy. In the short term it proposed to propagate the impeccably Leninist notion of 'All power to the soviets' in the hope that revivified elective assemblies could become genuine counterweights to the hitherto overwhelming might of the apparatus.

Support of the soviets and of popular initiative could have provided a short-term forum on which the Popular Fronts and the Democratic Union could work together, but in practice the claim to act as an opposition party proved deeply divisive, and there was little cooperation between them. The authorities regarded the Democratic Union with undisguised hostility and, although they did not ban it (as any previous leadership would have done), they obstructed its meetings and harassed its members, subjecting many of them to brief periods of detention for alleged minor offences. In August 1988 for example, when the Union went ahead with a banned meeting to commemorate the crushing of the Prague Spring, the police intervened and cordoned off the square: in the ensuing mêlée, some thirty people were injured and ninety-six arrested.

The creation of informal political associations had especial resonance in the non-Russian regions of the Soviet Union. There all the frustrations which impelled them in Russia were compounded by resentment at alien domination. Issues of history, culture and the environment bore an even more powerful emotional charge, and writers and scholars who could articulate them enjoyed even more respected status. The whole dynamic of *glasnost* thus thrust ethnic factors to the centre of the stage. As we have seen in Chapter 14, intellectuals were already chafing at Muscovite rule during the seventies. *Glasnost* enabled them to go on and mobilize whole peoples behind them. What was previously suppressed surged powerfully to the fore, uniting people of disparate social backgrounds and career paths. An explosive realignment of loyalties and political structures was the result.

Each nation has its own flashpoint, and each Communist Party has reacted in its own way to the unwonted challenge offered. There has thus been a varied spectrum of demand and response in the different republics.

At the peaceful, yet also most radical end of the spectrum, were the Baltic republics. Aspirations voiced in the seventies only by dissenters were espoused by scientists and cultural activists, then by broader public organizations, and finally, albeit hesitantly and incompletely, by the local Communist Parties themselves. The pace differed somewhat in each republic, Estonia taking the lead, Latvia following closely behind, while Lithuania, less threatened by foreign immigration, brought up the rear.

Starting from environmental issues, public protest soon moved on to the fundamental grievance of all Balts: their annexation in 1940, and the subsequent deportation of the flower of their nations. Gathering momentum throughout 1987 and 1988, demonstrations began to mark the fateful anniversaries: Independence Day, the day of the deportations (14 June), and the Nazi-Soviet Pact. Grimly enthusiastic crowds demanded full *glasnost* about the events which had brought about their slavery.

As in Russia, the next stage was the creation of organizations and programmes. In June 1987 the Latvian Writers' Union convened a meeting of all the country's cultural unions, which despatched a specific and radical set of demands to the 19th Party Conference: Latvia should become a sovereign state with Latvian as its sole official language, acknowledging membership of the Soviet Union, but having its own seat at the United Nations, its own military units with Latvian as the language of command, running its own economy and reserving the right to restrict immigration of non-Latvians.

The response of the local Communist Parties to these demands was quite sensible, at least after personnel changes at the top. Realising that this programme had the overwhelming support of the indigenous population, they decided it would be prudent to compromise with it, in order both to avert an explosion and to head off more extreme demands. When, therefore, People's Fronts (known in Lithuania as Sajudis – the Movement) were created to mobilize popular support for the creative unions' proposals, the Communists sought dialogue with them, and adopted a large part of their programme as a mandate for the 19th Party Conference.

In all three republics the founding congresses of the People's Fronts, held during October 1988, turned into festivals of national rebirth. Anthems were sung by huge crowds, national flags which had been illegal for nearly half a century were once more hung from public buildings, and in Lithuania a packed service of national rededication was held in the Roman Catholic cathedral newly restored to the Church after forty years as a picture gallery.

The implications of these national revivals for the structure of the Soviet Union were unclear, and deliberately left so by both sides. By the autumn of 1988 Estonia, Latvia and Lithuania were asserting that the Nazi-Soviet Pact was null and void, as a crude violation of the norms of international relations, and that therefore they were sovereign nations who had agreed of their own free will to be members of the Soviet Union. They would need, however, to renegotiate the tacit treaty which bound them with the rest of the Union, and in this process nothing could be taken for granted: certainly not the 'leading role of the party', nor the right of Moscow to decide the laws or administer the economy of the Baltic nations. The Estonian Supreme Soviet explicitly asserted its right to reject Soviet legislation which displeased it.

These pretensions diverged so strikingly from previous theory and practice that they could not go uncontested. Moscow remained content for the time being with verbal refutations, though there was a period of tension in early 1989 when it seemed that the imposition of direct rule was being contemplated. More vigorous was the reaction of the non-indigenous (mainly Russian) inhabitants of the Baltic republics themselves, who constituted half the population in Latvia and not much less in Estonia. They began to forge their own counterparts to the Popular Fronts in the shape of 'International Fronts' or 'Unity Movements', protesting against proposed restrictions on immigration and upholding the right to continue using Russian in public life. They warned that the republics were arrogating to themselves powers which undermined the constitutional integrity of the Soviet Union, and that this trend was encouraging 'extremists' intriguing to detach the Baltic from the Union altogether.

By the spring of 1989 these movements were bringing large numbers of mostly Russian workers out on to the streets to parade with red hammer and sickle and protest against 'creeping counter-revolution'. They threatened to strike in the major industries in order to remind the Balts just how weighty was the contribution of the non-indigenous peoples to their economies. The International Fronts are of great significance as the first popular movement to defend the status quo against the changes wrought by perestroika. In the emergent era of mass politics they could turn out to be as important a catalyst as were the Ulster Unionists in the politics of early twentieth-century Britain.

In Armenia, a nation over the centuries uprooted and scattered between various empires, the most deeply-felt issue is Nagorny Karabakh, a mountainous and pastoral region traditionally populated mainly by Armenians, but incorporated into the Azerbaidjan Republic by a decision of Narkomnats in 1921. The ethnic affront of this incorporation is deepened by the way in which, in a one-party state, administrative subordination affects all aspects of life: the allocation of housing, jobs, education and economic projects all tends to favour the Azerbaidjani minority. In 1988 the resentment burst into the open. A Karabakh Committee was formed, consisting mainly of writers, scholars and journalists, as well as of officials acting in a private capacity. It placed branches in factories, offices and educational establishments – rather like the Communist Party, and in rivalry to it. It brought at least half a million people out on to the streets of Erevan in February, demanding the return of Karabakh to the Armenian Republic. It pushed a similar resolution through the Armenian Supreme Soviet.

The response of the Azerbaidjanis was immediate and violent: in the industrial town of Sumgait, on the shore of the Caspian Sea, dozens, possibly hundreds of Armenians were murdered in a pogrom which went on for two days, with what many Armenians thought was the connivance of the local Azerbaidjani authorities. Moscow's response was more measured, but also negative. It eventually declared direct rule of Karabakh from Moscow, and sent troops in to patrol Erevan and protect minorities fleeing from their homes. It used the confusion caused by the devastating earthquake of December 1988 to arrest the eleven leading members of the Karabakh Committee, only to bow to popular pressure and release them again in June 1989.

The Georgians had no single overwhelming issue like that of Karabakh, but rather an accumulation of gnawing grievances: the threat from neglect and misuse to their ancient monasteries, the increasing use of the Russian language for official purposes, the immigration of Russians, the destruction of the Aragvi valley by construction work on the projected Caucasian Mountain Railway, pollution caused by the Baku oil refinery, and the anti-Georgian separatism of some of the minorities within their own republic, especially the Abkhaz. The Communist Party failed to respond constructively to any of these grievances, so that there was a steady drift in public opinion towards the irreconcilable end of the Georgian political spectrum: the Society of Ilya Chavchavadze (named after a late nineteenth-century writer now thought to have been murdered by the Bolsheviks) and the National Democratic Party, who proclaimed that 'the revival of Georgian independence would set right a great historical injustice. It is worth living, fighting and dying for that.'

In April 1989 the National Democrats brought hundreds of thousands of people out on to the streets of Tbilisi and instituted all-night vigils, backed by hunger strikes, calling for independence from the Soviet Union. The demonstrations were peaceful, if unwontedly trenchant in their demands, yet special Ministry of the Interior riot troops were flown in, while more and more ordinary Georgians surged out into the streets and squares to protect the hunger strikers. Early on the morning of 9 April, it is not known on whose orders, army and MVD troops dispersed the crowds forcibly, using clubs and sharpened spades. Some reports speak of drunken soldiers 'butchering women and girls with military shovels'. The authorities admitted that 19 people were killed, while Georgians maintain that the figures were much higher; more than 200 people were injured. It was the worst act of violence inflicted by the Soviet authorities on their own people since Novocherkassk in 1962.

In the Central Asian republics Brezhnev's 'trust in cadres' had helped to consolidate a still semi-feudal political system, in which local leaders built up networks of patronage, promoting their own acquaintances, local favourites or extended families, while keeping Moscow happy with inflated figures for cotton output and the learning of Russian. Old-style nepotism combined with the nomenklatura system and the planned economy to create formidable edifices of corruption which some observers have compared to the mafia. Local party leaders embezzled money from Moscow for non-existent cotton production and diverted the proceeds to stimulate whole branches of the black economy which both remedied shortages of goods and services and also provided lucrative jobs for favourites.

This system kept the whole region quiet, but had seriously damaging effects. It increasingly isolated Central Asia from the rest of the Union, as the figures for intermarriage and immigration showed in the censuses of 1970 and 1979: outsiders felt unwelcome there, while Central Asians themselves were reluctant to quit the security of tribal protectionism to take up jobs going begging elsewhere in the country. Moreover, since favours were dispensed along ethnic lines, the corruption kept relations between nationalities tense. Russians in particular tended to be excluded from the networks and to feel discriminated against. Worst of all, the rapacious and wasteful use of water to irrigate cotton depleted the Amu-Darya and Syr-Darya rivers, lowering the water level of the Aral Sea and allowing salty marsh and desert to encroach on its banks. This environmental degradation endangered the supply of clean drinking water and threatened to alter the whole climate of the region, with deleterious effects for the cotton on whose behalf the irrigation had been undertaken in the first place.

Attempts to root out the corruption began under Andropov in 1983, and by late 1986 all five republican first party secretaries had been replaced, while criminal investigations were being conducted into their affairs and those of their subordinates. These proceeded with great difficulty, probably because it transpired that the tentacles of corruption stretched to Moscow itself, as was demonstrated in the trial of Brezhnev's son-in-law, Yury Churbanov.

Local resistance to this alien inquisition burst out in December 1986, when Kunaev, first party secretary in Kazakhstan, was dismissed and replaced by a Russian, Gennady Kolbin. Why Gorbachev permitted himself this egregious violation of the custom that the top party job should go to a local is not clear: perhaps he could not find a Kazakh whom he could trust to root out corruption. At any rate the affront provoked two days of rioting in the Kazakh capital, Alma-Ata, starting among students, who are the most nationally conscious element and also the most vulnerable to any undermining of ethnic protectionism.

Much worse communal violence erupted in the summer of 1989 in a number of areas of Central Asia. The most serious was in the Fergana valley, a fertile cotton-growing area of Uzbekistan. Uzbek youths in half a dozen towns attacked the homes of Meskhetians, deported there in 1944 by Stalin and never permitted to return home. Economic uncertainty aggravated by the abandonment of the Siberian rivers project had intensified the competition for jobs and official favours, and revived old resentments about having an alien people dumped in their midst. The violence was unleashed by a dispute about the price of strawberries in the market, where Meskhetians are adept traders: it exemplifies the way in which economic grievances can often be superimposed on ethnic ones. Some observers suggested that the Uzbek youths were unusually well armed, perhaps by elements in the local mafia. At any rate, in the end MVD special troops had to be flown in to protect and evacuate Meskhetians after at least a hundred people had lost their lives.

Although Popular Fronts have made their appearance in the Central Asian republics, they have not gained the popularity which has come their way in the European parts of the Soviet Union, perhaps because ethnic feeling there is still semi-tribal rather than civic in nature. It is striking, too, that communal violence has so far mainly been directed against immediate neighbours, often fellow Muslims, rather than against Russians or other Europeans.

In Bielorussia and Ukraine the closeness of the local peoples to the Russians has affected the evolution of the national movements. Russians like to consider both peoples as honorary members of their own nation who happen to speak a different 'dialect'. Taken together, the three Slav peoples make up a bloc consisting of nearly three-quarters of the Soviet population, whereas Russians on their own constitute barely a half. Accordingly, the Soviet state has encouraged a policy of quiet Russification, using parents' natural inclination to send their children to Russian-language schools, where they will get accustomed to speaking the imperial language fluently.

In Ukraine, the erosion of the language was taken up as a campaign in 1987 by the Writers' Union, and it soon joined with other sensitive issues, like the environment – especially keenly felt after the Chernobyl explosion – the persecution of the Uniate Church, and the 'blank spots' of Ukrainian history and culture, meaning not just Stalin's brutality but the way in which Russians had for centuries slighted the distinctiveness of Ukraine.

So far things had developed much as in the Baltic. The next stage should have been the formation of a Popular Front. But here the Ukrainian authorities, led by Shcherbitsky, the last survivor from Brezhnev's Politburo, took a totally different line from their Baltic counterparts. Unable to imprison national activists for long spells, as they had done in the seventies, they harassed them and forbade their meetings, or detained them for brief periods on minor charges. Even so, after a big ecological rally in Kiev in November 1988, an initiative group met, including representatives from the Writers' Union and informal associations. They managed to publish a draft programme for a Popular Front in the Writers' Union weekly (presumably the only paper that would carry it). It was similar to the equivalent Baltic documents, giving support to perestroika and calling for 'genuine sovereignty for Ukraine', the full range of human rights, a self-managed economy and the 'granting of the status of state language in the Ukrainian SSR to Ukrainian'. 'The practice of parental free choice in the language of education . . . leads,' it added, 'to national nihilism.'

Because of the authorities' attitude, however, the Ukrainians have not yet been able to hold a full republican congress of the Popular Front. Here the Bielorussians have got in ahead of them, though their own Communist Party is no more favourably disposed. Much of the impetus for the expression of national feeling in Bielorussia has derived from the language question, the nuclear fallout from Chernobyl (much of which fell directly on Bielorussia), and from the discovery of a mass grave of Stalin's victims in the Kurapaty Woods outside Minsk. An informal society called 'Martyrology' was set up to promote the idea of a memorial to them, and to call for a public commission to carry out an independent investigation of Stalin's crimes in Bielorussia.

Together with other informal groups, Martyrology organized an anti-Stalin demonstration in Minsk in October 1988, but the authorities sent in riot police with truncheons, tear gas and water cannon to disperse it. Hereupon all-Union *glasnost* came to the rescue: Vasil Bykau, Bielorussia's leading writer, wrote an article of protest in the Moscow press, and the Bielorussian Writers' Union announced that it would accept signatures at its premises from anyone who wished to register as members of the 'Renewal' Popular Front. The Lithuanians also rallied round, and offered premises for Renewal to hold its first national congress in June 1989.

This is not the only example of cooperation among the national movements of the Soviet Union. A coordinating committee was set up in June 1988, and by early 1989 it represented all the major nations except the Muslims and – the Russians. The committee addressed an appeal 'To the Russian Intelligentsia', accusing them of not having 'grasped the primary axiom of democracy: nations cannot be free if they oppress others, or if they serve as instruments of such oppression.'

The Russians are in a strange and frustrating position, since, while their language and culture is indeed used as an 'instrument of oppression', they nevertheless *feel* like a minority discriminated against almost as much as the other nations. Their language is not in danger, but otherwise they have analogous complaints to all the other nations in the Union about the degradation of their environment, the undermining of their culture, religion, history and traditional way of life. In one or two respects, they have more to complain of: they have no Communist Party, national capital or Academy of Sciences distinct from those of the Soviet Union as a whole. This is a direct result of the hybrid nature of the first constitution of the Union (see pages 117–18) and its subsequent manipulation by the Communists.

The advent of perestroika has in some ways heightened the paradoxical inferiority complex of the Russians. The vague and brooding sense of being victimized has been sharpened both by the revelations of *glasnost* and by the surge of anti-Russian feeling in the other republics. It was well articulated by the writer Valentin Rasputin, who suggested at the Congress of People's Deputies that there was an anti-Russian conspiracy afoot, and asked sarcastically if the Russian Republic should perhaps secede from the Soviet Union.

Not much in their education has prepared today's Russians to diagnose the true reasons for the repression they have suffered in what to outsiders looks like their own empire, and so they tend to put the blame on the Communist Party's traditional scapegoats, the 'imperialists', or even to revive the bogies of pre-revolutionary Russian nationalism, the Freemasons and the Jews. The Russians' own movement for the protection of the environment and historical monuments, *Pamyat* (Memory), was soon hijacked by those eager to blame the Jews for all the wrongs suffered. The *Pamyat* manifesto poses defiantly the questions which genuinely trouble many Russians: 'Who has defiled our history and culture? Who has been undermining our economy and devastating our agriculture all this time? Who has been destroying the nation with ideological and alcoholic drugs?' The members of *Pamyat* parade in black shirts, embroidered with a bell, the symbol of the ancient Russian folk assembly, the *veche*. At some of its meetings excerpts have been read from the *Protocols of the Elders of Zion*, the tsarist police forgery which purported to show how a Jewish conspiracy was planning to achieve dominion over the whole world and rule it through a mixture of coercion, propaganda and secret police informers. Ironically, this nightmare vision is not a bad approximation to the realities of the totalitarian state, which is doubtless why such a fabrication retains its hold over today's listeners.

Pamyat has supporters in high places, otherwise it would not be allowed to publish its materials in the press, nor does it enjoy the wholehearted patronage of the Communist Party: it is too disreputable (indeed probably illegal in its propaganda of racial hatred) and too divisive. The more temperate face of Russian nationalism is that of the 'revivalists' (see pages 421–2), who have their stronghold in the Writers Union of the RFSFR and in the journal *Nash sovremennik* (Our Contemporary). The 'revivalists' accept the need for free speech and a radical critique of the past – indeed they were the most forthright exponents of such a critique during the seventies – but they warn of the 'excesses' of Western culture – pop music, pornography and commercialism – riding in on the back of perestroika. They are also suspicious of the free market schemes proposed by the radical economists, fearing that they will lead to social polarization, impoverishment and a loss of community spirit. What they propose instead is akin to the ideas of Schumacher or the Green Parties of Western Europe: 'civilised cooperatives', drawing on the traditions of the Russian peasant commune and working man's artel.

The danger for Russian patriots is that, in fending off the excesses of free speech and the market economy, they will throw themselves into the arms of the leviathan state whose works they themselves revile. Apparatchiks under pressure and looking for mass support have much to gain from a tacit alliance with them, together with the International Fronts in the non-Russian republics, and a nod and a wink in the direction of *Pamyat*. Such a conservative bloc has considerable potential in the age of *glasnost*, for it offers alluring if unsatisfactory solutions to the ethnic and economic problems which beset the leadership.

The ethnic tensions would be much easier to resolve if the Soviet economy were performing more strongly. Taking his

cue from the Novosibirsk report, Gorbachev has tried to
decentralize the command system in industry by reducing the
number of compulsory output targets and granting more
decision-making power to individual enterprises, giving them
the power to conclude contracts with each other and with
customers rather than always gearing their production to the
instructions of the ministries. He has also closed down the
Central Committee departments once responsible for detailed
monitoring of the economy, and reduced the industrial
ministries. In practice, however, it transpires that the
remaining ministries are well able to rephrase what used to
be their commands into contractual orders, leaving the
enterprises – who in any case have absolutely no experience
of seeking their own customers – to carry on as before.

In agriculture, too, though Bukharin has been rehabilitated
and individual households are permitted to rent plots of land
for up to fifty years, there has been no resolute disavowal of
the collective principle. Kolkhozniks have been slow to
respond to the invitation to become farmers, partly because
collective farms and local authorities are reluctant to lease
them land, and partly because they themselves have no
experience of independent husbandry. Even more important,
probably, is the government's failure to demonstrate whole-
hearted commitment to private agriculture: villagers have
seen the party's agricultural policy change many times, and
are unlikely to gamble their future on private smallholdings
until they are convinced the authorities mean to give them
unswerving support. To inspire such conviction, it would be
necessary to slim down the kolkhozy to something like West
European cooperatives, offering insurance, agrarian advice,
bulk purchasing and cheap credit, while the government
would have to free food prices and invest heavily in the rural
infrastructure of roads and schools and the like. Probably
only such a demonstrative package of measures could end the
decades of rural demoralization and depopulation, and
restore confidence to those who have to produce the food.
This is crucial to Gorbachev's reform programme, since most

of the population will assess him not least by what they can buy in their groceries.

Gorbachev's other major economic innovation, the introduction of cooperatives (essentially private enterprise) in the field of retailing and services, has had somewhat more success, but in a manner which has proved unsettling for the economy as a whole. In many towns restaurants have appeared, along with hairdressers, fruit and vegetable stalls, motor repair workshops and so on, where supplies are more reliable and the quality usually better than in the state sector – but then the prices are three or four times higher. Many Soviet citizens use their services, having cash to spare and not much to spend it on, but they resent the profiteering. This is not just sullen Russian egalitarianism. Cooperative traders are operating in conditions of extreme scarcity and are able, therefore, to get away with charging high prices. Probably they exacerbate that scarcity by entering into corrupt deals with officials in the material-technical supply sector of the planned economy. In short, the new private economy is conspiring with the old sclerotic public one to aggravate the shortages and profit by them. The frustrations thus bred in the public often take ethnic forms when, as often happens, customer and trader are of different nationality.

As with agriculture, the uneasy situation of the cooperatives is partly the fault of the government's half-heartedness. Until they can operate in a stable framework of rational prices, private property, contract law, commercial banks and a stock exchange, cooperatives will continue to behave in a grasping and semi-criminal manner, anxious to secure quick profit as an insurance against the unknown future.

Overall, there is not much doubt that the early stages of reform have made the economic situation worse. Many everyday stock items like sausage meat, cheese and soap are now rationed in most Soviet cities, an indignity not suffered since the immediate post-war years. Nor has the government yet taken measures which seem adequate to overcome the difficulties.

Of itself the economic problem may not be enough to endanger Gorbachev's position, but it strengthens the people's impression, gained over decades, that the authorities promise more than they can deliver, that they are unable or unwilling to disrupt vested interests sufficiently to bring about real and lasting change. This certainly seemed to be the reason for the first serious outbreak of labour unrest since Khrushchev's time, which erupted in the Kuzbass coalfields in July 1989 and then spread to the Donbass and elsewhere. As usual in Soviet labour disputes, the miners presented a whole repertoire of demands, embracing not just pay and working conditions, but covering also housing, recreation, social welfare, medical provision and food supplies. The common factor in their demands was resentment of the apparatus's privileged way of life and distrust of its promises. The miners by-passed the official trade unions and formed their own strike committees, which patrolled the streets during the strike, maintaining order and keeping alcohol out. Furthermore, in many pits they demanded the right to participate in management, and to take decisions about how the revenue earned there should be spent.

Gorbachev supported most of the workers' demands, indeed could claim to be endeavouring to achieve them. At the same time he recognised that paralysis of a major source of energy would be crippling to the whole economy and therefore also to his reform programme, and he televised several appeals to the miners to return to work. They probably realised that to weaken Gorbachev would be to negate any hope of serious improvement, and reluctantly drifted back to their pits.

The place of the industrial workers in the emergent political constellation is crucial. Of course, they have a long-term interest in the fulfilment of Gorbachev's reforms, and in the greater freedom, self-management and prosperity that should result. But in the shorter term, they have much to fear from the intermediate stages of perestroika: shortages, higher prices and the possibility of becoming unemployed. If in fear of these they join the conservative bloc I have sketched above, they will constitute a formidable contribution to the forces resisting change. No doubt that is why Gorbachev tried to appeal to them over the heads of the apparatus.

The ambiguities of Gorbachev's political system were well summed up in the sessions of the new Congress of People's Deputies in May and June 1989. It convened without its procedures or even its functions fully defined, and this lack of clarity enabled Gorbachev repeatedly to act as the decisive arbiter, which he did in a virtuoso display of the new 'presidential democracy'. But it also enabled Andrei Sakharov to propose that the Congress should itself assume the function of drafting and debating new laws, instead of delegating it to a haphazardly chosen one-fifth of its membership in the Supreme Soviet.

In the elections to the Congress, the complexities of the nomination procedure ensured that nomenklatura candidates were usually elected. But the exceptions were unexpected and conspicuous. In a few towns Popular Fronts and other informal associations proved sufficiently well organised to convince people that an anti-establishment vote was worth casting. In Leningrad, where Yury Solovyov, an alternate member of the Politburo, failed to gain the minimum 50 per cent of votes required by an unopposed candidate, demonstrations were held with placards reading 'If there is only one name on the list, cross it out!' In the Baltic the Popular Fronts more or less determined the outcome of the ballot, and only official candidates receiving their endorsement were elected. In Moscow popular discontent found a convincing spokesman in the person of Boris Eltsin (ousted from the Politburo eighteen months earlier for excessive radicalism), who achieved a poll of 90 per cent in defeating the party's official nominee.

The elections showed that public resentment at the nomenklatura elite was widespread and waiting to be mobilized. They gave considerable moral authority to those deputies prepared to take an oppositional stance in the

Congress itself. Official candidates were nevertheless in the majority and dominated proceedings in what was supposed to be the main business of the Congress, the election of the head of state and of the Supreme Soviet.

If one believes, however, with John Stuart Mill, that one of the main functions of a representative assembly is to educate the public and stimulate political debate, then there is no doubt that the Congress was a triumph for the opposition. It was televised live from beginning to end, and many people stayed off work to watch it. They saw a concentrated display of information about all sides of Soviet life, such as not even the new-style press had vouchsafed to them before. They saw generals interrogated on their crowd control methods, ministers grilled on their fitness for office, government policies roundly questioned, and even Gorbachev himself criticized for his frequent interventions.

Overall both the Congress and the preceding elections gave the Soviet public new confidence in their ability to affect political processes, and a higher level of information with which to do so. These gains almost certainly helped to impel the miners to undertake the strikes which followed shortly after. They make any eventual recourse to authoritarian rule both more expensive and more uncertain. The apparatus retains control over the levers of power, and over the legislative process, but it faces for the first time a more or less coherent opposition bloc, led by Boris Eltsin, which has a lot of support from a well-informed public and from most of the informal associations. There remain marked disagreements over priorities between the Russian and non-Russian radicals, but what unites this opposition is the demand to abolish article 6 of the constitution, on the 'leading role of the party', and recognition that the government should be answerable to the Congress of People's Deputies and to the Supreme Soviets of the Union Republics.

In the few short years he has been in power, Gorbachev has in one sense transformed the Soviet scene beyond recognition. He has encouraged or at least tolerated the emergence of a limited political pluralism and of freedom of discussion which is beginning to reach those sacred objects of the Soviet tabernacle, Lenin and the October revolution. Yet the party's monopoly, broken now in culture and ideology, has still not been fully shaken off in the political and economic spheres. The formerly tight ship run by the apparatus through its nomenklatura patronage system is storm-tossed and leaking in places, but still very much afloat and ready to repel boarders.

Gorbachev has tried to return to the humanist principles which once underlay Marxism. Yet he himself is the child of a political apparatus whose main preoccupations are to maintain its grip on power and to strengthen the Soviet Union as a great power. He came to office at a time when those two aims were becoming incompatible, and this compelled him to reopen all political issues. He has taken Lenin as his guide, and in doing so has begun to unravel the solutions which Lenin devised to the dilemmas which faced *him*.

To a greater extent than is usually realised, Lenin was a divided personality. He shared with previous Russian revolutionaries the belief in a humane and democratic future society. Where he differed from them was in hard-headed realism and the determination to achieve power at all costs. He craved a historical theory which would provide absolute certainty, and in Marxism he thought he had found it. 'Marxism is all-powerful because it is *true*', as he was fond of repeating. The unacknowledged and ultimately incongruous mixture of science and prophecy in Marxism was exactly what appealed to Lenin, and to solve the mismatch between them he invented the 'party' as a hierarchical and disciplined organization dedicated to exercising power in the name of a proletariat which could never do so.

The 'party', though not inconsistent with the European Marxist tradition, was an important addition to it. It was able to appropriate the 'Soviet' revolution of 1917 and thereafter to substitute itself for the workers, and indeed for the people as a whole, deriving legitimacy from them, but exercising power in such a way as to trample their interests underfoot.

This is the fateful process which Gorbachev is trying to reverse, taking as his lodestar the Lenin of the years 1921–4, when, free from the responsibilities of war (and, towards the end, of political power itself), he was able to reflect on the system he had created. Lenin knew that something had gone seriously wrong and, although he was incapable of diagnosing the underlying causes of the malaise – indeed he made things worse by increasing the authority of the Central Committee – the works of his last years are full of warnings against bureaucratism, Communist arrogance, chauvinism and the fascination with administrative solutions to all problems.

Gorbachev has proved much more effective than Lenin at acting on these warnings. He has understood as Lenin never did the importance of mobilizing the forces of society against the party apparatus. He has tried to secure the bases of his authority both in the party and in the public by setting up the new elective legislative assemblies. He is endeavouring to dominate both, and yet also give both their freedom. He wants to use them as a weapon against the party without allowing them to supplant the party as the leading force in politics. It has been a dazzling display of Soviet-style Bonapartism whose outcome at the moment is unforeseeable.

One thing seems to me certain, however. Even if Gorbachev is overthrown, or is forced to trim back perestroika severely, one day his reforms will have to be resumed. They represent the only hope of a happier future for the peoples of the Soviet Union, and also the only way in which the country can maintain anything like its present influence in the world. The human and material resources for a prosperous, humane future are present in abundance: the Soviet Union *could* be the 'economic miracle' of the twenty-first century. But first the transformation of the political system, now at last boldly undertaken, needs to be carried through to completion.

Chronology

1917

Feb.	February revolution; formation of Petrograd Soviet
Mar.	Abdication of Nicholas II; formation of Provisional Government
Apr.	Lenin's return to Russia
June	1st All-Russian Congress of Soviets
	Kerensky's offensive
July	July days in Petrograd
Aug.	Kornilov coup
Oct.	October revolution; 2nd All-Russian Congress of Soviets
	Decrees on peace, land
Nov.	Declaration on the Rights of the Peoples of Russia
	Decree on workers' control
Dec.	Armistice on German front
	Creation of Cheka
	Creation of Vesenkha
	Finland proclaims independence

1918

Jan.	Constituent Assembly
	Ukrainian Rada declares independence
	Creation of Red Army
	Legislation on 'separation of church and state'; Patriarch Tikhon anathematizes the Bolshevik regime
Feb.	(1st/14th) Introduction of Gregorian calendar
Mar.	Treaty of Brest-Litovsk
	7th Party Congress
	Extraordinary Assembly of Delegates from Works and Factories
	Bielorussia declares independence
May	Georgia, Armenia, Azerbaidjan declare independence
July	Socialist Revolutionary rising in Moscow and elsewhere
Aug.	Whites capture Kazan
Sept.	Red Terror declared
Nov.	German withdrawal from occupied Russian territory
	Kolchak seizes power in Omsk
	Muslim Communist Party merged with Russian Communist Party

1919

Mar. 8th Party Congress; creation of Politburo and Orgburo
Oct.   Denikin reaches Orel, and Yudenich the suburbs of Petrograd

1920

Mar. 9th Party Congress
Apr. Poland invades the Ukraine
Aug. Red Army fails to take Warsaw
       Outbreak of Tambov peasant insurrection
Oct.   Polish–Soviet armistice
Nov. Red Army defeats Wrangel in Crimea
Dec. Central Committee directive on Proletkult

1921

Feb. Creation of Gosplan
       Red Army invades Georgia
       Workers' unrest in Petrograd
Mar. Kronstadt revolt
       10th Party Congress; birth of NEP
       Treaty of Riga with Poland

1921–2 Famine on the Volga; government demands surrender of church
            valuables for famine relief

1922

Feb.   Cheka reorganized as GPU
Mar.–Apr. 11th Party Congress; Stalin becomes General Secretary
Apr.   House arrest of Patriarch Tikhon
June–July Trial and execution of Metropolitan Veniamin
Aug.   Capture of Enver Pasha
Dec.   Formation of Union of Soviet Socialist Republics

1923

Apr. 12th Party Congress
       First *sobor* of Living Church

July   USSR Constitution published
Summer   'Scissors crisis'

1924

Jan.   Death of Lenin
May   13th Party Congress

1925

Jan.   Trotsky dismissed as war commissar
Apr.   14th Party Conference; 'socialism in one country' accepted
June   Central Committee resolution on literature

1926

Oct.   Trotsky expelled from Politburo

1927

May   Rupture of diplomatic relations with Britain; war scare
Dec.   15th Party Congress; collectivization of agriculture
        resolved

1928

Spring Grain procurement crisis
May   Shakhty trial
July   Central Committee sent the first batch of 'thousanders' to col-
        lege
Oct.   Beginning of 1st Five Year Plan (to Dec. 1932)

1929

Apr.   Law on 'religious associations'
Autumn Start of forced mass collectivization and dekulakization
Nov.   Bukharin expelled from Politburo; defeat of Right Opposition

1930

Mar.   Stalin's *Pravda* article, 'Dizzy with success'
Apr.   Suicide of Mayakovsky
Nov.–Dec. Trial of 'Industrial Party'

1931

Mar.   Trial of Mensheviks

1932

Apr.   Central Committee resolution 'on the reformation of literary-
          artistic organizations'
Second Ryutin's programme circulates in the Central Committee
half
Oct.   Opening of Dneprostroi hydro-electric scheme
Dec.   Introduction of internal passport and *propiska*

1932–4 Famine in Ukraine and elsewhere

1933–7 2nd Five Year Plan

1933

May   Opening of Belomor Canal

1934

Jan.   17th Party Congress
July   GPU reorganized as NKVD
Aug.   1st Congress of Union of Soviet Writers
Dec.   Assassination of Kirov

1935

Jan.   Death of Kuibyshev

Feb.   Model collective farm statute
Aug.   Introduction of 'Stakhanovite' labour
Sept.   Reintroduction of ranks in Red Army

1936

Feb.   Communist Academy absorbed into Academy of
        Sciences
June   Death of Gorky
        New family law, making divorce more difficult
Aug.   Trial of Zinoviev, Kamenev and others
Sept.   Yezhov succeeds Yagoda as head of NKVD
Dec.   Promulgation of 'Stalin Constitution'

1937

Jan.   Trial of Radek, Pyatakov and others
Feb.   Death of Ordjonikidze
May–June Dismissal, arrest, trial and execution of Tukhachevsky
        Powers of Red Army political commissars restored

1938–   3rd Five Year Plan
June 1941

1938

        Stalin's *Short Course* published
Mar.   Trial of Bukharin, Rykov, Krestinsky, Rakovsky, Yagoda and
        others
Dec.   Introduction of 'labour book' for workers
        Beria succeeds Yezhov as head of NKVD

1939

Mar.   18th Party Congress
Aug.   Nazi–Soviet Pact
Sept.   Invasion of Eastern Poland
Nov.   Outbreak of Finnish war

1940

          Closure of *rabfaki*
Mar.   Peace concluded with Finland
June   Annexation of Baltic states
Aug.   Absenteeism at work made a criminal offence
          Assassination of Trotsky in Mexico
Oct.   Introduction of fees for higher and upper secondary education

1941

22 June German invasion of USSR
30 June GKO established
3 July Stalin's first broadcast
Sept.   Beginning of Leningrad blockade
          Fall of Kiev
Oct.   Moscow in direct danger; partial evacuation of the city
Dec.   Wehrmacht thrown back from Moscow

1942

Sept.   Wehrmacht reaches Stalingrad
Oct.   Restoration of officers' full status in Red Army
Nov.   Soviet offensive encircles German 6th Army in
            Stalingrad

1943

Jan.   Surrender of German 6th Army in Stalingrad
          Vlasov's Smolensk proclamation
July   Battle of Kursk
Sept.   Re-establishment of Patriarchate

1944

Jan.   Leningrad blockade finally lifted
June   'Second front' established in France
Aug.–Oct. Warsaw rising
Sept.   Vlasov establishes KONR

1945

Feb.   Yalta conference
            Election of Patriarch Alexei
9 May   Surrender of Germany
July–Aug. Potsdam conference

1946–50 4th Five Year Plan

1946

Aug.   Central Committee decree attacking Akhmatova and Zosh-
        chenko
        Central Committee decree establishing network of
          party high schools
Sept.   Decree 'on measures to liquidate breaches of the
          kolkhoz statute'

1946–7 Famine in the Ukraine

1947

Sept.   Establishment of Cominform
Dec.   Currency reform

1948

Jan.   Murder of Mikhoels
Feb.   Communist coup in Czechoslovakia
June   Yugoslavia expelled from Cominform
Aug.   Lysenko's victory at the Agricultural Academy
           Death of Zhdanov
Autumn   Disappearance of Voznesensky; Leningrad purge
Nov.   Dissolution of Jewish Anti-Fascist Committee

1948–9 Collectivization of agriculture in Baltic region

1949 Closure of Jewish State Theatre in Moscow

1950

June Stalin's article on linguistics, attacking Marr
July Law on workers' councils in Yugoslavia

1951–5 5th Five Year Plan

1952

Oct. 19th Party Congress

1953

Jan. Discovery of 'doctors' plot' announced
Mar. Death of Stalin; Malenkov becomes prime minister
May Revolt in Norilsk labour camp
July Arrest (and execution?) of Beria; revolt in Vorkuta labour camp
Sept. Khrushchev confirmed as first secretary of CPSU

1954

Pospelov Commission begins investigation of Stalin's
repressions
May Revolt in Kengir labour camp

1954–6 Height of 'virgin lands' campaign

1955

Feb. Bulganin replaces Malenkov as Prime Minister
May Establishment of Warsaw Pact
Khrushchev and Bulganin visit Yugoslavia

1956

Feb.   20th Party Congress; Khrushchev's 'secret speech'
Apr.   Criminal liability for absenteeism at work abolished
June   Workers' riots in Poznań, Poland
        Fees for higher and upper secondary education
            abolished
Oct.   Gomulka becomes first secretary of Polish United Workers'
            Party
        General strike and street demonstrations in Budapest
Nov.   Soviet intervention in Hungary; Kadar becomes first secretary
            of Hungarian Workers' Party

1957

June   Central Committee plenum backs Khrushchev against 'anti-
            party group'
Oct.   Zhukov dismissed as defence minister

1958

Feb.   Khrushchev replaces Bulganin as prime minister
Oct.   Pasternak awarded Nobel Prize for literature
Dec.   Publication of new criminal code
        Educational reforms promulgated

1959–65 Seven Year Plan

1959

        Khrushchev launches maize campaign
Sept.   Workers' unrest in Temirtau (Kazakhstan)

1960

May   Death of Pasternak

1961

Closure of Monastery of the Caves, Kiev
Apr.   First manned Soviet space flight
        First arrests at Mayakovsky Square unofficial poetry readings
July   Legislation restricting role of priest in parish councils
Oct.   22nd Party Congress; new party programme; Stalin removed
        from mausoleum

1962

June   Workers' strikes and rioting in Novocherkassk
Oct.   Cuban missile crisis
Nov.   Publication of Solzhenitsyn's *A Day in the Life of Ivan Deniso-*
        vich

1963

Mar.   Khrushchev addresses Writers' Union, warning of 'bourgeois
        influences'
Autumn Very poor harvest

1964

Apr.   Fire at the Ukrainian Academy of Sciences
Oct.   Central Committee plenum; Brezhnev replaces Khrushchev as
        first secretary of CPSU

1965

Mar.   Central Committee plenum approves agricultural
        reforms
Sept.   Central Committee plenum approves Kosygin's economic re-
        forms
Dec.   Demonstration on Pushkin Square calling for observance of
        Soviet Constitution
        Eshliman and Yakunin criticize Council for Affairs of Church in
        letter to Supreme Soviet

1966–70 8th Five Year Plan

1966

Feb.   Trial of Sinyavsky and Daniel
Mar.   Demonstration by Baptist Initsiativniki at Supreme Soviet building in Moscow
      23rd Party Congress

1967

May   Andropov succeeds Semichastny as head of KGB
June   Arab–Israeli war

1968

Jan.   Trial of Ginsburg and Galanskov
      Dubček becomes first secretary of Czechoslovak Communist Party
Apr.   First issue of *Chronicle of Current Events*
Aug.   Warsaw Pact invasion of Czechoslovakia

1969

Jan.   Formation of Initiative Group for Defence of Civil Rights
July   Aliev replaces Akhundov as first secretary of Azerbaidjan CP

1970

      First issue of *Ukrainsky Visnik*
Feb.   Removal of Tvardovsky from editorship of *Novyi mir*
Mar.   Sakharov, Turchin and R. Medvedev write to Brezhnev
Apr.   First issue of Jewish samizdat journal *Exodus*
Dec.   Two Jews sentenced to death – then reprieved – in Leningrad for hijacking airliner
      Workers' rioting in Poland; Gierek replaces Gomulka as first secretary of Polish United Workers' Party

1971–5 9th Five Year Plan

1971

Feb.   Mass Jewish demonstration at Supreme Soviet building; beginning of large-scale Jewish emigration to Israel

Apr.   24th Party Congress

1972

    First issue of *Chronicle of Lithuanian Catholic Church*

Jan.   Widespread arrests and searches among Ukrainian intellectuals

May   Riots in Kaunas (Lithuania) following self-immolation of R. Kalanta

    Shcherbitsky replaces Shelest as first secretary of Ukrainian CP

Sept.   Shevardnadze replaces Mzhavanadze as first secretary of Georgian CP

1973

Apr.   Central Committee plenum; Andropov and Gromyko join Politburo

1974

Feb.   Deportation of Solzhenitsyn from USSR

1975

Aug.   Helsinki agreement on European Security and Cooperation

Oct.   Sakharov awarded Nobel Prize for peace

1976–80 10th Five Year Plan

1976

    Formation of Helsinki Watch Groups in various republics

Feb.–Mar. 25th Party Congress

Apr.	Ustinov becomes minister of defence
June	Workers' unrest in Poland
Sept.	Formation of KOR in Poland

1977

| June | Brezhnev replaces Podgorny as president of USSR |
| Nov. | New Soviet Constitution published |

1978

Apr.	Khalq coup in Afghanistan
	Street demonstrations in Tbilisi in defence of Georgian language
July	Trial of Shcharansky

1979

Jan.	Three 'Armenian nationalists' executed
Apr.	Brezhnev awarded Lenin Prize for literature
Dec.	Soviet military intervention in Afghanistan

1980

Jan.	Sakharov exiled to Gorky
July–Aug.	Olympic Games held in Moscow
Aug.	Workers' unrest in Gdańsk and elsewhere in Poland; formation of Solidarity
Oct.	Street demonstrations in Estonia
Dec.	Death of Kosygin; Tikhonov becomes prime minister

1981–5 11th Five Year Plan

1981

| Feb.–Mar. | 26th Party Congress |
| Dec. | Jaruzelski declares martial law in Poland |

1982

Jan.   Death of Suslov
May   Fedorchuk replaces Andropov as head of KGB;
        Andropov enters CP Secretariat
Sept.   Last Helsinki Watch Group disbanded
Nov.   Death of Brezhnev; Andropov becomes General Secretary of
        CPSU

1983

Aug.   Andropov falls seriously ill

1984

Feb.   Death of Andropov; Chernenko becomes General Secretary of
        CPSU
Dec.   Death of Marshal Ustinov

1985

Mar.   Death of Chernenko; Gorbachev becomes General Secretary of
        CPSU

1986–90 12th Five Year Plan

1986

Feb.   27th Party Congress
Apr.   Explosion at the Chernobyl nuclear power station
June   8th USSR Writers' Union Congress
Dec.   Riots in Alma-Ata
        Gorbachev releases Sakharov from administrative exile in
        Gorky

1987

July   New law on the 'socialist enterprise'
Aug.   Foundation of FSOK

1988

Feb.   Demonstrations in Armenia over Nagorny Karabakh
Mar.   Pogrom in Sumgait
Apr.   Gorbachev receives Patriarch Pimen
May   Formation of Democratic Union
June/July 19th Party Conference
Sept.   Gorbachev is elected President of the USSR
Dec.   Earthquake in Armenia

1989

Mar.   Elections to Congress of People's Deputies
Apr.   Soldiers forcibly disperse crowds in Tbilisi
May/June Congress of People's Deputies and first sessions of reformed
            Supreme Soviet
June   Riots in Fergana Valley and other parts of Central Asia
July   Coalminers' strike in Kuzbass, Donbass and elsewhere.

Statistical Tables

A gap indicates that no information is available.

A. Population of the Soviet Union (in millions)

1914	140.4	(estimate)
1926	147.0	
1939	170.5	
1940	194.1	(including newly annexed territories)
1950	178.5	
1959	208.8	
1970	241.7	
1979	262.4	
1989	286.7	

Sources: F. Lorimer, *The Population of the Soviet Union*, Geneva: League of Nations, 1946, pp. 36, 112. *Naselenie SSSR*, Moscow: Izdatel'stvo politicheskoi literatury, 1983, p. 8. *Current Digest of the Soviet Press*, vol 41, 1989, p. 17.

B. Class Composition of the Population, by official Soviet classification (in percentages)

	Workers	Individual peasants	Collective peasants	White collar	Bourgeoisie, landowners
1913	14.6	66.7	—	2.4	16.3
1924	10.4	75.4	1.3	4.4	8.5
1928	12.4	74.9	2.9	5.2	4.6
1939	33.7	2.6	47.2	16.5	—
1959	50.2	0.3	31.4	18.1	—
1970	57.4	—	20.5	22.1	—
1979	60.0	—	14.9	25.1	—
1987	61.8	—	12.0	26.2	—

Source: *Naselenie SSSR*, Moscow: Politizdat, 1980, p. 143. *Narodnoe Khozyaistvo SSSR za 70 let*, Moscow: Finansy i Statistika, 1987, p. 12.

C. Selected Indices of Industrial and Agricultural Production

	1913	1922	1928	1932	1940
Steel (m. tonnes)	4.3	0.3	4.0	5.9	18.3
Coal (m. tonnes)	29.2	11.3	35.4	64.3	165.9
Oil (m. tonnes)	10.3	4.7	11.7	21.4	31.1
Electricity (milliard Kw hours)	2.0	0.8	5.1	13.4	48.6
Automobiles (thousands)	—	—	0.8		145
Tractors (thousands)	—	—	1.3	48.9	31.6
Wool cloth (m. metres)	107.7	37	97	93.3	119.7
Leather footwear (m. pairs)	60	6.8	58	86.9	211
Overall:					
Industrial group A (capital goods: 1913 = 1)	1		1.55		13.4
Industrial group B (consumer goods: 1913 = 1)	1		1.2		4.6
Grain (m. tonnes)	76.5	50.3	73.3	69.6	95.6
Meat (m. tonnes)		2.2			4.7
Milk (m. tonnes)		24.5			33.6
Sugar (m. tonnes)	1.3	0.2	1.3	0.8	2.2
Cows (m. head)	24.9 (1916)		29.3	22.3	22.8
Pigs (m. head)	17.3		22.0	10.9	22.5

Note: There are strong grounds for treating Soviet economic production statistics with considerable scepticism, as I have indicated on pp. 202–3 and 382. Nevertheless, they can be useful for making very broad comparisons over time, or between one branch of the economy and another.

	1945	1950	1960	1970	1980	1986
Steel (m. tonnes)	12.3	27.3	65.3	116	148	161
Coal (m. tonnes)	149.3	261.1	510	624	716	751
Oil (m. tonnes)	19.4	37.9	148	353	603	615
Electricity (milliard Kw hours)	43.2	91.2	292	741	1294	1599
Automobiles (thousands)	74.7	363	524	916	2199	
Tractors (thousands)	14.7	109	239	459	555	595
Wool cloth (m. metres)	53.6	155.2	439	643	762	670
Leather footwear (m. pairs)	63	203	419	679	743	801
Overall:						
Industrial group A (capital goods: 1913 = 1)	15	27.5	89.4	213.8	391.4	493
Industrial group B (consumer goods: 1913 = 1)	2.7	5.7	15	30	49.8	63
Grain (m. tonnes)	47.3	81.2	126	186.8	189.1	210.1
Meat (m. tonnes)			8.7	12.3	15.1	18.0
Milk (m. tonnes)			61.7	83.0	90.9	102.2
Sugar (m. tonnes)	0.5	2.5	6.4	10.2	10.1	12.7
Cows (m. head)	22.9	24.6	34.8 (1961)	39.8 (1971)	43.3	42.9
Pigs (m. head)	10.6	22.2	58.7 (1961)	67.5 (1971)	73.9	77.8

Sources: A. Nove, *An Economic History of the USSR*, London: Allen Lane, 1969, pp. 14, 191, 387, 291. *Strana sovetov za 50 let: sbornik statisticheskikh materialov*, Moscow: Statistika, 1967, pp. 28–9, 51, 86. *Narodnoe khozyaistvo SSSR: statisticheskii sbornik*, Moscow: Gosudarstvennoe statisticheskoe izdatel'stvo, 1956, pp. 75, 85, 87, 91, 118. *Narodnoe khozyaistvo SSSR, 1922–87*, Moscow: Finansy i Statistika 1982, pp. 52–3, 271, 275; 1987, pp 5–6, 255.

D. Party Membership and Social Composition, according to the party's own classification

	Numbers (thousands)			Social origin (%)		
	Full members	Candidates	Total	Workers	Peasants	White collar
1921	733		733			
1924	350	122	472	44.0 (18.8)	28.8	27.2
1927	786	426	1212	55.1 (39.4)	27.3 (13.7)	17.6 (46.9)
1930	1185	493	1678	65.3 (46.3)	20.2 (12.0)	14.5 (41.7)
1935	1659	700	2359			
1940	1983	1417	3400			
1945	3966	1795	5760			
1950	5511	829	6340			
1956	6768	406	7174	32.0	17.1	50.9
1961	8472	803	9276	34.5	17.5	48.0
1966	11548	809	12357	37.8	16.2	46.0
1971	13810	645	14455	40.1	15.1	44.8
1976	15058	636	15694	41.6	13.9	44.5
1981			17430	43.4	12.8	43.8

Note: Figures in brackets reflect the members' current occupation, a category which the party ceased to report after 1932. Variable criteria were used in drawing up these categories, so the figures are not very reliable (see above, p. 144, and Rigby, pp. 158–63). Even so, the discrepancy between 'social origin' and 'current occupation' is striking.

Sources: T. Rigby, *Communist Party Membership in the USSR, 1917–67*, Princeton University Press, 1968, pp. 50–3, 116. *Current Digest of the Soviet Press*, vol. 28 (1976), no. 35, pp. 1–3; vol. 33 (1981), no. 38, pp. 1–3.

E. Educational Level of Party Members (in percentages)

	Higher	Secondary	Incomplete secondary	Primary
1919	5.0	8.0		87.0
1922	0.6	6.3		92.7
1927	0.8	7.9		91.3
1939	5.1	14.2		
1947	6.3	20.5	23.7	49.5
1956	11.2	25.8	29.6	33.4
1961	13.3	29.6	28.6	28.5
1965	15.0	32.7	27.9	24.4
1971	19.6	36.7	24.9	18.8
1976	24.3	41.0	20.3	14.4
1981	28.0	44.1	17.1	10.8

Sources: T. Rigby, *Communist Party Membership in the USSR, 1917–67*, Princeton University Press, 1968, p. 401. *Current Digest of the Soviet Press*, vol. 28 (1976), no. 35, pp. 1–3; vol. 33 (1981), no. 38, pp. 1–3.

F. Social Welfare Expenditure

	1940	1950	1955	1960	1965	1970	1975	1980	1986
Total (milliard rubles)	4.6	13.0	16.4	27.3	41.9	63.9	90.1	117	155
Per capita (rubles per annum)	24	72.8	84.4	128.5	182.5	264.4	354	441	554
of which (in milliard rubles):									
Welfare payments and social insurance	0.9	5.8	7.2	13.5	14.4	22.8	34.6	45.6	65.8
Education	2.0	4.4	5.2	7.3	13.2	18.7	25.1	31.6	39.4
Health care	1.0	2.2	3.1	5.0	6.9	10.0	12.9	17.2	20.9
Housing subsidies	0.1	0.5	0.7	1.2	2.3	3.4	4.9	6.9	9.8

Sources: A. McAuley, *Economic Welfare in the Soviet Union*, University of Wisconsin Press, 1979, p. 262 (partly calculated from); *Narodnoe Khozyaistvo SSSR, 1922–87*, Moscow: Finansy i Statistika, 1982, p. 419; 1987, p. 435

G. Housing Construction (million square metres)

1918–28	203
1929–32 (1st Five Year Plan)	56.9
1933–37 (2nd Five Year Plan)	67.3
1938–June 1941 (3rd Five Year Plan)	81.7
July 1941–1945	102.5
1946–50 (4th Five Year Plan)	200.9
1951–55 (5th Five Year Plan)	240.5
1956–60	474.1
1961–65	490.6
1966–70 (8th Five Year Plan)	518.5
1971–75 (9th Five Year Plan)	544.8
1976–80 (10th Five Year Plan)	527.3
1981–85 (11th Five Year Plan)	552.2

Source: *Narodnoe Khozyaistvo SSSR, 1922–87*, Moscow: Finansy i Statistika, 1987, p. 425.

H. Population of the Main Nationalities (in thousands)

	1959	1979	1989	% claiming fluent Russian (1979)	(1989)
Russians	114,114	137,397	145,072	100	100
Ukrainians	37,253	42,347	44,136	49.8	56.2
Bielorussians	7,913	9,436	10,030	57.0	54.7
Uzbeks	6,015	12,456	16,686	49.3	23.8
Tatars	4,968	6,317		68.9	
Kazakhs	3,622	6,556	8,138	52.3	60.4
Azerbaidjanis	2,940	5,477	6,791	29.5	34.4
Armenians	2,787	4,151	4,627	38.6	47.1
Georgians	2,692	3,571	3,983	26.7	33.1
Lithuanians	2,326	2,851	3,068	52.1	37.9
Moldavians	2,214	2,968	3,355	47.4	53.8
Chuvashes	1,470	1,751			
Latvians	1,400	1,439	1,459	56.7	64.4
Tadzhiks	1,397	2,898	4,217	29.6	27.7
Mordvins	1,285	1,192			
Turkmens	1,002	2,028	2,718	25.4	27.8
Estonians	989	1,020	1,027	24.2	33.8
Bashkirs	989	1,371			
Kirgiz	969	1,906		29.4	35.2
Germans		1,936		51.7	
Jews		1,811			

Sources: *Strana sovetov za 50 let: sbornik statisticheskikh materialov*, Moscow: Statistika, 1967, p. 19. *Naselenie SSSR*, Moscow: Izdatel'stvo politicheskoi literatury, 1983, pp. 128–9. *Radio Liberty Report on the USSR*, 20 October 1989, pp. 2–3.

I. Population of the Union Republics (in millions)

	1940	1959	1970	1979	1989	1979 % of basic nationality to population
RSFSR	110.1	117.5	130.1	137.4	147.4	82.6
Ukraine	41.3	41.9	47.1	49.6	51.7	73.6
Bielorussia	9.0	8.1	9.0	9.5	10.2	79.4
Uzbekistan	6.6	8.3	11.8	15.4	19.9	68.7
Kazakhstan	6.1	9.2	13.0	14.7	16.5	36.0
Georgia	3.6	4.0	4.7	5.0	5.4	68.8
Armenia	1.3	1.8	2.5	3.0	3.3	89.7
Azerbaidjan	3.3	3.7	5.0	6.0	7.0	78.1
Lithuania	2.9	2.7	3.1	3.4	3.7	80.0
Moldavia	2.5	2.9	3.6	4.0	4.3	63.9
Latvia	1.9	2.1	2.6	2.5	2.7	53.7
Estonia	1.1	1.2	1.4	1.5	1.6	64.7
Kirgizia	1.5	2.1	2.9	3.5	4.3	47.9
Tadjikistan	1.5	2.0	2.9	3.8	5.1	58.8
Turkmenistan	1.3	1.5	2.2	2.8	3.5	68.4

Sources: *Strana sovetov za 50 let: sbornik statisticheskikh materialov*, Moscow: Statistika, 1967, p. 16. *Naselenie SSSR*, Moscow, Politizdat, 1980, pp. 27–30; *Current Digest of the Soviet Press*, vol. 41 (1989), no. 17, pp. 17–20.

Bibliography

The works listed here are those which I found most useful in preparing this study. The editions quoted are the ones I have used, not necessarily either the first or the most recent. Where an English language edition is available, I have quoted that.

* indicates works which I feel would be especially useful to someone unfamiliar with the subject.

† indicates a particularly thorough and comprehensive treatment of the subject.

General

* R. J. Hill and P. Frank, *The Soviet Communist Party*, London: Allen & Unwin, 1981.

* A. Nove, *An Economic History of the USSR*, London: Allen & Unwin, 1969.

* ——, *Stalinism and After*, London: Allen & Unwin, 1975.

J. Armstrong, *The Politics of Totalitarianism*, New York: Random House, 1961.

H. J. Berman, *Justice in the USSR*, New York: Vintage Books, 1963.

C. E. Black (editor), *The Transformation of Russian Society: aspects of social change since 1861*, Harvard University Press, 1960.

H. Carrère d'Encausse, *A History of the Soviet Union, 1917–53*, 2 vols., London: Longman, 1981.

J. S. Curtiss, *The Russian Church and the Soviet State, 1917–50*, Boston, Massachusetts: Little, Brown, 1953.

W. C. Fletcher, *The Russian Orthodox Church Underground, 1917–70*, Oxford University Press, 1971.

M. Geller and A. Nekrich, *Utopiya u vlasti*, 2 vols., London: Overseas Publications Interchange, 1982.

Nigel Grant, *Soviet Education*, third edition, Harmondsworth: Penguin Books, 1972.

R. Hingley, *The Russian Secret Police: Muscovite, Imperial Russian and Soviet political security operations, 1565–1970*, London: Hutchinson, 1970.

History of the Communist Party of the Soviet Union (Bolsheviks) (edited by a commission of the Central Committee of the CPSU[B], Moscow: Foreign Languages Publishing House, 1939 (and numerous other editions: the standard Stalinist version of its subject – see above, Chapter 8).

J. Hough and M. Fainsod, *How the Soviet Union is Governed*, revised edition, Harvard University Press, 1979.

A. Inkeles and R. Bauer, *The Soviet Citizen: daily life in a totalitarian society*, New York: Atheneum, 1968.

B. Kagarlitsky, *The Thinking Reed: intellectuals and the Soviet state, 1917 to the present*, London: Verso, 1988.

G. Kline (editor), *Soviet Education*, London: Routledge & Kegan Paul, 1957.

V. I. Lenin, *Collected Works,* 45 vols., Moscow: Progress, 1963–70.

——, *What is to be Done?* (edited by S. V. Utechin), Oxford: Clarendon Press, 1963.

——, *State and Revolution*, London: Central Books, 1972.

M. Lewin, *The Making of the Soviet System*, London: Methuen, 1985.

B. Lewytsky, *The Uses of Terror: the Soviet secret service,* London: Sidgwick & Jackson, 1971.

Maksudov, 'Pertes subies par la population de l'URSS, 1918–58', *Cahiers du monde russe et soviétique*, vol. 18, no. 3 (1977).

M. Matthews, *Privilege in the Soviet Union*, London: Allen & Unwin, 1978.

R. H. McNeal (editor), *Resolutions and Decisions of the Communist Party of the Soviet Union*, 5 vols., University of Toronto Press, 1974–82.

Narodnoe khozyaistvo SSSR, 1922–82, Moscow: Finansy i statistika, 1982 (basic statistical information on the economic development of the USSR).

Narodnoe khozyaistvo SSSR, Moscow: Statistika (a yearbook containing summaries of economic information).

Narodnoe khozyaistvo SSSR za 70 let, Moscow: Finansy i Statistika, 1987.

Naselenie SSSR po dannym vsesoyuznoi perepisi 1979 goda, Moscow: Politizdat, 1980 (a brief compendium of demographic information).

A. Nove, 'Is there a ruling class in the USSR?', *Soviet Studies,* vol. 27, no. 4 (October 1975).

S. N. Prokopovich, *Narodnoe khozyaistvo SSSR,* 2 vols., New York: Chekhov Press, 1952.

Resheniya partii i pravitel'stva po khozyaistvennym voprosam, 1917–82, 14 vols., Moscow: Politizdat, 1967–83.

T. H. Rigby, *Communist Party Membership in the USSR, 1917–67,* Princeton University Press, 1968.

Sbornik zakonov SSSR, 1938–70, 3 vols., Moscow: Izvestiya, 1968–71 (texts of important laws).

Leonard Schapiro, *The Communist Party of the Soviet Union,* second edition, London: Eyre & Spottiswoode, 1970.

J. V. Stalin, *Problems of Leninism,* Moscow: Foreign Languages Publishing House, 1945.

——, *Collected Works,* 13 vols., Moscow: Foreign Languages Publishing House, 1952–5 (no more published).

R. C. Tucker, *The Lenin Anthology,* New York: Norton, 1975.

——, *Political Culture and Leadership in Soviet Russia from Lenin to Gorbachev,* Brighton: Wheatsheaf, 1987.

A. Ulam, *Lenin and the Bolsheviks,* London: Fontana, 1969.

——, *Stalin: the man and his era,* London: Allen Lane, 1974.

L. Volin, *A Century of Russian Agriculture: from Alexander II to Khrushchev,* Harvard University Press, 1970.

M. S. Voslensky, *Nomenklatura: die herrschende Klasse der Sowjetunion,* Vienna: Molden, 1980.

——, *Nomenklatura: anatomy of the Soviet ruling class,* London: Bodley Head, 1984.

T. Ware, *The Russian Orthodox Church,* Harmondsworth: Penguin Books, 1963.

Geoffrey Wheeler, *The Modern History of Soviet Central Asia,* London: Weidenfeld & Nicolson, 1964.

S. White, *Political Culture and Soviet Politics,* London: Macmillan, 1979.

1. Introduction

* N. V. Riasanovsky, *A History of Russia*, Oxford University Press, 1977.

† M. T. Florinsky, *Russia: a history and an interpretation*, 2 vols., New York: Macmillan, 1960.

† H. Seton-Watson, *The Russian Empire, 1801–1917*, Oxford University Press, 1967.

J. Blum, *Lord and Peasant in Russia from the Ninth to the Nineteenth Century*, Princeton University Press, 1961.

J. S. Curtiss, *Church and State in Russia: the last years of the Empire, 1900–17*, Columbia University Press, 1940.

L. Haimson, *The Russian Marxists and the Origins of Bolshevism*, Harvard University Press, 1955.

R. E. Johnson, *Peasant and Proletarian: the working class of Moscow in the late 19th century*, Leicester University Press, 1979.

J. L. H. Keep, *The Rise of Social Democracy in Russia*, Oxford University Press, 1963.

Richard Pipes (editor), *The Russian Intelligentsia*, Columbia University Press, 1961.

M. Raeff, *The Origins of the Russian Intelligentsia: the 18th century nobility*, New York: Harcourt, Brace & World, 1966.

——, *The Well-ordered Police State: social and institutional change through law in the Germanies and Russia, 1600–1800*, Yale University Press, 1983.

G. T. Robinson, *Rural Russia under the Old Regime*, London: Collier-Macmillan, 1967 (reprint of 1932 edition).

R. Service, *Lenin: a political life*, vol. 1, London: Macmillan, 1985.

F. Venturi, *Roots of Revolution: a history of populist and socialist movements in 19th century Russia*, New York: Knopf, 1960.

A. Wildman, *The Making of a Workers' Revolution: Russian Social Democracy, 1891–1903*, Chicago University Press, 1967.

2. The October Revolution

* Sheila Fitzpatrick, *The Russian Revolution*, Oxford University Press, 1982.

* Leonard Schapiro, *1917: the Russian revolutions and the origins* *of present-day Communism*, London: Temple Smith, 1984.

* ——, *Origin of the Communist Autocracy: political opposition in the Soviet state*, second edition, London: Macmillan, 1977.

† W. H. Chamberlin, *The Russian Revolution*, 2 vols., New York: Grosset & Dunlap, 1965 (reprint of 1931 edition).

† J. L. H. Keep, *The Russian Revolution: a study in mass mobilisation*, London: Weidenfeld & Nicolson, 1976.

R. R. Abramovitch, *The Soviet Revolution, 1917–39*, London: Allen & Unwin, 1962.

O. Anweiler, *The Soviets: Russian workers', peasants' and soldiers' councils, 1905–21*, New York: Pantheon Books, 1974.

A. Ascher (editor), *The Mensheviks in the Russian Revolution*, Cornell University Press, 1976.

J. Bunyan and H. H. Fisher (editors), *The Bolshevik Revolution, 1917–18: documents and materials*, Stanford University Press, 1934.

V. Chernov, *The Great Russian Revolution*, New York: Russell & Russell, 1966 (reprint).

R. Daniels, *Red October: the Bolshevik revolution of 1917*, London: Secker & Warburg, 1968.

M. Ferro, *Des Soviets au communisme bureaucratique*, Paris: Gallimard, 1980.

M. Florinsky, *The End of the Russian Empire*, New York: Collier Books, 1961.

G. Gill, *Peasants and Government in the Russian Revolution*, London: Macmillan, 1979.

M. Gorky, *Untimely Thoughts: essays on revolution, culture and the Bolsheviks, 1917–18*, London: Garnstone Press, 1968.

L. Haimson (editor), *The Mensheviks*, University of Chicago Press, 1974.

T. Hasegawa, *The February Revolution: Petrograd 1917*, Seattle and London: University of Washington Press, 1981.

D. H. Kaiser (editor), *The Workers' Revolution in Russia, 1917: the view from below*, Cambridge, CUP, 1987.

George Katkov, *Russia 1917: the February revolution*, London: Longman, 1967.

——, *Russia 1917: the Kornilov affair,* London: Longman, 1980.

M. McCauley (editor), *The Russian Revolution and the Soviet State, 1917–21*, London: Macmillan, 1975.

R. Medvedev, *The October Revolution*, London: Constable, 1979.

S. P. Melgunov, *The Bolshevik Seizure of Power*, Santa Barbara, California: ABC-Clio, 1972.

P. N. Milyukov, *Political Memoirs, 1905–17*, University of Michigan Press, 1967.

R. Pipes (editor), *Revolutionary Russia: a symposium*, Harvard University Press, 1968.

A. Rabinowitch, *The Bolsheviks Come to Power*, New York: Norton, 1976.

O. Radkey, *The Election to the Constituent Assembly of 1917*, Harvard University Press, 1950.

——, *The Agrarian Foes of Bolshevism: promise and default of the Russian Socialist Revolutionaries, February–October 1917*, Columbia University Press, 1958.

John Reed, *Ten Days that Shook the World*, London: Lawrence & Wishart, 1961 (reprint).

W. G. Rosenberg, *Liberals in the Russian Revolution*, Princeton University Press, 1974.

R. Service, *The Russian Revolution, 1900–27*, London: Macmillan, 1986.

S. A. Smith, *Red Petrograd: revolution in the factories, 1917–18*, Cambridge University Press, 1983.

N. Sukhanov, *The Russian Revolution, 1917: a personal record*, Oxford University Press, 1955.

L. Trotsky, *History of the Russian Revolution*, London: Gollancz, 1932–3.

A. Wildman, *The End of the Russian Imperial Army*, 2 vols: Princeton University Press, 1980, 1987.

3. War Communism

* D. Footman, *Civil War in Russia*, London: Faber & Faber, 1961.

† P. Avrich, *Kronstadt 1921*, Princeton University Press, 1970.

† S. F. Cohen, *Bukharin and the Bolshevik Revolution*, London: Wildwood House, 1974.

† R. Daniels, *The Conscience of the Revolution: Communist opposition in Soviet Russia*, Harvard University Press, 1960.

† Leonard Schapiro, *Origin of the Communist Autocracy: political opposition in the Soviet state*, second edition, London: Macmillan, 1977.

† R. Service, *The Bolshevik Party in Revolution: a study in organisational change, 1917–23*, London: Macmillan, 1979.

520   Bibliography

R. R. Abramovitch, *The Soviet Revolution, 1917–39*, London: Allen & Unwin, 1962.

Angelika Balabanova, *My Life as a Rebel*, New York: Greenwood Press, 1968.

A. Berkman, *The Russian Tragedy*, Sanday, Orkney: Cienfuegos Press, 1976.

M. Bernshtam (editor), *Nezavisimoe rabochee dvizhenie v 1918 godu*, Paris: YMCA Press, 1981.

——, *Narodnoe soprotivlenie kommunizmu v Rossii: Ural i Prikam'e, noyabr' 1917–yanvar' 1919*, Paris: YMCA Press, 1982.

V. N. Brovkin, *The Mensheviks after October: socialist opposition and the rise of the Bolshevik dictatorship*, London: Cornell University Press, 1987.

N. Bukharin and E. Preobrazhensky, *The ABC of Communism*, Harmondsworth: Penguin Books, 1969.

J. Bunyan (editor), *The Origin of Forced Labor in the Soviet State, 1917–21*, Johns Hopkins University Press, 1967.

General A. Denikin, *The White Army*, Gulf Breeze, Florida: Academic International Press, 1973 (reprint).

Isaac Deutscher, *The Prophet Armed: Trotsky, 1879–1921*, Oxford University Press, 1974.

I. Getzler, *Kronstadt 1917–21: the fate of a Soviet democracy*, Cambridge University Press, 1983.

D. L. Golinkov, *Krakh antisovetskogo podpol'ya*, Moscow: Politizdat, 1975.

K. V. Gusev, *Krakh partii levykh eserov*, Moscow: Sotsekgiz, 1963.

——, *Partiya eserov*, Moscow: Mysl', 1975.

P. Kenez, *Civil War in South Russia, 1918–20*, 2 vols., University of California Press, 1971–7.

George Leggett, *The Cheka: Lenin's political police*, Oxford University Press, 1981.

R. Luckett, *The White Generals*, London: Longman, 1971.

M. McCauley (editor), *The Russian Revolution and the Soviet State, 1917–21*, London: Macmillan, 1975.

S. Malle, *The Economic Organisation of War Communism, 1918–21*, Cambridge University Press, 1985.

E. Mawdsley, *The Russian Civil War*, London: Allen & Unwin, 1987.

J. M. Meijer (editor), *The Trotsky Papers, 1917–22*, 2 vols., The Hague: Mouton, 1964–71.

O. Radkey, *The Sickle under the Hammer: the Russian Socialist Revolutionaries in the early months of Soviet rule*, Columbia University Press, 1963.

——, *The Unknown Civil War in Soviet Russia: a study of the green movement in the Tambov region, 1920–21*, Stanford, California: Hoover Institution Press, 1976.

T. H. Rigby, *Lenin's Government: Sovnarkom, 1917–22*, Cambridge University Press, 1979.

Victor Serge, *Memoirs of a Revolutionary, 1901–41*, Oxford University Press, 1963.

T. Shanin, *The Awkward Class: political sociology of a peasantry in a developing society, Russia 1910–25*, Oxford University Press, 1972.

4. The Making of the Soviet Union

* Robert Conquest (editor), *Soviet Nationalities Policy in Practice*, London: Bodley Head, 1967.

† A. Bennigsen and C. Lemercier-Quelquejay, *Islam in the Soviet Union*, London: Pall Mall Press, 1967.

† E. H. Carr, *The Bolshevik Revolution, 1917–23*, vol. 1, London: Macmillan, 1950.

† R. Pipes, *The Formation of the Soviet Union*, revised edition, Harvard University Press, 1964.

A. Bennigsen and S. Wimbush, *Muslim National Communism in the Soviet Union*, Chicago University Press, 1979.

Norman Davies, *White Eagle, Red Star: the Polish-Soviet war, 1919–20*, London: Macdonald, 1972.

S. L. Guthier, 'The popular base of Ukrainian nationalism in 1917', *Slavic Review*, vol. 38, no. 1 (March 1979).

T. Hunczak (editor), *The Ukraine, 1917–21: a study in revolution*, Harvard University Press, 1977.

F. Kazemzadeh, *The Struggle for Transcaucasia*, Oxford: George Ronald, 1951.

B. Krawchenko, *Social Change and National Consciousness in Twentieth Century Ukraine*, London: Macmillan Press, 1985.

M. Lewin, *Lenin's Last Struggle*, London: Faber & Faber, 1969.

M. Olcott, 'The Basmachi or freemen's revolt in Turkestan, 1918–24', *Soviet Studies*, vol. 33, no. 3 (July 1981).

J. Reshetar, *The Ukrainian Revolution, 1917–20*, Princeton University Press, 1952.

O. Subtelny, *Ukraine: a history*, University of Toronto Press, 1988.

R. Suny, *The Baku Commune, 1917–18: class and nationality in the Russian revolution*, Princeton University Press, 1972.

R. G. Suny, *The Making of the Georgian Nation*, London: I. B. Tauris, 1988.

A. L. Unger, *Constitutional Development in the USSR*, London: Methuen, 1981.

N. P. Vakar, *Belorussia: the making of a nation*, Harvard University Press, 1956.

5. The New Economic Policy and its Political Dilemmas

* M. Lewin, *Lenin's Last Struggle*, London: Faber & Faber, 1969.

† J. Azrael, *Managerial Power and Soviet Politics*, Harvard University Press, 1966.

† E. H. Carr, *Socialism in One Country, 1924–26*, vols. 1 & 2, London: Macmillan, 1958–9.

† S. F. Cohen, *Bukharin and the Bolshevik Revolution*, London: Wildwood House, 1973.

† A. Erlich, *The Soviet Industrialisation Debate*, Harvard University Press, 1960.

† B. Knei-paz, *The Social and Political Thought of Leon Trotsky*, Oxford University Press, 1978.

† M. Lewin, *Russian Peasants and Soviet Power*, London: Allen & Unwin, 1968.

† R. C. Tucker, *Stalin as Revolutionary, 1879–1929*, London: Chatto & Windus, 1974.

B. Bazhanov, *Vospominaniya byvshego sekretarya Stalina*, Paris: Tret'ya Volna, 1980.

V. P. Danilov, 'K kharakteristike obshchestvenno-politicheskoi obstanovki v sovetskoi derevne nakanune kollektivizatsii', *Istoricheskie zapiski*, vol. 79 (1966).

——, *Sovetskaya dokolkhoznaya derevnya*, 2 vols., Moscow: Nauka, 1977–9.

——, *Rural Russia under the New Regime*, London: Hutchinson, 1988.

Isaac Deutscher, *Trotsky: the prophet unarmed*, Oxford University Press, 1959.

M. Fainsod, *Smolensk under Soviet Rule*, London: Macmillan, 1958.

S. Fedyukin, *The Great October Revolution and the Intelligentsia*, Moscow: Progress Publishers, 1975.

P. Kenez, *The Birth of the Propaganda State: Soviet methods of mass mobilization*, Cambridge University Press, 1985.

D. J. Male, *Russian Peasant Organisation before Collectivisation*, Cambridge University Press, 1971.

Olga Narkiewicz, *The Making of the Soviet State Apparatus*, Manchester University Press, 1970.

R. Pethybridge, *The Social Prelude to Stalinism*, London: Macmillan, 1974.

Yu. A. Polyakov, *Perekhod k NEPu i sovetskoe krest'yanstvo*, Moscow: Nauka, 1967.

E. Preobrazhensky, *The New Economics*, Oxford: Clarendon Press, 1965.

M. Reiman, *Die Geburt des Stalinismus*, Frankfurt am Main: Europäische Verlagsanstalt, 1979.

W. G. Rosenberg, 'Smolensk in the 1920s: party-worker relations and the "vanguard" problem', *Russian Review*, vol. 36, no. 2 (April 1977).

Victor Serge, *Memoirs of a Revolutionary, 1901–41*, Oxford University Press, 1963.

T. Shanin, *The Awkward Class: political sociology of a peasantry in a developing society, Russia 1910–25*, Oxford University Press, 1972.

Y. Taniuchi, *The Village Gathering in the mid-1920s*, University of Birmingham: Centre for Russian & East European Studies, 1968.

I. Ya. Trifonov, *Ocherki klassovoi bor'by v gody NEPa*, Moscow: Gospolitizdat, 1960.

Nina Tumarkin, *Lenin Lives! The Lenin cult in Soviet Russia*, Harvard University Press, 1983.

6. Revolution from Above; 7. Stalin's Terror; 8. Stalinist Society

* M. Lewin, 'Society and the Stalinist state in the period of the five-year plans', *Social History*, vol. 1, no. 1 (May 1976).

* J. Millar and A. Nove, 'Was Stalin really necessary? A debate on collectivisation', *Problems of Communism*, vol. 25, no. 4 (July–August 1976).

† Kendall Bailes, *Technology and Society under Lenin and Stalin*, Princeton University Press, 1978.

† R. Conquest, *The Great Terror*, revised edition, Harmondsworth: Penguin Books, 1971.

† ——, *Harvest of Sorrow: Soviet collectivisation and the terror-famine*, London: Hutchinson, 1986.

† R. W. Davies, *The Industrialisation of Soviet Russia*, 2 vols., London: Macmillan, 1980.

† M. Fainsod, *Smolensk under Soviet Rule*, London: Macmillan, 1958.

† Sheila Fitzpatrick, *Education and Social Mobility in the Soviet Union, 1921–34*, Cambridge University Press, 1979.

† S. Schwarz, *Labour in the Soviet Union*, London: Cresset Press, 1953.

† A. Solzhenitsyn, *The Gulag Archipelago*, 3 vols., London: Collins/Harvill, 1974–8.

† R. C. Tucker, *Stalinism: essays in historical interpretation*, New York: Norton, 1977.

V. Andrle, *Workers in Stalin's Russia: industrialisation and social change in a planned economy*, Brighton: Harvester, 1988.

P. Barton, *L'institution concentrationnaire en Russie, 1930–57*, Paris: Plon, 1959.

D. R. Brower, 'Collectivised agriculture in Smolensk: the party, the peasantry and the crisis of 1932', *Russian Review*, vol. 36, no. 2 (April 1977).

R. Conquest, *Kolyma: the Arctic death camps*, London: Macmillan, 1978.

D. Dallin and B. Nicolaevsky, *Forced Labour in the Soviet Union*, London: Hollis & Carter, 1948.

D. Dalrymple, 'The Soviet famine of 1932–4', *Soviet Studies*, vol. 15, no. 3 (January 1964).

V. P. Danilov (editor), *Ocherki istorii kollektivizatsii sel'skogo khozyaistva*, Moscow: Politizdat, 1963.

R. W. Davies, *The Soviet Economy in Turmoil, 1929–30*, London: Macmillan, 1988.

V. Z. Drobizhev and A. I. Vdovin, *Rost rabochego klassa, 1917–40gg.*, Moscow: Mysl', 1976.

Harold Eekman, *Inside Stalin's Russia: memories of a diplomat, 1936–41*, London: Triton Books, 1977.

Karl Eimermacher, *Dokumente zur sowjetischen Literaturpolitik*, Stuttgart: Kohlhammer, 1972.

D. Filtzer, *Soviet Workers and Stalinist Industrialisation*, London: Pluto Press, 1986.

Sheila Fitzpatrick (editor), *Cultural Revolution in Russia, 1928–31*, Indiana University Press, 1978.

K. Geiger, *The Family in Soviet Russia*, Harvard University Press, 1968.

Evgeniya Ginsburg, *Into the Whirlwind*, London: Collins/Harvill, 1967.

Hans Günther, *Die Verstaatlichung der Literatur*, Stuttgart: Metzler, 1984.

Maurice Hindus, *Red Bread*, London: Jonathan Cape, 1931.

Ronald Hingley, *Russian Writers and Soviet Society, 1917–78*, London: Weidenfeld & Nicolson, 1979.

Holland Hunter, 'The overambitious first Soviet five-year plan', *Slavic Review*, vol. 32, no. 2 (June 1973).

Istoriya sovetskogo krest'yanstva i kolkhoznogo stroitel'stva v SSSR, Moscow: Izdatel'stvo Akademii Nauk, 1963.

Khrushchev Remembers, 2 vols., Harmondsworth: Penguin Books, 1977.

Lev Kopelev, *No Jail for Thought*, London: Secker & Warburg, 1977.

——, *The Education of a True Believer*, London: Wildwood House, 1981.

V. Kravchenko, *I Chose Freedom: the personal and political life of a Soviet official*, London: Robert Hale, 1947.

H. Kuromiya, *Stalin's Industrial Revolution: politics and workers, 1928–32*, Cambridge University Press, 1988.

Nadezhda Mandelstam, *Hope against Hope*, Harmondsworth: Penguin Books, 1975.

——, *Hope Abandoned*, Harmondsworth: Penguin Books, 1979.

Yu. Margolin, *Puteshestvie v stranu ze-ka*, New York: Chekhov Press, 1952.

Roy Medvedev, *Let History Judge: the origins and consequences of Stalinism*, New York: Knopf, 1971.

Yu. A. Moshkov, *Zernovaya problema v gody sploshnoi kollektivizatsii*, Izdatel'stvo Moskovskogo Universiteta, 1966.

Boris Nicolaevsky, *Power and the Soviet Elite*, London: Pall Mall Press, 1966.

M. Olcott, 'The collectivisation drive in Kazakhstan', *Russian Review*, vol. 40, no. 2 (April 1981).

A. Orlov, *The Secret History of Stalin's Crimes*, London: Jarrolds, 1954.

Raisa Orlova, *Vospominaniya o neproshedshem vremeni*, Ann Arbor, Michigan: Ardis Press, 1983.

N. S. Patolichev, *Ispytanie na zrelost'*, Moscow: Politizdat, 1977.

R. Redlikh, *Stalinshchina, kak dukhovnyi fenomen*, Frankfurt am Main: Posev, 1971.

R. Schlesinger (editor), *The Family in the USSR: documents and readings*, London: Routledge & Kegan Paul, 1949.

John Scott, *Behind the Urals: an American worker in Russia's city of steel*, London: Secker & Warburg, 1943.

V. Shalamov, *Kolymskie rasskazy*, London: Overseas Publications Interchange, 1979.

L. Siegelbaum, *Stakhanovism and the Politics of Productivity in the USSR, 1935–41*, Cambridge University Press, 1988.

Andrew Smith, *I Was a Soviet Worker*, London: Robert Hale, 1937.

Gleb Struve, *Russian Literature under Lenin and Stalin, 1917–53*, Oklahoma University Press, 1971.

N. Timasheff, *The Great Retreat: the growth and decline of Communism in Russia*, New York: Dutton, 1946.

L. Trotsky, *The Revolution Betrayed*, London: Faber & Faber, 1937.

R. C. Tucker and S. F. Cohen (editors), *The Great Purge Trial*, New York: Grosset & Dunlap, 1965.

C. Vaughan James, *Soviet Socialist Realism*, London: Macmillan, 1973.

L. Viola, *The Best Sons of the Fatherland: workers in the vanguard of Soviet collectivisation*, Oxford University Press, 1987.

9. Religion and Nationality under the Soviet State

* Robert Conquest (editor), *Soviet Nationalities Policy in Practice*, London: Bodley Head, 1967.
* Pierre Pascal, *The Religion of the Russian People*, London: Mowbrays, 1976.

* D. Pospielovsky, 'The renovationist schism in the Russian Orthodox Church', *Russian History*, vol. 9, parts 2–3 (1982).

† A. Bennigsen and C. Lemercier-Quelquejay, *Islam in the Soviet Union*, London: Pall Mall Press, 1967.

† W. C. Fletcher, *A Study in Survival: the church in Russia, 1927–43*, London: SPCK, 1965.

† W. Kolarz, *Russia and her Colonies*, London: George Philip, 1952.

† ——, *Religion in the Soviet Union*, London: Macmillan, 1961.

Robert Conquest, *The Nation Killers*, London: Sphere Books, 1972.

L. Kochan, *The Jews in Soviet Russia since 1917*, second edition, Oxford University Press, 1972.

L. Kopelev, *The Education of a True Believer*, London: Secker & Warburg, 1977.

H. Kostiuk, *Stalinist Rule in the Ukraine: a study of the decade of mass terror, 1929–39*, New York: Praeger, 1961.

A. Krasnov-Levitin, *Likhie gody, 1925–41*, Paris: YMCA Press, 1977.

——, *Ruk tvoikh zhar*, Tel Aviv: Krug, 1979.

I. S. Lubachko, *Belorussia under Soviet Rule, 1917–57*, University of Kentucky Press, 1972.

R. Misiunas and R. Taagepera, *The Baltic States: the years of dependence, 1940–80*, London: Hurst, 1983.

M. Olcott, 'The collectivisation drive in Kazakhstan', *Russian Review*, vol. 40, no. 2 (April 1981).

D. Pospielovsky, *The Russian Church under the Soviet regime, 1917–82*, Crestwood, NY: St Vladimir's Seminary Press, 1984.

G. von Rauch, *The Baltic States: the years of independence, 1917–40*, London: Hurst, 1974.

M. Rywkin, 'L'Islam parallèle en Union Soviétique', *Cahiers du monde russe et soviétique*, vol. 21, no. 1 (January 1981).

——, *Moscow's Muslim Challenge: Soviet Central Asia*, London: Hurst, 1982.

R. S. Sullivant, *Soviet Politics and the Ukraine, 1917–57*, Columbia University Press, 1962.

R. Taagepera, 'Soviet collectivisation of Estonian agriculture: the deportation phase', *Soviet Studies*, vol. 32, no. 3 (July 1980).

Philip Walters, 'The Living Church, 1922–46', *Religion in Communist Lands*, vol. 6, no. 4 (winter 1978).

10. The Great Fatherland War

* M. McKintosh, *Juggernaut: a history of the Soviet armed forces*, London: Secker & Warburg, 1967.

* Alexander Werth, *Russia at War, 1941–45*, London: Pan Books, 1965.

† T. J. Colton, *Commissars, Commanders and Civilian Authority: the structure of Soviet military politics*, Harvard University Press, 1979.

† A. Dallin, *German Rule in Russia, 1941–45*, London: Macmillan, 1957.

† John Erickson, *The Road to Stalingrad*, London: Weidenfeld & Nicolson, 1975.

† ——, *The Road to Berlin*, London: Weidenfeld & Nicolson, 1983.

† D. Fedotoff White, *The Growth of the Red Army*, Princeton University Press, 1944.

† G. Fischer, *Soviet Opposition to Stalin: a case study in World War II*, Harvard University Press, 1952.

† Albert Seaton, *The Russo-German War, 1941–45*, London: Barker, 1971.

N. M. Aleshchenko, *Moskovskii sovet v 1941–45*, Moscow: Nauka, 1976.

John Armstrong, *Soviet Partisans in World War II*, University of Wisconsin Press, 1964.

Yu. V. Arutyunyan, *Sovetskoe krest'yanstvo v gody velikoi otechestvennoi voiny*, second edition, Moscow: Nauka, 1970.

S. Bialer (editor), *Stalin and his Generals*, New York: Pegasus, 1969.

A. Chuyanov, *Na stremnine veka: zapiski sekretarya obkoma*, Moscow: Politizdat, 1977.

Eshelony idut na vostok: iz istorii preobrazovaniya proizvoditel'nykh sil SSSR v 1941–42, Moscow: Nauka, 1966.

M. P. Gallagher, *The Soviet History of World War II: myths, memories and realities*, New York: Praeger, 1963.

L. Gouré and H. Dinerstein, *Moscow in Crisis*, Glencoe, Illinois: Free Press, 1955.

P. Grigorenko, *Memoirs*, London: Harvill Press, 1983.

M. Harrison, *Soviet Planning in Peace and War*, Cambridge University Press, 1985.

The Memoirs of Marshal Zhukov, London: Jonathan Cape, 1971.

A. V. Mitrofanova, *Rabochii klass v gody velikoi otechestvennoi voiny*, Moscow: Nauka, 1971.

A. Nekrich, *22 June 1941* (edited by V. Petrov), University of South Carolina Press, 1968.

N. S. Patolichev, *Ispytanie na zrelost'*, Moscow: Politizdat, 1977.

Yu. P. Petrov, *Stroitel'stvo politorganov, partiinykh i komsomol' skikh organizatsii armii i flota, 1918–68*, Moscow: Voennoe izdatel'stvo, 1968.

P. N. Pospelov (editor), *Sovetskii tyl v velikoi otechestvennoi voine*, Moscow: Mysl', 1974.

Harrison Salisbury, *The Siege of Leningrad*, London: Secker & Warburg, 1969.

V. Shtrik-Shtrikfeldt, *Protiv Stalina i Gitlera: General Vlasov i russkoe osvoboditel'noe dvizhenie*, Frankfurt am Main: Posev, 1975.

K. F. Telegin, *Ne otdali Moskvy!*, Moscow: Sovetskaya Rossiya, 1968.

J. Thorwald, *The Illusion: Soviet soldiers in Hitler's armies*, New York: Harcourt, Brace, Jovanovich, 1975.

N. Voznesensky, *The War Economy of the USSR in the Period of the Great Patriotic War*, Moscow: Foreign Languages Publishing House, 1948.

Alexander Werth, *The Year of Stalingrad*, London: Hamish Hamilton, 1946.

11. The Last Years of Stalin

* M. Djilas, *Conversations with Stalin*, London: Hart-Davis, 1962.

* F. Fetjö, *A History of the People's Democracies: Eastern Europe since Stalin*, second edition, Harmondsworth: Penguin Books, 1974.

* Alexander Werth, *Russia: the post-war years*, London: Robert Hale, 1971.

† Robert Conquest, *Power and Policy in the USSR*, London: Macmillan, 1961.

† Loren Graham, *Science and Philosophy in the Soviet Union*, London: Allen Lane, 1973.

† D. Joravsky, *The Lysenko Affair*, Harvard University Press, 1970.

† V. Mastny, *Russia's Road to the Cold War*, Columbia University Press, 1979.

Svetlana Allilueva, *Twenty Letters to a Friend*, London: Hutchinson, 1967.

Vera Dunham, *In Stalin's Time: middleclass values in Soviet fiction*, Cambridge University Press, 1976.

T. Dunmore, *The Stalinist Command Economy: the Soviet state apparatus and economic policy, 1945–53*, London: Macmillan, 1980.

W. Hahn, *Postwar Soviet Politics: the fall of Zhdanov and the defeat of moderation*, Cornell University Press, 1982.

Khrushchev Remembers, 2 vols., Harmondsworth: Penguin Books, 1977.

W. O. McCagg, *Stalin Embattled, 1943–48*, Wayne State University Press, 1978.

Zh. Medvedev, *The Rise and Fall of T. D. Lysenko*, Columbia University Press, 1969.

A. Nekrich, *Otreshis' ot strakha: vospominaniya istorika*, London: Overseas Publications Interchange, 1979.

V. Perel'man, *Pokinutaya Rossiya*, 2 vols., Tel Aviv: Vremya i my, 1976–7.

E. Strauss, *Soviet Agriculture in Perspective*, London: Allen & Unwin, 1969.

I. M. Volkov (editor), *Sovetskaya derevnya v pervye poslevoennye gody, 1946–51*, Moscow: Nauka, 1978.

12. Khrushchev and de-Stalinization

* F. Fejtö, *A History of the People's Democracies: Eastern Europe since Stalin*, second edition, Harmondsworth: Penguin Books, 1974.

* R. and Zh. Medvedev, *Khrushchev: the years in power*, Oxford University Press, 1977.

* E. Strauss, *Soviet Agriculture in Perspective*, London: Allen & Unwin, 1969.

† Robert Conquest, *Power and Policy in the USSR*, London: Macmillan, 1961.

† C. Linden, *Khrushchev and the Soviet Leadership, 1957–64*, Johns Hopkins University Press, 1966.

† A. McAuley, *Economic Welfare in the Soviet Union: poverty, living standards and inequality*, Wisconsin University Press, 1979.

† M. McCauley, *Khrushchev and the Development of Soviet Agriculture: the Virgin Lands programme, 1953–64*, London: Macmillan, 1976.

† K. E. Wädekin, *The Private Sector in Soviet Agriculture*, University of California Press, 1973.

Paul Barton, *L'institution concentrationnaire en Russie, 1930–57*, Paris: Plon, 1959.

Edward Buca, *Vorkuta*, London: Constable, 1976.

V. Bukovsky, *To Build a Castle: my life as a dissenter*, London: André Deutsch, 1978.

S. Cohen, *An End to Silence*, New York: Norton, 1982.

S. Cohen, R. Sharlet and A. Rabinowitch (editors), *The Soviet Union since Stalin*, London: Macmillan, 1980.

Chris Harman, *Bureaucracy and Revolution in Eastern Europe*, London: Pluto Press, 1974.

P. H. Juviler, *Revolutionary Law and Order: politics and social change in the USSR*, London: Collier-Macmillan, 1976.

Khrushchev Remembers, 2 vols., Harmondsworth: Penguin Books, 1977.

Bill Lomax, *Hungary 1956*, London: Allison & Busby, 1976.

Bernice Madison, *Social Welfare in the Soviet Union*, Stanford University Press, 1968.

Mervyn Matthews, *Education in the Soviet Union: policies and institutions since Stalin*, London: Allen & Unwin, 1982.

V. Micunović, *Moscow Diary*, London: Chatto & Windus, 1980.

R. Pimenov, 'Odin politicheskii protsess', *Pamyat'*, nos. 2 & 3 (1979–80).

S. R. Rozhdenstvenskii, 'Materialy k istorii samodeyatel'nykh politicheskikh ob"edinenii v SSSR posle 1945 goda', *Pamyat'*, no. 5 (1982).

L. Schapiro (editor), *The USSR and the Future: an analysis of the new programme of the CPSU*, New York: Praeger, 1963.

Joseph Scholmer, *Vorkuta*, London: Weidenfeld & Nicolson, 1954.

Alexander Solzhenitsyn, *The Gulag Archipelago*, vol. 3, London: Collins/Harvill, 1978.

Michel Tatu, *Power in the Kremlin from Khrushchev to Kosygin*, London: Collins, 1968.

Alexander Werth, *The Khrushchev Phase*, London: Robert Hale, 1961.

13. The Soviet Union under 'Developed Socialism'

* J. Cracraft (editor), *The Soviet Union: an interpretive guide*, Chicago: Bulletin of the Atomic Scientists, 1983.

* Hedrick Smith, *The Russians*, London: Times Books, 1976.

† A. Brown and M. Kaser (editors), *The Soviet Union since the Fall of Khrushchev*, second edition, London: Macmillan, 1978.

† B. Kerblay, *Modern Soviet Society*, London: Methuen, 1983.

† G. Lapidus (editor), *Women in Russia*, Brighton: Harvester Press, 1978.

† H. Gordon Skilling, *Czechoslovakia's Interrupted Revolution*, Princeton University Press, 1976.

V. Belotserkovsky, 'Workers' struggles in the USSR in the early sixties', *Critique*, nos. 10–11 (1979).

S. F. Cohen, *An End to Silence*, New York: Norton, 1982.

I. Efimov, *Bez burzhuev*, Frankfurt am Main: Posev, 1979.

V. Fišera (editor), *Workers' Councils in Czechoslovakia, 1968–9*, London: Alison & Busby, 1978.

Betsy Gidwitz, 'Labour unrest in the Soviet Union', *Problems of Communism*, vol. 31, no. 6 (November 1982).

G. Golan, *Reform Rule in Czechoslovakia: the Dubček era, 1968–9*, Cambridge University Press, 1973.

G. Grossman, 'The "second economy" of the USSR', *Problems of Communism*, vol. 26, no. 5 (September 1977).

V. Haynes and O. Semyonova, *Workers against the Gulag*, London: Pluto Press, 1979.

M. Lewin, *Political Undercurrents in Soviet Economic Debates*, London: Pluto Press, 1975.

M. McCauley (editor), *The Soviet Union after Brezhnev*, London: Heinemann, 1983.

Zh. Medvedev, *Andropov*, Oxford: Blackwell, 1983.

Alex Pravda, 'Is there a Soviet working class?', *Problems of Communism*, vol. 31, no. 6 (November 1982).

R. Remington (editor), *Winter in Prague: documents on Czechoslovak Communism in Crisis*, Cambridge, Mass.: MIT Press, 1969.

T. Rigby and B. Harasymiw, *Leadership Selection and Patron-Client Relations in the USSR and Yugoslavia*, London: Allen & Unwin, 1983.

B. Ruble and A. Kahan, *Industrial Labor in the USSR*, New York: Pergamon, 1979.

A. Shtromas, *Political Change and Social Development: the case of the Soviet Union*, Frankfurt am Main: Verlag Peter Lang, 1981.

'Soviet workers: the current scene', *Problems of Communism*, vol. 13, no. 1 (January 1964).

J. Valenta, *Soviet Intervention in Czechoslovakia, 1968: anatomy of a decision*, Johns Hopkins University Press, 1979.

A. Yanov, 'Essays on Soviet society', *International Journal of Sociology*, vol. 6, nos. 2–3, 1977.

V. Zaslavsky, *The Neo-Stalinist State*, Brighton: Harvester Press, 1982.

I. Zemtsov, *Partiya ili mafiya? razvorovannaya respublika*, Paris: Les Editeurs Réunis, 1976.

14. Religion, Nationality and Dissent

* H. Carrère d'Encausse, *Decline of an Empire: the Soviet socialist republics in revolt*, New York: Newsweek Books, 1979.

* Zh. Medvedev, *Soviet Science*, Oxford University Press, 1979.

* J. Rubenstein, *Soviet Dissidents: their struggle for human rights*, London: Wildwood House, 1980.

†L. Alekseeva, *Soviet Dissent: contemporary movements for national, religious and human rights*, Middleton, Connecticut: Wesleyan University Press, 1985.

† J. Azrael, *Soviet Nationality Policies and Practices*, New York: Praeger, 1978.

† L. Churchward, *The Soviet Intelligentsia*, London: Routledge & Kegan Paul, 1973.

† J. Dunlop, *The Faces of Contemporary Russian Nationalism*, Princeton University Press, 1983.

† Christel Lane, *Christian Religion in the Soviet Union: a sociological study*, London: Allen & Unwin, 1978.

A. Amal'rik, *Zapiski dissidenta*, Ann Arbor, Michigan: Ardis Press, 1982.

A. Bennigsen and M. Broxup, *The Islamic Threat to the Soviet State*, London: Croom Helm, 1983.

A. Bennigsen and C. Enders Wimbush, *Mystics and Commissars: Sufism in the Soviet Union*, London: C. Hurst, 1985.

A. Bennigsen and C. Lemercier-Quelquejay, *Islam in the Soviet Union*, London: Pall Mall Press, 1967.

M. Bourdeaux, *Religious Ferment in Russia: Protestant opposition to Soviet religious policy*, London: Macmillan, 1968.

——, *Patriarch and Prophets: persecution of the Russian Orthodox Church today*, London: Macmillan, 1969.

A. Brumberg (editor), *In Quest of Justice: protest and dissent in the Soviet Union today*, New York: Praeger, 1970.

V. Bukovsky, *To Build a Castle: my life as a dissenter*, London: André Deutsch, 1978.

J. Chiama and J. F. Soulet, *Histoire de la dissidence*, Paris: Seuil, 1982.

V. Chornovil, *The Chornovil Papers*, New York: McGraw-Hill, 1968.

Robert Conquest, *Courage of Genius: the Pasternak affair*, London: Collins/Harvill, 1961.

Robert Conquest (editor), *The Last Empire: nationality and the Soviet future*, Stanford, California: Hoover Institution Press, 1986.

Ivan Dzyuba, *Internationalism or Russification? A study in the Soviet nationalities problem*, London: Weidenfeld & Nicolson, 1968.

Jane Ellis, *The Russian Orthodox Church: a contemporary history*, London: Croom Helm, 1986.

Zvi Gitelman, 'Are nations merging in the USSR?', *Problems of Communism*, vol. 32, no. 5 (September 1983).

Max Hayward (editor), *On Trial: the case of Sinyavsky and Daniel*, London: Collins/Harvill, 1967.

M. Hopkins, *Russia's Underground Press: the Chronicle of Current Events*, New York: Praeger, 1983.

G. Hosking, *Beyond Socialist Realism: Soviet fiction since 'Ivan Denisovich'*, London: Granada, 1980.

'Iz otcheta soveta po delam religii – chlenam TsK KPSS', *Vestnik Russkogo Khristianskogo Dvizheniya*, no. 130 (1979).

R. Karklins, *Ethnic Relations in the USSR*, Boston, Massachusetts: Allen & Unwin, 1986.

L. Kochan (editor), *The Jews in Soviet Russia since 1917*, second edition, Oxford University Press, 1972.

Zh. Medvedev, *Ten Years after Ivan Denisovich*, London: Macmillan, 1973.

R. Misiunas and R. Taagepera, *The Baltic States: the years of dependence, 1940–80*, London: Hurst, 1983.

R. Orlova, *Vospominaniya o neproshedshem vremeni*, Ann Arbor, Michigan: Ardis Press, 1983.

M. Popovsky, *Science in Chains*, London: Collins/Harvill, 1980.

T. Rakowska-Harmstone, 'The dialectics of nationalism in the USSR', *Problems of Communism*, vol. 23, no. 3 (May 1974).

P. Reddaway, *Uncensored Russia*, London: Jonathan Cape, 1972.

Religion in Communist Lands (a quarterly journal issued by Keston College – gives up-to-date information on all varieties of religion in the Soviet Union).

E. Rogovin Frankel, *Novy Mir: a case study in the politics of literature, 1952–58*, Cambridge University Press, 1981.

M. Rywkin, *Moscow's Muslim Challenge: Soviet Central Asia*, London: Hurst, 1982.

Andrei Sakharov, *Sakharov Speaks*, London: Collins/Harvill, 1974.

M. Shatz, *Soviet Dissent in Historical Perspective*, Cambridge University Press, 1980.

G. W. Simmonds (editor), *Nationalism in the USSR and Eastern Europe in the Era of Brezhnev and Kosygin*, University of Detroit Press, 1977.

R. L. Tökés, *Dissent in the USSR: politics, ideology and people*, Johns Hopkins University Press, 1975.

V. S. Vardys, *Lithuania under the Soviets: portrait of a nation, 1940–65*, New York: Praeger, 1965.

A. Yanov, *The Russian New Right*, Berkeley, Calif.: Institute of International Studies, 1978.

15. The Soviet Union in the 1980s

*James Cracraft (editor), *The Soviet Union Today: an interpretive guide*, 2nd edition, London: Chicago University Press, 1988.

A. Aganbegyan, *The Challenge: economics of perestroika*, London: Hutchinson, 1988.

Yu. V. Andropov, *Speeches and Writings*, Oxford: Pergamon, 1983.

——, *Izbrannye rechi i stat'i*, Moscow: Politizdat, 1983.

A. Arnold, *Afghanistan's Two-party Communism*, Stanford, Calif.: Hoover Institution Press, 1983.

N. Ascherson, *The Polish August: the self-limiting revolution*, Harmondsworth: Penguin Books, 1982.

H. Bradsher, *Afghanistan and the Soviet Union*, Durham, North Carolina: Duke University Press, 1982.

A. Brown and M. Kaser (editors), *Soviet Policy for the 1980s*, London: Macmillan, 1982.

Mark Frankland, *The Sixth Continent: Russia and the making of Mikhail Gorbachev*, London: Hamish Hamilton, 1987.

T. Garton Ash, *The Polish Revolution: Solidarity, 1980–82*, London: Jonathan Cape, 1983.

M. Goldman, *USSR in Crisis: the failure of an economic system*, New York: Norton, 1983

Mikhail Gorbachev, *Perestroika: new thinking for our country and the world*, London: Collins, 1987.

V. Haynes and M. Bojcun, *The Chernobyl Disaster*, London: Hogarth Press, 1988.

B. Komarov, *The destruction of Nature in the Soviet Union*, London: Pluto Press, 1980.

M. McCauley (editor), *The Soviet Union under Gorbachev*, London: Macmillan Press, 1987.

D. Marples, *The Social Impact of the Chernobyl Disaster*, London: Macmillan Press, 1988.

Zh. Medvedev, *Andropov*, Oxford: Blackwell, 1983.

Dev Murarka, *Gorbachev: the limits of power*, London: Hutchinson, 1988.

N. P. and R. S. Newell, *The Struggle for Afghanistan*, Cornell University Press, 1981.

A. Shtromas and M. Kaplan (editors), *The Soviet Union and the Challenge of the Future*, vol 1: *Stasis and Change*, New York: Paragon House, 1988.

J. Steele and E. Abraham, *Andropov in Power*, Oxford: Martin Robertson, 1983.

Martin Walker, *The Waking Giant: the Soviet Union under Gorbachev*, London: Michael Joseph, 1986.

C. E. Ziegler, *Environmental Policy in the USSR*, London: Frances Pinter, 1987.

Index

(Principal entries on a particular subject are given in bold type)